"The Broadw

Robert Russell Bennett

Drawing by Irma Selz; © 1951 *The New Yorker Magazine*, Inc. Used by permission.

This caricature of Bennett accompanied Herbert Warren Wind's *New Yorker* article on Bennett, "Another Opening, Another Show."

"The Broadway Sound"

The Autobiography and Selected Essays of Robert Russell Bennett

Edited by

George J. Ferencz

University of Rochester Press

First published 1999
Softcover edition published 2001
Transferred to digital printing 2007

University of Rochester Press
668 Mt. Hope Avenue, Rochester, NY 14620, USA
www.urpress.com
and Boydell & Brewer Limited
PO Box 9, Woodbridge, Suffolk IP12 3DF, UK
www.boydellandbrewer.com

ISSN: 1071–9989
ISBN-13: 978–1–58046–022–4 (hardcover)
ISBN-13: 978–1–58046–082–8 (softcover)
ISBN-10: 1–58046–022–4 (hardcover)
ISBN-10: 1-58046–082–8 (softcover)

Library of Congress Cataloging-in-Publication Data

Bennett, Robert Russell, 1894–
The Broadway sound : the autobiography and selected essays of Robert Russell Bennett / edited by George Ferencz
p. cm. — (Eastman studies in music. ISSN 1071–9989; v. 12)
Includes bibliographical references and index.
ISBN 1–58046–022–4 (hardcover: alk. paper)
1. Bennett, Robert Russell, 1894– . 2. Composers—United States—Bibliography. I. Ferencz, George Joseph. II. Series.

ML410.B4498A3 1999
780'.92—dc21
[B] 99–29425
CIP

A catalogue record for this title is available from the British Library.

This publication is printed on acid-free paper.
Printed in the United States of America.

Contents

Photographs

Musical Examples

Eastman Studies in Music

(ISSN 1071–9989)

1. *The Poetic Debussy: A Collection of His Song Texts and Selected Letters* (Revised Second Edition)
Edited by Margaret G. Cobb

2. *Concert Music, Rock, and Jazz since 1945: Essays and Analytical Studies*
Edited by Elizabeth West Marvin and Richard Hermann

3. *Music and the Occult: French Musical Philosophies, 1750–1950*
Joscelyn Godwin

4. *"Wanderjahre of a Revolutionist" and Other Essays on American Music*
Arthur Farwell, edited by Thomas Stoner

5. *French Organ Music from the Revolution to Franck and Widor*
Edited by Lawrence Archbold and William J. Peterson

6. *Musical Creativity in Twentieth-Century China: Abing, His Music, and Its Changing Meanings* (includes CD)
Jonathan P.J. Stock

7. *Elliott Carter: Collected Essays and Lectures, 1937–1995*
Edited by Jonathan W. Bernard

8. *Music Theory in Concept and Practice*
Edited by James M. Baker, David W. Beach, and Jonathan W. Bernard

9. *Music and Musicians in the Escorial Liturgy under the Habsburgs, 1563–1700*
Michael Noone

10. *Analyzing Wagner's Operas: Alfred Lorenz and German Nationalist Ideology*
Stephen McClatchie

11. *The Gardano Music Printing Firms, 1569–1611*
Richard J. Agee

12. *"The Broadway Sound": The Autobiography and Selected Essays of Robert Russell Bennett*
Edited by George J. Ferencz

13. *Theories of Fugue from the Age of Josquin to the Age of Bach*
Paul Mark Walker

14. *The Chansons of Orlando di Lasso and Their Protestant Listeners: Music, Piety, and Print in Sixteenth-Century France*
Richard Freedman

15. *Berlioz's Semi-Operas: "Roméo et Juliette" and "La damnation de Faust"*
Daniel Albright

Foreword

From just about the time when Robert Russell Bennett abandoned his rural Missouri farm life for whatever awaited him in New York City in 1916, Broadway theater life seems to have been waiting for his arrival. And we have been waiting these countless years for him to tell the great Broadway story as no other member of its endless parade of creators and collaborators could do. And do it he does, though he warns us that it's "impossible to put together a lot of memories like these without, as Cornelia Otis Skinner used to say, 'dropping names with a dull, sickening thud.'"

How else could he deal with all the great at whatever station they stood, or the niche from which they, too, could emerge in the putting together of a theater work? There are stories here about his enormous output of scores of other men's music, and much, too, about his own.

Irving Berlin's name is, appropriately, the first one "dropped" in Bennett's autobiography, the songwriter's name being "the first [he] ever saw on a popular song." Berlin is lovingly recalled as "song-writer number one, at least in our era. . . . If any youngster is ambitious as a song-writer a long look at Irving Berlin should be a required study."

Vincent Youmans, Cole Porter, Richard Rodgers, Oscar Hammerstein II, Jerome Kern, Alan Jay Lerner, Frederick Loewe, Serge Rachmaninoff, George Enesco, and Philip J. Lang, too—they of his time are all here in depth and in Russell Bennett's own way.

Bennett writes of a January 1948 performance he and Louise attended, with the League of Composers sponsoring an unusual Carnegie Hall appearance by the Goldman Band:

> I suddenly thought of all the beautiful sounds the American concert band could make that it hadn't yet made. That doesn't mean that the unmade sounds passed in review in my mind at all, but the sounds they made were so

Bennett and Frederick Fennell, Eastman Theatre, 1958. Photo © Louis Ouzer, courtesy of Frederick Fennell. Used by permission.

Inscribed "To Frederick Fennell with such thanks as only a writer of music can owe such an understanding performer." The Eastman Wind Ensemble, with Fennell conducting, was performing *Symphonic Songs for Band*, which they recorded the following spring for Mercury Records.

> new to me after all my years with orchestra, dance bands and tiny "combos" that my pen was practically jumping out of my pocket begging me to give this great big instrument some more music to play.

A few years later when his pen had jumped to the paper there came the great *Suite of Old American Dances* and then 1957's *Symphonic Songs for Band.* And I'm pleased to have conducted the University of Rochester's Eastman Wind Ensemble recordings for Mercury Records, helping ensure these pieces' deserved popularity. Russell's close association with the enormous commission project of Robert Austin Boudreau and his American Waterways Wind Orchestra, too, produced a series of unusual compositions. That pen had indeed "jumped" to these happy enrichments of the wind repertory.

Chapter Nine begins with *Victory at Sea*, twenty-six half-hour shows for NBC Television. Richard Rodgers was the composer, providing Russell initially with three main themes. Bennett observes that scoring each week's episode "was physically about like orchestrating a complete Broadway musical every ten days to two weeks"—and the remainder of Rodgers's role as "composer" consisted of nine additional musical themes. Excerpting his tale of the U.S. Navy as the series evolved into a super documentary is not possible; it simply has to be read—and to be heard; to close this tiny observation on that vast subject, Bennett reminds us "how powerful a string of musical notes can be in human ears."

On Friday, October 16th, 1959, I was in Boston where Arthur Fiedler and I cut the ribbon—one-quarter-inch magnetic recording tape—to open the city's Hi-Fi Show. Russell saw this in the press and tracked me down at my hotel to say that he too was in town at the Hotel Touraine, working on the new show that he intended to be his farewell to musical theater. He was busy scoring in one room, with three copyists down the hall preparing the orchestra parts. He said it was a "dream" show with which to conclude his Broadway career, Mary Martin being perfect in her starring role. It was *The Sound of Music*—ignoring high-fidelity. And Russell's joy in what he was putting on paper was completely sincere and totally contagious.

Bennett's life and his work also were a remarkable physical triumph, for he was a classic case of the devastating effects first of polio and then arthritis on the human body. But they stopped him not at all, even when they affected his writing hand—every note in his manuscript remained clear. We visited when we could, and our last meeting was for dinner with him and Louise at the Warwick Hotel, shortly before he began work on his *Autobiography for Band* and these charming memoirs.

I know of no biography that covers territory which we all should know as it is so warmly expressed in this fascinating life of Robert Russell Bennett.

Frederick Fennell
December, 1997

Frederick Fennell (b. 1914) is a conductor and recording artist of world renown. The Eastman Wind Ensemble, which he established at the Eastman School of Music in 1952, has been taken as a model by more than 20,000 wind ensembles in schools throughout America, as well as in Japan and other countries. His contributions are explored in *The Wind Ensemble and Its Repertoire: Essays on the Fortieth Anniversary of the Eastman Wind Ensemble*, edited by Frank J. Cipolla and Donald R. Hunsberger (Rochester: University of Rochester Press, 1994).

Acknowledgments

Many individuals, organizations, and institutions have assisted me in chronicling Russell Bennett's life and career. Both this volume and my earlier *Robert Russell Bennett: A Bio-Bibliography* have benefited immeasurably as a result.

I am fortunate that so many who knew Russell Bennett have helped me to get to know him: Josef Alexander, Vera Appleton, Walter Lanier "Red" Barber, Mary Ellin Barrett, Leon Barzin, Robert Biddlecome, Gerald Bordman, Robert Austin Boudreau, William David Brohn, Carmen Carrozza, Helen Grady Cole, Adele Combattente, Ainslee Cox, Anna E. (Mrs. Russel) Crouse, Richard De Benedictis, Fred de Cordova, Assunta Dell'Aquila, Alfonso Dell'Isola, Agnes De Mille, Morton Gould, Frances Greer, Mary Rodgers Guettel, George J. Guilbault, Albert Hague, James Hammerstein, William Hammerstein, Kitty Carlisle Hart, Dorothy Cadzow Hokanson, Cham-ber Huang, Donald B. Hyatt, Milton Katims, Milton Kaye, Miles Krueger, Burton Lane, Mrs. Phil Lang, Eleanor Lawrence, Eddy Lawrence Manson, Bernard Mayers, Lyle "Spud" Murphy, Donald Pippin, Gordon Pope, David Raksin, Sid Ramin, Paul Renzi, Jr., William D. Revelli, Trude Rittman, Aaron Rosand, Edith Sagul, Herbert Spencer, Franklyn Stokes, Herbert Stothart, Jr., Hugh Thompson, Virgil Thomson, J. "Billy" VerPlanck, Audrey Walker, Myron Welch, Margaret Whiting, Jack Wilson, Herbert Warren Wind, and George Zevitas. Their letters and interviews bear witness to their admiration for a special colleague and friend.

Invaluable assistance was provided by the staff members at the New York Public Library, Free Library of Philadelphia, Los Angeles Public Library, Metropolitan Toronto Reference Library, State Historical Society of Wisconsin, Music and Recorded Sound Divisions of the Library of Congress (Elizabeth Auman, et al.), and the libraries at Beloit College, Brigham Young University, Idaho State University, Indiana University, The Juilliard School of Music (Jane Gottlieb), Louisiana State University, University of Arkansas, University of

California at Los Angeles (Stephen Fry, Brigette Kueppers), University of Colorado, University of Wisconsin–Madison, and here at the University of Wisconsin–Whitewater.

William D. Hilyard first introduced me to Bennett's compositions three decades ago. Many others are to be thanked for their assistance and encouragement: Larry Blank, Lance Bolling, Jon Alan Conrad, David Lewis Crosby, Bill Everett, Ed Flesch, Frank Hudson, and Larry Stempel. Judy McCulloh and an associate examined an early version of the manuscript, and their input was useful in shaping this volume into its final form.

I appreciate the enthusiasm of my colleagues at the University of Wisconsin–Whitewater, especially J. Michael Allsen, Janet Barrett, Michael Benson, Linda Hurstad, and John Stone. Christian Ellenwood formatted the musical examples. A pair of my institution's Research Grants made possible research travel to New York, Philadelphia, and the Library of Congress.

Assisting with illustrations were Ruta Abolins (Wisconsin Center For Film & Theater Research), Fran Achen, Dee Bergstrand and Lucille Ullery (Freeman, Mo.), Eileen Darby, Amy Dawson (Cleveland Public Library), Nicholas Firth (President, BMG Music), Jill Frisch (*The New Yorker*), Marty Jacobs (Museum of the City of New York), Kristine Krueger (Academy of Motion Picture Arts and Sciences), Cathleen R. Latendresse (Henry Ford Museum), Delores Massiah (Corbis/Bettman), Denise Morrison (Kansas City Museum), Louis and Helen Ouzer, Dennis Dale and Nicole Omdahl (UW–Whitewater). The reprinting of Irma Selz's drawing was underwritten by a gracious gift from the Cristine Ferencz Howe Subvention Foundation (Trenton, Michigan).

I am especially indebted to:

Frederick Fennell, who graciously supplied a Foreword, and also for his lengthy replies to my inquiries;

Robert Shaw and Nola Frink, his administrative assistant at the Atlanta Symphony Orchestra;

G. Thomas Tanselle (John Simon Guggenheim Foundation), who arranged access to materials relating to Bennett's fellowship;

Roy Benton Hawkins, whose 1989 dissertation was based in part on Bennett's memoirs;

Gayle Harris, who worked with Bennett at NBC and later at the Library of Congress, and who lovingly chronicled his professional work and assisted me in many ways;

Theodore Chapin and Bruce Pomahac (Rodgers & Hammerstein), who have freely shared their knowledge and the resources of their organization;

Annette Kaufman, an enthusiastic and faithful correspondent for several years. She and her husband Louis vividly brought to life the film and concert music scene in late-1930s Los Angeles and have introduced me to several of Bennett's Hollywood associates;

Kean K. McDonald, who is to be thanked for nearly a decade of cordial cooperation with my inquiries. It was he who, following publication of my earlier *Bio-Bibliography*, extended an invitation to edit his grandfather's memoirs. Jean Bennett, too, has also helped me get to know her father better—and I thank her especially for her assistance with photographs.

Thanks go to the Hal Leonard Corporation for permission to use the following lyrics and/or musical excerpts:

"Can't Help Lovin' Dat Man" (p. 126). Lyrics by Oscar Hammerstein II, Music by Jerome Kern. Copyright © 1927 PolyGram International Publishing, Inc., Copyright Renewed, International Copyright Secured, All Rights Reserved.

"The Song Is You" (pp. 124–25). Lyrics by Oscar Hammerstein II, Music by Jerome Kern. Copyright © 1932 PolyGram International Publishing, Inc., Copyright Renewed, International Copyright Secured, All Rights Reserved.

"The Way You Look Tonight" (p. 257). Words by Dorothy Fields, Music by Jerome Kern. Copyright © 1936 PolyGram International Publishing, Inc. and Aldi Music, Copyright Renewed, All Rights for Aldi Music Administered by The Songwriters Guild of America, International Copyright Secured, All Rights Reserved.

"Why Do I Love You?" (p. 103). Lyrics by Oscar Hammerstein II, Music by Jerome Kern. Copyright © 1927 PolyGram International Publishing, Inc., Copyright Renewed, International Copyright Secured, All Rights Reserved.

The University of Rochester Press's Sean M. Culhane (Director) and Louise Goldberg (Production Manager), along with Eastman Studies in Music editor Ralph Locke, cannot be thanked enough for their patience, assistance, and support.

I appreciate the encouragement provided by my parents, brothers, and sisters. Thanks are also due to my wife Jane, a fine musician and musicologist who—more than a decade ago—suggested that I begin my study of Russell Bennett's singular "life in American music."

George J. Ferencz
Whitewater, Wisconsin
Summer 1998

Editor's Introduction

"Orchestrations by Robert Russell Bennett" was one of the most common of credits on Broadway's "golden age" playbills and original-cast LPs. The phrase served both to honor him for his principal role in shaping America's "Broadway sound" and, regrettably, to obscure many other commercial and artistic accomplishments.

Robert Russell Bennett (15 June 1894–18 August 1981) orchestrated all or part of more than three hundred shows between 1920 and 1975. He became the first-choice collaborator for America's leading theater composers, including Irving Berlin, George Gershwin, Jerome Kern, Frederick Loewe, Cole Porter, and Richard Rodgers. Always capable of providing "whatever the composer left out," he dominated the field of theater orchestration for decades, shaping the orchestral fabric that clothes much of the Broadway canon.

The many "symphonic picture" Broadway medleys crafted by Bennett have been performed on countless occasions by amateur and professional orchestras alike. High school and college bands regularly include a pair of his original works among their most-played repertoire. Yet the reader of Bennett's memoirs will likely be surprised to learn of the breadth of his composing and arranging for the concert hall, Hollywood, and network radio and television—all of this in addition to a half-century of theater work.

A student of Nadia Boulanger in the late 1920s, Bennett eventually completed more than 175 original compositions in a variety of genres: symphony, opera, wind band, incidental music, choral and vocal works, and keyboard and chamber music. His creations were widely performed by America's most acclaimed soloists and orchestras, especially in the 1930s and 1940s. Fortunately, recent revivals of Bennett's "golden age" Broadway orchestrations have brought about a renewed interest in this most-neglected aspect of his career—the music he wrote when he *wasn't* enriching someone else's melodies with orchestral color and rich counterpoint.

One of the recurring touchstones of Bennett's memoirs is his self-confessed musical snobbery—rooted, he tells us, in the thorough training that his musician-parents provided for him. It is his denigration of Broadway as "boiling the pot"—with an allied diffidence concerning his own contributions—that has always surprised those who have come to know Bennett through the loving touches he bestowed on decades of Broadway musicals. Even as he was being honored as "the dean of American arrangers" in the national press, Bennett wryly observed that "The way you get to be 'dean' of anything is to live longer than everyone else." Late in his career, he recounted his correspondence with a young researcher who had been eager to hear all about his work with Broadway's famed songwriters and lyricists:

> This boy was just starry-eyed about these people. . . . He was very disappointed with me that I didn't just come right in and say, "Oh yes, see what we did!" because I just couldn't say that. And finally . . . he kept writing back and was getting more and more angry at me for not falling in with his ideas of how *vastly* important this whole racket is. And I finally said, "There isn't any use in my trying to answer all your questions because the fellows that work in musical shows—the composers, the lyric writers, the actors, singers, producers—they're all wonderful people, they had this-and-that idiosyncrasy, this-and-that weakness, and this-and-that strength. But the truth of the matter is, twenty-seven bars of Beethoven's opus 84 [the incidental music for *Egmont*] is worth the whole output of musical comedy since I *started* working on it." . . . (laughter) . . . I never heard from him again![1]

Immediately after confessing his snobbery to the reader of his memoirs, however, Bennett professes his admiration for the unique abilities and instincts of the songwriters he had worked so closely with: "I doubt very much that any greater talents have ever existed than those of our American song-writers of the last seventy-odd years. What they arrive at is often a pure sequence of tones and syllables that is as inevitable and individual as any detail of art can be."

These two points of view—perhaps incompatible, perhaps not—run happily in counterpoint through his autobiography, always tempered by his conviction that posterity is the true arbiter of any music's worth.

Beginning in the 1930s, the American press regularly solicited articles from Bennett, and we are fortunate that he graciously complied, time and again. Because his autobiography is rarely technical in nature, I have appended eight of Bennett's published essays concerned with the arranger's craft. All of his

---

[1]Bennett interview with George J. Guilbault for WGBH radio, Boston, 1 October 1977.

writing is infused with his gracious personality, and these essays tell us much about both Bennett's *métier* and the man himself, whether written for the lay reader (*New York Times*) or the amateur or professional musician (*The Etude, International Musician, Modern Music, Harp News, Music Journal*). His theater-orchestrator contemporaries—Hans Spialek, Don Walker, Philip J. Lang, and Ted Royal among them—received scant mention (or column space) in newspapers or periodicals of the 1930s, 40s, and 50s, making Bennett's behind-the-scenes glimpses of his profession in these articles—and of course in the autobiography—all the more valuable today.

To these must of course be added Bennett's most extensive discussion of his specialty, *Instrumentally Speaking* (1975). Written but a few years before these memoirs, it provides those with a fair musical background a distillation of his lifetime of experience in theater and "legitimate" scoring—and is long overdue for a rescue from its out-of-print status.

Russell Bennett has been unfailingly lauded by those who knew him: "a true gentleman"—"the nicest guy in the music business"—"an unsung hero." And those aware of his unique contributions to others' musical-theater or television scores may wish that his memoirs would find him more willing to criticize the well-known personalities he had worked with. But this was clearly not his nature; he once wrote:

> The wild rush to expose all great men and women as "human beings after all" has its less fortunate features . . . only true saints can escape the natural desire on the part of those who know them to scream out the less glamorous features of the hero's life. . . . The funny things that have happened to me in the fields of my efforts in music are most of them based on the foibles and narrowness of my famous contemporaries—as well as on my own. . . .[2]

Three decades later, he spoke—if a bit disjointedly—with the same voice:

> In this book that I'm writing now—they asked me to write a book about Broadway, and the movies, and TV, which I turned down because I knew they wanted me to say something dirty. And, I don't want to say anything dirty about anybody. . . . I started this thing [interview] off in the very beginning by saying there would be no red faces—they have no market here. Oscar Levant had . . . two or three cute books that he wrote; but he really hurt a few people. You know, the great thing about it is: the more you talk, the less you say. . . .[3]

---

[2]Letter to Verna Arvey (wife of composer William Grant Still), 9 July 1945.

[3]Guilbault, interview.

Bennett completed his memoirs in 1978. As with most of his published writing—*Instrumentally Speaking* included—it was drafted in longhand. A typescript copy was then prepared from the handwritten draft by an assistant. Bennett next made some modest additions and deletions while correcting many of the typist's transcription errors.

I was able to examine both the penciled holograph and the Bennett-corrected typescript; the latter was favored when resolving the few discrepancies that existed between the two. Some material has been re-sequenced, with an eye toward consistency of chronology and subject matter; most of these relocated passages, however, are only a few paragraphs in length. Several obvious spelling and punctuation errors, missing words, etc., have been corrected without comment—and my chronological re-sequencing has allowed for a few transitional sentences here and there—but I have otherwise refrained from assuming Bennett's voice, with all editorial additions clearly indicated.

Because most of the material that Bennett deleted from the typescript was from the conclusion of the final chapter, his memoirs come to a somewhat abrupt end with his "latest" (1978) wind-band composition, *Autobiography for Band.* I have added a brief Epilogue with the aim of bringing his life's chronicle to a more satisfying conclusion.

Bennett set himself apart from his arranging peers through his prolific output of concert works; he likely surpassed his colleagues, too, in terms of the sheer number of pages of manuscript orchestration completed during his six decades as a commercial orchestrator. *Victory at Sea* alone necessitated the grinding out of more than five thousand pages of orchestral score over little more than a year, the sort of feat that has given rise to speculation among Bennett's fellow arrangers that he produced more musical manuscript in his lifetime than *any* composer or arranger, past or present.

Bennett's own working title for his remembrance was "Nor Is Not Moved—A Music Arranger's Story":

> The man that hath no music in himself,
> Nor is not moved with concord of sweet sound,
> Is fit for treasons, stratagems, and spoils;
> The motions of his spirit are dull as night,
> And his affections dark as Erebus;
> Let no such man be trusted.
>
> (*The Merchant of Venice*)

The Shakespeare reference is a telling one, as is Bennett's concession that his settings of others' melodies might remain his best-known creations. Though his compositions are infrequently programmed beyond America's shores, his orchestrations for many a Broadway perennial continue to reach new generations of theater-goers all around the globe. We trust that Bennett, experienced in collaborative enterprises, would have accepted with a rueful smile our decision to give the book a more straightforward title, which recognizes him as the principal architect of an essential contribution—the "Broadway sound"—to the cultural life of his century.

NOTES ON THE EDITION:

Throughout the autobiography, I have sought to provide clarifying annotations about the projects and people—many now a bit obscure—to which Bennett alludes.

[These annotations have been set as separated paragraphs, indented, in brackets, and in a different type, as seen here.]

Those interested in learning more details about Bennett's original works and theater, film, and television credits, may wish to consult my earlier *Robert Russell Bennett: A Bio-Bibliography* (1990), though a few additional compositions and arrangements have surfaced since its publication.

The chapter-by-chapter summaries in the table of contents have been added in an attempt to make the riches of the autobiography a bit easier to survey.

The Autobiography of
Robert Russell Bennett

Prologue

Irving Berlin and I, being contemporaries as far as the calendar goes, pursued in a certain way parallel careers. He is said to have consciously avoided the study of music for fear it would dam the flow of fabulous song that was in him. He never said that to me, but he was widely quoted [as saying it].

When I heard it I immediately thought of that brilliant contrapuntist Giuseppe Verdi, but at that moment I realized that a very similar unprovable idea had already staked out its claim on me. We were parallel, moving in opposite directions—as I recall geometry doesn't cavil at that. I was sure I never would learn all I had to know.

How it got there has never been clear to me, but a piece called *The Lady with the Red Dress* was on our piano one day when I was about ten years old. I opened it and began to play it. My piano-teacher mother, who was pretty well known for brooking no nonsense, hit the ceiling. *The Lady with the Red Dress* was ragtime, and ragtime was trash. If I ever hoped to be a musician I'd better not play one more bar of it.

As incredible as its seems, I don't remember ever playing one more bar of it.

And my mother had begotten an incurable life-long musical snob.

The parallel business with Irving Berlin has a little difficulty getting started, for an obvious reason: nobody ever looked over Irving's shoulder and poured music lessons in his ear, while my whole taste and instinct had to be planted, watered and cultivated in a garden full of rags—"Down Home Rag,"[1] "Twelfth Street Rag,"[2] "Put Me to Sleep with an Old-Fashioned Melody and Wake Me Up with a Rag."[3] If you played the piano for the kids you played ragtime (or old-fashioned melodies). If you got a playing job, more of the same.

---

[1]By Wilbur C. Sweatman (1911), with lyrics by W. Lew Brown.

[2]By Euday L. Bowman (1914); three later versions incorporated lyrics by James S. Sumner (1919), Spencer Williams (1929), and Andy Razaf (1942).

[3]By Harry Jentes, with lyrics by Richard Howard and Samuel M. Lewis.

Max (seated) and Louis Dreyfus, c. 1930. Photo courtesy of Nicholas Firth, BMG Publishing.

Irving Berlin's music excepted, the Dreyfus brothers published the creations of Broadway's "Golden Age" almost singlehandedly.

And what was wrong with this? Nothing, unless you were an incurable musical snob. I remember saying to Nadia Boulanger many years later that "Tea for Two" would always sound a little cheap to me, and I remember her saying, "I don't find that at all! I think it is a real find—'une vraie trouvaille.'" Nadia Boulanger, a sort of divinity to all of us, didn't cure me. "Tea for Two," along with about all the two-hundred-and-fifty-odd theater scores I've sat with, slept with and lived with, still sounds a little cheap to me.

They are all distant relatives of *The Lady with the Red Dress.*

So Irving Berlin's train and mine pass each other on parallel tracks, and I shall always have an elusive worry that those ever-lovin' rags may have disqualified me for listening to the music of Prokofiev, Messiaen—and Bach; Irving, in the other direction, never broke down in his refusal to know the treble clef when he saw it, and he went from rags to riches.[4]

[4]Bennett seemed ever aware of the inconsistencies of his self-confessed snobbery: "I'm forever selling Broadway short. . . . I always turn to the classics when I listen for my own pleasure. If a piece is signed Serge Prokofiev, I'll pay strict attention to it, even though the music may be worse than Irving Berlin's!" (Roland Gelatt, "Music Makers," *High Fidelity*, July 1968, 20).

It's hard to disprove that the point of view of an incurable snob must be seasoned with contempt or envy or both. If this is your conclusion (and it is a justifiable one), let me say that I doubt very much that any greater talents have ever existed than those of our American song-writers of the last seventy-odd years. What they arrive at is often a pure sequence of tones and syllables that is as inevitable and individual as any detail of art can be.

So then, what am I complaining about?

Well, a good friend of mine, Abram Chasins,[5] a musician of authority, once gave me a quote that I've repeated many times: "Talent is the essential thing. Genius is what you do with it." Here is a day-dream, perhaps, but it contains a guess at the answer to an old question among music lovers. Might it be possible that one of history's greatest talents, Franz Schubert, once wrote three or four heavenly melodies for a symphony and completed two movements, only to have the great genius, Franz Schubert, abandon the whole project? It would be impertinent to try to break the idea down any further, but, to quote Oscar Hammerstein's Carmen Jones, "To think a little ain' 'gin no law."

To get full mileage out of the four-letter word ["snob"]—and that seems to be exactly what my wandering pen is bent on doing—one has to realize that snobbery has no edge unless it is a little preposterous. A real patrician background wipes all the outlines out and gives the attitude a new name. I'm thinking now about the publisher of a large majority of the scores of the musicals that gave the Golden Age of the American Musical its name—Mr. Max Dreyfus. He was a slight, soft-spoken man with his roots in the German Scharzwald, a man who quietly took over the destinies of the words and music of Broadway. His success, I think (along with a good many others'), was due as much to his general education and capacity for learning as to his music studies. An outstanding trait of Max Dreyfus, according to the tune writers of Tin Pan Alley, was that he never knew a hit when he heard one. The many writers of songs are many of them writers of books, wherein they tell with great glee of how Max listened to their score and turned it down, later having to come to them and ask to publish their music.

If this volume goes where I think it will, there may be several stories that clear up little confessions like this. During the year at the old Metropolitan Opera House they often had a season of matinee performances of Wagnerian operas. Max's office (and the publishing firm) was only about six blocks from the Metropolitan. Time and time again he would see me around the office and say, "Russ, get your hat and coat."

---

[5]American pianist, composer, and author Chasins (1903–1987) was music director of WQXR and WQXR-FM radio (operated by the *New York Times*) from 1946 to 1965.

And we would be off to the Met.

One time in February we had just heard a fantastic performance of *Tristan*, with Kirsten Flagstad, Lauritz Melchior, and others of the top stars, Arthur Bodanzky conducting. We left the place in silence. After two of three blocks I noticed Max carrying his hat in his hand and the temperature was about 8° Fahrenheit. I said, "You'd better put your hat on, Max. It's cold!" He looked at me and said, "How about yours?" We put on our hats and walked to the elevator door at 62 West 45th Street, where we would find a lot of the songwriters laughing, joking, playing their latest for their colleagues and friends.

Before the elevator picked us up I heard Max Dreyfus say, mostly to himself, "And still the boys upstairs want me to like their music!"

But Max Dreyfus was not a snob. He was born and raised to love and keep in his heart the Allegretto from Beethoven's Seventh, which has less "tune" than Rodgers and Hart's "Johnny One-Note."

Chapter One

I was born in Kansas City which, in spite of what a shocking number of people think, is not in Kansas. One time in London, where I was making the orchestrations for a new musical, I had supper at the Kit Kat Club with Ernest Truex, a brilliant and beloved light-comedy actor. He played the lead in many hits and was very much at home in London.

As we sat there a party was seated at the next table with quite a bit of nobility, not to say royalty, among the assembled. Ernie was telling me a bit about each member of the group and something made me say:

"No, I'm from Missouri,"—something a little hard to swallow.

He said quickly, "Are you really from Missouri?"

I said "yes."

He said, "No kidding! So am I! What town were you born in?"

"Kansas City."

"So was I! What street were you born on?"

"Cherry Street."

"So was I!"

We were born ten blocks apart.[1] When it gets closer than that it qualifies for a plot of some kind of something. Probably musical.

What I know of my ancestry doesn't take long to tell, nor would it explain anything if offered in evidence. On my father's side, the Bennetts, the family apparently chose to let sleeping dogs lie and no detail of their history reached my young ears except that my father's father was kicked in the head by a mule that helped draw a cannon about in the American Civil War. This got my grandfather a pension and he owned five hundred acres of pretty good land near a tiny town in Missouri, just south of Kansas City.

---

[1] Some sources give Rich Hill, Mo. as the birthplace of Ernest Truex (1889–1973). Bennett was born at 2425 Cherry Street, according to his 1981 *Kansas City Star* obituary; in the *Star* of 19 June 1894, it is listed as 2426 McCoy Street. The latter address also appears in the 1894 *Hoye's City Directory of Kansas City* (Missouri).

I never heard what became of the mule, but he seems to be as far back as the family legend went, from my point of view. My grandfather was a tall, gaunt man, rather impressive and rather pompous. He played hoe-down fiddle with the tailpiece of it down against his chest instead of under his chin.

He was tall and gaunt and also powerful. An unhappy spot in my childhood was an afternoon when George Riley Williams, who did chores and errands for Grandpappy, was supposed to be sawing firewood and was loafing on the job. Granapy (our name for the old fellow) went out and gave him a sound thrashing.

George Riley fell to and sawed wood furiously, but it wasn't in me to understand why. Even now I'm sure I should have put on a convincing act as a wounded martyr about to die.

My grandfather came from the days of slavery, and as a matter of fact was helping to raise and support George Riley and his sister because their parents, neighbors on a nearby farm, were too poor to feed themselves.

His [Granapy's] four sons, raised on the farm, all became professional musicians, all brass players. They formed a brass quartet: George (my dad) first trumpet, Jim (the third son) second trumpet, Louis (the youngest) trombone and Charles (the second son) tuba.

Their mother married at the age of sixteen, outlived them all but Louis, and died at the age of a hundred and one.

The other half of me is a Bradford, and the Bradfords were not prone to keep their name a secret. One of my million Bradford cousins once showed me a book about our relatives. One of us was a girl born when they named girls Patience, Prudence, Faith and the like. She went through life with the name Submit Murdock.

My Grandfather Bradford, it seems, was a bit impressed with his family connections and brought the old governor[2] into the conversation once in a while. My mother had three sisters but only one brother. He would always tease his father and say, "The line ends with me. I'm never going to marry."

He stuck to his guns until he was in his forties, but a handsome siren came one day and changed his mind, as handsome sirens do. They had one son, who now has sons and the line goes on. I often think what a great answer to all this it would be if the story could be wrapped up, like a W. S. Gilbert libretto, something like this: there was indeed a man named Bennett with John Smith when he came to Virginia, and my father's father came from Virginia, so what if . . . ?

---

[2]William Bradford (1590–1657), a passenger on the Mayflower and longtime governor of the Plymouth colony.

I'll tell you what if! If that Bennett had been our great-great-great-etc. we would have heard about it far into the night, since he got here thirteen years before William Bradford did. Any historical fact with the proper spirit would have arranged itself to be that way for our amusement, but you know how historical facts are—no sense of humor.

There are probably thousands of volumes in the libraries dealing with human memory and I could read and study them all without being any nearer to what I'd like to know that I am. It's simple: what determines the age at which we are suddenly blessed with an almost photographic mind, memorizing words, retaining clear pictures, collecting facts more accurately than we ever shall again in our lives, when one day earlier and all the days before that remain a complete blank?

Sometime before I was four years old my mother was looking over her sewing machine and had the heavy part raised up on its two hinges. I came up, reached out my right hand and the thing fell and almost cut off an inch of my middle finger.

What do I remember of that accident? Absolutely nothing—no noise, no pain, no screams! But two or three days later two doctors came to change the bandage and I remember how they looked, what they did with gauze, scissors, etc., and how it hurt. Many details and many things said about it are clear in my mind, but not one moment of the day it happened do I recall.

I have no trouble recalling some efforts to make me into a comedian, when a "straight-man"—usually my father—would say, "What did you do when the sewing machine fell on you?" I would answer, "I yelled bloody murder." Big laugh. This was repeated many times with big success.

I didn't write the script, needless to say, but I was a quick study.

What makes any off-hand study of man's memory practically useless is something we all know: memory is almost synonymous with concentration. Stories of two great rememberers of my time testify to this. Arturo Toscanini and Dimitri Mitropoulos, orchestra conductors, left a trail of wonderment behind them, no matter how advanced the minds of their associates were.

With Toscanini[3] it may have been a little more natural to concentrate than with Mitropoulos. Toscanini had such myopia that he could only read a page a few inches from his face, and it seems to us that part of the concentration could be automatic, although I certainly don't know that to be true.

---

[3]Arturo Toscanini (1867–1957) made his U.S. debut in 1908, having established himself in Europe as an esteemed opera and symphony conductor. From 1937 until 1954 he led the NBC Symphony, which the radio network had created for him. During 1952–53, Bennett led the same NBC Symphony personnel in recording sessions for the twenty-six *Victory at Sea* episodes.

Two stories about these giants will always stay with me. One was told by the concertmaster at the opera of a rehearsal for the premiere of a new work (I believe it was by Puccini, but that was not part of the tale). The score and orchestra parts were delivered during the rehearsal of the first two acts, and Maestro Toscanini had never seen the score.

He called a recess of one hour to allow him to read it once through. Then the orchestra came back and the rehearsal went on. After several minutes of music the maestro stopped and said to one of the horn players, "Forte-piano! The G is forte-piano!" The player took time to find the note and then said, "Sorry, maestro, it says forte." Toscanini handed the unopened score to the concert-master and said "Look on page 41 (for example) and see how the G in bar three is marked."

It took Mr. Davis a little time to find the note, but finally he found it. It was marked ***fp*** (forte-piano). The copyist had missed the ***p***.

Some of the stories of Mitropoulos[4] are hard to believe unless you have seen them unfold before your own eyes. One I was fairly close to is typical. He presented a symphony of Morton Gould with the New York Philharmonic.[5] Morton gave him the score one afternoon. The next day they had lunch together and Mitropoulos gave it back to him. He brought up several questions about the music, singing the phrases as though reading the score. A few days later he called the publisher and asked if he might have the orchestral parts sent to him; he wanted to proof-read them. A natural question—in fact two natural questions—were asked of him: why did he take on the tedious work of correcting the parts himself, and didn't he need the score book? The answer: he wanted to know how each page of each musician's part looked, in case of questions; no, he didn't need the score, he knew that already.

No doubt many, many equally impressive memories are to be found in all branches of human expression. These and others that have come to me seem to suggest that such capacities are, at birth, lying somewhere in the human spirit waiting to be tested and demonstrated, and (the reason for bringing the point up) that they are gone today and here tomorrow.

"'Twas nothing, something," to continue getting my quotes backwards.[6] It becomes "something" somewhere about the age of four, younger in some cases.

---

[4]The American career of conductor (and composer) Dimitri Mitropolous (1896–1960) began in 1937 with the Minneapolis Symphony; he went on to lead the New York Philharmonic in the 1940s and 50s. Like Toscanini, he routinely conducted from memory.

[5]Probably Gould's Symphony No. 3, which premiered 28 October 1948.

[6]"Who steals my purse steals trash, 'Tis something; 'Twas mine, 'tis his. . . ." (*Othello*).

Sometime soon after the joust with the sewing machine I may be said to have become conscious of Beethoven. The smashed finger must have been by that time what it still remains, a big scar with no pain. My mother was practicing a Beethoven G-major sonata [op. 14, no. 2] and one day I went to the piano, reached up and "faked" the tune of the finale for two or three bars.

Obviously, I didn't do anything about the sharps. I probably couldn't have reached the black keys, but the performance was apparently slow enough for the doting relatives to recognize it and the performance had to be repeated a few times.

As a child-prodigy story it's not worth much–Mendelssohn or Mozart would no doubt have played the whole movement—but it might be cited in connection with the enormous number of Broadway tunes I had to take down from the piano some years later.

One more fact, interesting but not startling, should be noted here before the story moves forward. Interesting because it seems to indicate a reason why, when the uncomfortable question of self-support had to be answered, I often took on the job of music arranging. It was noted by friends and neighbors as well as family that, whenever two or more persons played music together during the day, I was sure to leave whatever I was doing and come in to listen. One person could practice all day and not be more than noticed, but as soon as more than one started to tune up or give other signs of duets or trios, they were sure of having an audience of one: me. This seemed so natural to me that I never even thought of it, but neighbors, being nosy creatures, talked about it. Any kind of ensemble playing was more exciting than climbing fences and trees, bouncing a ball, rolling a hoop or flying a kite.

Looking into life through the other end it seems evident that orchestration was bound to get me.

What did get me sometime before I was five years old was a thing now called polio—poliomyelitis. I never heard that name for it during the first thirty or more years of its stay with me, but there is no question about my remembering it. It moved in quite some time before Dr. Jonas Salk[7] was born, and quite some time before our doctors knew much about it.

---

[7]Salk (1914–1995) developed the first polio vaccine, widely used in the U. S. beginning in the 1950s.

I was put to bed ill. This was no novelty for my family. My sister and I between us spent a lot of our earlier days ill, poor Beatrice more than I. The best doctors my parents could find were called, and no one has ever suggested that any better ones could have been found. After some consultation they diagnosed the illness as typhoid malaria. That name has a musical sound to me, and I kept it as sort of souvenir.

I never knew much about what they gave me for my "typhoid malaria" but, whatever it was, I was able to get out of bed after about three weeks. As I started to put my feet on the floor my mother said, "Now, son, don't try to walk too fast, you'll be weak after being in bed so long."

I took two steps and crashed. Of course that got me a big scolding. "I told you not to walk too fast," etc., etc.

Back to bed.

I don't have as clear a picture of the days that followed. I know there were short walks and long sits in chairs, and somewhere in here I learned that alphabet well enough to spell things out loud and have people tell me what it said. At this time we were in a war with Spain. Two pictures (cartoons) on page of the *Kansas City Times* on two different days remain with me. One was of a ship on which as cargo was a packed market basket about a third the size of the ship. The family told us that the basket was the one we packed to send to the starving Philippine children the week before. The other front page picture was of the battleship Maine blowing up. That was also explained to us—not successfully, however.

But the next vivid picture is clear indeed: my mother setting up a varnished box about the size of a shoe box, with strings or wires coming out of a little engine of some kind. At the end of each wire was a handle with a wet sponge that she passed up and down my right leg, shooting little needles into the flesh. Of course I hated it, but must admit it fascinated me a little. Whether I liked it or not it went on for months. Electricity was looked on as the ultimate answer for every question as I was growing up.

I have no idea whether the doctors of fifty or more years later would laugh at my mama's therapy or not, but several batters that tried to beat out a bunt to me at third base some years later might have hesitated to testify against her. Taking a peek down the passing years a fundamental human trait seems hard to argue down. When a defect in the body takes early permanent residence like that it never really registers in the mind and character.

When I got thrown out trying to take an extra base I don't remember ever thinking what I might have done with two good legs. This writing may well be the first time the point ever came up. After the tennis court became the scene of my poor achievements as an athlete, the tournament players beat me because they were better players. That was and is the beginning and the end of the story. Sometimes when particularly ashamed of my performance I tried to find an excuse in the body, but bodies are not just sitting around waiting to say "I'm sorry!"

These conclusions seem to be valid in a case where the affliction comes in early. It must surely be a different story when the routine of living has been established—even partially established. My deep sympathy goes to one friend who got polio after her third child was born—to one of my best tennis-playing friends who got it at the age of eighteen and had to start all over as a left-handed player—or to the late Franklin D. Roosevelt, who was stricken as a mature man. All of them must remember what a complete body is like and miss it. Not so those of us to whom infantile paralysis was really infantile.

This, in one way or another, holds an unexpressed promise that the subject of the beast that was felled by Dr. Jonas Salk will never need to find its way onto these improvised pages again. I hope that will be the case, even though the very nature of improvised anything makes it rash to promise anything with too sober a face.

More and more, as these reflections pass by, I marvel as the wastefulness of the young human spirit. This of course is merely adding one more testimony to the incredible improvidence of youth, but when dealing with the squandering of that rich photographic mind that is dropped in our laps one begins to search for words.

My father was engaged to play the cornet in a concert band at the Boulder, Colorado chautauqua the summer my sister was three years old and I five.[8] Mother, sister and I went with him to Denver and out to Boulder and, as I write, rich mental trophies come by like a circus parade. Pikes Peak, the other mountains that look a half mile away and are actually twenty-five, and pine trees, the goldenrod, even an eagle or two!

And what did this fabulous memory so recently lavished on me choose to notice and retain? Only the great, big horse fly that lit on my poor sister's shoulder and bit her, hurting so much that she was ill. She, being three then, doesn't even remember being there.

I must pause to qualify this a little. I do remember being told about Pikes Peak [about a hundred miles south of Boulder] and do remember having it

---

[8]Actually, Summer 1898, just after his fourth birthday. The June 1898 *Texas-Colorado Chautauquan* also notes that Bennett's uncle Louis—a trombonist—joined George Bennett as a performer-instructor at the three-week session.

pointed out. It was there with clouds around it, but it failed to get its message across to me. They must have oversold it somehow.

Next big impression: Omaha, Nebraska. Why were we there? It would clutter this thing up miserably to make guesses based on something I knew later, even if that could be fully trusted, which it can't. What belongs to the story is that we were in a new world. My father had an office where they had something new to us, and wonderful: electric lights.

Beatrice and I spent one Sunday afternoon turning a hanging bulb on and off and on and off. Magic! I assume Papa had some business to clean up in the office and put us in the hall—where the light was—to get rid of us. Mr. Thomas Alva Edison may never have achieved a more complete success in his whole career!

We were in Omaha only a few months—I didn't count them, but a little work on the calendar shows that we made another move by the time the twentieth century arrived. The pictures that remain of Omaha are short—but with plenty of variety. We lived in a new little house in South Omaha. I know it was new because I was given a pocket knife for my sixth birthday and proceeded at once to cut slices out of a brand-new window sill of the house. There seems no appropriate remark except to quote Polly Damrosch (Mrs. Sidney Howard), with whom we were chatting eons later at a party where several nieces and nephews were scampering around among the grown-up guests. Polly's remark was, "Children should be abolished." She not only came by a few of them when she married Sidney, but they added a few of their own. That's all the abolishing she did![9]

The house in Omaha had a front porch and on it I put on a dramatic show one morning. Somehow I had developed a routine of going into a prima donna's temperamental outburst whenever my sister got punished for being naughty. I would throw myself face down on the floor and hit it with fists and kick it with toes while the spanking was going on. And yelling.

The last of these performances was on the porch while the discipline was being carved out inside the front room. That evening a man who lived next door asked me what the matter with me was that morning, and insisted on getting an answer. I had no reply, and tried without success to drop dead.

One other recollection of Omaha is the world-shaking discovery that there was another boy named Russell. It wasn't a common name for a boy, in spite of the fact that James Russell Lowell was a generation or two before me. And to mess this paragraph up so we'll never get out of it, I have a first cousin

---

[9]She was the daughter of American conductor Walter Damrosch, who founded the School of Music and Fine Arts at Fontainebleau. Sidney Howard, the Pulitzer-Prize-winning playwright, authored several screenplays, including 1939's *Gone with the Wind.*

named Lowell, named for the writer. It seems Lowell's mother and mine plotted the whole thing before we were born. My dad was very fond of a famous comedian named Sol Smith Russell and they gave us family names Louis and Robert, plus the names we were to be called, Lowell and Russell.

Well, Russell Dietrich was within a month of my age and lived just two doors away from me—and who are we to pretend that that was unimportant?

As I file this report second thoughts about the sudden appearance of the photographic mind are stirring a bit in their sleep. If the young mind could take and keep any picture it chose, how did it happen that not one detail of moving a household from Kansas City to Omaha, and from Omaha to the next spot, stayed with me? I loved trains, I loved trips, I have many mental pictures of steam engines that scared me to death, of the red coaches on the trains that went to Topeka, of the sound of unseen trains with haunting whistles that seemed to call to me on a quiet evening. Why was it that this brain—that a bit later seldom bothered to read teaching pieces more than once or twice before practicing them—never took the trouble to record a major move of many miles with all our possessions?

Our next move turned out to be drastic. Papa and Mama (we actually called them that in our early youth) must have done some long thinking before deciding, but they moved us into the north half of the big white house on my grandfather's Missouri farm.

My father and his three brothers were raised on some part of the same property, but my poor mother had no idea of what she was getting into. She was afraid of every bug, bee, animal or natural phenomenon she saw. When a cow came into the front yard she stayed in the house. She was a graduate of a college in Kansas, where, one would suppose, she must have learned something about a cow, but I can attest personally to the truth of the story. She hated the whole thing, yet somehow brought her Boston birth and background under a tight rein and came through.

Papa was a different story. Like nearly all farmer boys, he was a dreamer who idealized people and trusted them. If he had a bull to sell and someone came to buy it, my father would ask the buyer to stay and have dinner with us after the deal was complete. Of course that cost us a good part of the whole profit, and you can imagine what my New England mother thought of that!

Their career as farmers got off to quite a bad start. The first year brought no rain, and corn simply dried up and died without developing any ears at all. The second year made up for it: the rains came, a creek and a river became a lake, with its shore in our front yard. We sat and watched the neighbors' furniture float by on the way to sea (or the Gulf of Mexico). Again, no corn. Corn for the pigs, for the chickens and even for the cattle. I have no idea how they kept us alive, but we even had a "hired hand" a good part of the time. He got thirty dollars a month. Many times at the end of the month, two ill-clad little creatures would come to the back door and a tiny voice would say, "Poppy wants his money." I gathered that the little visitors were not greeted with big smiles, but don't remember a time when they came for nothing. Mother was a successful piano teacher and may have kept us from missing any meals, but it's much easier to believe that her earnings were not touched for daily expenses.

There's no use trying to guess how we got along. Irving Berlin told his wife Ellin that, in spite of the fact that his father left the family when Irving was a tiny tot, his mother dug in and took over the job, and he never remembered a time when they were cold or hungry. However, there is nothing in that for my original "parallel" theory to feed on. Midwestern farmers at the turn of the century were a remarkable breed, who fought it out with nature and survived.

Grandfather Bennett's five hundred acres lay adjacent to the town of Freeman, Missouri; it was a buggy ride of about a mile to the railway station, the post office, or the stores. The population of Freeman was never much more than two hundred and teaching music was hardly a source of wealth as it was in Biblical times.

For my sister and me the farm and the town just about filled in all the blank spaces. The day was never long enough. Our mother elected to keep us out of public school and took the job over herself. We had readin', writin', and 'rithmetic for three hours every morning after we had practiced the piano and in the afternoon we practiced again.

Only from things overheard it seems that the idea of keeping us at home for our schooling brought on a lot of criticism from the neighbors and townspeople, but to Mama we were still invalids and she carried the day, somehow. When we finally went to the public school I had one year of grammar school and two years of high school. Then a flowery Valedictory address and a diploma. That's as far as the Freeman, Missouri, high school went.

That about sums up my academic training, and when I've faced large groups of young undergraduates, all eager to learn from me, I think again and again what many teachers must think: that the real education is so much more than memorizing information, training minds to make creative use of it and pointing out directions of deeper thought. The great treasure is being acquired by sitting next to a contemporary, feeling a part of his or her reaction, sharing his or her bafflement at times and saying "Move over!" telepathically time and time again. Not only in these subtle influences is the school—and college—man or woman better trained for the job of living, but in the

Bennett with his mother, May Bradford Bennett, and sister, Beatrice, c. 1900. Photo courtesy of Jean Bennett.

outer contacts, the everyday give and take, the affections and disaffections of normal citizenship.

This the self-educated and the drop-out must do largely without.

The real story of our education, my sister's and mine, has to begin with music. Music was not the frosting on the cake with us, it was both cake and frosting. In spite of a hearing problem, dad had a band rehearsing and playing for picnics and ball games in a very short time and we had a family orchestra almost as soon. And almost as soon as we two started piano lessons we had violins (half- and three-quarter size at first) and I had a cornet for my ninth birthday. Beatrice was practicing the piano one morning, playing a piece called "The Naughty Pixie Mocking His Mother." We decided it would be fun for her to play the mother's part and let me do the Naughty Pixie's part on the cornet. We started, and when I played the notes on the cornet they sounded a tone too low. (It was a B flat cornet, for advanced thinkers.)

Hardly missing a beat I began to transpose the tune up to G from F to make it fit. When we came to the end we laughed like idiots. Thus went my first job as a music arranger.

I doubt that anyone alive ever disliked practicing any more than I did. From the day Mama stopped my "improvising" and made me count and play what was written, music had a few less charms. Oddly enough I was much

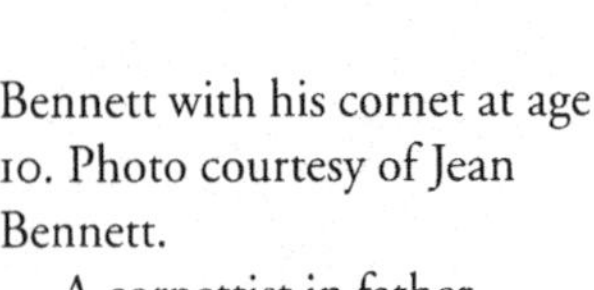

Bennett with his cornet at age 10. Photo courtesy of Jean Bennett.

A cornettist in father George Bennett's band (1904), Russell quickly became the ensemble's utility member, who could "borrow a horn and play whatever was missing at rehearsals, parades and celebrations."

more content to do purely physical exercises over and over than to repeat those compositions of Czerny[10] and Kreutzer,[11] which may last a long time as physical problems, but they died for me as music after one or two hearings. The fingers needed them, but the ears didn't. I never practiced as much as I should have, especially on the band instruments. As I was growing up it got to be a routine for me to borrow a horn and play whatever was missing at rehearsals and even for parades, celebrations, etcetera. I didn't get very good on them, but I met a lot of nice horns.

The time I wished with all my heart that I had practiced harder was when my dad and I went to play in the band at a week-long affair in northern Missouri and on the first day I found myself playing the first trombone part. I tried to trade parts with the third trombone man, but the conductor of the

---

[10]Austrian pianist-teacher Carl Czerny (1791–1857), a student and associate of Beethoven, was an astoundingly prolific composer. He is best known for his pedagogical works, especially the *Complete Theoretical and Practical Pianoforte School.*

[11]Rodolphe Kreutzer (1766–1831) composed the Etudes that are still widely used as study material for violinists.

concerts caught us in the act and made us trade back. My lips felt like mattresses and it was a good thing the band-leader was well filled with choice liquids most of every day.

There's no substitute for practice as well as no substitute for talent.[12] All those who imagine they can get by with that big thing [talent] they have should have had to listen to our [band's] Prelude to Act III of *Lohengrin.*

At the end of the engagement we were paid in silver dollars. My father had somewhere else to go before returning to Kansas City, where we were housed at that particular time, so he gave me his money to take along with mine. We filled an empty music-stand case with dollars and I got home at three or four in the morning with almost one hundred of them in tow. The street-car from the railroad station stopped six blocks down the hill from our house and, after climbing three or four of those blocks, I stumbled and dropped the music-stand case. Down rolled the dollars with a silvery ring in the silent morning air.

It must have been a good show, me scrambling after them, but I was the only audience and I didn't enjoy it much.

There were a number of men in Freeman who were quite capable as instrumentalists, and we got together and played standard orchestra music fairly often—overtures like *Semiramide* or *William Tell,* the waltzes from *Faust* or the ballet music of Leo Delibes. I remember our clarinet player, whose tone in the lower register was quite rich and gave me a life-long fondness for the instrument. As a group we played for Sunday school and church, an occasional oyster-supper, or one of those charity affairs where the girls brought baskets and the baskets were auctioned off to the merry young gentlemen, who had to guess which ones to bid on in order to eat supper with their favorite girls.

I don't believe anybody ever paid the orchestra for their music, but they nearly always got a basket of pickled beets and hard-boiled eggs for their pains.

A word about my dad is still due. His hearing weakness started, my grandmother told me, when his father and mother brought him in a mover-wagon from Illinois to western Missouri when he was one year old. He developed an ear ache and his mother had no way to get help for him. It must have been serious for him as a playing musician through his years as first trumpet in the Grand Opera House in Kansas City, but a strange thing about it was that he could hear music that was pianissimo much more easily than he could hear speaking voices.

---

[12]Cf. *Kiss Me, Kate* conductor Pembroke Davenport's comment, "There's no substitute for talent" (Bennett's essay, "Fools Give You Reasons," below).

His forte (or his fortissimo) on trumpet was rich and thrilling by everybody's account. I never heard him play virtuoso music on the violin, but his tone was full of authority and he was a member of a good string orchestra in Kansas City. I was told by a quite famous astrologer once that most of my talents and instincts came from my mother. I suppose if I dispute that Aries will butt me and Leo will roar, but I prefer to think of the morning when my dad came home from a buggy ride to the town, stopped the horse and said to me, "Stand out there beside the horse's head." Quite mystified, I stood by the horse's head and Papa threw a shiny, white baseball at me. Of course I missed it and it rolled to the front yard fence, but there lay one of the major influences, as far as I'm concerned. It's a little romantic and amusing to speculate on just how far I should have gone with baseball with a free choice, but it's honest to say that listening to a great performance of Beethoven's Ninth and seeing a no-hit, no-run ball game are awfully well matched as thrills.

I learned about then that Papa was the star pitcher of the town and had a blazing fast ball and great control. That was before I was born.

There must be something pathological about the way I love a ball, something for experts to work on. My "twin" cousin Lowell came to live with his (and my) grandparents when we were about twelve, and he and our several cousins who came to visit the farm all got so they wanted to hide when they saw me coming with a fielder's glove. Not that they didn't like baseball, but enough was enough. In order to keep one of them at it I would bet them they couldn't "burn me out" with me wearing only a thin glove. They might have been smart enough to realize that Lowell's father, when young, used to catch behind the bat wearing a kid glove when Papa was throwing his fast ball past batters.

Near the top of the story is my sister Beatrice, left-handed and getting tall, who got so she could strike out nearly all the boys. This was not socially good for her, but I paid her back by sewing doll clothes with her. I still remember the general line of fashion for the years 1906, –07 and –08.

This is a good place to report a compliment paid me by Lowell's quite a bit younger sister, Bonnie. She also came to live in the big white house with our grandparents and we all of us played together at whatever the games were. Bonnie was not more than seven or eight years old when her grandmother was asking her with whom she liked to play. She said, "I like to play with Russell. He's big, but he has a small mind."

At the age of thirteen I was over six feet tall, skinny and awkward. Youngsters, especially boys, made fun of me and I was never relaxed and natural with them. Once or twice in school I grabbed boys by the shoulders and shook them. One said I hurt his sore neck and was done in while another picked up a club and hit me over the head. Both incidents left me most miserable. I boxed and loved that, but when there was any bitterness I had no answers. Two or three years before that I went along with my father to a festival a good many miles east of us where he was conducting the band. This was before I played and I just hung around and listened at a distance.

A bunch of noisy teenage boys decided to make my life miserable every afternoon. I tried to be one of the gang but had no chance when they all hooted, laughed at me and pushed me all over the place. This went on all week until one day an angel came along. He was eighteen or nineteen years old, I imagined, and he came up, looked the situation over and said, "Here! You let my friend alone!" and proceeded to kick them in the stomach, grab one boy and use him for a club to hit two or three others, and so on. The party didn't last long. The whole gang just disappeared and never came back. I found out his name, Harry Pratt, and that he had a sister Susie Pratt, but I never saw him again. If I ever get to Heaven I'm sure he'll be working as an angel and I'll look him up.

At Freeman High School we played a good deal of baseball and even though the game was such a love of mine I got very little respect. My schoolmates had made up their minds that I couldn't possibly be a ball player, so they wouldn't let me pitch, catch behind the bat, or play in the infield. That left only the outfield, where I was practically as bad as they thought I was. But all this time I was studying books on batting and pitching, and I could almost recite the baseball rules from end to end.

One day came the happy ending. In a matchup of some kind and for some reason they put me in to pitch for our side. Then the joy that every performer knows: when the spotlight is on and all eyes are on you, you suddenly forget to be nervous and start thinking how beautiful the thing you are doing is and wishing you never would have to do anything else.

I'm sure we must have played nine innings and some of my adversaries may have made a hit or two, but all I could think of and remember was throwing strikes and my catcher, Earl Enloe, dancing up and down for joy, coming out once or twice to the mound and saying, "What's got into you, anyway?"

There were no trophies or cheers, but after the game Earl, the catcher, and I were walking down the town street and we passed two fellows playing catch. They, for some reason, hadn't been at the game.

I, feeling pleased with the world, called to one of them, "You're quite a ball player, Leonard!"

Leonard turned to me and said, "Well, you cain't fan me, Wampus." Wampus was one of my disrespectful nicknames.

Earl let out a whoop and said, "Can't, eh? He fanned Walter Dale three times!"

Leonard stopped everything and said, "Huh?" with disbelief in every muscle.

That was my trophy and my applause.

Back to music and farming, but baseball will be back, I'm sure.

Chapter Two

A five hundred acre farm in the Missouri Valley is almost a universe in itself. We had hills you could almost call mountains, great trees and small brooks running into a creek running into a river and a lake covering two or three acres. In winter we skated and coasted and made snowmen, spring and summer we fished and swam and in autumn we shot rabbits, quail and ducks. And—oh yes—we raised corn, wheat, rye and alfalfa, and of course hogs and cattle; we had no sheep or goats but some neighbors did. Haying time was a big week, as was the harvesting. Add the berry picking, wild honey and wild strawberries, putting up jars of jelly and "preserves," filling the ice-house with ice in the winter for use in the spring and summer, milking cows, churning for butter, turning the separator for cream, gathering eggs and taking them in to sell for ten cents a dozen at the market—what have I left out?

In there somewhere was an education in music and more and more composing and orchestration. The "education" part of it at this point was mostly my mother and I playing symphonies arranged for two players at one piano and sonatas for violin and piano. It was also a part of life for me to read a Beethoven piano sonata before going to bed every night. Music at that period for me was top-heavy with Bach and Beethoven. One summer day when we were having a lawn party some of the guests asked me to play the piano for them through the open window. I improvised on a couple of tunes they knew, without making any musical history, and then one of the wags said in a loud voice, "Play a duet, Russell!" This got a big laugh, but I said, "I'll play a quartet," and played a four-voice fugue in C from Bach's *Well-Tempered Clavier.* Nothing could have fallen flatter. Mama explained that it was four voices, etc., but the whole crowd was in trouble.

I left the piano, a slightly bigger snob than ever. Now, in looking back, I wonder if Cole Porter had left three of the voices out and done a lyric like "I wonder why in the morning, morning will never be the same again. I wonder why," how high it would have been on the hit parade.

It seems to me that the three things on the farm that did me the most good were the mile walk to school and back, pitching hay, and making believe. It's not likely that there would have been any baseball, tennis, handball or skating but for those two miles a day at that time. As for pitching hay, the weight of the pitch-fork full of hay lifted up to the wagon is a test of strength, and when it doesn't come back and bury you you can feel yourself meeting the test with certain satisfaction.

When it comes to making believe, poems and books have been written, pictures have been painted and songs have filled the air about how a farmer boy dreams—and it's true, or was when I was one of those. If we could get through to Gertrude Stein, she would probably tell us that a dream is a dream is a dream—which I could take to mean "so what?" If that was not what she put into her microphone it was what came out on my loudspeaker anyway.

On those farm jobs with long hours of purely physical effort, what a farm boy dreams may not be important even to him, but turning anybody loose with his dreams is a big invitation.

One of my biggest assignments besides pitching loads of hay every season was cultivating corn. How they do it with modern machinery is clear out of my world now, but then we had a team of horses—sometimes one horse—who drew a machine along the corn rows and destroyed weeds while it made a "dust-mulch" to draw the moisture up from the soil and make the corn grow. One of my horses was named Dolly. She was my favorite and I hated her. I hated her because she was blind and wind-broken and went down the corn rows with a perplexed look on her face. Hate is the wrong word. I always felt like crying when I looked at her worried forehead and heard in her panting sound the rhythm of the Kreutzer Sonata,[1] first movement. It was a sacred thing to let the horses rest after a certain number of corn rows and poor Dolly had been overworked at some time. One young horse of ours named John died of heat prostration when one of the hired hands forgot to rest him. The hired man's standing fell pretty low for as long as people remembered—anywhere from twenty minutes to what? (There we go with that human memory question again—these were mostly oldsters, who are good forgetters.)

It used to make him furious when one of the town whittlers and tobacco juice spitters would say, "I hear yuh killed a horse fer George Bennett!" Of course he had already convinced himself that John died of some other cause. Whether he was right or they were we couldn't get John back.

---

[1]Beethoven's Sonata for Violin and Piano, Op. 47, dedicated to Rodolphe Kreutzer.

Presumably the social life in the little town and around it amounted to something like everywhere else. Most of the evening get-togethers were for grownups but our parents certainly kept us up on what was going on. There were book clubs and card clubs and discussion clubs, and Beatrice and I got a full report the next morning on almost everything. The card clubs didn't play bridge. At that particular period the popular game was called High Five (also known as Pedro). Those who didn't join the game got their kicks talking about those who did—it was wicked to play cards because people gambled on cards. (As my papa said, they didn't seem to mind people owning horses.)

One boy said to another boy, "We're gonna church your mother!"[2] The other boy, not having any idea what that entailed, said, "Why?"

The answer was, "For playin' cards."

I'm afraid that helps explain why I was Valedictorian when I graduated from high school. Anyhow, if ever a penny was bet on the game of High Five I never heard of it.

During the week of graduation someone gave a party and I was asked to it. All my contemporaries and others were there. After refreshments we all joined in a game I had never heard of; they started for some reason with me and said, "Choose a partner." An older boy said in my ear, "Pick a pretty girl." I picked a girl named Ula, who was indeed pretty, but she was not one of my favorites. This was because I didn't know what was coming up next, and something inside was mixing up paint to make my face red.

It turned out to be a kissing game—the first and last ever for me, not for any reason but it just turned out that way. We played several games with several names but not Post Office, the only one I'd ever heard of up to then. Finally my dad came by from some lodge meeting to pick me up and walk home. With his usual humor he said, "It's time to go home, you've kissed everybody good night."

Girls were always a bit magic to me—all of them. That would be part of the farmer boy's dreams in my case. But I somehow managed to build up a dream-world wherein all the females were what they pretended to be—delicate, fragrant and a tiny bit distant.

There was always poetry in a courtship but almost none in a mating. And yet some memories contradict that. A girl neighbor of ours in Kansas City met a nice looking boy and married him and when they had just come back from their honeymoon I ran into them in the park one evening. We chatted

---

[2] I.e., report her to church authorities, or perhaps have her tried before the congregation.

for a moment and they turned and went up the path and out of sight arm in arm. The picture was pure beauty to me and haunted me for several days.

Still and all almost any girl I noticed bounced up on a pedestal (where she probably had no desire to be) and there she seemed to remain, rather untouchable in my thoughts. From the age of fourteen or fifteen I began to plight my one-sided troth to a certain idol to whom I was faithful but never met. Down the block a bit lived a smallish girl named Esther Burke and the fun began. She was my constant dream—by day and quite often at night.

The leading lady in these passionate dreams was always chosen from a neighborhood in Kansas City during our rather rare visits at the home of Mama's oldest sister. She was married to a man of Dutch descent who tuned pianos and really deserves a good deal of space in this story, but probably won't get it. His top salary as far as I ever heard was around twenty-five dollars a week; he had several emergencies in his family that had to be financed by him, but he owned four quite nice homes in the city toward the end of his life. He not only showed us all that the way you spend it, or don't spend it, is the true measure of an income, but he was a great friend for a young musician—a well-balanced pro with fine tastes and enthusiasms.

We still spent most of our time in the country, where Esther had no serious competition. Then one day on the trolley car appeared a girl rather bigger than Esther, whom I had seen once before on the same side of town and recognized—dark hair and fair skin, a pretty creature indeed. She was on the car often, sometimes quite near me, but I never would have dared speak. I found out her name, Mary Cook. My informant knew her slightly but said Mary Cook was a Catholic and hard to get to know well. I never knew her at all—only knew that I loved her and "kept myself wholly unto her."

There were probably more male virgins around me at that time than I realized, but it seemed to me all the boys I knew spent all their waking hours thinking and talking of "her straight leg and quivering thigh and that which doth adjacent lie"—as William S. so prettily put it.[3] Their appropriate vocabulary was not so elegant but neither was it confined to four-letter words, as is popularly supposed. Personally, even if I hadn't been faithful to some "one and only" I always spent all my time at the piano playing ragtime and popular ballads whenever I went to parties, when all the pairings started.

But the other reason I never went to the school of "doin' what comes naturally" calls for a big *Dal Segno*. (For those fortunate characters who got

---

[3]"By her fine foot, straight leg, and quivering thigh / And the demesnes that there adjacent lie" (*Romeo and Juliet*).

through so far without practicing music, that means "go 'way back to where the man says and do it all over again.") So *dal segno*, timewise.

As far as I know, all my poundings on the piano were (aside from the imitating of Beethoven reported above) about the same as that of all kids who had suddenly found a new way to make a loud noise. At some time the sounds must have begun to sound a little more agreeable because my mother's exact words when she put the printed notes before me were, "I have something here that you might like to play." (Sort of sneaked up on me like.) I was eight years old.

I was nine when I "composed" a piece—meaning it was in such shape that its all three strains could be repeated any number of times without changing from playing to playing. Both parents were much too impressed, I thought, but it was not to be the last time I took bows for things which didn't amount to much. My papa wrote a very neat staff of music and had a few short compositions and arrangements of his own. Somehow (presumably with his help) I arranged the little ditty for band and the band played it at a rehearsal. Precocious? Not from what I have read of so many of our big heroes. And from word of mouth as well. The European young start so early that they are veterans at the age of nine. A beautiful story is that of a little six-year-old girl who studied piano somewhere in Europe. She worked with a local teacher (I think it was in Russia) and every six months was brought to Paris for a master-lesson with Nadia Boulanger. When I was in Paris the little pupil came in to play her assignment—twenty Preludes and Fugues of Johann Sebastian Bach. She played them all for Mademoiselle Boulanger—and divinely! Much pleased, Mlle Boulanger said to the little musician, "And how do you like Bach?"

The answer was, "I don't like him."

"And why do you not like him?"

"I don't like for everybody to talk at the same time! I like for one to speak and the others to listen."

This is largely a musician's story, but is not unrelated to the folks at the lawn party who didn't take to Mr. Bach's four-voice fugue when I played it for them.

Here we are at the point where a songwriter is supposed to have said, "And then I wrote," etc. It gets quoted often when songs are being played, but the reason that underlies the uncomplimentary laugh is often forgotten. What's really amusing—or was—is that the tunesmith couldn't write two bars to save his soul. He called in a music arranger and sang, whistled, or one-fingered it on the piano and the arranger took it from there.

The typical story is that it caught on and made a hit. The arranger got paid by the page—say, a total of fifty dollars, and the composer made a pile—something in five figures for him to lose when the market crashed.

And then I wrote . . . I not only wrote, I made a little theater out of some packing boxes, designed scenery (doll-size) with a curtain that really rose and fell, set out to do a libretto and construct a whole musical comedy. None of these ever got finished but they all got started. The only things that got finished were some piano solos written and submitted to the publishers of the music magazine *The Etude*, Theodore Presser in Philadelphia.[4] The first pieces I sent them were elaborate and ambitious and they were returned to me with, I must say, great courtesy, and every evidence that the editors had really taken time to look them over. Then one day I tried an experiment. I sent them a shorter piece, much easier to write and containing nothing that I would call new in it.

In the mail came a letter saying they could accept the composition and give me fifteen dollars and fifty printed copies.

Much rejoicing. Papa said, "The main thing is you got fifteen dollars" and Mama jumped down his throat. It meant much more than the fifteen dollars, etc.

(It could just as easily have been the other way around, I'm sure I needn't add.)

The publishers took one more piano piece and a duet for violin and piano on the same terms.[5] Along about here Mother, sister and I moved to, and spent most of our time in Kansas City where I studied harmony and composition with the conductor of the Kansas City Symphony Orchestra. A dear man originally from Denmark, a composer of some beautiful orchestral works and a pupil of Engelbert Humperdinck—the real Engelbert Humperdinck,[6] Carl Busch—Sir Carl Busch, knighted at the Danish court—was a master of strict harmony and counterpoint and an exponent of elegance in music.

[Carl Reinholt Busch (1862–1943) studied at Denmark's Royal Conservatory with Niels Gade and J. P. E. Hartmann, emigrating to the U.S. in 1887. He founded the Kansas City Symphony (later the Philharmonic), which he led from 1912 until 1918. Busch praised Bennett as the most gifted of his students, one who could "solve the most difficult problems in counterpoint with the greatest ease."[7] Bennett later returned the compliment:

---

[4] *The Etude*, published monthly from 1896 until 1957, was widely read by America's music teachers and amateur musicians.

[5] *June Twilight* appeared in the July, 1913 *Etude*; *Echoes of Palermo*, two months later. The January 1914 issue included Bennett's violin-and-piano *At Sundown: Romance*.

[6] A curiosity of contemporary popular music is singer Arnold George Dorsey's (b. 1936) use of the name of German composer Engelbert Humperdinck (1854–1921) professionally, and his international success with this unlikely stage name. The singer's followers are said to be largely unaware of his namesake.

Carl Busch, c. 1912. Photo from the Kansas City Museum, Kansas City, Mo. Used by permission.

Composer Carl Busch was founder and first conductor of the Kansas City Symphony.

"As a teacher, Sir Carl was very thorough and preached the gospel of the old fundamental rules. When you studied with him, you could say that you had studied harmony, counterpoint and fugue without blushing."[8] Still, until his pupil's success as a composer was well established, Busch fretted about Russell's commercial-music distractions: " . . . everytime {that Bennett returned to Kansas City to visit} I would ask him when he was going to stop that cheap business."[9]]

We rented a furnished house (or several, one at a time) and I helped pay for it improvising music for the silent screen on piano or organ.[10] There were little moving picture houses all over the city, and all had to have music of some kind. One job that has some memories was across the river in Kansas

[7]*Kansas City Times*, 3 May 1929.

[8]1972 letter from Bennett to Donald Robert Lowe, quoted (271) in Lowe's dissertation, "Sir Carl Busch: His Life and Work."

[9]*Kansas City Times*, 3 May 1929.

[10]Bennett remembers his first professional engagement as "the day I got a card in the American Federation of Musicians and marched over the cable-car tracks [in Kansas City] playing the euphonium in E. W. Berry's band for the Priests of Pallas parade." This was evidently 1 May 1912, the date he joined Local 34 of what was then the "Kansas City Musicians' Association." Though occasionally late with a dues payment while living in New York or in Europe, Bennett never resigned and was awarded life membership in 1960.

City, Kansas, on the main street, where we had three reels of pictures and two acts of vaudeville—admission five cents except on Saturday and Sunday, when it was ten cents. We rehearsed and changed the show twice a week.

The orchestra was violin, trumpet, drums and piano. Our leader was Leo Forbstein, who some time later became general music director for Warner Brothers Pictures in California. His violin playing was quite exciting to me at the time, but when he got in pictures, I don't believe he ever took the instrument out of its case.

Our brass section (the one trumpet) was a charming man with a nice tone when his lip wasn't sore. The drummer didn't read music very well, so he was quite likely to add a few licks after the rest of us had finished—not even noticing that the overture was over.

To get to the Victor Theater in Kansas City, Kansas, from where I lived in Kansas City, Missouri, one took a trolley car that passed over a viaduct not very far from the stock yards. In the summer the soft breezes from the south brought an odor with it that was not like any other I've every known. I've smelt animals, dead and alive, as well as a great many other "fragrances," as the cosmetics merchants like to call them, but this was completely without its equal. Not in repulsiveness either, nor was it seductive. Just vaguely awful, warm and unavoidable.

Leo Forbstein's next job was in a new theater where they had a fairly nice three-manual organ on which another boy and I played (on alternate weeks) from nine in the morning till two p.m., then from five till seven-thirty. Every week we exchanged and played from two to five and seven-thirty to midnight. I list these hours because they were responsible for a serve that mowed down many tennis players who were clear out of my class as the years went by.

The other organist was a young husband who had a very young son. My partner's name was Harry Frank and we both loved tennis so much that we got up every morning between six and seven to drag our bodies out to a public tennis court and play until one of us had to dash to the theater to play the organ at nine. Being a husband and father he couldn't always get to our rendezvous at all, at which point I stood alone and served and served for more than an hour. When I have aced one or two of the glamour boys of tennis I have been careful to send my silent thanks to the Franks—Mrs. and the young son.

At certain times of the day we switched from the organ to the piano to form a trio with Leo and a fine cellist named Julius Leib. The last I heard of Julius Leib he was the conductor of the San Diego Symphony Orchestra.[11]

---

[11]Leib was the Hamburg-born pupil and protégé of conductor Arthur Nikisch at the Leipzig Conservatory before coming to the U. S. in 1915. He spent his later years teaching at

Some time later Harry and I changed our every-other-week routine and I had to do the early morning shift every day in order to take on another job. This was in a legitimate theater—meaning in this case not a movie—where a stock company played a performance every night and two or three matinees a week. Watching this troupe work was an education and an inspiration. I don't think we ever worked as hard on the farm as these actors, directors and stage workers did. A week's work amounted to three, really: studying and learning one part, rehearsing an entirely different one, and performing the third one for an audience eight to ten times.

Sounds like fun, eh? Maybe for a few days, providing you didn't have to do it or get sacked. All I did was play in the orchestra except for a few bits on the stage or off-stage when called upon.

Two jobs and nothing to do with my spare time but try to learn music. Harmony and counterpoint in the theater basement while the actors shouted and stomped on the stage overhead. Sometimes at the cinema [Hanson's Arcadia] it was possible to turn on a mechanical device that would play ragtime and such during two reels of comedy picture at a stretch. That was a good time to practice real concentration with the exercise book in my lap, writing double counterpoint invertible in the octave, tenth and twelfth[12] while the rafters rang with "The Chicken Reel," "The Oceana Roll," or "In the Shade of the Old Apple Tree."[13]

Holding two jobs and getting two salaries was great fun until I went to bed one night and not only couldn't sleep—I couldn't breathe. Something was wrong and I was scared. Big afflictions don't give you big warnings as a rule, so the chances are there was nothing drastic moving in on me, but my mother insisted on calling our family doctor in. She, a powerful woman named Richardson, checked the lungs and heart, and found nothing wrong. But she practically commanded me to quit one of my theaters and march down to the Y.M.C.A. and join a physical culture class. The reason I so rapidly obeyed her command may have been that the body was hungry for some of the activity of the farm years—or it may have been because even our early morning

San Diego State College, conducting the city's Symphony Orchestra and Star-Light Opera Company. Leib died in 1957 while leading a Star-Light performance of Richard Rodgers's *South Pacific*—with Bennett's orchestrations.

[12]Bennett had earlier quipped: "[I] studied with Carl Busch . . . and with Nadia Boulanger in Paris, can write double counterpoint invertible in the octave, tenth, and twelfth—and Fred Astaire likes my saxophone parts" (program note for the Carnegie Hall premiere of Bennett's *Hexapoda* for violin and piano, with the composer accompanying Louis Kaufman, 20 March 1940).

[13]These three pieces (the first an instrumental work) are by Joseph M. Daly (1910), Lucien Denni and Roger Lewis, (1911, revived for use in the 1941 film *Mildred Pierce*), and Egbert van Alstyne and Harry H. Williams (1911) respectively.

tennis had been crowded out now—there must have been some explanation for my untypical surrender. Anyway there began a fairly long affair with the Y.M.C.A. The handball court and the handball crown [crowd?] soon took in a new addict.

By now it must be unnecessary to make a pompous point of what took up my time and thoughts when the normal lads and ladies were getting down to basics. This, however, is why I made the big *dal segno* pages and pages ago. A wise old doctor once told me that it was a fact that when the monks in any old order showed signs of breaking their vows of celibacy, their leaders gave them more work to do.

I gave up the organ job and stayed with the legit—the stock company. Except for one or two special weeks, that meant only eight performances a week—time for more intensive study, preparing to be what by this time I most wanted to be, an opera conductor, preferably a Wagnerian opera conductor.

I must say I did learn a lot of scores, but whatever I did was practically nothing compared with what I did not do. And what I did do included joining a fine tennis club and playing as much tennis as I wanted to for the first time.

What I did not do was set my sights on the post of principal conductor of the Metropolitan Opera House in New York and sacrifice pleasure, friends, family and years of my life if need be on the altar of that one ambition. With that as a program I should probably have ended up as an associate director at Stuttgart, Mannheim or Mainz, a disappointed old Herr Kappellmeister.

Instead I waited for music to come to me, doing each task as I was expected to do it, never at all sure of making good but trusting fate to steer for me. Fate chose to guide me to many beginnings:

I was making sounds in the darkened theater when John Bunny and Mary Pickford crossed the screen.

I was writing violin and piano parts when engineers were at their wits' end to record them for the phonograph.

I was knee deep in oom-pahs, vamps-till-ready, verses and repeat choruses when the "Golden Age of the American Musical" was beginning.

The Wireless—or Radio, depending on where you were—almost sneaked in on me, but they were still on earphones when I sneaked in on them.

Sound pictures, too, almost got started behind my back. I was in Paris when a young artist told me she was interested in learning to draw pictures for animated films. A man was in Paris at the time that she hoped to talk to because he was developing a technique for the medium. His name was Walt Disney. My first film job was almost two years after that.

Last stop for fate and me, Television. I was interviewed in the first building ever erected for TV—in Erie, Pennsylvania[14]—and Channel Five in New York broadcast a *Music Box Opera* of mine as one of the first musicals on people's living room screens.

The next big pot-boiler hasn't come over the horizon far enough to be recognized yet, but when it does, I'll probably still be looking for work. It would be hypocritical to curse my fate, but when I think of the second act of *Die Meistersinger* I think it couldn't have been bad in Mainz. "Lobet sei der Herr!"

My father acquired a farm and built a nice house on it at the eastern edge of Freeman in 1910. We moved in just before I finished my "education," and there was less than a year left of my life as a farmer. However, there was time left for the biggest and most impossible of the farmer-boy dreams.

This time I didn't wait till I saw her. Just read about her in the papers. Her parents lived in Slater, Missouri, but she was in Paris and London, making headlines as a coloratura soprano at L'Opéra and Covent Garden. She was five feet tall and weight around one hundred. The nearest I ever came to her was at two recitals she gave in Kansas City within the next two or three years. I bought a seat in the second balcony for both recitals.

When my mother was displeased with me she invariably shook her head sadly and said, "Poor Felice!" The idol's name was Felice Lyne. I once met a girl who said she knew Felice Lyne and she pronounced the last name like "Lynne," with a short *i* sound of the *y*. That's all the authority I can muster as to the pronunciation.

We had an exciting life together, except for the moments when I found myself carrying a five-gallon pail of milk a quarter of a mile beyond where it was supposed to go. Of course I knew for the five years that this went on that she as I perceived her didn't exist, but if you read a few pages of the famous philosophers, what does?

This fairy-tale has two endings. Ending number one came when I walked through the streets of New York, realizing that it was a simple matter to find her and tell her whatever was tellable of the story. The idea was impossible because I had nothing to offer of importance in her world. So the story died a lingering death.

I've never gone to a psychiatrist, but I don't need one to tell me the true reason I chickened.

---

[14]In April 1949, while Bennett was in town to guest-conduct Fritz Mahler's Erie Philharmonic in his *Overture to an Imaginary Drama*. WICU television had moved into its new building but a month earlier.

Ending number two is much simpler. My mother sent me a newspaper clipping only a year or two later saying Felice Lyne had died.[15]

In a biography of Oscar Hammerstein (the first), the impresario of the Manhattan Opera House in New York, I came across a reference to Felice Lyne, coloratura soprano. She was singing at the Manhattan and came to the boss's office with some kind of grievance.[16] They argued and she slapped his face.

Knowing producers as I do the story could have no effect on Felice's memory unless I knew what Mr. Hammerstein said to her. If he was like his grandson, Oscar II, the verdict would be very different from the verdict if he was like his son Arthur.

The stock company at the Auditorium in Kansas City flourished for a season, but ran into difficulty. One of the principal character actors took over the artistic direction and we coasted for more than half of my second year with them. We ended working a week or two without salary, and then pouf!

I worked around. Phonographs had been invented but loud-speakers were still in the future, so a free-lance playing musician got work if anybody wanted to hear music. Two seasons on second violin in the Symphony Orchestra, band dates on trombone or baritone, two summers as piano-conductor in a beer garden in Fairmount Park (near where Harry Truman, who also played the piano, lived), a few weeks at a grill room where the orchestra was a banjo and a piano. The banjo player was the contractor. He was a trumpet player who took up the banjo because it was a "new" fad all over the country. All he, or nearly everybody, could play on it was chords. As the piano was the only thing that played the tune I nearly broke my right hand banging it out. I was fighting a losing battle because it was the loudest banjo I ever heard.

One day a friend of mine met my banjo player-leader-employer by chance and reported to me that they had spoken of me. He asked Mr. Banjo how I was and Mr. Banjo said, "He's fine, but I wish he wouldn't play so loud."

The nearest thing to a steady engagement I played in this period was on piano with a good-sized dance-concert orchestra at the Muehlbach Hotel Grill. The hotel was and is on Twelfth Street—I always supposed it was for this street that the "Twelfth Street Rag" was named—I don't think I ever cared enough to look it up, but the "Twelfth Street Rag" is bound to turn up in

---

[15]Bennett is mistaken about her early death, as she lived until 1935. Following her European successes, Felice Lyne had returned to the U.S., being featured principally with the Boston Opera Company.

[16]According to Vincent Sheehan's *Oscar Hammerstein I: The Life and Exploits of an Impresario*, 73, Lyne had been kept waiting at a rehearsal, as the conductor had been summoned to Hammerstein's office.

these pages because it plays a tiny part in a tiny drama that we'll stumble over before long. The days of our orchestra were numbered because by this time the dance bands, later called name bands, were beginning to organize. Paul Whiteman and Jack Hylton[17] were getting ready to start a vogue. What I didn't know, never having heard what they were doing, was that the sound of the new organizations was sensationally new to the "hep" crowd because they had special new arrangements for their small groups. What this meant, besides a few new bars composed by the arranger, was that every harmony was complete in each section instead of up to twelve men trying to make like thirty.

Added to this each player was a top man on his instrument and they rehearsed and rehearsed and rehearsed. Hotel men probably had no idea why they had to pay so much more for these groups, but they did and the price of cocktails went on up.

In following this report from one point of view it would seem that destiny just missed something here: dance orchestras all springing up and each needing its own private music arranger, and me looking elsewhere for work.

No worry—destiny knows what it is doing!

---

[17]Whiteman (1890–1967) was the most visible proponent of "symphonic jazz" and one of America's most popular dance-band leaders in the 1920s and early 1930s. Gershwin's *Rhapsody in Blue* was written for Whiteman's ensemble, orchestrated by his arranger Ferde Grofé, and premiered at the bandleader's celebrated 1924 Aeolian Hall concert in New York. Jack Hylton, Whiteman's British counterpart, led a dance orchestra that likewise featured virtuoso musicians playing highly stylized arrangements. Though the ensemble's recordings were distributed in the U.S., Hylton was never able to organize an American tour with his group.

Chapter Three

"Looking elsewhere for work," toward the end of August in 1916, I gathered up my life savings—$140—and took a railroad train to New York City. Arriving at Pennsylvania Station I had to put a nickel in a pay telephone to ask at the West Side Y.M.C.A. how to get there. Following instructions I came up with another nickel and got on a trolley car headed uptown. It was one of those summertime cars with no walls at all and the trolley wires were down where the cable used to be (see Powell Street in San Francisco for where that was). It was nice to be where the streets were so simply and clearly marked at every corner.

There was a small thunderstorm just as I settled down in my dormitory room and I wondered if it was a growl or a twenty-one-gun salute. I decided it was a small thunderstorm. The Y.M.C.A. was just about ideal: kind of a combination of club and home, complete with friends, neighbors and handball players.

It took less that a week to get settled in the new quarters, but then the roof fell in. Or rather, a young man name Brown Schoenheit came in to live in the room next to mine. He was in New York to study flute with Georges Barrère,[1] who was as good as any for the title of the all-time greatest.

Brown Schoenheit had spent two years in Boston studying flute and harmony with the first and second flutists of the Boston Symphony Orchestra. He was from Kansas City and for reasons never clear to me he purposely checked in as my next-door neighbor. I certainly had not come to New York to bum around with a boy from Kansas City, Missouri, and his appearance was timed to remind me of an especially asinine trick I had played on myself the afternoon my train was coming into New York. There was a quite chic young New York girl with whom I had chatted and had one meal in the din-

---

[1]The French flute virtuoso (1876–1944) came to the U.S. in 1905; he was a member of the New York Symphony Orchestra and later taught at the Institute of Musical Art and the Juilliard School.

ing car, and as we were coming to the end of the trip she said she would like to introduce me to a few of her friends.

My answer: I would have neither the time nor the money to have any social life at all, thanks just the same.

("Hell hath no fury," etcetera.) She should have kicked me.

Never mind; I kicked myself for two years in this lonely, lonely town.

Brown turned out to be not hard to take in a crowd of friends like we had at the Y. He was colorful, had a whole deck of jokes and stories to keep us laughing, and was indeed a talented flutist. I have him to thank for the fact that I wrote a fairly successful *Rondo Capriccioso* for four flutes while we were neighbors. It was first published by The New York Flute Club and had its first public performance at a Flute Club concert. The players could easily have been ranked one, two, three, and four in the world if flutists were tennis champs.

[The piece, written in 1916 and published six years later, was premiered by Barrère, William Kincaid, George Possell and (probably) Lamar Stringfield. Kincaid, a longtime friend of Bennett's, was for many years principal flutist for the Philadelphia Orchestra. Stringfield went on to receive the Pulitzer prize in composition and direct the North Carolina Symphony and the Knoxville (Tenn.) Symphony. He was soloist for the 1947 premiere of Bennett's *A Dry Weather Legend* (flute and orchestra) in Knoxville.

The *Rondo Capriccioso* was the first Bennett composition to circulate widely. It appeared on programs by "flute clubs" across the U.S., and was championed by Barrère and by Leonardo DeLorenzo, who often played it with his flute students at the Eastman School in the 1920s and 30s. Chappell republished the piece in 1962, incorporating Bennett's minor revisions.]

Brown Schoenheit had two great interests, Girls and Music. Mostly girls, when I knew him. The last time I heard from him he was business manager of the Kansas City Symphony, having lost his front teeth.[2] With them went what I remember best—a very "manly" tone on the flute. When Barrère first heard him the Master said, "Do not make war on ze flute—make love!"

"Cher maître Georges" knew very well how to do both—on the flute, I mean. I heard him.

After a few trips to the musician's union, looking for a playing job of some kind, I had some good advice from one of the popular dance-band leaders of the

[2]Bennett's 1948 *Six Souvenirs* for two flutes and piano begins with a movement dedicated to Schoenheit.

day. He had a friend who sold violin music on the ground floor at G. Schirmer's. He might know about an opening for a man who writes music.

I went right down to Schirmer's (the name was rather a famous one, being on at least half of the great music I was raised on) and met Mr. Otto Flaschner of the violin department.

Mr. Flaschner wasted no time. He said, "Go up to the sixth floor and ask for Mr. Rober. Maybe we could use you here." I did and they did.

The man in charge of arranging, proof-reading and copying, Mr. Charles Greinert, put me to work copying a piano part of something I didn't recognize. It had big chords and lots of notes and figures on it. At the end of the day I was a little ashamed of my output but Mr. Greinert seemed to think it was respectable. We were paid by the page and I started to figure whether I would be able to eat, even if I worked full time. It wasn't hopeless.

The rate per page was surprisingly small. I heard a little old German fellow ask Greinert what he should charge a page for what he was doing. In a tired little voice, when he heard the rate, the little old fellow said, "That's a hell of a price!" Mr. Greinert's answer was simple: "Don't do it, then!" At the end of the first week my pay was twelve dollars.

But I was working.

After a few weeks the boss came to my desk and told me to go to Freeport, Long Island, and to the home of Mr. William Furst to help him finish scoring a film.

It turned out to be a full-evening-length show featuring Geraldine Farrar as Joan of Arc. William Furst[3] had spent a good part of a year in California writing a 100% background score for an orchestra of forty-odd men, but he had run out of time to write out the full score. After a few minutes' talk he gave me a pile of sheets of his original sketches and we both sat down to finish the opus. After an hour I heard him behind me looking over my shoulder. He said, "You know your business," and went back to work. I stayed in his house for almost a week, during which time a blizzard buried us in about three feet of snow.

Mrs. Furst managed miraculously to come up with three meals a day and between us Mr. and I came up with a symphonic score for *Joan the Woman.* He got me into the second violin section of the orchestra and gave me a chance to take over the conducting, which was quite beyond me, since I only knew the part of the score that I had orchestrated—among other inadequacies.

---

[3]Furst (1852–1917), a one-time orchestra director at San Francisco's Tivoli Theatre, was a leading composer and conductor of incidental music and theatrical specialty numbers, often in association with producer David Belasco. Furst's score for *Joan The Woman* was his last.

But my real flop was just before the opening in New York[4] when they took the film to Washington for a preview before a white-tie-and-tails crowd. William Furst stayed in New York and sent me to play the whole score on a grand piano all by myself. At that time I had no idea at all what was in eighty percent of the music. So I sat down to play and watch the picture for the first time. I improvised as I had for the first running of a five-cent picture show at 15th and Brooklyn Avenue in Kansas City, but I was not enjoying myself. Just as I was beginning to develop some kind of theme for poor Joan, the pedals of the grand piano fell off.

At intermission time the director of the picture, Mr. Cecil B. DeMille, came up and complained about the music. He couldn't have liked it any less than I did, and I was actually glad the miserable pedals had fallen down. It was a practical thing that he could see for himself and may have seemed like an alibi of some kind to him.

In the movies you are only concerned with the opinion of one man. This is a moving picture axiom.

I played violin in the reduced orchestra at the theater for a few weeks, but was not a complete success with only two second violins playing. Another place where I didn't practice enough. There was only one official complaint: I didn't play loud enough. The truth is the tone wasn't good enough. I still looked on Schirmer's arranging and copying as my job, so I offered to quit without notice at the theater. They were glad, I know, to get me out of there, but were really more kind than they needed to be.

The next break in the routine at Schirmer's is a story that goes back quite a ways. There was a very fine actor named Guy Bates Post, who brought his show through Kansas City every two or three years in those days, and when I was still there I heard some of my friends or family say that they never missed a play with Guy Bates Post for one reason: he always carried a little lame violin player who played between the acts with the most gorgeous tone they had ever heard on the violin.

I never knew how it happened, but one day I had a phone call from this very violinist. His name was Maurice Nitke and he asked me to come to his hotel. He had written a new piece for violin and piano and needed an arrangement of the accompaniment. It was quite a charming piece and we became friends on the spot.

When I got to New York I looked him up and we visited a bit.[5]

---

[4]24 December 1916.

[5]Guy Bates Post (1875–1968) appeared on the New York stage for several decades; moving to Los Angeles in the 1930s, he worked occasionally in Hollywood. Polish musician Maurice

One day he called me and asked me to put some music in order and play in the orchestra with a production of *Peter Ibbetson.* The cast included Constance Collier, Laura Hope Crews, John Barrymore and Lionel Barrymore. As you might imagine, this was quite a cast and the show quite a success.[6] It played to the end of the season, reopened in the fall, then played what was called the Subway Circuit before closing. The Subway Circuit was a name for the Bronx Opera House and one or two other neighborhood theaters.

One evening during the performance in the Bronx, some men were sitting in a box just off the stage, doing a lot more laughing than the scene called for. Ben Kauser was on the stage with John Barrymore, serving him in some way, when Barrymore raised his voice and said, "Antoine, what do you suppose those asses are laughing at?"

Whatever it was, they were quieter for the rest of the evening. I never heard any more to the story than that, if there was any more.

Lionel Barrymore was a pretty well schooled musician,[7] wrote some chamber music and knew what he was talking about. In another scene in *Peter Ibbetson* Lionel (as his brother John's uncle) was supposed to sit down at the piano and play Liszt's *Fourteenth Hungarian Rhapsody* for a few bars. They put a piano behind the scene, Lionel mimed and I furnished the sounds he was supposed to make. The director told me it didn't necessarily have to be Liszt's *Fourteenth Hungarian Rhapsody* as long as it was loud and showy. I happily agreed, since I would have had to send out for two more hands to come near playing the Liszt piece.

What I played (and Lionel pretended to play) may sometimes have been just as hard to play as the *Fourteenth* if written out and practiced. Such is the nature of improvisation, but in any case it was never the same thing twice. When I could see him through the scenery it was remarkable how Lionel could make his whole body look like he was playing what I did, whatever it was.

During the run of *Peter Ibbetson,* I made a big try to do something that I didn't know couldn't be done. In the orchestra that played for the performance was a brilliant young lady harpist who eventually was to travel all over the world as a soloist with John Philip Sousa's band. She was tiny. Her dimensions were just about identical with those of Felice Lyne, my dream wife.

Nitke was the leading conductor-violinist for New York's legitimate theater (especially productions featuring the Barrymores), though he eschewed musical-comedy work.

[6]Opening at the Republic Theater, 17 April 1917.

[7]Barrymore (1878–1954) was an eager concert-goer early in his career. His large works were programmed occasionally by America's major orchestras, and he was nominated for ASCAP membership in 1944. The actor starred in MGM's series of *Dr. Kildare* films, and contributed a theme to the score of *Dr. Kildare's Strange Case* (1940).

Of course I got out a brand new, shiny pedestal from my unlimited supply and put her name on it: Winifred.[8] Looking at her on her pedestal I could find no detail of personality with a red light on it: nothing could stop me but mature judgment and that was in short supply. I reasoned that I had really dreamed Felice up—invented her, when all was said and done—so why not just move the dream into a new body?

It sounded easy.

Winifred had a nice mother who spent nearly all of her time in New York with her daughter. They were Canadians. Whenever we did any "going together" I always invited her mother. I don't believe it ever occurred to me to do it any other way: lunch, dinner, movies, Coney Island—always three tickets. We were alone together waiting for our cues in the theater but talks were short and usually in whispers. We never talked of marriage. If I thought of it—of money and apartments and children—I also thought of how much I had left after a week of multiplying some of the lunch checks by three.

The theater season ended and the company was laid off for the summer, to return in September. Mother and daughter went to Canada and I got on their train to ride to the 125th Street Station of the New York Central with them. Mother wanted to take our picture on the train platform but thought it would look silly if we posed hand in hand; the conductor said "All aboard" and no picture was taken.

I spent a good deal of the summer with my mother, father and sister. Sister was by this time having a number of commissions as a painter. Her latest work was a mural for a new bus station in Kansas City which she and Gertrude Fryman were painting together, putting the picture on the wall. Both of them were on a high scaffold. Gertrude, like Beatrice, is left handed. Many characters from the neighborhood came by and stopped to crane their necks and look on. One particular citizen looked for a long time as if fascinated and finally said, "Do you have to do that stuff with your left hand?"

Beatrice's speaking voice was always down toward the range of Boris Goudonof and everybody laughed when she boomed out, "You do if you're left handed."

I found a neighborhood movie to work at and had a quiet two months or so in the west, as New Yorkers in those days called anything west of Newark, New Jersey. I missed little Winnie, but it didn't ache. After all, it was the normal thing not to have Her with me in the flesh. Her letters to me were sweet and discreet. Mine to her, as far as I can analyze them at this distance, were letters to a wife of several years. To someone who belonged to me and to whom I belonged.

---

[8]Winifred Bambrick, Sousa's harpist from 1923 until 1930.

It's hard to see how even a dreaming farmer-boy could be so ignorant of women. After a few days back at work in the theater, my dream-girl squared off and let me have it. It had been an awful summer because my letters were not what she needed and expected and now I seemed to be avoiding her. This was not really true, but it might as well have been. My reply was sincere but not any help at all. We had no immediate future and there was no use pretending we had. Our countries were at war and at that time we all believed the slogans. There were many such reasons.

Neither of us got angry or dramatic, but Felice had never turned on me like that and I couldn't understand what went wrong. As time went on I felt like trying to explain the whole story to Winnie and her mother, but didn't know how to explain something I didn't understand.

Some years later she played in the theater orchestra for a musical with my orchestrations. Her harp playing was more beautiful than ever.

By the time *Peter Ibbetson* closed its career I was no longer at the Y.M.C.A. Two other "Y" men, Harold Probasco, cartoonist from Binghampton, and John Marony, a lawyer-poet from Oswego, New York, shared a two-room place with me on the ground floor at 65 West 69th Street. We were the three inhabitants of a mythical kingdom called Boobania. We were three young nuts, but not quite nuts enough to set to music. Just pleasantly unpredictable. I wasn't always able to keep up with the other two.

I had never really deserted my connection as a copyist, editor, and arranger at Schirmer's, so I was sitting at my workbench when one of my bosses came in with a most impressive lady named (of all names) Winifred. Mrs. Winifred Edgerton Merrill needed a composer to help her work something out musically, something she didn't describe to me at the time, but she asked me to take home a few pages of black dots spread all over musical staves and see what they suggested to me. Completely in the dark I made notes out of all the black dots, chose certain things arbitrarily—such as time, accidentals, etc. The only noticeable characteristic in the resultant melodic line was its tendency to sound Slavic in many spots.

We had an appointment on a certain day and I was interested when she asked me if any of it sounded Russian. Then she tried to clear the charade up a little for me: every form, line or point in nature may be expressed in mathematics by reference axes or coordinates.

We didn't get quite that far in the book at Freeman High School, so I just sat and looked stupid while she went on. What she had given me was the Russian National Anthem (the words) written in Russian and translated into higher mathematics, the black dots being at every dot or intersection of lines, one at each extremity of a straight line and three to express every simple curve.

I learned later that Mrs. Winifred Edgerton Merrill was the first woman Ph.D. at Columbia University. Her subject was Mathematical Astronomy.

It was her hope that a person's signature, written across a musical staff, would furnish a melodic line expressive of that person's character, and possibly his or her mood at the time of signing.

Like all the complexities of science, the whole scheme is relatively simple if you sit still and let the other man talk. It was not hard to take a signature to a letter, or on a check, and reduce it to the points that express it. And if you have the signature on a music staff or draw a staff through it you can take down all the dots, even if you only went to Freeman High School. We prepared a book that Schirmer printed in a fine edition,[9] containing the signatures of twenty of the most prominent men of the era reduced to music.

Mrs. Merrill collected the signatures of then-president Woodrow Wilson, ex-presidents Taft and Roosevelt, Enrico Caruso, John Philip Sousa, John Wanamaker[10] and fourteen others. In choosing rhythms, key signatures, harmonies, etc., the musician must find the most simple and satisfying idiom in each case, never allowing any preconceived musical idea to take over.

I remember a review of Mrs. Merrill's book in some music magazine where the critic concluded, "But it is on its musical value that one must judge . . . " etc. That shows you what you are up against when you face the critics with something new. I always wanted to meet that fellow and ask him what he thought musical value had to do with it.

In the course of helping to prepare the book, Mrs. Merrill and I met several times and she invited me to lunch one day at her home. Her "home" was an estate on the shore of Long Island Sound, Orienta Point near Mamaroneck, New York. There she ran a fashionable girls' school with around one hundred pupils in residence. The school was named Oaksmere and housed students from every part of the U.S.A.

At the luncheon I met Mrs. Merrill's daughter Kitty (whose real name was Winifred) and her son Captain Hamilton Merrill. The feature of the day for me was the Captain's uniform. In World War I, as it came to be known, a lot of us of military age believed sincerely in our mission. Everything about war was unattractive, but going through it with our orders in our hand gave our lives a meaning that later generations may understand but I doubt if they feel it. I didn't stand in line waiting to get into the enlistment centers, but it added up to several tries, and when the draft came up they marked me for

---

[9]*Musical Autograms*, 1918.

[10]He founded the successful Wanamaker's department stores in Philadelphia (1876) and New York (1896) and was later Postmaster General under President Benjamin Harrison.

"limited service." I pleaded for a chance to join the big action. One of the examiners said, "You want to go, don't you!" but he said it almost without the exclamation point, and I could tell that it was nothing new to him.

So when I met a captain in full regalia in his own home—it sounds now like a play by Booth Tarkington, but it was a nice day.

By this time I had several ambitious songwriters who depended on me to take down their melodies and fill out their accompaniments in shape for publishing or for submitting to publishers. A little business built itself up and represented a fair living until the U.S.A. decided what to do with me.

One day along here somewhere my friend Mrs. Merrill called and asked me to have lunch with her at the Biltmore Hotel. There were two other women at her table, a member of the faculty at the Merrill School and "another daughter that you haven't met."

Mrs. Merrill, as a flesh and blood woman, had always frightened me a little. She symbolized a highly educated, socially superior human being with whom I would never attempt to match strides, and yet she was important to me and always would be. I knew, if only vaguely, that I was hungry for her to have a daughter for me to love.

The daughter I had met carried a spear, a shield, and a coat of mail an inch thick as far as I was concerned, but now I consciously felt myself saying, "This game isn't over yet." It didn't sound as ridiculous as it should have.

To my great surprise, when a communication came from the Draft Board it was marked "1-A." That meant the trenches and no more nonsense about limited service. How it happened I never knew. Whether they changed my status as a result of my appeal or somebody goofed doesn't matter. I waited for a couple of weeks and no call came, so I went back to them and asked if they had anything for me.

After going through several papers they said there was no opening in my line, but since I had been on a farm I could probably handle an assignment as a teamster in Jacksonville, Florida. Did I want it? Yes.

Another wait. The call for a teamster in Florida fell through and I gave the Draft Board an address in Kansas City and left town. In Kansas City another long wait. It began to look like the U.S.A. didn't like me. Then I got a very strange telegram: "Are you going to Camp Dix on July 10?"

Since when did the Army ask you? I wired back, "I'll go to any camp in the country whenever you say."

The answer: "Report to the draft board where you are and save railroad fare." I ended up in Camp Funston, Kansas.

So this was the army. So these were the heroes. If there was a patriot among us he was hard to spot. We lined up and filed past a barn window from which they threw out some clothes and shoes. They herded us into a shed with a cement floor and showers overhead. It was evident that some of my neighbors hadn't had much experience with shower baths. Somehow we all stumbled through what we had to do, and as we all grouped and went to the next spot some old soldier (probably a veteran of some two and a half months) would call out to us, "Where ya from, boys?" Some one of us would say "Wichita!" or "Topeka!" or whatever, and the "old soldier" would say, "You'll like it!"

The first time a little feeling crept into the blood was at twilight when a lone bugle sounded "Call to Quarters" from somewhere. The bugle was in A flat, to my surprise.[11] It was enough at least to remind me of the captain's uniform that was a part of my ambition.

That ambition never left me, but it got some rude jolts. After a solid night's sleep I awoke at First Call (still in A flat) and went through the routine. ("Oh, How I Hate to Get Up in the Morning" is one of many Irving Berlin songs that I never could have written. I was always eager to see what was next.) We were all ordered to gather after breakfast and a young corporal addressed us as a group. When he finished I wondered whether it would really have been so bad in "limited service" or as a civilian. A corporal is not to be expected to have Major General Leonard Wood's education or his stage presence, but this corporal!

He began with something like, "Now you fellers all think yer goin' on a picnic here. Git that outa yer nut! You ain't even privates yet! You're recroots and yuh keep yer mouth shut 'n' do what yer told!"

And I thought "I'm not a private yet, but I'll have to be one, and then a corporal—and if that's how you have to be—oh my God!"

That day we all went though a physical check-up and when I walked into the big room a man looked at me and put a big blue circle on my chest. At the end of my check-up they pointed to a door and said, "Go in there." I found myself in a small room with a first lieutenant of the Medical Corps. He looked at the blue circle and said, "What's the matter with your feet, young man?" I said to him, "I can beat you playing tennis, Dr. Kyger!"

We had belonged to the same tennis club. I told him about those dirty words "limited service," but he said, "If I put you into the infantry you'll have an overseas examination and I'll be in trouble." But he must have done it anyway because, after training for a rather short time I was told I was an "act-

---

[11]The standard-issue military bugle was pitched in G, not A flat. Yet instruments were built to varying pitch standards at the time, hence the then-common labeling of wind or keyboard instruments as "high pitch" or "low pitch." The international standardization of A = 440hz took place in the 1930s, after a long history of controversy.

ing Second Lieutenant, conductor of the 70th Infantry Band." History kept repeating itself, putting me in the big show.

And what a band it was! Fifty-one men, one of whom could play. He was a cornetist and played with a circus band, had a fine tone and was in every way a pro. The rest of them were fine fellows, ranging from grade C bandsmen to harness makers. To the brass (so-called) in the army, my bandsmen wouldn't be any less musicians than the recruits were soldiers. It seems like it ought to be that way, and maybe I'm too tough on them, but at least one music critic agreed emphatically—the colonel, our commanding officer. He hated the way they played the National Anthem.[12] I knew better than to ask for suggestions as to how to improve it.

However, he sent down orders to go out on the drill field one morning and practice *The Star Spangled Banner.* Pretty soon he came by across the field on his horse, listened to us and called over, "That's much better!" Of course it wasn't, and I didn't know enough about teaching amateur bands to pursue the matter any further. To add insult to injury (unquote), the last time he complained he told me my band was a disgrace to the flag. Thinking quickly over the hard time I'd had to be there at all I wanted to laugh in his face. Instead I gave him my most stylish salute and marched out without waiting to be dismissed. On the way out of his office I told the adjutant that we would play "Dixie" that night and see if the colonel knew the difference.

After swearing, tearing my hair and yelling through many days of rehearsal I decided to try another approach and speak softly, helping each player with his difficulties and being a nice, kindly old maestro to see if that got any better results. It would be nice to report that solved our problems, but it didn't. I couldn't tell a bit of difference.

At that time there was a bad epidemic of flu that swept the country.[13] The band gave concerts every day next to the camp hospital and it was a rare day that we didn't see a corpse or two being carried out. You didn't dare let yourself think too much about it. The epidemic was still raging when they began the overseas examination. I got sent up early for mine, possibly be-

---

[12]Though generally accepted as such for some time, and advocated for ceremonial use in U.S. Army and Navy manuals beginning in the 1890s, *The Star Spangled Banner* was not officially designated the National Anthem until 1931. Among those who worked to galvanize public support and prompt Congressional approval were John Philip Sousa, the Daughters of 1812, and "Believe It or Not" creator Robert Ripley.

[13]The first recognized cases of the "Spanish flu" are believed to be those reported on 4 March 1918 at Camp Funston. Estimated total deaths worldwide range between twenty and forty million, yet this influenza pandemic is rarely mentioned in U.S. history texts and is unknown today to most Americans. The virus was finally isolated in the late 1990s using tissue samples from victims entombed in Alaska's permafrost for eight decades.

cause during a cross-country march of (they said) eight miles to where the division was to pass in review, my right foot almost split open and a good many soldiers knew about it.

That wasn't the only trouble I had that day. I was playing the euphonium and my other euphonium player fell ill and fell out during the march to the parade ground. That left only one of us to stand and play one march (*Our National Anthem*)[14] eighteen times without interruption. The mouthpiece never left my lips till the whole division had gone by. After the first three or four repeats my lips stopped getting tired and just went on and on.

I've often thought since then that it couldn't have been as tough for me as it was for those within earshot that had to listen to the same march for fifty-four minutes.

A few days thereafter came the "overseas." I showed the medicos what I could do with my feet and one of them at one time said to the other two, "What do you suppose he does that with?" Neither of them could guess. But they flunked me.

No overseas. No more infantry. No more dreams about a captain's uniform. I walked up to our barracks trying to hold back tears, and as luck would have it met our commander (he had replaced the music critic some time before). He stopped and I managed to tell him about the overseas business.

He said, "I don't think we're any of us going." He was right. The next day orders came in: "No more transfers and no more promotions."

That didn't mean the war was over for me. They sent me to a detention camp where I did guard duty once and spent twenty-four of the worst hours of my entire life. I'd much rather be a prisoner than do that "two on and four off" routine. Two long hours walking around a closed canteen, waiting for the officer of the day to sneak up on me, which he did in the blackest part of the night and scolded me for my attempt to do "present arms." When I told him I'd never carried an army rifle before he had no reply. Just disappeared in the dark.

The detention camp was only for two or three days. Then they moved me to camp headquarters and—you guessed it—limited service.

We didn't know it, but there was no fight left in the Kaiser by this time and everybody had to stay in place while the machines of war ground to a halt. Soldiers sat around with nothing to do but complain, and wonder why they couldn't just go out and bum a ride home. In our headquarters company each of us had a three-day program that never varied.

We had one day off, one day on K.P., one day policing the barracks and latrines, and da capo ad infinitum—to mix up the languages a bit. They had

---

[14]This is perhaps E. E. Bagley's popular march, *National Emblem.*

a piano in one building and I played a song called "Smiles"[15] for the soldiers at least twenty times a day.

One day a stranger came up to me and said, "Come down to the Zone at six-thirty tonight. I've got a job for you." I was a little mystified and showed it.

He said, "You're a piano player, aren't you?"

I took a long chance and said "Yes."

He said, "Come to the stage door of the Star Theater at six-thirty."

When I got to the stage door I introduced myself to a man with a musical instrument in his hand and he went to get the piano parts of the show and gave them to me. I asked where the leader of the orchestra was so I could run down the routine of the acts and not make a fool of myself.

He looked a little puzzled and said, "You're playing the piano, aren't you?"

Me: "Yes."

He: "Well, you're the leader."

My hair stood up. When I'd played and conducted a vaudeville show in Kansas City I bought a package of five sticks of chewing gum and chewed the whole package all through the first performance of a new bill, just to keep from going stark, staring mad at all the things that happen. But at least I'd had a rehearsal there.

I grabbed the piano book and made for the dressing rooms to get some idea of the danger spots from the acts themselves.

I had good luck. Two of the four acts I had played at the beer garden in Kansas City and the other two were not too complicated. One of the teams, after a warm greeting, showed me something new, a four-year-old daughter I hadn't met.

When we started the performance and had played about sixteen bars of the overture, the little four-year-old presented herself in the orchestra pit, climbed up in my lap and sat there through the whole show and two or three reels of movies that wound up the evening. She was a real pro, and never budged till the last curtain fell.

There followed the period of greatest affluence of my entire life: twenty dollars a week at the theater and thirty a month as a private in the army. And no expenses!

To earn the pay in the Army the programs were never varied. One day shooting pool in a nearby pool hall, one day washing dishes (three hundred sets for three hundred soldiers) and one day as the admiral, they called it—in charge of the vessels . . .

---

[15]The 1917 evergreen by Lee S. Roberts (music) and J. Will Callahan (words).

In the 70th Infantry Band we were still privates even though we were all "acting something-or-other" until, I presumed, we should be sent to the front.

"We were still privates" with twenty-two sad exceptions. After I had been in the camp headquarters job only a few days I went back to visit the band and was greeted by the news that out of the fifty-one of us, twenty-two had died of the flu.

I couldn't bring myself to ask which of the boys got it. It seemed like such a sad way to die for one's country.

All through my military "career" I found time to write many letters to Miss Louise Merrill and she made a good job of keeping up her end of the correspondence. She understood French and German. If my down deep ambition to be a top opera conductor had been down deep enough those two languages, plus Italian, would have been part of me by then, but they weren't.

When the regular leader at the Star Theater got well, or got out of the guard house, or whatever it was, my season there ended. Almost immediately thereafter, one of the two corner cafés on the Zone needed a piano player and I went to work there. There already was an excellent violinist, a member of the medical corps and a nice man to meet. His first name was Lyall but I blush to say I didn't ever call him anything else and didn't retain the last name.

He remains a pleasant memory, partly because in the café across the street, where they served Mulo, or near-beer, just as our place did, there was a fabulous little lady piano player named Edythe Baker, who was a particularly sweet sweetie of Lyall's. We went in to hear her one evening during a break at our shop, and I don't believe Josef Lhevinne or Vladimir Horowitz could ever have played the "Twelfth Street Rag" in octaves faster or more cleanly than she did. It took my breath away.

That, as my long-time friend Jerome Kern used to say, is Part One of the story. Part Two: when I went to London with a musical show a good many years later one of the stars of the show was Edythe Baker, who had become such a toast of London town that her picture occupied a full page of one of the glamour magazines right across from the picture of a beautiful and beloved duchess. Moral: all young ladies should learn to play the "Twelfth Street Rag." In octaves yet![16]

---

[16]Kansas City native Edythe Baker left for New York as a teenager. She worked as comedian Harry Fox's accompanist and was later hired by Ziegfeld. Her appearance as pianist-singer in 1923's *Big Boy* (with Al Jolson) was one of many in Lee Shubert's productions.

Long, empty days strung out, with three hundred limited service men sitting around, listening to rumors and grousing. One evening I had an idea. Twenty or thirty of us were sitting around on our bunks waiting for bedtime and I claimed the floor to say, "Guys, two or three of us are divinity students. Why not do what Enoch Arden's wife[17] did—pray for a word of divine guidance? One of you who can pray ask for a word from the Almighty, telling us what to do. I have a Bible here. I'll shut my eyes, put one finger on the text and see what we can find out."

It was agreed. The boy's prayer was sincere and beautiful.

I closed my eyes, opened the book, and put the index finger down. Without changing the place I handed the Book to my nearest neighbor and he began to laugh what is sometimes called a mirthless laugh.

The Book said "In your patience possess ye your souls."

Out of the clear came the end of this for me. One day a letter came from Mrs. Merrill, saying she was to give a talk on Musical Autograms to an important group in Chicago. She hoped I could get permission from Uncle Sam and play the music for them.

A look at my uniform, the only one they ever gave me, suggested that my wealth would have to be invested in a clean, new uniform, especially since we were to appear at a women's club. That meant asking my commander if he could promise me a furlough at the time of the Chicago appearance.

In the days of my dreams of honor and promotions I had practiced standing at attention and saluting, but in the Trade Test section—my branch of the Headquarters Company—it was not unusual to see a private or a corporal walk up to the captain's deck, lean over at ease and say, "Cap'n, c'n I git a pass to go see m' wife over the week-end?" I had even heard the captain say, "Not until you learn to salute" once. So I wasn't going to miss a chance to show off when I made my request. Taking my case to the captain, I explained the need to buy a new uniform in time for the date if the furlough could be granted. He said he would take care of the matter for me and I went into my act as I thanked him, marched out of the orderly room and back to my bunk. As I passed out the door I could almost feel some of the men saying, "What's that soldier doing here?"

In a matter of minutes the top sergeant came into the barracks and said, "Bennett, the captain wants to see you."

The captain made it brief. He said, "Bennett, I'm going to speak to the colonel and recommend a discharge for you. You're too good a man to waste any more time here. You'll hear in a few days. That's all."

---

[17]Annie, in the Tennyson poem "Enoch Arden."

I'm sure it was the salute that did it.

Exit the would-be soldier. Goodbye, captain's uniform. Forever.

Mrs. Merrill's talk to the ladies in Chicago went extremely well. The principal of a fine school knows just how to talk to a group that has no idea what he or she is talking about. I had taken a few of their signatures and converted them by our mathematical process into music. They listened to each piece as I played it and then discussed each personality as it showed in the music. There was mostly polite silence until I came to a spot in the study of Mrs. Frank Gordon where I said, "There is quite a bit of humor in this character"—and the house came down—laughter and applause.

It seems Mrs. Gordon was the court jester among her contemporaries and that was the trait they all knew about. I had known her slightly before but had never seen that side of her. We had found out a good many things like that, just through the process—moods, instincts, even important turns of fate like a bad accident or a grave illness that has deeply affected the lives of those who signed their names.

As with so many of the half-revealed truths that tease the spirit of man, it's a waste of time to try to laugh a thing like this off. The poets predict and science keeps coming up with full vindication time and time again. However, neither the poet nor the scientist can fill in all the blanks, and out of these empty spaces come religions—each man to his own—cults, revelations, and fanaticism.

One word seems to guide useful minds through the dark spaces: faith. Faith in what gets many answers, but it must be deep and unshakable. The miracle workers of art and literature are so often those who never think to question the beliefs just as they are given them, that it must leave the agnostic mind completely bewildered time and again.

My many attempts to explain and also to unsettle the accuracy of Mrs. Merrill's reference axes in getting at the fundamental traits of people convinced me that the truth was there, but there are some imponderables. How accurately, for instance, can the language of music be translated from sounds to ideas? And, before that, how far can we trust the sensitivity and the creative disciplines of the composer (maybe "arranger" would be a better title) who adds rhythm, key signatures, tempo and so forth to the little dots that offer their secrets to him?

With him comes the inevitable point in the message wherein someone has to say "I think it goes this way" instead of knowing and going to the blackboard with chalk in hand to fill in the blanks.

Some of Mrs. Merrill's close friends, well acquainted with the world of supply and demand, were convinced that we had a salable product. With their encouragement I tried to hang out my shingle and lure people into buying their Autograms,[18] but writing each one and analyzing the music when written took several hours and I had neither the time nor the salesmanship to build up such a business. It never got out of the gate.

The summer of the year 1919 was when I learned how low one could get in funds without sinking. There was apparently no bottom, even in high-priced New York. Twenty cents bought dinner for many a long string of evenings. Ten cents for a bowl of soup, five cents got me a jelly doughnut and five more a glass of milk. Coming out of the Army I weighed 183 pounds. By September 1st I weighed 159, but I honestly never felt better.

Every week or ten days Mrs. Merrill would invite me to Oaksmere for lunch and somehow I raised enough money to get there and back. In June I spoke to Louise of marriage and her answer was yes if I was sure I wanted it that way. It was a good answer because I was terrified at the distance I had to go before I could even pretend to be a husband and provider. A few war bonds, gathered together here and there, went for an engagement ring and that's when I went over to twenty-cent dinners.

Twenty-cent dinners and a serious look for work. Mr. Charles Greinert, who had been my boss at Schirmer's, told me to get in touch with Mr. George Moody at a publisher's called F.T.B. Harms and Francis, Day and Hunter. I sent Mr. Moody a note requesting an interview, and went out to Southampton, Long Island to arrange music and conduct an orchestra of five for *The Mask of the Queens* by Swinburne. The performance was an affair for charity. There were two good reasons to be glad I took it on. One was that it had a remarkable man named Francis Markoe, who did the reading of Swinburne's poetry. He became a very warm friend and we never lost touch with him for years—"we" of course being my not-yet wife and me.[19]

The other nice memory of the trip to Southampton was Beniamino Gigli, one of the world's great tenors. His accompanist had at the last minute been unable to join him in a short recital during our stay and the joy of accompanying this great artist is unforgettable. I can only guess how comfortable or otherwise he was in the performance but he was utterly charming about it.

When I got back to the "apartment" shared with Harold Probasco and John Marony, I was appalled to find a note from Mr. Moody, of F.T.B. Harms and Francis, Day and Hunter, saying "Come in the morning." The message

---

[18]Bennett's daughter Jean relates that the short-lived Musical Autograms shop was on Lexington Avenue.

[19]Markoe (1884–1960) was an enterprising society leader with a special flair for organizing civic events. Two of his early successes were important roles in staging the coronation pageant for King George V (1910) and, six years later, the 200th anniversary celebration at Yale University.

was almost a week old, and it looked like I'd missed the boat. However, reached by telephone, all he said was, "Come in the morning."

In the morning, without anybody knowing it, I kept an appointment with the Golden Age of the American Musical.

Mr. George Moody of Harms was a famous professional musician from Iowa and we may be said—in our own vernacular—to have hit it off like a house-afire. He handed me a song copy of "An Old Fashioned Garden" from a show called *Hitchy-Koo of 1919* by Cole Porter, and we didn't need to discuss the nature of "print orchestrations" music. I don't know when George Moody first had to take a paper-knife and separate the parts of a printed orchestration, but I was already an old hand at the age of twelve. They were referred to as "for fifteen and piano" but anybody who could count that high knew it was sixteen parts or more.

He just asked a question or two and I nodded my head.

When would I bring it in? Day after tomorrow. That was about as long as they could wait for them. What would I charge him? Twelve dollars. (I don't know yet where the figure came from.)

"Day after tomorrow" he gave me a song from *The Ziegfeld Follies* to arrange for band (that's the one that plays in the park during the summer). When that was finished another show tune was ready for orchestration, and the factory was in full operation.

These arrangements were printed and sold to orchestras and bands all over the country—given to a few whose playing of them was a plug for the show or the music. In hotels, cafés, at social evenings and dance halls where the orchestra might be almost any number of musicians, they all used the same music to play from.

> [George Moody recalled: "A couple of weeks after Bennett had come to work for us, I happened to mention to him that the band at the old Hotel Pennsylvania was doing a very neat job on his arrangement of 'An Old-Fashioned Garden.' Russell got excited, like a kid. He'd never heard an arrangement of his played by a classy New York hotel band. He insisted we go down to the Pennsylvania that very evening, which we did. It was a hell of a good arrangement, by the way. It would still play today. As a matter of fact, Russell put real music into all those stock arrangements he did for us. They'd all play today."[20]]

The exception was, of course, the bands that were springing up with their own special arrangers.

---

[20]Quoted in Herbert Warren Wind, "Another Opening, Another Show," *The New Yorker*, 17 November 1951, 58–59.

Another place where they got our arrangements without paying for them was at the recording studios where they made discs (and, at first, cylinders), and where the engineers were struggling bravely to make a violin sound like a violin and a piano resemble a piano.

The person (or persons) who thought up the name "The Golden Age of the American Musical" naturally listens to and looks for different sounds and sights than I do, but it seems from where I sit that the age could start much earlier than they seem to think. There seems to be a tendency to think of *Show Boat* (Edna Ferber, Oscar Hammerstein II, Jerome Kern—1927) as "away back when" in discussing the subject.

I had a lot of gray hair when I sat with Kern and took down the tunes before making the *Show Boat* rehearsal copies for voices and piano. It seems very much wasteful to start our arbitrary "age" after the classics of Victor Herbert, the lovable little masterpieces of Boulton, Wodehouse and Kern, and such shows as *Maytime, The Student Prince, Sally, Sunny, Wildflower*, and *Rose Marie* had closed.[21]

That person (or persons) who thought the name of the epoch also seems to enjoy the idea that this or that number, some dance routine, some other this or that, revolutionized the musical theater. Hooray!

Nobody that I ever knew in the theater sat down to conceive of a conception, as a composer friend of ours used to say, without asking his Muse, or the ghost of Aeschylus, or somebody, to send him (or her) a brand new revolutionary idea.

I suppose we who toiled through the Golden Age did no less than revolutionize the whole world of make-believe, and that someone, someday, will sit down and tell us when and how it happened. In any case it will be a surprise to us who did it.

Just about as our arrangement factory got in full gear my mother-in-law-to-be asked me to teach harmony (and piano) at Oaksmere two days a week. This meant getting on an early train every Tuesday and Friday whether there was time for the proverbial eight hours the night before or not.

I can't pretend I was ever a good teacher, but the girls at the school were some of them quite talented and the head of the piano department was Eugene Heffley, a simply wonderful man to know and work in music with. A train ride of forty minutes four times a week with a man known and loved by all the musicians great and small of our time was beyond price.

---

[21] *Maytime* (1917) and *The Student Prince* (1924), music by Sigmund Romberg; *Sally* (1920) and *Sunny* (1925), Jerome Kern; *Wildflower* (1923), Vincent Youmans and Herbert Stothart; *Rose Marie* (1924), Rudolf Friml and Stothart.

Two of Mr. Heffley's piano pupils at the school one or two years were Pauline and Elsa Heifetz, whose brother was and is a pretty familiar man of music.[22] One of the Heifetz girls later married S. N. Behrman, and Sam Behrman used to like to tell of the Heifetz' Russian father and his angles on life. His comment on Oaksmere—also often called The Merrill School—was "The Sherill School (sic) where they teach backhorse!"

Translated, it means he didn't quite approve of horseback riding lessons. The two sisters also took harmony lessons from me but I never heard any quotes from father about that.

Hamilton Merrill—called Jim by his intimates—had a younger brother Edgerton—known to all as Pete. Both brothers were tennis players and both were left-handed. Added to that there were four or five good tennis courts on the school grounds. Both of these left-handers were of the type that was always hard for me to beat, and not because they were southpaws. No matter how I studied the great tournament players of the day, and in spite of the power I could put in a serve, the type of player who could make my life miserable was always a man who went to school and college and played tennis as a part of his daily program without taking it too seriously.

Somehow they were always ready to keep the ball in play and let me beat myself. This I obligingly did, while making some spectacular shots in the course of the set.

Jim was the captain whose uniform I so idealized. He went on to a career from the bottom to the very top of a nationally important manufacturing corporation. Pete did something similar in, of all things, the Army. While in college (both Merrills went to M.I.T.) he was in R.O.T.C. He resented the fact that the darned old war had to end before he got into it, but he went into business, married and had children, and at the same time worked his way up from the cavalry's lowest possible rank without missing a grade. When World War II began he was a lieutenant colonel. He was sent to Asia, made a full colonel and, at the end of his life, buried in Arlington Cemetery with full military honors.

Politics, a game quite beyond the grasp of a vast majority of those who play at it, would call for many points of view in looking at a career like that, but it was easy to feel a presence of fulfillment as we followed the colonel to his grave among the patriots.

Back to 1919. Louise Merrill and I were married in the big white house at Oaksmere the day after Christmas. My bride was just about as far away in every detail from what my boyhood dreams had predicted that I was not quite

---

[22]Violinist Jascha Heifetz (1901–1987) recorded Bennett's 1940 *Hexapoda* for Decca Records, as well as two movements from his 1947 *A Song Sonata.*

sure I was there. I only knew that it would have been unthinkable to be anywhere else. Humility is often thought to be an attribute of the great, but when it is unfeigned and yours, you can feel like calling for an ambulance.

A voice told me that a majority of marriages are made with no more idea of how in heaven's name one is going to live up to the contract than this, but I was never a long-shot player in any gambling game and I had a terrible time finding my own voice to repeat the words of the ceremony.

The reception after the wedding was unique in that I was not asked to play the piano. Maurice Nitke was there with his beautiful violin, and the affair was light-hearted enough to scare away all earthly concern. We enjoyed the fun. Edward, the Merrill chauffeur, picked us up in the Winton, and we were off to take the train to Kansas City and thence to Freeman. The honeymoon was a nice home-made affair. My grandmother said Louise looked like my Aunt Etta, but I couldn't for the life of me think what Aunt Etta looked like, or even if I'd ever met her.

Neither the bride nor the groom actually knew anything about mating, but neither do the bees nor the birds, as far as I ever heard. The one thing everybody there had was a good laugh at everything that was funny. With both my father and his mother there, there were plenty of laughs, and there'll never be a better audience than Louise M. Bennett.

Back in New York in time for the young ladies at Oaksmere to return to classes, we settled in a small apartment across the street from the Lexington Opera House. The location had nothing to do with it, but we had seen the Chicago Opera in *Louise* and *Pelleas* there a month before. The routine of arrangements day and night and two days a week at school took up after the slight interruption. Some of the show tunes that went through our mill were destined to be noted—"Swanee" of Gershwin, Jerome Kern's "Look for the Silver Lining," Victor Herbert's "I Might Be Your 'Once-in-a-While'" and "Just a Kiss in the Dark," Cole Porter's "What Is This Thing Called Love?"—these come to mind.[23]

Three unrelated things happened during the year that have to go into the books: we spent the Decoration Day weekend at the Merrill place when burglars came into the apartment in New York and cleaned us out; we sat watching a tennis match in the National Tournament at Forest Hills while an airplane crashed only a short distance behind us; and our daughter was born.

The only unusual feature of the burglary was the insurance paid us. They gave us cash to cover all but some bits of silver that they could buy and replace for us, paying "a little less than we would have to pay." Adding it all up,

---

[23]Bennett is mistaken about Porter's "What is This Thing Called Love?"; the song was written a decade later, in 1929.

we were given a few dollars more than our total coverage. According to the popular idea, big corporations never do that sort of thing.

The airplane at the tennis club flew very close to the stadium full of people and began to sputter. I waited for what seemed like a long time, during which I was in the cockpit hoping for some kind of miracle. It may have missed the big crowd as much as half a mile, but it shook the whole planet, or seemed to.

As to the birth of our daughter, I had a feeling of panic similar to the one that clutched my throat at our wedding: whoever told me I could be a father to a real live daughter?

By this time the sounds of Maurice Nitke's fiddle were filling theaters with music for one of New York's really artistic producers—Arthur Hopkins—and Hopkins was planning a production of Shakespeare's *Macbeth* with Lionel Barrymore as the Scottish king. They were musically ambitious enough to give me a twenty-one piece orchestra and say "Go at it!" I was grateful. It would be a shame to let a musician go through life without writing an incidental score for at least one Shakespeare play.

Seriously though, it was a lovely engagement, albeit rather a short one.[24] The critics of the New York newspapers resented it; many years later Lionel and I spent an afternoon together in Hollywood and he was still chuckling over a wise-crack of Heywood Broun in his review of the production. He opened his effort with "Lionel Barrymore opened last night in 'Macbeth.' Lay on, Macduff, lay off McBride."[25]

To the generations who don't know who or what McBride was I would say, "Look in the yellow pages under Ticket Brokers." The ability of Lionel Barrymore to enjoy repeating this daily-paper witticism at the expense of something he spent so many long hours to build would not surprise anyone who knew him well.

Arthur Hopkins tried two more Shakespeare plays with the Barrymores: *Romeo and Juliet* with Ethel and *Hamlet* with John.[26] John Barrymore's *Hamlet* had quite a success in New York and he took it to London, where it ran ten weeks. The production paid me fifty dollars a week for the music, but John neglected paying me the royalty during the whole London run.[27] He

---

[24]*Macbeth* received 28 performances at the Apollo Theatre, opening 17 February 1921.

[25]Lyricist Howard Dietz (*Dancing in the Dark*, 142) attributes the "lay off" remark to drama critic Kelcy Allen, whose reviews appeared in *Women's Wear Daily*.

[26]*Romeo and Juliet* opened 27 December 1922 at the Longacre Theatre, again with incidental music by Bennett; it ran for 29 performances. *Hamlet* was presented at the Sam H. Harris Theatre, where the first of its 101 performances took place 16 November 1922.

[27]Bennett composed his incidental music for *Hamlet* for an ensemble of three trumpets, timpani, string quartet (led by violinist Maurice Nitke), and musical saw. The last was, in his

spoke of owing me five hundred dollars a good many times, but never got around to doing anything about it. It was worth more to me to make mean little remarks about it to his adoring fans than if I had it, so he still owes me the money. Or his ghost does.[28]

The official name of F.T.B. Harms and Francis, Day and Hunter was changed to simply Harms, Inc. somewhere along here. Nobody had called it anything but just "Harms" anyway. My family (of three) spent one or two summers at Oaksmere in a building that had a squash court in it and one of the tennis courts in front of it. I invited some of the Harms gang out one day for something like lunch and tennis. George and Ira Gershwin were among them, and George and I played six sets of tennis. Like everything that George enjoyed doing, he was instinctively good at tennis. There was no need to temper the wind to the shorn lamb. The shorn lambs kept me very busy.

By this time it was possible to draft a set of important steps toward becoming a successful arranger of popular music:

1. Find a job with a publisher who has under contract a great "stable" of popular composers and lyric-writers, such as Jerome Kern, Victor Herbert, Vincent Youmans, George Gershwin, Cole Porter, Oscar Hammerstein II, Dorothy Fields, Otto Harbach, and P. G. Wodehouse.
2. Either write fast or do without much sleep, or both.
3. Be sure your bosses can read music and also English.
4. Make sure also that the shows where the music is played and sung are big hits wherever possible before the material gets to you.

These rules may not all be indispensable, but I can only speak from personal experience.

I'm sure that if this simple formula gets into the proper hands it will meet with the same response as Oscar Hammerstein's page in *Variety*'s annual special issue [4 January 1944]. After eleven years of no luck at all, Oscar's holiday greeting said, "I've done it before and I can do it again!" and listed all of his flops.[29]

He expected (maybe) laughs, but what he is reported to have got was poor, baffled souls wondering what on earth he was bragging about.

---

words, "concerned only with the wailings of the ghost" (letter to Henry Allen Moe, John Simon Guggenheim Foundation, 14 January 1928).

[28]Barrymore died in 1942.

[29]*Sunny River* (1941, with Romberg), *Very Warm for May* (1939, with Kern), *Three Sisters* (1934, with Kern), *Ball at the Savoy* (1933, an adaptation of a Hungarian operetta), and *Free For All* (1931, with Richard Whiting) preceded Hammerstein's 1943 successes with *Oklahoma!* and *Carmen Jones*.

Under chemical analysis, the four rules above are sure to be found to be pretty close to the truth.

The top boss at Harms was Max Dreyfus, of whom I spoke several pages ago. The next general direction of this tale begins with him. He called me into his office one morning and told me of what arrangers of music enjoy hearing: a new job. This time it was really new.

Arthur Hammerstein was producing a new musical with a well-known comedian, Frank Tinney, as a star; lyrics by Oscar Hammerstein II and music by Herbert Stothart, who was also music director. Orchestrations for the production by me, with what help I needed from Maurice De Packh, a well-known show arranger. Orchestrations for the pit were an important part of a score, and were supposed to be done by the composer as a part of his job. Victor Herbert, pretty well recognized as the ideal composer of theater music, did all his own arrangements and they were models for all of us to shoot at.[30]

But the vast majority of Broadway's tune-writers didn't know their ankles from their uncles when it came to the orchestrations and that's how we all got to assume a certain importance.

There was probably never a tune-writer in the world so simple-minded that he didn't have many ideas as to how the orchestra should sound playing his music, but the craft of putting the sounds on a piece of paper and having a bunch of musicians sound that way is something else.[31]

There had been an arranger named Frank Saddler, whose arrangements just sparkled no matter who wrote the tunes.[32] By this time, however, he had

---

[30]"Jerome Kern once made an arrangement for orchestra of about 16 bars of one of his melodies while we were on the road together. That night, after we had played the arrangement, he said to his music director, 'Did you notice the 16 bars that I arranged? They were no good—and that's why that old fellow over there was the greatest of them all,' pointing to a picture of Victor Herbert on his piano." (Bennett letter to Edward N. Waters, quoted in Waters, *Victor Herbert: A Life in Music* [New York: Macmillan, 1955], 574).

[31]S. N. Behrman writes: "If you have some tune jingling in your head, you have only to go to Harms and, provided you can get by Max's Irene [Gallagher, his secretary]—and by Max, hum it or play it with one finger to Russell Bennett and it will presently emerge fully arranged or scored, suavely and colorfully, for a modern orchestra. It is as if an aspiring writer who could neither read nor write were to go into Scribner's, whisper an idea to the editor, and get it written for him in novel form by John Galsworthy. . . . The completeness of the [Harms] organization, its equipment to transform into sophisticated musical speech the stammering inspirations of these random Homers, fill a writer who has to go through it in longhand with the profoundest envy" ("Profiles: Accoucheur," *The New Yorker*, 6 February 1932, [23]). Similarly, columnist John Chapman remarks: "A program credit, instead of stating 'Orchestrations by Russell Bennett,' should read: 'You can thank Mr. Bennett for the music sounding nice. All he had to start with was a one-finger piano outline of eight song choruses" ("Mainly about Manhattan," New York *Daily News*, 17 May 1937).

[32]Bennett had earlier observed: "When you went to one of those Kern shows at the old Princess Theatre, you just sat back and wondered what delightful touch [Saddler would] treat

died of a heart attack and most of the show music was being arranged by two successors, Maurice De Packh[33] and Stephen O. Jones[34]. They were colorful men in totally different ways.

Songwriters told me that when they played their numbers for Maury De Packh he was very likely to say, "That's lousy! What the hell can I do with it?" But he would turn out a fine orchestration and all would be happy. Steve Jones was an entirely different human being. He was rough, profane and full of fun. Whatever they played for him he said, "Beautiful!" It was his favorite word. "How do you like this song, Steve?" "Beautiful!"

"Is the bass drum loud enough?" "Beautiful!"

[Hans Spialek, Bennett's arranging colleague at Chappell, tells of any early out-of-town assignment with Jones, orchestrating the 1926 show *Margery*:

> Stephen Jones, although in his late forties, was sort of a lanky, tousle-haired, boisterous nature boy, endowed with rare musical instinct, taste and talent. . . . Besides being in charge of arranging and copying, he was the co-composer of "Margery." My trouble with him was that I could never find him. Insane about golf, leaving the hotel usually at the break of dawn, he only showed up for dinner in the course of which he would give me the necessary instructions. On the day of the opening, he called me around five a.m. to his room. Informing me that we'd have to work very fast as he'd forgotten entirely about a number in the show that had to be orchestrated. Determined to finish the job as fast as possible, we both

---

the music to next. He'd have two violins playing a duet against the melody, and then some whimsical bass progression, or he'd come up with a low woodwind that was just right for some little looker with a little voice. One fine idea after another" (Wind, "Another Opening, Another Show," 60). See also Bennett's remarks about Saddler in the essay below ("Orchestration of Theatre and Dance Music").

[33]Bennett and De Packh also worked together in Hollywood on Gershwin's *Shall We Dance* and Kern's *I Dream Too Much*. A disciple of Frank Saddler (they'd shared duties on Gershwin's 1919 *La La Lucille*), De Packh felt that the intrusion of jazz-band instrumentation and scoring into the theatre pit had caused his mentor's "life work [to] crumble to ruin" (letter to the *New York Times*, 3 February 1929). De Packh's efforts to affirm the "artistic worth" of "that friendless orphan, the theatre orchestra" included a spring 1928 concert by his De Packh Symphonic Ensemble. He moved to Hollywood in the 1930s, eventually becoming one of 20th Century-Fox's busiest arrangers.

[34]Jones (1880–1967), a native New Yorker, collaborated with Bennett on *Lady Be Good!*, *Wildflower*, and *No, No, Nanette*. He contributed songs to several 1920s musicals, including *Captain Jinks*, *Poppy*, and the "follow-up" show *Yes, Yes, Yvette* and worked as an (uncredited) orchestrator as late as *Carousel* (1945).

> settled down to work. But only for a few minutes. The temptation of the very sunny spring day and an obviously severe bite from his golf bug were too much for him. He jumped up, grabbed his golfbag, telling me, "You can orchestrate that, yourself," and off he went.[35]]

He would be sitting on his front porch chatting with friends and you would hear his wife call out from inside the house, "Steve, if you're going to talk that way you'd better come inside!"

But his orchestrations were the daintiest things you could imagine. His trademark—or one of them—was a habit of coming to a climax in a big brassy chorus and suddenly doing the next four bars with an oboe, two clarinets and a bassoon. At an orchestra rehearsal once in my hearing his wife, sitting next to him, said, "Steve, that's lousy!"

Steve said, "You know I always do that."

She said, "I know you do, but it's no good."

When Frank Saddler was alive he did the arranging for Jerome Kern. The Kern-Saddler combination was one of Broadway's little aristocracies, causing George Gershwin to talk a bit about a Gershwin-Bennett team once or twice. Nothing much came of that—not that we didn't join forces often enough.

It doesn't read like much of a promotion to be taken off the music that is sent to all the corners of the globe and put on the music that's only played in one place eight times a week, but the original sounds of a show score are desperately important to the whole enterprise, at least to all the minds involved in the birth of the child. It's a sensitive job and it calls for several talents not directly artistic.

One of the responsibilities of the assignment is to pack up and join the troupe for at least a part of the out-of-New York tryout. There would be new dance routines, even entirely new songs, and "fixes" to keep the music up-to-date with this and that new idea.

The social side for the music arranger or arrangers depended in those days on what free time there was, if any. Some of that social side could involve you in one way or another even when you were too busy to look up from the pages in front of you.

The name of this show (my first[36]) was *Daffy Dill.* The star in the show was, as noted, Frank Tinney.[37] Frank Tinney's off-stage vocabulary was not made to order for nice, quiet people sitting on their front porches on a warm

---

[35]Hans Spialek, "A Passing Note" (unpublished memoirs), 140–141.

[36]I.e., the first for which he was the principal (credited) orchestrator.

[37]Youmans's *Daffy Dill* opened 22 August 1922. Frank Tinney (1878–1940) was a small, baby-faced comedian who had established himself in vaudeville before appearing in musical comedies.

August evening in Long Branch, New Jersey. But that's what they got and where they got it. He would come outside the stage door during the show's intermission and breathe the nice fresh air—and turn it blue. His voice was deep and resonant, and I never cared to turn up in the neighborhood again.

As the show went through its tryout weeks, Tinney had two constant companions, a baby-doll blond and an olding Irishman who always went around in the clothes of a priest. He probably was a priest at some time or other.

One night after the show the authors and the producers went out for a few hours on the town—Asbury Park by this time. Frank Tinney went with them without telling the baby-doll blond or the "priest" where he was going. My room at the hotel was on the same floor as the Tinney entourage and I was treated to quite a performance. Baby-doll was screaming up and down the hall, wild with rage at being left there, screaming and weeping while the house detectives and the little old "priest" tried desperately to shut her up. Half of the hotel must have been wondering what was going on. It was nightmarish, but what puzzled me as I sat there and tried to work on a few bars of music for the next performance, was Mrs. Frank Tinney. I knew she was in her room nearby. I had been told that she always came on the road with his shows; she liked the excitement. The last time the noisy ones paused in front of my door, the blond was calling Frank Tinney all the dirty names in the book when the little old companion managed to cool her enough to say, "See here! I've known Frank Tinney for many years and I love him. You mustn't talk about him that way!" And the high soprano voice, through tears, "You don't love him half as much as I do!"

When the sun was high, Herbert Stothart, the composer and music director of the show, came by my room and reported that he had just peeked into Tinney's room and Tinney's black hair was quite a contrast to a mass of blond hair beside it, and all was calm.

I hope Mrs. Tinney enjoyed the excitement.

The next assignment was a revue called *The Greenwich Village Follies.* It was the third edition of a new series with the same general purpose as the already famous *Ziegfeld Follies.* It probably was not a landmark of any kind but it was jammed with colorful personalities. The over-all director was a man who might have been referred to as a [bit mad] if he hadn't looked like a senator. His name was John Murray Anderson and he was, I must say, a real artist, especially with stage pictures and lighting.[38] Watching him at rehearsals

---

[38] In addition to his own revues, Anderson (1886–1954) directed several editions of the *Ziegfeld Follies* and such musicals as *Life Begins at 8:40* (1934), *Jumbo* (1935), and *Three To Make Ready* (1946).

was more entertaining to some of us than the show could ever be. He had a high-pitched intense voice, and one of his habits was to give his own special name to each member of the cast and chorus and call him or her by that name during the entire run of the play. Some of his names for people were unusual, to say the least.

As a sample from this show, there was a tall, blond male dancer with a lock of hair that kept falling over his forehead. Murray Anderson called him Seed Catalogue. "Now, Seed Catalogue, you go left and turn up-stage—no, no, NO!—stage left, Seed Catalogue!"

The 1922 *Greenwich Village Follies* had a very pretty score by Louis Hirsch. He seems completely forgotten as far as I know, but if one is to remember any show music at all "Just A Love Nest" from the show *Mary*, "Going Up!" from the play of the same name, or "Nightingale Throw Me a Rose" and "Sixty Seconds Every Minute" from *The Greenwich Village Follies* should have reached my ears from the ocean of loud-speakers around us, but none have.[39]

The music director of the show was Alfred Newman. He was less that twenty years old at the time but from then until he died one of the very top figures in Hollywood music forty-odd years later, I never saw a sign of immaturity.[40]

The opening night of the show was in New Haven, Connecticut. Big and complicated as it was, it was running pretty smoothly and successfully until the middle of the finale of Act I, when all of a sudden Alfred Newman leapt from the podium to the piano and began to play music two or three pages further down. I looked on the stage and saw a pair of featured dancers making a grand entrance for their pas de deux—a minute and a half too soon. With what help I could offer the musicians I found the right spot to join in with Al Newman's piano playing and the whole thing got back on the track.

The opening performance seemed in general to be successful, even though no single department of any musical ever got through an opening on the road without contemplating suicide. In any case, before they go to buy the poison they nearly all wind up at a party of some kind. I ran into one in somebody's suite at the Taft Hotel, next to the theater. There were plenty of vivid characters there, among them Irving Caesar, who was a lyric and sketch writer as

---

[39]Louis Hirsch (1881–1924) scored his biggest popular success with the song "Hello Frisco" from the 1915 *Ziegfeld Follies.*

[40]Newman (1900–1970) had studied to be a concert pianist but, of necessity, worked in theater and vaudeville in New York. As leader of 1920's *Greenwich Village Follies* and *George White's Scandals* he became Broadway's youngest-ever musical director. A conducting student of William Daly (who led most of Gershwin's shows), Newman began work in Hollywood in 1930 and, ten years later, began two decades as 20th Century-Fox's Musical Director.

well as a very articulate off-stage comedian, good for a laugh or two in any company. He wrote the words to three of the biggest hits I remember: "Swanee" with George Gershwin, "Tea for Two" and "I Want to Be Happy" with Vincent Youmans.

They motioned me to a chair beside a lovely French "diseuse" who had two solo spots in the show. She spoke no English. Caesar was on the telephone talking to Lindy's restaurant in New York and ordering a supper to be sent to some address on First Avenue. He's hard to quote, but he must have had the restaurant dizzy and everybody at our party at the Taft was holding his sides.

Bert Savoy, of the team Savoy and Brennan, was sitting on the other side of the French lady. He was a fabulous impersonator who played a gorgeous gal in the act and didn't bother to change much when he was off-stage. Every time Irving Caesar got a roar of laughter, Bert Savoy would turn to me and say, "Tell her!" meaning translate the whole thing into French for the beautiful diseuse.

It might be interesting to know what a good interpreter could have done with Caesar's material.

Daffy Dill and *The Greenwich Village Follies* were the first two of a long parade of Broadway's song and dance creations for which I inked in everything musical under the top line. They came in all sizes and successes but I never had a favorite. I never had a favorite show or a favorite song. A normal thing, since music arranging is a way of keeping out of debt, would be to delight in "Dahomey" from *Show Boat* for which an hour of work once brought me about fifty-one dollars, and to try to forget "I Could Have Danced All Night" from *My Fair Lady.* I don't remember what the union scale was for that two [?] pages of score, but it wasn't fifty-one dollars.

Or, sitting on my home-made perch as a musical snob, should I enjoy *any* of Broadway's hits? No?

That would be like not liking to pet a pussy-cat or hating the Kentucky Derby. Every bar in a musical comedy score is there because it's good and it's up to the orchestra to feel that and take it from there. Sometimes that's easy and sometimes it's hard. Apparently there is no ratio between the success achieved and the effort required.

You keep looking for this. You hear someone [an orchestrator] who plays everything on the piano "to see how it sounds" slaving through the night over two or three bars and you wonder how gay and spontaneous it can possibly sound when finished.[41] Yet somehow when it gets to the audience the passage sounds as if it came with the original inspiration.

---

[41]Bennett's colleagues have concurred that he orchestrated without reference to a piano, and almost always in ink—while perhaps carrying on a conversation or listening to wife Louise

The original inspiration, normally, comes through the original composer. Nearly all show composers carry around a conviction that everything in their score is their own creation, whether they write it down or not, and they are a lot nearer right that you might think. No matter how rich or poor a composer's idiom may be a sensitive arrangement of his music is pretty well bound 'round by what the tune-writer does. This may be too technical to make good reading, but when a precocious student asks me, "Where does Dick Rodgers end and you begin?" they've given me a hard question to answer.

Irving Berlin, working with the arranger, would sometimes stop at a chord and say, "Is that the right harmony?"

We would say, "It's probably not the one you want. How about this?" We would strike a chord and he would say, "No, that's not it," or his face would light up and he'd say, "That's it!"

Which means that his inner ear was way ahead of his fingers on the black keys of the piano.[42] The right harmony, as he called it, was a part of the original inspiration, whether he could play it for you or not.

An old account book shows that I worked on twenty-two shows a year for the next three or four years. That counted everything from two or three songs or dances (to help a fellow toiler meet his deadline) to complete scores from cover to cover.[43] Some of the plays were glamorous enough to be remembered, some were disasters. Most of them were neither, but each was vital and strenuous while being born. Long, brain-flogging nights and days of worry and finally relief when somehow the curtain went up with all the music in the musicians' books.

If the music arranger's contribution is not as much of a feature as some people seem to think should be in a big hit, so is his contribution spared most of the impact of a dire failure. Sometimes I felt quite guilty at seeing all my close associates so defeated while I was looking up trains to take me to the next job. Maybe the scales were balanced a bit when they all had a great big hit and were dreaming of a vacation in Barbados while I was packing up to join another free-for-all in some rehearsal hall.

---

reading poetry to him in one of several languages. Richard Rodgers remarks that Bennett "probably has the most amazing powers of concentration of anyone I've ever known. . . . I remember walking into his [London] flat one morning to discover him working diligently on the score [to Rodgers's *One Dam Thing After Another*, 1927] while listening to music blaring from a radio" (*Musical Stages*, [New York: Random House, 1975], 101).

[42]Berlin is said to have composed his songs in the key of G flat (or F sharp) major, which uses a predominance of black keys. He had special transposing pianos made for his use so that songs he played could be made to sound in any key.

[43]Official "orchestrations by" credits are unreliable, often listing only a show's principal orchestrator. Uncredited assistance to a colleague was commonly referred to as "ghosting" in Bennett's arrangers' circle.

Jerome Kern had a lot of his great career behind him when we joined forces. He was just about everybody's favorite tune-writer in those times and it's not easy to find his superior, all things considered. My first show with him in New York was *Stepping Stones*, starring Fred Stone and his daughter Dorothy. The lyrics were by Anne O'Day.

Fred Stone was a veteran of countless big and little hits, dating back almost beyond my memory.[44] He was famous among other things for a fantastic performance in *The Wizard of Oz*, but to single one out among his accomplishments is like saying, "Beethoven, the composer of the Ninth Symphony." In *Stepping Stones* he sang and danced a number (with his daughter) called "Raggedy Ann." They were both dressed to look like floppy dolls, Raggedy Anns, that were popular at the time. The only person that didn't like the number at all was Fred Stone. He never liked the song or the strenuous dance routine that went with it, even though the audiences were all for it.

Jerry Kern thought maybe some of the rather busy orchestral arrangements might be getting in the way of Fred's feet. Kern and I did what we used to call a "you-do-this" arrangement: the orchestra men took their pencils and gave the ears much less work to do. They did the whole number twice in the "new" version as Fred and Dorothy danced it. It looked and sounded perfectly acceptable to us and Kern asked Fred how it felt.

Fred said, "What did you do to it? I couldn't hear any difference!"

So "Raggedy Ann" went back the way it was before. The last time I ever saw Fred Stone it happened to be just as he and Dorothy were coming offstage at the end of that very number. He was still muttering, "I can't do it" and "It's no good." He was still not at all happy, and of course the audience still was. They kept applauding and Dorothy was saying, "Daddy, we're a hit! Listen to them!" as they went to take another bow.

He was an endearing figure on the stage but not so to the old stage-door man at the Globe Theater. The old fellow complained sadly that Fred Stone never gave him a tip in all the time he was there.

The second show I did for Jerome Kern was called *Sitting Pretty.* It was not successful enough to be in the history books,[45] but it gets into them for another reason: it was the last collaboration of the team of Bolton, Wodehouse and Kern. This trio formed one of the happiest teams of all times.

---

[44]Acrobatic dancer Fred Stone (1873–1959) was a circus and minstrel show veteran before making his Broadway debut in 1901's *The Girl from Up There*, followed by *The Wizard of Oz* in 1903.

[45]Ninety-five performances beginning 8 April 1924.

Guy Bolton wrote the libretto, Pelham G. Wodehouse the lyrics and Jerome Kern the music in several shows that could only be described as adorable. Much of the essential character of their plays came, I believe, right from the character of Wodehouse and there must be thousands of people who need no further recommendation. His many, many books, most of them about "Jeeves," kept on appearing until he died in the middle nineteen-seventies.

Guy Bolton was a great craftsman, and as full of color as they come. There was a saying among the light-hearted and light-headed theater people that nobody knew whether he was an American or an Englishman. Both countries claimed him; in New York they said he was English and in London—oh well, you know how those smart characters are.

Sitting Pretty was on the tryout tour for eight weeks, and were I forced to choose the high spot in my theatrical career it would be hard to rule out eight weeks as a fourth at bridge with Bolton, Wodehouse and Kern.

The show came to the Morosco Theater in New York, where no musical had ever succeeded. *Sitting Pretty* did nothing to change that. But we were speaking before of the Globe.

The Globe Theater brings up the ghost of Charles B. Dillingham, great producer of many a more memorable hit musical. One of these was *Sunny* with Marilyn Miller, Jack Donahue, Mary Hay and Clifton Webb in the cast. It reportedly cost two hundred and fifty thousand dollars and they were dollars then; that much for a production was just about unheard of. Dillingham was a real gambler, as I found out when *Sunny* opened in Philadelphia. With a quarter of a million at stake and top people in all departments the ingredients must have been there, but they were certainly hard to find on the opening night. Nothing seemed to work and after the first act I was standing in the back of the theater wondering if part of the disaster was my fault. To my consternation here came Charles B. Dillingham. I was busy trying to think of one thing nice to say about his show when he broke into a broad smile and said with his big voice, "Well, it's better than it was last night, isn't it?"

And it kept getting better and better and ended up one of the best. A song called "Who?" didn't hurt it a bit. Those were the days when a very successful song in the show brought in a lot of customers. They didn't drown you in a hit song in all the media then and you went to the theater to hear and see it sung and danced. Around that time a modest show called *Little Jessie James* ran a year, by everybody's agreement because it had one particular song in it. Name of song: "I Love You."[46]

---

[46]*Little Jessie James* (which was not concerned with the famed outlaw) opened on 15 August 1923. Its songs were by Harry Archer, and in the pit was Paul Whiteman's orchestra.

The music director of *Sunny* [Gus Salzer] was for some years considered the best man in town. In connection with the redoubtable Mr. Kern he could be remembered for the small thing that has something rather larger by the tail, as far as the hidden meanings of melodies go. Jerome Kern told me that way, way back there when Kern was having his first success with Broadway shows, Gus Salzer was the conductor of one of them.[47] Kern had a song in it called "The Same Sort of Girl." Toward the end of the melody it climbs up to its top note and drops down a perfect octave in a quite original way. I remembered an arched eyebrow at that spot the first time I ever played the tune on the piano, but Kern told me that when he played it for Gus Salzer he saw a tear appear on the hard-boiled music director's cheek.

This is the sort of thing that must be believed but is not to be understood. The piano pupil plays thousands of octaves up and down the scale every week, from lesson to lesson; and yet here comes the little son of a Newark business family with one octave that makes a listener "all weepy," as Julie Andrews once said to me.[48]

It was years later that we did *Sunny* but Gus Salzer was still in there pitching and still hard-boiled.[49]

During the rehearsal of the show, I was making notes on the routine of a dance featuring Clifton Webb and the girls. It was quite an athletic number and Clifton came down from the stage to ask me how I liked it. The answer was "Very much. Isn't it a rather hard number to do?"

"Yes it is," he said, "it's very hard to do it with the girls." Gus overheard us and said, "I know, you'd rather do it with the boys." Clifton snapped back, "I don't do that either, you bitch!"

Oscar Hammerstein, maker of cigars and impresario at the Manhattan Opera House in New York, was spoken of briefly a while ago. His grandson, Oscar Hammerstein II, was just beginning his long career now, but his son Arthur, uncle of Oscar II, was already one of the successful producers of musical comedy on Broadway.[50]

Arthur Hammerstein was very loyal to his music director Herbert Stothart, a former professor of drama at the University of Wisconsin. Between

---

[47] *The Girl from Utah*, 1914.

[48] The Broadway successes of Julie Andrews (b. 1935) include *The Boy Friend* (1954), *My Fair Lady* (1956) and *Camelot* (1960)—these latter two Lerner and Loewe musicals orchestrated by Bennett and Philip J. Lang—which preceded her work in motion pictures.

[49] In addition to 1925's *Sunny*, Salzer conducted Kern's *Have A Heart* (1917), *Sally* (1920), *Dear Sir* (1924), *Lucky* (1927), and *Sweet Adeline* (1929). Less than a year before his death he was musical director for Bennett's own *Hold Your Horses* (1933).

[50] Arthur Hammerstein's productions include *The Firefly* (1912), *Wildflower* (1923), *Rose Marie* (1924) and *Song of the Flame* (1925). He built New York's Hammerstein Theatre in 1927.

them they went on a big shopping tour for collaborators for Herbert on the music of Arthur's shows.

No one could find fault with their taste in collaborators: Vincent Youmans, Rudolf Friml, and George Gershwin. With Youmans he did the score for *Wildflower*, a solid success helped a great deal by trying something quite new at the time: a broadcast over radio of a live performance at the theater.

Vincent Youmans had a very keen ear and as a melodist he may easily have been what many of his contemporaries said, the most gifted of the whole lot. One of his gifts was definitely not for diplomacy. He made a good many uninspired remarks that one had to learn to translate. Arthur Hammerstein turned on him once and said, "Is that all you know, and you're writing music for my show? Get out of here!"

> [Bennett elsewhere relates the entire incident: "Vincent Youmans may have been the most talented of all our tune writers; he may also have been the most naive (not excluding Gershwin, for whom the word seems to have been reserved). In a show for Arthur Hammerstein we had four cellos in the orchestra, which was conducted by Herbert Stothart. Youmans, Stothart and Hammerstein were discussing a dance routine wherein the orchestra leaped rather frantically from key to key. Arthur, whose ears were conservative, was worrying for fear we were getting too ambitious for his public. After some talk between Arthur and Herbert a light suddenly came over Vincent's face. 'Tell you what you do,' he beamed. 'Put it in the cellos.' Never have I seen a more incredulous face than Arthur Hammerstein's. 'Are you writing music for me, and don't know any more than that?' he boomed. 'Get out of here, and stay out!'"[51]]

Fortunately Vinnie didn't take the order seriously. I never kept any book on just how big the sale of song copies and records was on the shows, but his songs for *Wildflower* must have done well. One piece I remember from my own personal perch was "The Bambalina." The orchestration, particularly of the dance, made a great hit with everybody. It flowed in Steve Jones's arrangement, to my great joy. When the deadline is bearing down on you as the arranger of the full score of a show and you call in a fellow-worker, the worst fate is for his arrangement to have to be re-done whether anybody has time or not. When it turns out to be a little masterpiece like "The Bambalina" was you feel like jumping over the moon.

---

[51] "From the Notes of a Music Arranger," *Theater Arts*, November 1956, 89.

For *Rose Marie* the collaborator was Rudolf Friml, and the musical theater had never seen a bigger success, according to the statisticians. With a dramatic libretto by Otto Harbach and Oscar Hammerstein II it had a first-act curtain nothing short of thrilling.

That a big hit is in the eye of the beholder got a very good demonstration right under my eyes in the case of this one. Two friends of ours, Marion Green, a singer with a beautiful baritone voice, and Gretl Urban, a successful scene designer, went to the opening-night performance together. Marion Green, or "Bill" as we all called him, had had high hopes of playing the lead in the show, but didn't get the part.

At the end of the exciting first act Bill said to Gretl, "Well, I wanted this show to be bad, but I never dreamed it would be this bad!" And she quite agreed with him.

And you don't have to miss getting a part in it to hate the biggest success. Many sincere playgoers are inclined to shy away from plays that get rave notices. Not a pose, but the result of many disappointments.

Jerome Kern, in his position as the established leader of theater composers, was used to dictating the terms of who did what, especially in the preparation and publication of his music. My boss, as far as I had a boss, was really Max Dreyfus, who with his brother Louis owned the firm of Harms, Inc. They assigned us to whichever performance we worked for, took care of our bills for work as we delivered it, no matter who eventually paid for it. Kern, of course, had his choice of any of us he wanted.

Conflicts of one production with another were always possible, but in fact seldom got to be a serious problem.

While *Rose Marie* was in rehearsal and my department was under full steam, I got a call from Jerome Kern asking me to meet him in Max Dreyfus's office the next morning.

We met and went in to see Max together. Jerry, looking like a tough little bulldog, walked up to Max's desk while I stood ill-at-ease in whatever shadow I could find.

Kern said, "I hear Russell Bennett is working on some other show. I need him on mine."

Max said, "Are you in rehearsal?"

Kern: "No, but I need him." (Silence.) "What are you going to do about it?"

Now I was really ill at ease, because I had just heard that Rudolf Friml had tried to arrange his music in *Rose Marie* for the orchestra. Arthur Hammerstein had heard some kind of rehearsal of it and threw it out of the show.

That just about doubled my load of work for the out-of-town opening.[52]

Kern stood there looking Max Dreyfus in the eye like Wotan killing Hunding—except that Hunding died and Max didn't. Max finally said quietly, "Well, Jerry, it will be the way you want it."

Jerry didn't stomp out, but the effect was the same. I waited and said to Max, "What shall I do?"

He said, "Go ahead with what you're doing."

No serious conflict ever came of it. Kern actually had two different shows in preparation at that time and one of them got to the point where it kept me from leaving New York when *Rose Marie* went on the road for its tryout. Maurice De Packh went with it and nobody lost any sleep over the problem. Certainly not we arrangers because we weren't going to get much sleep anyway.

I doubt that Mr. Jerome David Kern ever thought of it again.

Rose Marie did very well on the tryout and came back to New York in good shape.

Something you won't see very often in these pages is "I don't remember," but the fact is I don't remember whether I wrote a fancy overture for the New York opening or not. If so, it was obviously quite forgettable.

I do remember the overture to *Wildflower.* It had a soft ending—an experiment in show overtures at the time. The producer was very disturbed by this earth-shaking departure and I assumed I would be asked to bring it in line with tradition. In fact, being almost completely surrounded by other musical obstetrics, I forgot to ask and no one told me what was decided about it. A couple of months later Steve Jones (whose arrangement of "The Bambalina" was so good in the show) said one day, "That overture with the soft ending is the only one I ever heard in the theater that gets applause every performance."

It was nice of John Q. Public to give me that nod of approval. John Q. doesn't usually waste much approval on me—and vice versa.

The third collaborator for Herbert Stothart in an Arthur Hammerstein musical was George Gershwin. The name of the play was *The Song of the Flame.*

Gershwin had already won fame with his *Rhapsody in Blue*, and his fans surrounded him, turned his head, in fact turned it so far around that it was

---

[52]"Arthur Hammerstein . . . wouldn't open the show unless he had a new orchestration [to replace Friml's] of the song ["Indian Love Call"], which he was counting on to be the big hit, and started looking for Bennett. He located him in a private hospital, confined to bed with a badly sprained back incurred in the semifinals of a Y.M.C.A. handball tournament. With a nurse at his side to keep remolding the pentagon of pillows supporting him, Bennett dashed off a memorable orchestration of "Indian Love Call" on a scratch-pad" (Wind, "Another Opening, Another Show," 46). (But see p. 149.)

on straight again. He was still full of youthful fun that protected him from being a social liability.

During the tryout of *The Song of the Flame* he didn't spend much time working with us, but paid us a couple of visits. In his fur coat and smoking a very large cigar, he only needed the beard to look like Johannes Brahms in the very flesh. While he was stopping by he played me a little minuet strain that has always stayed with me and always will. You might win a few bets if you played it for tune-detectives and started a discussion about whose melody it was. It may [be] that this little piece of pure beauty went into a Gershwin score some place, some time, but all I know about it is what he played me one morning when he was visiting his own show.[53]

The music of *The Song of the Flame* must not have been a success with the producers. Toward the end of the tryout I was asked to arrange a new number for which they used an all-Russian melody with a new lyric. They called it "Don't Forget Me."

In spite of the great sympathy that must be between the music arranger and the people on the stage it has not been my experience that one makes many long friends with the members of the cast. There is no possible reason for this, and once in a while a big exception stands out. An especially attractive juvenile lead was in several of the many shows I worked on during the period. His name was Jack Whiting, and no doubt a great many who have liked the theater will recall him with pleasure.

Ever since I was "promoted" (to whatever this was in the shows) my old friend Mr. George Moody had been looking for a man to do the show numbers for publication, and still wasn't satisfied with what he found. It was the old story—and also the perennial one—if you need a job you may be in trouble, if you need help, try and find it.

One day, out of a clear sky, Jack Whiting said to me that at the University of Pennsylvania he'd had a classmate who arranged music well, in Jack's

---

[53]Long after the composer's death, interest in "new" Gershwin works continues. The announcer on one of Bennett's *Ford Show* radio broadcasts once enticingly introduced a new Gershwin-Bennett medley: "You know, we're all present at a unique event in music right now. The event is possible because Robert Russell Bennett has a memory like the *Encyclopedia Britannica* crossed with the Manhattan telephone book. He's remembered several lovely unpublished Gershwin melodies from the many years he and Gershwin worked together. Some were written for shows that were never produced, others were improvised and forgotten—by everybody but Russell. They all have the distinctive Gershwin touch—as Russell says, he wasn't a one-finger thinker, he thought down into the harmony of the chords, and even into the harmonies of life itself. Russell has woven these unknown themes and melodies into a haunting fantasy for the Ford Orchestra—*The Gershwin Nobody Knew.*" An aircheck of this 1 July 1945 program survives.

opinion, and it turned out he was right. Mr. Moody, of Harms, "imported" Jack's classmate, Walter Paul, and he more than made good.[54]

Jack had another classmate, Douglas Fairbanks Jr. From being classmates, they also became relatives. Douglas's mother, Beth, and Jack got married and really did live happily. She was an outstanding person and their companionship was lovely to see.

Douglas Jr. was very unlike his unbelievable silent movie star father, but he had an important career that kept him covering a lot of territory. His mother once told my wife Louise that the only time she ever saw her son was when her husband brought him around.

That same Marion Green, who hated *Rose Marie*, has also a high spot on our list of friends. We introduced him to Gretl Urban, his companion of that evening. Gretl was the daughter of Josef Urban, famous as the designer of the scenery of many operas at the Metropolitan Opera House for years.

"Bill" Green was a featured performer in a revue that opened in Chicago in the mid-twenties. I quote it because of a personal interest in one of the songs he sang. Lewis Gensler was the composer of the songs in the revue and he had set the poem "The Raven" of Edgar Allen Poe as one of the numbers. Sung by Bill with his God-given voice it had some real class.

The show was built around none other than that old trouper Raymond Hitchcock. (I tip my hat as his name comes up here. "An Old Fashioned Garden," Cole Porter's song, was in a Raymond Hitchcock revue [*Hitchy-Koo, 1919*], and that song was my entrance music to orchestration for Broadway.) When Gensler, the composer, was getting a little enthusiastic about having "The Raven" in a show of this kind, old Raymond tried to help the composer keep his feet on the ground with a little advice. In his deep, scraping voice he said, "My boy, you mustn't expect the public to have a vocabulary of more than twelve words, including 'wheat,' 'manure,' and a few others."

During the dress rehearsal at the theater I was, as is often the case, at the hotel with two copyists, rushing out the last few cues to be ready for the opening night in a few hours.

The telephone rang. It was Lew Gensler with panic in his voice, saying, "Russ, you'll have to conduct 'The Raven' at the performance tonight. This fellow can't possibly do it!"

I said "yes" to get rid of him and dived back into the unfinished cues on the desk. At almost curtain time I got to the theater and for the first time

---

[54]Paul turned out many "stock" arrangements and helped orchestrate Porter's *DuBarry Was a Lady* (1939), *Something for the Boys* (1943) and *Kiss Me, Kate* (1948). Born in France, he also did commercial arranging of symphonic music under his full name, Walter Paul Dauzet.

realized that they were dead serious and expected me to do the whole scene without a rehearsal—and without a white tie and tails, incidentally. I couldn't, and don't still, believe the change was that important, but they looked awfully desperate and I gave in.

The time came to go into the pit and one of the Chicago orchestra men met me at the door saying "Are you a member of the union?"

"Yes."

"May I see your card?"

"I don't have it with me."

So he barred the way and a feeling of emancipation began to creep over me. I started to turn away as I said, "Okay, you won't let me do it?"

This bothered him and he said, "Can you get your card tomorrow?"

By this time the lights were changing and the conductor of the show was smiling and handing me the baton.

Bill Green sang gloriously and the number brought down the house.

Toward midnight, after the tumult of the evening subsided, Green, Gensler and I walked to the hotel from the theater and Gensler was in heaven over the success of his song. In his joy he made a rather innocent remark. He said, "Fellows, if 'The Raven' goes this way in provincial Chicago, think what it will do in New York!"

Bill stopped dead and said, "Provincial Chicago, eh? Everything really artistic I ever did on the stage got much more in Chicago than it ever did on Broadway!"

Lew Gensler looked incredulous, but there was not any way to bring him back to earth that evening. Nor any need to.

I think I heard that "The Raven" was not even retained in the New York production. A hit in Chicago and "quoth the raven, nevermore."

Several producers in the New York theaters went to seek advice from astrologers or clairvoyants of some kind as to dates to go into rehearsals, dates to open shows, etc. Many another sound-thinking businessman was not ashamed to look to the stars for help in making decisions.

A name one heard very often at that time was Evangeline Adams. Many of our friends knew her and swore by her. Students of astronomy like Mrs. Merrill are likely to be interested in astrology, even though they may not take it seriously. Another, much less well-known among my friends, was a favorite among theater people as a "medium," Marie Juliette Pontin. Several men pretty high in show business wouldn't make a move without Mrs. Pontin's advice. I was curious to know what attracted all these grown men and women to the lady, so I called and made an appointment. Her office told me to come in at a certain hour and asked me the exact hour of my birth.

During the last three or four years I have been skimming over in this report, time spent in theaters as a writer of whatever wasn't already written in their music, there was so much to learn—about people, about language, about business, about survival (multiplied by three)—that the future of the distinguished conductor of Wagnerian opera was hardly even taken out and dusted off with any regularity. However, it still slept in the master bedroom—while it slept. I got as far as learning to speak pretty fair French, as well as some Italian and German, gained at least a nodding acquaintance with the operas and kept on dreaming.

I met a fine musician named Chalmers Clifton,[55] conductor at the time of the American Orchestral Society, who graciously welcomed me at his rehearsals and even turned the baton over to me once or twice. These visits were worth a lot to me, but took a good deal of time away from boiling the pot.

When the time of my appointment with Mrs. Pontin came, I realized that I should bring in some kind of purpose, some need for her advice, rather than come as a curious sight-seer, so I more or less improvised a problem. I would ask her to help me decide whether I should spend time with the conducting and "kibitzing" or devote full time to my Broadway clients.

I waited a very short time in a very pleasant waiting room and Mrs. Pontin parted two heavy, dark-red curtains and came toward me in a flowing robe, extending her hand and saying, "Good morning, Mr. Bennett! You wanted to see me about a change you are making in your professional life. Come in."

She led me into a sort of office where she had two large charts filled with figures spread out. I told her very briefly of my desire to be a conductor or find a post where I was concerned with serious music. I'm sure that what I told her was not any more than this paragraph long.

She had my chart in front of her beside the chart of the conductor of the New York Philharmonic Orchestra at the time, William Von Hoogstraten, and she proceeded to compare our two talents and capabilities in great detail.[56]

I gathered from her that the stars had no objection whatsoever to my forging ahead as a maestro and she was also inclined to worry a little about nervous tension, saying that handball and tennis dragged on the same nerve centers as music, and were therefore not to be trusted as relaxation. She recommended ballroom dancing.

---

[55]Bennett later listed Chalmers Clifton (1889–1966), as well as Carl Busch and Nadia Boulanger, as references on his 1927 Guggenheim fellowship application. Clifton taught at Columbia in the early 1930s and later directed the WPA's Federal Music Project in New York City.

[56]William Von Hoogstraten (1884–1965) was associated with the New York Philharmonic from 1922 until 1938; he spent the remainder of his career conducting in Europe.

I told her that I had yet to dance a step and had no assurance that it would be possible. Whereupon she showed herself to be a human female by saying, "I shouldn't recommend it if I didn't know you could do it."

I never took up dancing and did continue playing handball and tennis, but I could see why so many theater people swore by her. How she knew before I said a word exactly what I had decided to ask her, or why she had me on her desk with the conductor of the Philharmonic already—this is the sort of thing I long since stopped trying to explain away. My own brief forays into the subconscious have shown me what a waste of time trying to peek is.

Chapter Four

Three passengers on the *DeGrasse*, a medium-sized ocean liner of the French Line, were three Bennetts: Louise, Beatrice Jean, and Russell. Jean was about five and a half years old. The sailing date was April 17, 1926. We were about to become Parisians. This change was not brought on by the stars; only as a part of the incurable desire to keep up with music.

I did, however, consult Mrs. Pontin about the date to sail. We had chosen the *DeGrasse* from what we could learn about boats and when Mrs. Pontin gave me three or four dates as favorable, the departure date of the *DeGrasse* was on her list.

On the boat, as soon as we got our sea legs we acquired two new friends: a French lady of a generation and type that Broadway and Hollywood never heard of—pouring a little water in her wine ("better for the stomach that way") and knowing a simple answer to every travel question, usually giving you the answer quietly before you asked—and one of the flutists of the New York Symphony Orchestra, who was on his way to study composition with somebody I'd never heard of: Nadia Boulanger.

He had met Mlle. Boulanger when she was in New York to play an organ concerto with Walter Damrosch, whose orchestra was the one to which our new friend belonged.[1] His name, he told us, was Quinto Maganini, and nobody at any ad agency ever did a job of selling like he did of his new teacher.[2]

---

[1]On 11 January 1925, during her first visit to the U. S., Boulanger premiered Aaron Copland's Symphony for Organ and Orchestra with Damrosch's New York Symphony.

[2]Maganini (1897–1974), an Oakland native, had been wooed away from the San Francisco Symphony by Damrosch. He studied flute with section-leader Barrère while also remaining active as a composer; his flute quartet, *The Realm of Dolls*, was widely played in the 1920s. Maganini conducted both the New York Sinfonietta and his Maganini Chamber Symphony in the 1930s; he later (1939–1970) led the Norwalk (Connecticut) Symphony. Bennett may have met him prior to his 1926 trip to Paris, as Maganini had taken part in an earlier (20 January 1924) New York Flute Club performance of the *Rondo Capriccioso*.

I had written to a very much esteemed composer in Paris named Paul Vidal, asking him to consider taking me on as a pupil, but before we landed at Le Havre I was about sold on Quinto's fabulous lady.

We checked in at the Hotel des Deux Mondes (I never did ask what "two worlds" they had in mind[3]), stayed there a few days and went to Tours to visit Roger Salabert and his wife and daughter for a long weekend. Roger Salabert was a member of the music publishing firm Francis Salabert et Cie., and the firm was in turn connected with Harms, Inc. of New York.

There was an idea behind all this that I might have some work as a music arranger in France, but it will surprise no one to hear that nothing came of the idea, whoever had it. Roger and his family were sweet to us. Such hospitality is not typical of that part of the world and, sadly enough, Roger died in New York only a few months later, leaving us socially very much in their debt. Some friends of theirs rented us a couple of rooms in their house in St. Cloud, just outside of Paris, where we lived for our first two or three months as Parisians.

No word came from M. Vidal in answer to my letters from New York and I sent a note to Mlle. Boulanger. Less than a week later I joined the Boulangerie ("the bakery"), a name the mass of pupils gave her studio and all who frequented it.

The third and last time I had visited Mrs. Pontin in New York she was concerned with a "dynamic woman" I was to meet who would cause, in her words, "separation tendencies" with my wife. She seemed to take the situation quite seriously and was evidently anxious to find ways to help me steer a straight course through rough waters. Never having given even a thought to what it would be like to be without my wife no matter what lovely, highly emotional creature was pretending in the New York theater to be ready for goodness knows what, I simply couldn't conceive of this mysterious dynamic woman taking over.

Not until four or five years after Nadia Boulanger and I began poring through music and philosophy did it dawn on me that she must be Mrs. Pontin's enchantress, and I can't possibly understand how anybody with such superhuman abilities could make such a wild shot.

Eloping with Nadia Boulanger would be just like falling in love with Pikes Peak.

After another three or four weeks a note came from M. Vidal saying he would be glad to see me and take me as a pupil. By now there was no turning back, and it was only a question of what to say to him. I ended up waiting as

---

[3]The hotel's letterhead then featured maps of the Western and Eastern Hemispheres.

long as he had to reply and then honestly forgot it until I was ashamed. Therefore the hoped-for meeting never took place. Maybe we'll meet some day at harp practice.

Nadia had a sister Lili who was, by any judgment I can muster, a composer worthy to stand with the great. She died in her mid-twenties, a musician sincerely respected by all her contemporaries. I recall this because it may just possibly have something to do with what follows here.

On my first visit at the Boulanger studio at 30, rue Ballu, in Montmartre, I stated my aims and desires, after showing Mlle. Nadia a short symphony I had written to submit in a prize competition sponsored by the magazine *Musical America.* The prize had been won by Ernest Bloch[4] and my symphony received honorable mention. (Nadia said, "Qu'est-ce que ça vous rapporte?"—"What does that get you?")

After she had read the first movement I told her I always believed that too much music was being written and, rather than add to it my hope was to be a part of some of the great music already ours—preferably as a conductor, etc.

Her answer, very sincerely and clearly given, and I'm sure I can quote and translate it accurately: "I understand you perfectly. I had exactly the same decision to make and I made it just as you are. But I see so many ideas here that I doubt that you have a right to make that decision. If everybody did that we should have no more music written."

I once read that Schopenhauer, the old German philosopher, was reminded that if the women of this earth were all done away with, as he seemed to recommend, the human race would soon be extinct. His answer was—and I wish I could quote him exactly—what possible turn of events could be better than that?

I couldn't in all sincerity give Mlle. Boulanger the same answer. She, with typically French courtesy, refused to call me her pupil, but she wrote out the Greek modes for me and recommended I take themes from Frescobaldi and write some contrapuntal etudes in the Greek scales. That was about all the mental exercise she ever prescribed. The rest was something like four years of examination and discussion of contemporary music and musicians, and poets, and philosophers, and theology. With Louise she talked more about politics and world events. Looking back, it is hard to see how the woman had enough hours to go to concerts, join us at supper after concerts and other events, and, after those years had passed, to be one of the most faithful correspondents

---

[4]Bloch's prize-winning orchestra work was his "epic rhapsody" *America.* The other "honorable mentions" went to Samuel Gardner (*Broadway*), Louis Gruenberg (*Jazz Suite*), and Wintter Watts (*The Piper*). Bennett's symphony was his first, dedicated to Carl Busch.

I have ever known. And it was not that we were especially favored in this way. Somehow all the Boulanger pupils marvel at the time she took to remain loyal to them and keep in touch.

The period we spent as Parisians was almost identical with the time spent by William L. Shirer in France. The length of time and the dates as reported in his memoir[5] that I saw recently fit like a glove. The remarkable thing is that it's not a small world after all. The boulevards where we walked and the shops and the restaurants were just about the same but not one of the dazzling names he drops was in my world at all.

One semi-exception would be Charles Lindbergh. Louise and I were at the Club Interallié for an afternoon reception in his honor the day after he landed. The man that wrote the song "The Raven," Lew Gensler, and Mrs. Gensler had asked Ambassador Herrick to include us among the guests.

One of the great attractions at the Wednesday afternoon teas that were a permanent institution at the Boulanger studio was Nadia's mother. An international group if there ever was one was sure to be there and Mme. Boulanger sat near the door where she greeted every guest as a particularly beloved monarch would greet her subjects.

She was a Russian. One had to believe the generally accepted idea that she was of the old Russian nobility, but if I attempted to put together all these intimate facts you would discover at some point that I don't know what I'm talking about. The only point that I can make with authority is that standing near her and hearing her one had to feel the presence of the genuine article. A sample of one such occasion should need no elaboration. We chatted at one of the Wednesday teas for a minute or so and I stepped aside as the guests came by.

A young American came and was having quite some trouble finding the appropriate French words, so Madame Boulanger said most charmingly, "Speak English. I understand it." He was put at ease, said his few little nothings and went for his cup of tea.

The next guest went into Russian and they chatted for a few moments. As he left her she chuckled and said to me, "Once a year I speak Russian." Then three more young persons came in together. They were enjoying themselves and told Madame Boulanger so. In the course of this it came out that they were Italian.

Madame Boulanger said, "Do you know why I never speak Italian?"

One of them said, "No. Why?"

---

[5]Shirer's *20th Century Journey: A Memoir of a Life and the Times* (New York: Simon and Schuster, 1976).

She said, "Because I don't know how."

I'm afraid that what I've just written, without the charm and the good humor of her voice, will fail to give any idea of how enchanting she was. I know that fine biographies are being written of both Lili and Nadia Boulanger. I hope they have some room for more about Madame Boulanger.

The American students at the "Boulangerie" at that time were so plentiful that it amounted to a phenomenon. Part of that impression came from the presence of the American Academy at the Palais de Fontainebleau. Mlle. Nadia spent a certain time every week there in the summer and one summer my family and I took a place on the rue Royale for a pleasant change. If you took a stroll on a balmy evening there you were as likely to meet a young American whose name would be headline material in the U.S.A. world of music in a very few years as you would be to meet any particular native or a party of young French lovers on an evening stroll.

We saw a good deal of our boat companion Quinto Maganini all through the Parisian years. His name sounds like the fifth son of a little Italian organ grinder, but he was really a rather tall, fun-loving American with great energy and lots of talent. And of course was an outstanding flutist. We'll pay him several visits as these pages wander on.

Many of our fellow Parisians who became close friends were headed for importance in the world of the arts through the years. One of Nadia Boulanger's organ pupils whom she admired very much was a quiet, likable man from the Chicago territory named Barrett Spach. The name was pronounced like the German word for bacon—Speck. He was later to become organist and music director of Chicago's Fourth Presbyterian Church, where he remained until he died of a heart attack thirty-one years later.

In Paris he was very fond of a little Swiss girl named Nellie, who had a divine soprano voice. All of us were rooting for them to head for a wedding—all of us, that is, except Nellie and Barrett. He used to drop in *chez nous* once in a while to consult the ouija board trying to find out why the two of them never caught fire. Ouija didn't know any more than they did, as far as I could gather.

Some time later Barrett married a girl in Chicago who had a divine contralto voice. The marriage was most happy, so the gods knew what they were doing. As usual.

Barrett and Maurine (Mrs. Spach) furnish a fine example of something I said about Nadia Boulanger just a while ago. She remembered his birthday and sent greetings every year as long as he was alive. Not only that, but she sent a message of remembrance to Maurine every year until she herself was almost ninety.

When I think how hard it is to keep up with personal correspondence and then think of multiplying it by the number of pupils—she must have been touched by a fairy wand that multiplied her.

Each of the young talents with burning-bright futures that were so plentiful would no doubt be a story worth telling from the point of view of each of the others. Barrett Spach always had a good influence on me. I even wrote a sonata for the organ[6] and he and I sat in one of the churches in Paris while Nadia Boulanger gave a very good performance of it one morning. At sight, of course.

A very different relationship was that between Roy Harris and me. We played tennis a few times, and we talked a lot about a lot of things. What Roy never said to me in so many words is what most of his associates quoted him as saying and believing: "It's nonsense to study musical theory. Better just sit down and write what you have to say in music."

If he had said that directly to me something would have come up that has not been touched on here for a while: the old snob. I should have said that if I wanted to deal with primitive talents alone, I should certainly never have left Broadway.

The nearest we ever came to bringing up the point and laying it on the table, came some years later when I heard one of Roy's most serious works [likely his Fifth Symphony]. It was on the program of the Chicago Symphony Orchestra at Carnegie Hall one evening and after the concert we met by chance at the Russian Tea Room.

I said, "Roy, they always told me you didn't believe in studying music, and what's this I see and hear? The last movement of your piece called 'Double Fugue'!"

His answer is a good quote: "Well, what y'gonna do?"

Although we were both raised in almost identical surroundings, and in the same part of the U.S.A., I'm not at all sure how to spell the quote. It seemed to mean to say that he had had to break down and spend hours and hours with musical theory in self-defense.

I'm not sure that's what he meant.

In the little villa in St. Cloud we were fairly comfortable. Our young daughter had a governess part of the day and she also went to a little school

---

[6]The Sonata in G (1929), Bennett's sole composition for organ, was dedicated to Barrett Spach—later a professor at Northwestern University—who assisted with the published registrations. Cast predominantly in the phrygian mode (and with a slow movement in three keys simultaneously) the piece invariably startles those who know only Bennett's more conventional works. The Sonata in G enjoyed a certain "avant garde" vogue for decades, featuring in the repertories of Melville Smith, Catharine Crozier (Mrs. Harold Gleason), and David Craighead.

not far away. She had to become a French girl. At that age that was not very difficult. She told us they gave her something like an onion to eat and after tasting it she said (in French), "Ooh, that burns!" They corrected her and said, "No, no! It is not hot! It pricks the tongue (Ça pique la langue)." Of course they were both wrong; it doesn't stick into anything any more than it burns it. Such is the charm and the discomfort of each new language.

It was interesting to see how easily she slipped into a new tongue at that age, and also to see the years take away—tiny bit by tiny bit—her memory and her concentration. After a month or two in Berlin (later) she was at home enough in German to pick out the longest prayer at bedtime (just so she could stay up that much longer, I suspect). Two or three years later she was asked in Vienna why she didn't like it as much as most of us did and she said, "Man muss Deutsch sprechen (You have to speak German)."

We stayed in St. Cloud until after the French National Tennis Tournament that year. The club where they played was right there in St. Cloud, and French tennis was enjoying its finest hour just at that time. [René] Lacoste, [Henri] Cochet, [Jean] Borotra, [Jacques] Brugnon—all the top players of three or four years were there.

Louise found an apartment at 30, rue De Saix, in Paris, where we really settled down some time in June, and I don't think we ever lived where we felt more at home. The place was across the street from a cavalry headquarters—a *caserne de cavalerie.* (I don't know how to translate the name or tell the exact institution it was.) All I do know is a bugle call one heard every few hours. I asked someone who should know how the call was originally written, but all I know even now is how it sounded.[7]

[7]This melody appears in Bennett's 1929 *"VU (Seen in Paris)": 20 Etudes in Miniature* for piano. Each etude is a vignette from one of the twenty arrondissements (precincts) of Paris; the fifteenth, (Vaugirard)—"La Caserne de Cavalerie (The Cavalry Barracks)"—includes Bennett's "bugle call." Selections from *"VU"* were premiered on Jose Iturbi's Carnegie Hall recital of 30 November 1932, and the piece was published by Éditions Raoul Breton (Paris) in 1934.

The Eiffel Tower is a stone's throw to the northeast and to the west is a subway (Metro) station with the prettiest name any subway station ever had: La Motte Piquet Len Grenelle [La Motte-Piquet Grenelle].

For a man who was not anxious to be a composer, I turned out a lot of music in Paris: orchestral, chamber music, piano music, a setting of an old French poem by De Fontenelle published in 1728—my piece was a ballet on the stage with soloists, chorus and orchestra in the pit—a song cycle with words by Chaucer [*Three Chaucer Poems*] (this was with string quartet) and so on and so on, but this was not uninterrupted.[8]

The De Fontenelle poem was "Endimion" and one of the principal characters was The Great God Pan. In the fall of our first year there [1926], the Great God Kern, flanked by my own personal demi-god Max Dreyfus, got me: They were doing a setting of Edna Ferber's *Show Boat* with the adaptation and lyrics by Oscar Hammerstein. I don't remember that they offered me half of the Guaranty Trust Company or anything else beside steamboat tickets and the per-page rate for orchestration, but we locked up our little apartment and, as French residents, paid a visit to New York.

We went into a furnished apartment in Bronxville, New York, near where both of the above-named deities lived. I took down some of Jerry 's songs from his performance at the piano. They had signed Paul Robeson and I don't know whom else for the cast, but one fine morning Kern told me the news. Their producer, Mr. Florenz Ziegfeld, didn't have any money. *Show Boat* was on the shelf.

We were looking up boats to "go home" on, but there were two or three rather big productions in or near rehearsal and we stayed to pick up a little financial stability.

In the middle of the winter we returned to France where we were technically residents. We crossed the Atlantic Ocean on the *France*, a larger ship than the *DeGrasse*, and older. There was some evidence that we had a few fellow passengers that are famous for deserting sinking ships on board, but we never saw them. Only saw that they are neat marauders indeed.

It was a surprise to me that such a smooth crossing was possible in January, but our steward, a rather elderly one, said he was on his ninety-second crossing, and there was no particular season for bad or good weather. "Just cross the ocean when you have to" was the way he put it.

---

[8]Bennett's orchestral works completed in Paris include his First and *Abraham Lincoln* symphonies, *Charleston Rhapsody* (chamber orchestra), *Paysage* (a tone poem premiered by Howard Hanson and the Rochester Philharmonic in December 1933), and *Sights and Sounds*. Two flute-and-piano works, *Dance* and *Nocturne*, were also composed there, as well as his violin sonata and the woodwind quintet *Toy Symphony*.

It's a nice romantic thing to say, and one must discount it on many counts, but there was indeed a sincere feeling of getting back home as we rode in a taxi across the bridge, across the Champs de Mars and up to the door of 30, rue De Saix. Life there took up just about where it left off. More music, more musicians, more reading in Italian and German—and more interruptions from the commercial world.

Kern and Hammerstein once [1940] wrote a song called "The Last Time I Saw Paris." I must some day write one called "The First Time I Saw London." It will be a little dramatic. Harry Ruby and Bert Kalmar were in London with a new show about to be produced and asked me to hop over the Channel and talk about some of their future plans. They had already written many a hit, and now were especially famous for "Three Little Words." The title was used for the film about their careers a few years later [MGM, 1950].

I always thought that, with all those generations behind me, there must have been an Indian or two among my ancestors. Therefore, when I had to go somewhere I didn't know, it was in my instinct just to go out and follow my nose until I got there. It sounds ridiculous, but it's uncanny how often I got where I wanted to be.

So I went to the Gare St. Lazare and bought a ticket for London, was told to change to a boat at Dieppe and change back to a train at New Havre. When I got to Rouen I did a very foolish thing: asked somebody if this was where I should take the boat for New Haven. Now an Indian would never have done that, and [so] I'm afraid there wasn't any Indian blood after all.

The person I asked said yes and I got off the train and found a boat. No doubt everybody in the world knew in those days about crossing the Channel. However bad they heard it was, it was. I know now that I had never been really seasick before nor have I ever been since. The thing went on for three or four hours and at some point a very portly Briton in uniform came up to me and asked me for my ticket. I told him that I had had only a vague idea of where I wanted to go, and no idea at all that I should ever get there. He was quite understanding, but said, "I shall have to claim thirty-one shillings extra fare." All of which means that I was supposed to take the right boat at Dieppe and not at Rouen. I should probably have been as sick on the right boat, but it would have saved me thirty-one shillings.

When we edged up to English soil I followed the crowd on wobbly legs and was asked for my passport by a nice looking man who asked me a question. I tried very hard to find one word that I could recognize in any language and gave up.

"I'm so sorry," I said. "I've been miserably ill on that boat and have apparently no ears or mind to understand the question. Do you mind repeating?"

I could tell that he repeated exactly what he had said before, but had no success understanding him. One or two words did convince me that he was speaking English. I suddenly had an idea. I said, "Do you speak French?"

"Yes, sir."

"May I have your question in French?"

It worked. His French was perfectly understandable. He was afraid I was coming in to work for pay and he stamped the passport with something that said I had to get out of England by a certain date, which suited me just fine.

The length of the interview made me miss the London train. It was bitter cold and I had to wait over three hours for the next one. Some railroad men were gathered around a stove inside the station master's office and they offered me a chair near the stove.

In those three-odd hours the fellows never stopped talking and I assure you I never understood one thing they said. Not even one word for sure.

When I got to the hotel where Kalmar and Ruby were staying there was no room for me and day was almost over. Harry showed me his bed—an enormous one—and offered me half of it for the night. I accepted, and what happened is funnier when you realize that both of us, with our rough beginnings and uncomplicated personal lives, had a sum total of no instinct whatsoever toward closing the space between us.

The next morning, however, when I woke up I found I had put my right arm under his shoulders. When I got fully conscious and realized what I had done there seemed nothing to do now but die of embarrassment. As a matter of fact I did nothing of the sort, but heard myself saying, "Hello, Harry!" with a certain amount of affection in my voice and heard him say with somewhat similar affection, "Hello, Russell!"

Then we laughed like two utter asses.

At lunch that day with several young men of the London theater (maybe I should spell it "theatre"), Harry told the whole story on me and the whole table laughed, some a bit uncomfortably, I thought. But the big laugh came when one of them asked, "Well, what did you do about it, old boy?" and Harry answered, "I didn't do anything about it. It was nice!"

Kalmar and Ruby were a marvelous pair. I remember one day they were waiting in Grand Central Station for a train to go up to Westchester, and I said, "Oh, Bert, I just remembered. I owe you a quarter." I handed him the quarter. He said, "What do you owe me this for?" I told him I'd owed it to him for a couple of weeks, and tried to remind him when I'd borrowed it. Bert said, "Aw, forget it, you don't owe me any quarter!" So Harry came up to me, very confidentially and he said, "Do you know that's how Bert has made his pile—refusing quarters? After a while—it adds up!"

And Harry once really put me down. I said to him, "You know, the trouble with all of you popular songwriters is that you get an eight-bar phrase and you have to plug it all afternoon. You write a strain like 'Some enchanted evening,' and then you say a few bars later, 'All right, now in case you didn't hear it, you dumb clucks out there, "Some enchanted evening," here it is again.' And then a little bit later you say, 'All right, I know you've forgotten it by now,' so you say 'Some enchanted evening' again. But," I said, "you take a thing like 'La donna è mobile' from *Rigoletto*—listen to Verdi, he never goes back, never returns to the original statement; keeps on going, always something new!" And Harry quieted me down right away. He said, "Well, there've been popular songs like that. Have you ever listened to 'School Days,' by Gus Edwards?" And he was so right![9]

[Bennett at least once made the same point to Gershwin, urging him to avoid—in his concert works—melodies that persistently revisited their opening measures. Bennett was, after all, "always very ambitious for George, and he knew that." And so, in May 1928, at the Hotel Majestic in Paris, when Gershwin demonstrated his just-composed "blues" theme for *An American in Paris*, Bennett characteristically advised his friend, "George, this is what I wanted you to outgrow." Portions of Gershwin's next concert work, the Second Rhapsody (1931), were more to Bennett's satisfaction; its lyric central theme was "the best tune Gershwin ever wrote . . . such a grand, grand tune."[10]]

Many times I've watched the effect of Harry Ruby's friendly wit on a group of new acquaintances. The same with Oscar Hammerstein with his similar effortless humor. They would make a funny remark and everybody would laugh as though they weren't sure they should. Then after a few remarks anything Harry or Oscar said would get a hearty laugh whether it was funny or not. It's no wonder comedians, who depend on laughs for a living, often look as though they ate people.

The business in London was about a show coming up later in New York. Without going into a deep trance, I think it was *Top Speed* and that was our introduction to Ginger Rogers. It was also Ginger Rogers's introduction to the Broadway theater, unless I dreamed it. Ginger will trip in and out of this story more than once, especially after we get to Hollywood.

Kalmar and Ruby and I wound up our discussions in a day or two. You always had to allow extra time for laughs. The trip back to Paris, a bit better

---

[9]The preceding two paragraphs are interpolated from a Bennett interview (31) with Max Wilk for *They're Playing Our Song*.

[10]Bennett interview with Miles Krueger, New York, 8 September 1978.

planned this time, and again that feeling, stronger than ever, of getting back home as the taxi passed the Eiffel Tower. It was certainly nothing I could get a patent on. So many others have reported the same symptoms.

And again the routine, the concentrated effort to know music and be a musician, and again the interruptions, some of them very attractive.

I'd never met Richard Rodgers in New York, but Lorenz Hart and he were already making very pleasant noises in New York and London, and one day word came from somewhere that Richard would like to meet me in Paris.

When I saw him he had with him a very unusual and interesting man named Raoul Breton, who stepped gracefully into the chronicle, as will be seen.

Rodgers and Hart had a new show opening in London and they had some songs that could use arrangements. Would it be possible for me to pay them a visit of a few days when the production got far enough along?

The tiny voice of the Wagnerian conductor was, as usual, trying to attract my attention and say something, but it was still some time before I would have to go to London for Rodgers and Hart—so, oh what the heck? Jerome Kern's *Show Boat* was surely going to beckon in a few months anyway. . . .

The tiny voice died down after a few whimpers.

This not being a reference work it probably doesn't matter in the least, but all of this was taking place during the first half-to-three-quarters of the year 1927. The year before I had run across a very attractive poem called "The Easter Egg" by A. A. Milne and had proceeded to make a song of it for baritone voice and orchestra. It was written for two reasons and no other: one, because every time you write a piece of music you learn something, and two, because it's impossible to resist those five little parallel lines on a white piece of paper. What other reason might there be? Publication? At this point in my journey selling a few copies of music had no charm. Hearing a performance? If I've written out the reams of score I've had to on my job without already "hearing" one or more live performances of anything I do why don't I go back and give them all back their money?

It's true that once in a while a certain performer or group of performers may bring in a warmth of tone or other personal touch that can surprise and even please you, but for that you have to pay the price of many rehearsals and performances where they don't even play the right notes, or the conductor has no message from the page in front of him, or an airplane roars overhead.

"The Easter Egg" was fun to write, and was put with the rest of the manuscripts. It seemed a good idea to tell the author of the poem about it and I got a reply to my note, saying on a very small piece of paper in a very small script that he could not allow me to set his poem because the rights belonged to another composer.

I'd forgotten about that "rights" business.

One morning Nadia Boulanger, after one of our hour-long disagreements about composers or music, suddenly became serious and said, "There is something I want to tell you. I know the conditions under which you live here and work, and from this morning on my fee will be half of what it has been. There is nothing to discuss; it's settled."

I never knew just who said what to her, or why she suddenly did this. Also I never have known how many of her pupils were the object of this charity, but I did know that many whispers had been passed around among the Boulangerie that had left me quite unprepared for such a gesture.

It was quite unnecessary. What I got from her was a major part of what we had crossed the ocean for and that would normally be the last economy I would think of. However, I had no answer to offer except "thank you." And indeed we never discussed it further.

To add to that story is another that came out of a clear sky in almost the same way. She brought up the subject of a Guggenheim Fellowship one morning and asked me very briefly if I approved of the idea. Without really guessing what she was driving at I said I thought it was a very great thing. She said, "Good! I'm going to speak to Dr. —— and you'll hear from them." The blank space is not another dark spot in my memory. I didn't know the man she was going to speak to, nor did I really hear the name as she spoke it.

Again, all I could say was "thank you."

[Nadia Boulanger's undated latter of recommendation—in English—in support of Bennett's November 1927 fellowship application arrived at the Guggenheim offices on 11 January 1928:

> Robert Russell Bennett is a born, & an accomplished musician—his native gifts are served by one of the most complete technic one can expect to be reached. His form, his writing, his orchestration are absolutely achieved—and I have always wondered why he asked me advices—He is completely able to realize what ever he has planned—
>
> On the other hand his general culture is very fine, very large—and this twice striking, according with the fact that he earned his life {living} and his family's for long years.
>
> The Sonata for piano and violin has made a great impression on the Committee of the T.W.I. {?} and his songs with quartett's accompaniment[11] had last season a very bright impression.

---

[11]The *Three Chaucer Poems*.

> I can not insist too much of the value of Mr. Bennett{—}he is a true artist—and had he some freedom after so long struggle I feel quite sure that he would be able to give new proofs of his personality. ss/Nadia Boulanger[12]]

But as I sit here writing this bit of history down for the first time these many years later I am thinking that it must be what Mrs. Pontin, brilliant astrologer, took to be a love affair with a dynamic woman. The poor stars got confused, bless them!

[12]Courtesy of the Fondation Internationale Nadia et Lili Boulanger and the John Simon Guggenheim Memorial Foundation.

Chapter Five

I paid my visit to Rodgers and Hart in London and could see why the collaboration had already established so firmly on the Broadway scene. Nobody but a particularly hard-boiled you-know-what could listen to such blending of verse and air without losing his head and heart.

Soon thereafter back to *Show Boat* in New York. So many things have been written about that one that you'd think my job here would be short and easy. Maybe if there hadn't sprung up a big notion that the so-called Golden Age began with this particular play a reasonable perspective would put *Show Boat* a little farther up-stage, but it had enough happen to it to explain a lot of its notices. An orchestrator's-eye view is not likely to repeat much of what has already been told about it.

Jerome Kern laughed harder at one of my little jokes on the second day we worked together than anybody else ever did in my entire life. We worked in his living room in Bronxville, where he sat at the piano and played from his sketches, handing them over page by page.

On the first day he gave me the entire opening Act One. It involved the song "Make Believe" and yards and yards of music, both vocal and instrumental. I took home the great bundle of material and spent many hours writing out the voice parts and arranging the whole thing for piano and voices.

Before I describe the second day in the Bronxville living room it's important to report a meeting that the song writers had had a week or so before. They gathered to discuss what might be an important development in the modern theater: sound pictures. Sound pictures were mostly referred to as Vitaphone, a commercial name for the process, coined by one of the cinema giants.[1] Jerome Kern was at the meeting while they all tried to look into the future and be ready for the possible impact on their creative lives. Kern, according to the man who reported the meeting to me, sat silent through the

---

[1]At first licensed exclusively to Warner Brothers, the Vitaphone sound-on-disk process was developed by Bell Telephone's engineers.

whole discussion and finally got up, took his hat and gloves and said, "Gentlemen, I have enjoyed this discussion very much but I must tell you that you are wasting your time. It will never amount to anything."

Somebody said, "Jerry, we know it doesn't amount to anything now, but how can we tell about the future?"

Jerry said, "I'm afraid you didn't understand what I said. I said it will never amount to anything. Have any of you heard this Vitaphone?

They said no, they hadn't.

He said, "Well I have, and it will never amount to anything! Good day, gentlemen!"

Exit Jerome D. Kern.

When we started work on the second workday I brought in the vocal score of the entire Opening in a carefully prepared ink copy, as is usual, and, also as usual, a few indications as to what instruments in the orchestra would play certain phrases. At the end of the song "Make Believe" Ravenal sings:

> Might as well make believe I love you,
> For to tell the truth, I do.

On the word "do" the first line of the melody goes on with the tenderest possible playing of, obviously, a muted solo violin. I thought it would give Jerry a little chuckle if I indicated as wrong a sound as I could think of, and I remembered how he had spoken of sound pictures, so over the first tender note of the solo I put "English Horn and Vitaphone."

"A little chuckle," eh? When he came to the spot and saw what it said he let out a yell and burst into the biggest, loudest and longest laugh I remember ever hearing. He sat at the piano and laughed, then went over to the window and sat in a chair there and laughed as loud and long again.

Of course it wouldn't have been so funny by miles to anybody else in the world, but if there ever was anybody that was not anybody else, it was Jerome Kern.

The next thing in the score of *Show Boat* is now known to all as "Ol' Man River," but when he handed me his sketch it had no name and no lyric. It was thirty-two not wholly convincing measures that sounded to me like they wanted to be wanted. In the first place it starts with two harmonically powerful and self-reliant bars and then comes to a mud puddle and doesn't know where to put its feet for the next two. Perhaps that isn't important, but to a musical snob it is.[2]

Anyhow the Muse of Music never spat at either Jerry or me for not finding the chords that should have been there. I found some rather nice fills for

[2]Bennett's associates have consistently remarked upon his reticence and tactfulness. Yet he must have spoken more directly with Kern at least once, having volunteered to journalist

the ends of phrases and didn't worry about it until a few days later when I looked at it with Oscar Hammerstein's words written in. I didn't worry about it then either—just said to Jerry, "Gee, that's a great song!"

Kern said, "You didn't say that when I gave it to you." He knew as well as I did that it wasn't a song at all until Oscar came in with the words.

> [The "classic Broadway story" about the song—its veracity doubtful—is memorable:
>
> > Mrs. Kern and Mrs. Hammerstein arrived at a party, and their hostess introduced them. "This is Mrs. Jerome Kern," she began. "Her husband wrote 'Ol' Man River.'" "Not true," said Mrs. Hammerstein. "Mrs. Kern's husband wrote *dumdumdeedah, da dumdumdeedah. My* husband wrote 'Ol' man river, dat ol' man river'!"[3]]

If you watch a lot of people in an art gallery, you are bound to see that an overwhelming percentage of them get nothing out of a picture until they are told "what it's a picture of." Only then can they start being art critics. It seems evident that that same percentage must have a name for every phrase of music (in the form of lines in the language they speak) before they can react to it.

As to Oscar Hammerstein's words for "Ol' Man River" (he originally called it "Ol' Man Ribber"): reading them for the first time I was convinced that he was sent here to be a poet. Of course all the successful songwriters are poets and musicians in their souls, but why aren't we entitled to at least one or two Whitmans out of all that mass of talent? Or is that too much to ask?

There came a time, as everybody seems to know, in Oscar's life when everything he did in the theater was unlucky. I think it lasted almost eleven years.

During that time he and his wife Dorothy came to dinner with us in Paris, where they told us they were planning to find a house in the south of France and live there where Oscar could write poetry. The idea was a thrilling one, but I remember thinking at the time that it was too good to be true.

> [Bennett once described Hammerstein as "my closest and dearest friend in show business, all his years" and disclosed his response to Hammerstein's plan to remain in France:
>
> > I told him then, "Nothing on earth could ever make me happier than to hear that, because you have poetry in you—you have great

---

George Anderson: "When I was working on Jerome Kern's *Show Boat* his publisher said to him one day, 'Jerry, this is the finest thing you ever wrote,' and he replied, 'Well, I just wish Russell Bennett thought so'" (Pittsburgh *Post-Gazette*, 27 May 1974).

[3]Max Wilk, *OK! The Story of "Oklahoma!"*, 172.

> poems in you. But if you always stay in show business, where I've been, it'll never come out." He said, "Well, it's going to come out now. This is it." Then, a little bit later, along came *Carmen Jones* and then *Oklahoma!* and that was the end of Oscar as a poet. After that, he didn't care much about writing a great poem any longer. He was satisfied to write those lyrics, which he made into works of art. But they have it all . . . they all sound as if it's a poet trying to talk. It just burst out of him all the time![4]]

When a talent like that crosses my path I seem to get more ambitious for it than it is for itself, and I know deep down that all of us on this planet will do what we are to do. In other words, however deeply I felt the need to see another Walt Whitman come out of Oscar Hammerstein II, Oscar did what he was to do, and only in my dreams would he do more. And only in my dreams would I be perceptive enough to realize it if he did do more.

A bit of shop-talk about the good old days: In the good old days we had a room full of music copyists at the publisher's and they had none of the equipment of today: duplicating machines, mechanical erasers, transparent tapes, why go on? We brought in our scores of the last twenty-four hours and they wrote the parts for the musicians to read and play. When the time came to hit the road, one arranger went with the show and one copyist went with him to change routines, put in new material as the directors and choreographers needed it, or even put in whole new songs or dances.

My copyist on the tryout was a young Russian who later went to Hollywood and became one of the good orchestrators there. His name was Leonid Raab. Through the subsequent years he had a way of turning up wherever I was—London, Paris, Hollywood, wherever. In Hollywood, where the term "Yes man" was coined, Raab was often referred to as the No Man. No director, writer, producer or performer ever seemed to get any encouragement if they asked his opinion, but he was loyal and indefatigable.[5] One time when we were getting ready for a New York opening of a rather undistinguished play Raab and I took a room in a New York hotel where we both worked on a good-sized dance routine to be rehearsed with full company and orchestra at ten a.m. the next day.

I finished the score at some one o'clock in the morning and left the poor guy there to push on and take the whole piece to the theater before rehearsal.

---

[4]Wilk, *They're Playing Our Song*, 89.

[5]Raab worked for most of the major Hollywood studios. His principal association was with composer Franz Waxman at Metro-Goldwyn-Mayer in the mid-1940s.

He really was a "poor guy" when he finished at four a.m. and only then discovered that I'd directed him at the top of the last big section of the dance to transpose the whole thing into another key.

No machine has ever been invented even now, fifty-odd years later, to get him out of redoing the whole section. Four or five more hours work, but he did it and delivered it. Working through the night like that is not too unusual in our work, but not a great many helpers would just keep on writing without complaining bitterly to someone.

Jerry Kern was in a class by himself as a composer on the road with a new show. He used to invite a member or two of the troupe to have a bite to eat and a drink with him after the show and would include the arrangers and copyists—anybody who worked on the music with him. And a bite to eat and a drink always meant something like cold squab and champagne. You'd have to look quite a ways to find another man of his grace in his field.

We had everything ready for the [*Show Boat*] opening (in Washington, D.C.). In fact, we had about an hour and three quarters too much show ready. When the curtain went down on that first performance I looked at my watch with such tired eyes that nobody should quote me, but I saw it as seventeen minutes till one a.m.

It's never been clear to me why those of us who go through the last two or more weeks of rehearsal time with nowhere near what man considers a minimum amount of necessary sleep don't spring out of the theater and run to a bed as soon as the opening night curtain falls, but we don't. I suppose there are several explanations. One that sounds reasonable to me is that we're so glad not to have to meet a deadline in the next three hours that we feel like staying awake to enjoy this unusual freedom.

Without any philosophizing I said yes to the first man that said "Let's go somewhere." Somebody steered us to a night club. There we heard the pretty voice of the original "Julie" of *Show Boat*, Helen Morgan, just singing a song or two for the fun of it.

Someone came to our table and told me that everybody in the place wanted to hear "My Heart Stood Still" from a "new show in London."[6] Helen Morgan would sing it but nobody in the orchestra knew it, so nobody could play the accompaniment. They heard I had been with the show in London and would I please play it for her?

No, I wouldn't. I didn't care much for music after having finished the mile-high pile of scores for *Show Boat* a few hours before.

---

[6]Rodgers and Hart's *One Dam Thing After Another*—the song was also used in their *A Connecticut Yankee*.

But of course Helen soon came over to our table and said, "I'm mad at you," and I fell for her feminine wiles and went on the "stage" with her in a blinding spotlight to play "My Heart Stood Still."

I said to her, "What key do you sing it in?" and she said, "I don't know."

She didn't know and she didn't care. Her voice sounded good high or low or in between. So I started it in the original key and we did it. Of course it brought down the house and during the applause she gave me a kiss.

I think that's what happened but in the blinding glare I couldn't swear to it in a court of law. She said, "Let's do 'Bill'," so we did "Bill" for an encore. That was from *Show Boat* so we both remembered it pretty well just at that time.

> [Letter, 16 November 1927, Bennett (Willard Hotel, Washington, D.C.) to the John Simon Guggenheim Memorial Foundation: "I am today sending you an application for a fellowship. I realize I am too late and, as well as offering my apology, must leave my case to your judgment as does a recalcitrant schoolboy. . . . I got the application blanks the middle of last week, during which week, if it interests you, I was occupied in breaking all available records in the quantity of orchestra score turned out. This for the new Ziegfeld–Edna Ferber–Hammerstein–Kern opus, 'Show Boat'."]

As soon as the show could do without me I had to go to New York to get ahead with *Golden Dawn*—an operetta produced by Arthur Hammerstein, but rejoined *Show Boat* at the beginning of its second week, which was in Pittsburgh. They were writing a new song for the first scene of Act II.

Being an eye-witness to an event and then reading a report of it that even remotely resembles what you saw is an experience you probably never had. Very few have, and I have read and heard several versions of the conception and birth of this song that are not very close to what I saw. Kern and Hammerstein had taken suites at the William Penn Hotel in Pittsburgh. I got there on Monday morning and through the closed door of one of the rooms of the Kern suite I heard him playing, over and over, a very unsophisticated five-note phrase—over and over until I began to wonder if I had time to go out and have a Coke while he got past it.

Finally out he came, a dynamic little bundle of creative energy (the words weigh more than he did). I asked him why he needed to play his tune over so many times while the real invention goes on in the brain. He was a master of the unexpected answer. In typically crisp tones he said, "You're perfectly right!" and grabbed the paper he had written on to change two or three notes of his melody without taking it back to the piano. As far as I know these new notes are still a part of the tune.

As a matter of fact I do know, because he handed me his sketch then and there and I made a quick arrangement of it for voice and piano. So far no words, so a copy was sent to Oscar Hammerstein's room for words to be born.

After dinner that evening the door bell rang and a bell-boy brought in a sheet of paper on a tray. Kern read it with chuckles and called Hammerstein on the phone. With much laughter he said, "You left out a comma in the second line." Then he handed me the paper. It began:

"Cupid rules the day—
He's the naked boy
Who will show the way
To love's own joy."

Kern's hatred of the word "cupid" in lyrics was famous. In a little while another paper arrived with the words:

"Why do I love you?
Why do you love me?
Why should there be two
Happy as we?"

The next morning the dance director staged a fairly elaborate routine and Leonid Raab and I began to write the orchestra score and parts for the matinee the following afternoon. We met our deadline, the music director, Victor Baravalle, rehearsed the orchestra and the ensemble for about twenty minutes and the new number went into the matinee.

Kern was nowhere to be seen. After the show we heard he had gone to the movies. That would surprise nobody who knew Jerome Kern. We all knew how desperately he cared how the new number went, so Victor and I decided that when we met him for dinner we would not say a word about it.

We talked about everything except the show and Kern kept trying to remind us of it without showing any eagerness. At last, he couldn't stand it any longer. He blew up and cried, "Well, for God's sake come on! How did it go?"

I said to Baravalle, "You made that retard very gracefully at the end of the waltz. It just kept the whole thing together."

By this time poor Jerry was ready to weep, so Vic said to him, "The number felt very good. You ought to come over and see it when you have time."

There's no good reason to tell any stories here that can be heard or read elsewhere, but the story of the beginning of "Why Do I Love You?" (and Oscar's and Jerry's little private joke) has been so inaccurately told that it shouldn't be allowed to wander around loose.

Two more stories about the same play, one sad and the other—well . . . ?

Helen Morgan had her own night-spot in New York where she made a personal appearance whenever she could. When *Show Boat* got to Philadelphia [early December, 1927] before opening in New York she went in every night after the performance and sang there until they closed for the night.

Jerry Kern, for his own reasons, had her called for rehearsal in Philadelphia at ten every morning. When she told me about that I had to wonder just why he needed her so early.

One guess was that he didn't like her dividing her interest between the two jobs. I don't believe Norma Terris (Magnolia) or Howard Marsh (Ravenal) were called so early. When the company had gathered for the very first reading of the play, Jerry got a laugh by saying he had never had the pleasure of hearing Miss Morgan's organ. Maybe she didn't think it was as funny as he did. Whatever feeling there was between them, she told me once that she had a wonderful way to get to sleep and then wake up ready for work at ten in the morning:

"You take a stiff drink—I mean a very stiff drink—and it puts you right to sleep, then wakes you up full of ambition in two or three hours."

Hearing that, it was easy to predict her future—short!

She was lovely while she lasted.[7]

The other story is about Tess Gardella, known as Aunt Jemima. She played the part of Queenie, the fat cook on the show boat. On the stage or off, there could hardly be anyone else quite like her.

One of the tenderest and saddest scenes in Edna Ferber's novel (and Oscar Hammerstein's libretto) was called the boarding house scene. It's in the second act of the play and Frank and Ellie, comedians of the troupe on the boat, have discovered where Magnolia and Ravenal are living in Chicago, and are paying a surprise visit. While they are talking to Magnolia a note is brought into her from Ravenal, her gambler husband, saying goodbye and enclosing what's left of his money.

She looks at the letter, hands it to Frank and asks him to read it.[8] Theater being theater, he reads it aloud, making sure that those who paid for their seats hear it. Everybody in the house is fighting the tears back, but what those who paid for their seats didn't see one evening and the poor dears on the stage did see, was Aunt Jemima standing bent over in the wings with her skirts over her head, pointing one of the world's biggest behinds at them.

---

[7]Morgan died fourteen years later, at the age of forty-one.

[8]Actually, Ellie reads the letter.

Soft music.

Louise, Jean and I went back "home" by way of London. With us on the ship were Graham John, Guy Bolton and Jerome Kern. They represented the lyrics, book and music of *Blue Eyes*, beginning rehearsals and pointing for an opening soon.[9] As I look back on the dozen London productions that seemed so desperately important through the weeks we spent getting them going and then realize how desperately unimportant they seem as I try to tell this story I begin to wonder. Did the camera-mind take many pictures and neglect to develop them? Or did these assignments, heavy as they were, only represent an interruption in the journey back to the fairyland of twelve bass-notes instead of three? Of three, four, or five voices instead of one?

If the musical in Britain left me so unceremoniously, the people didn't. These fantastic minds and characters will go with me wherever I go for as long as I keep going.

Herman Finck, music director of the Drury Lane Theatre, for an example. I'm not at all sure of being able to bring you a fraction of his fascinating wit and resonant personality, even though it is fundamentally so simple. Evelyn Laye was the leading lady of *Blue Eyes.* She was one of the prettiest creatures of our era, but that is not the story. The story is that her father died at his home during a Saturday matinee of Evelyn's show, and the message was purposely not given to her until the evening performance was over.

She went home at once and spent Sunday and Monday with her family. They buried her father Monday afternoon and she went on with the show Monday night.

I was with Herman Finck a few evenings later when they told him the story. All he said was, "Humph! Father needn't to have died!"

When I told this to an old friend of Herman's, he told me his favorite Herman Finck story. A wonderful tenor of London, everybody's idol, was to sing at an annual "smoker" of the Savage Club one evening. His name was Harry Durth.

When it came time for the first song of his program, a piece by Gluck, he stood rather unsteadily while the pianist played the twenty-bar introduction and, when the magic moment came, opened his mouth and only a gulp came out. The accompanist smoothly went back to the beginning of the introduction and when he came to the spot again, the same thing happened.

The crowd was silent until from somewhere in their midst came the deep voice they all recognized, saying, "Oh Durth, where is thy sing?"

---

[9]The show debuted on 27 April 1928.

A very different sort of music director was Percy Fletcher. He conducted an English version of *Princess Charming*, originally Hungarian. Theater conducting was not his main interest. His music for band and orchestra was more played in Great Britain at that time than any other composer. Much too serious to be another Herman Finck, he was an entertaining fellow and his very seriousness was amusing.

He invited me to go to a broadcasting studio where they set us up to listen to one of the fine British brass bands—no strings or woodwind—playing the piece they had played to win the national championships for the year. The piece was called *An Epic Symphony* (no less) by Percy Fletcher.[10]

One day he and I had an hour or two with nothing calling for us at the theater. We were in Glasgow and we got a tram and got off at the end of the line to take a walk and see what the Scottish landscape looked like. After walking a ways we saw a young man riding a bicycle across a dirt road. The young man called over and asked something like an unsolved anagram in Swahili.

Percy laughed and said, "That's just what I was going to ask you!"

And I asked Percy, "Just what did he ask you?" because it was even less intelligible than what the man said to me in New Haven the morning I first set foot on British soil.

Oh well, the lad might have had some trouble with the English language in Freeman, Missouri, for that matter.

One more friend—I choose him at random, partly because he is so far removed from the professional world—Frank Benn, Francis Hamilton Benn, a London businessman whose business was something like lumber and building materials. We knew him because he was married to one of the girls that went to Oaksmere, Mrs. Merrill's school in New York.

Her name was Clara Boal and she was a grand-niece of W. F. Cody, better known as Buffalo Bill. She was therefore not British. The meeting of Frank Benn and Clara Boal would do credit to almost any romantic novel in literature. His business took him to the west coast of the United States and on one of his trips there his train stopped at a station at the same time as another one going in the other direction with Clara and her aunt at just the right window. Clara and Aunt were on their way to Europe and in a few seconds so was he.

According to his account, he looked through the window and said, "That's the girl I want to marry," got out of his train and into hers. The rest was up

---

[10]Fletcher (1879–1932) was, for many years, music director of London's His Majesty's Theatre. In 1926 his *An Epic Symphony* was the "test piece" for the brass band championships staged at the city's Crystal Palace. Bennett's *Three Chaucer Poems* (women's voice or voices with string quartet or piano), written the same year, were dedicated to Fletcher.

to his charm and salesmanship and when I met them they had a beautiful home and three nice children in The Boltons, a rather exclusive residential park in London.

One other little story of the Benns has no great bearing on his qualifications for my personal Who's Who, but it is not easy to leave out. He bid his wife and children goodbye one morning, took his luggage to the office and was just leaving for a trip to New York when something came up at his office that made it impossible to get away. He was heart-broken because it was the maiden voyage of the very latest and greatest ocean liner—the Titanic.

The show *Princess Charming* was first done in Budapest, with music by Dr. Albert Szirmai. Dr. Szirmai will drop in on us later. The producers of the London version, Messrs. Herbert Clayton and Jack Waller, could both of them be included among the unforgettables just sampled. They bought the material of the Hungarian show and proceeded to forget as much of it as they could, which is certainly not new in the theater, wherever you look.

They began by telling me what entirely new songs they needed. It was a little vague just who was to write these new songs, but I made a big mistake. Being under salary as an arranger, and knowing that an arranger's job is to furnish whatever is missing, I hit on an idea that will never cease to embarrass me. I wrote three songs in one evening—well, they looked like songs, anyway.

I took them in the next day and put them on the piano and explained that they were "dummy-songs." Dummy-lyrics were often written to help the poet toward a perfect fit with music that already existed; why not give these, designed to fit the situation in the play, to the songwriters and say, "This is the kind of number for this spot. Go to it, and good luck!"

When they started talking as though they now had their music, terror began to creep up my spine. I tried to explain that they were missing the point, and thought to quiet things down by saying, "What about the lyrics?"

That didn't work. Herbert Clayton said, "I think the lyrics are terrific." If ever a boy needed his mother, I needed mine then. In fact I shouldn't have been terribly surprised to see her come in the door with a copy of *The Lady with the Red Dress* in her hand.

I kept waiting and hoping for new songs to come in, but the orchestrations claimed their long hours and my prejudices and even my deficiencies as a Tin Pan Alley genius got pushed away back and forgotten.

We didn't stay for the London opening[11] and back in Paris not much time was lost thinking of *Princess Charming* except for two short difficulties. The first was when Clayton and Waller wrote, saying there was a claim that I had

---

[11]21 October 1926.

come too close to a song in *The Vagabond King* with the one I wrote when they asked for "something like the 'song of the Vagabonds.'" I hadn't heard the song (it was by Rudolf Friml) when I filled the order. I must say that if I had known it my "dummy-song" would never have been as close as it was, but you can't avoid something unless you know what you are avoiding.[12]

Anyway, nothing more came of the complaint. The next difficulty was much more serious to me. Max Dreyfus and some of his friends saw the show in London, one of his friends being Sergei Rachmaninov.

If I had to pick the one man in the world I least wanted to submit this material to it would have to be he. All he said when I met him in Paris was that he didn't care for the libretto. We had a few visits with his two daughters around this time. My music copyist-friend Leonid Raab was in the offing and he introduced us to a nice Russian restaurant where we got acquainted with blini—a Russian pancake with caviar that remains something special. Two sweet Rachmaninov girls and blini. If I ever get to the stage of sighing for the good old days that will be a good place to start.

By this time I was on a Guggenheim Fellowship and it was important to begin serious thinking about how to pay for it. They never send one a bill, but it's inconceivable that a student can believe he got a fellowship because of his big blue eyes. It certainly is a contract and a job.[13]

[Bennett's "Plans for Study" accompanied his Guggenheim application the previous November:

> I have been able to save enough money in the past few years to spend part of the last two in Paris, composing and studying with Mlle. Nadia Boulanger. . . . My situation is, briefly, that I shall be unable to continue this work for long enough to establish a position of any importance without financial aid. Even with financial aid it will require a great sacrifice on my part—a sacrifice I feel to be well worth while, however—and I enlist consideration of possible fellowship in the remarkable Guggenheim Memorial Foundation.
>
> Practically my entire life has been devoted to earning a living for self and family, and in New York I have developed an excellent income {"varying, from about $10,000 a year upward," he noted on the application} as an arranger. This, like all excellent incomes in New York, is merely a livelihood, and ceases the moment I take time to work on music of my own.

---

[12]Cf. Kern's remark below (p. 137) that Debussy was "the very greatest plagiarist, because he knew all music and was able to avoid it."

[13]His initial Guggenheim appointment was for a year beginning 15 May 1928.

I shall, if awarded a fellowship, spend another season with Mlle. Boulanger, after which I hope to be allowed to conduct in a small opera house in Germany. This latter opening is of great value to me, but there is of course little or no income attached to it and my acceptance depends entirely on my independence at the time.

As for my "expectation as to the publication of results of my study" I have a conviction that the music should prove its value to music before being rushed into print. Publishers there are who would print my efforts without too much question but I see no gain in their doing so.

My ultimate purposes—this is a hard one,—but I feel strongly equipped to join the young musicians that are beginning to put our real America into music, and thereto find myself irretrievably drawn. If I am given the opportunity of a fellowship I shall try hard to fulfill the obligation placed upon me.]

This thinking leads to the conclusion that the most immediate settlement of the account would be to create something that can be seen or heard and might cause enough stir to reach the ears of the boss. Obviously a long, slow climb as a conductor of opera would not in itself fill that order.

[Ira Gershwin's diary records Bennett's presence at two social affairs in Paris in May 1928. Dmitri Tiomkin, piano soloist for the upcoming premiere of Gershwin's *Concerto in F*, hosted a party on the 22nd also attended by the Gershwins, Maurice Chevalier, Jules Glaenzer, and "a host of painters, writers, musicians & critics," including Vladimir Golschmann, Arthur Honegger, Vladimir Dukelsky ('Vernon Duke'), Alexander Tansman, and Lazare Saminsky. Another soirée honored the Gershwins on May 31st—a "mixture of Mayfair, the Rialto and Left Bank" including Beatrice Lillie, Deems Taylor, Nadia Boulanger, photographer Man Ray, violinist Rudolf Kolisch and hostess Elsa Maxwell.]

Somewhere just at the time there appeared an announcement that RCA Records was opening two competitions for composers, one with a prize of twenty-five thousand dollars for a serious work for orchestra and one with prizes of ten thousand to the winner and five thousand to the "runner-up" for lighter style compositions.[14]

I thought of the fact that two or three years before I had been at the head of [*Musical America*'s] three or four "honorable mentions" (they were probably listed alphabetically), and there might be a chance to get one in this.

[14]The contest was announced in May 1928, the firm still known then as the Victor Talking Machine Company.

The judges for the serious work were surely hard to improve on—Serge Koussevitzky, Leopold Stokowski, Olga Samaroff, Rudolf [i.e. Rudolph] Ganz, and Frederick Stock. The John Simon Guggenheim Memorial Foundation would certainly give me a good grade if I could attract the attention of such a jury.

The more I thought of it the more it seemed worth a big try. The conditions of the contest said we were to be anonymous and that we could submit more than one work.

Of course the project that was forming meant a considerable infidelity to the conviction that was fundamental: that too much music was being written and that a career dedicated to performing and converting people to what I believed in was the noble one for me.

But that evening I made a rather pompous announcement to my wife and daughter, who were probably busy and not listening, that I would write two large works and enter them in the contest for the big prize and, if one of them got an honorable mention, I would move serious composition out of the fun-and-games department.

So now began the masquerade. I don't think there was any thought of being deceitful beyond the importance of being anonymous, but it happened we went to Berlin just after the score of the first work was completed on French manuscript paper and the second on German; I won't pretend I didn't think of it, but anonymity was just as important to me as it was to the contest and I fully approved of the "dirty work."[15]

Our five months in Berlin were five months of poverty. I had had visions of studying a bit with Paul Hindemith, whom both Nadia Boulanger and I admired. There was not a chance of raising the money to carry out that idea, so we just settled down, first at the Pension Regina and then in Eislebenerstrasse, near the Gedachtniskirche, where I worked on the second of the two big scores.

The main reason for going to Berlin blew up in our faces. There was a remarkable international person whose name and title in German was Herr Geheimer Hofrat Hugo Bryk there, and he was practically certain to be able to find a spot for me in some opera house in Germany. I had been counting on that for the future, just when depending on how fast I could talk German and a few other conditions.

Timing things perfectly, Hugo Bryk's secretary committed suicide and left notes involving Herr Bryk in some very nasty scandals. He couldn't do

[15]Bennett may have overestimated the effectiveness of this "deception." The two manuscripts are obviously in the same hand and must have been recognizable as such by Stokowski, Koussevitzky, and the other judges.

much for me or for himself under the circumstances. His name was completely cleared while we were there and I was invited to a stag dinner given by his associates to celebrate his return to his former power. I enjoyed the dinner very much but the opera-conductor's train was off the track.

We remained in Berlin past Christmas time. It was a little sad to realize that our landlady was able to give our child much nicer presents than we could ourselves, but the stay there was really a nice experience. Except for a constant feud between our maid and our landlady, there was nothing serious to interfere with the finishing strokes of the task I had taken on.

We very much enjoyed seeing quite a bit of the wife and two daughters of Ernest Bloch, the Swiss-American composer. He it was, now that I think of it, who wrote *America* and won the [*Musical America*] competition that brought me the honorable mention that keeps turning up.

Mrs. Bloch was a dear, and daughter Suzanne was a colorful pupil of Nadia Boulanger in Paris and Fontainebleau. Lucienne was a painter and sculptress, and also my tennis partner on the roof of the Peugeot Building in Passy for many outings. We were glad they were spending time in Berlin and especially glad at the end of our stay.

I hadn't heard much from my client Jerome Kern for quite a bit. He had passed through Paris going somewhere with Max and Victoria (Mrs.) Dreyfus some time before our move to Berlin, at which time he and the Dreyfuses went to a chamber music concert and heard Claude Levi and me play a rather experimental violin and piano sonata of mine for a hall full of young experimenters. You can imagine how seductive they found the then-modern idiom.

But now, in Berlin, came the request that I go to Paris and supervise the preparation of the music for the production of *Show Boat* at the Théâtre du Châtelet. Louise and Jean couldn't get ready to go with me and as soon as they were ready, Jean came down with the measles.

That was the point at which Mrs. Bloch was a friend indeed, helping the two of them wonderfully. I was tied up at the theater when they arrived in Paris and our organist friend Barrett Spach had to meet the train and bring them to the hotel.

All this dedication to my assignment, and if they had gone along the quay and picked up a man fishing in the Seine he couldn't possibly have done any worse job than I did. At every turn I met unsolvable problems and in every department I met only friendly, cooperative people who never thought of blaming me for what was happening.

But I had no place to pass the buck. The French language has no tonic accent, so the name they chose for the show, *Mississippi*, gets whatever accent it has on the last syllable. Try that on Mr. Kern's tunes and see what you can suggest.

My biggest contributions to the downfall were much more obviously my fault, however. One of the beauties was directly due to my orchestration. I had written a dance for the children in the convent scene. There were several compliments for the music until they heard it with the orchestra, but not thereafter. It's usually the other way around.

The charming person who played the piano for the kiddies to rehearse pounded out the notes as though she were driving each note into their little heads and somehow I got the idea that they wouldn't recognize it at all if the orchestra played it with its original delicacy. It was a disaster, all the more unfortunate because it was a new element in the scene and must have been under especially critical eyes. If it ever was a good idea I killed it.

I doubt that any of the lovely ladies and gentlemen of the production, from the producers, Messrs. Lehman and Fontane, to the ushers, ever fully realized what a big "help" I was.

A word about Paris, because we went back to being citizens of New York soon after *Mississippi.* Many friends, when we called ourselves Parisians, visited us, and most of them sang the same refrain—something like "Oh, yes, Paris is very nice, but you should have seen it in the old days!" I hope we're never tempted to say that. We've only been back once, and perhaps we'd better stay away—it's such a nice thing not to say!

Mademoiselle Nadia Boulanger had a look at my two entries in the RCA Victor Competition and we also went through discussions of several contemporary works before I went back to New York. One of my favorites among the contemporaries was Albert Roussel. He was a navy man, who spent years as a commanding officer in the French fleet in Indo-China (and, I assume elsewhere) but he had loved music all his life. When he retired in his forties he devoted himself to composition and produced many fine works. At the age of sixty he was given two gala concerts in Paris, one of his chamber music and one of his outstanding orchestral pieces.

We had a few opportunities to visit with Monsieur and Madame Roussel, utterly simple people, and utterly dedicated to the art of music. Another example of how humble and friendly a truly great artist can be.

Now [August 1929], we became New Yorkers again. We came back neither as victors nor vanquished. The purpose of the move to Europe had not been served in the slightest, but it was hard to believe we had lost the game. Certainly I had not advanced one inch in the ability to pick up a stick and make a group of performers deliver a message to an audience, but I did have a broader and more intelligent love for music than could be realized any other way. The future was hard to predict, but the past was not for sale at any price.

Our friend Quinto Maganini, whom we saw frequently in France, got a Guggenheim Fellowship at the same time I did. Whether or not in just the same way I never knew, but it was his impression that a few of our colleagues were not overimpressed with our qualifications. That is a quote from him. My fellowship was renewed for a second year, but when the call came to go from Berlin to Paris and work on the *Show Boat*-alias-*Mississippi* business I asked to be excused after three months. The Foundation has my undying gratitude and loyalty.[16]

When we settled in New York I had one important thing to learn: how to arrange music for the theater. Theater orchestration, like the Broadway theater itself, is always pressing. If a prize-fighter pressed that way he wouldn't keep the [championship] belt long. There must be fundamental values of some kind in the art, but sometimes you wonder. You can't blame them for making a dash for every new sound they can find, the competition being what it is, but my approach had always been to remember that several members of the troupe were being paid besides the musicians in the pit.

It sounds like sound thinking, but in order to make new sounds your servant and not your master, you need to hear each one and throw it out or help yourself to it according to what the show is trying to say.

Pardon the pedagogy, but it really seems necessary to explain why I had to take a lesson or two to come back from the outskirts of Parnassus to the Alley of the Shuberts without serious mishap. The only new gimmick that took me a little time to realize was the sound of three trumpets. Three and four of them had been in symphony orchestras for at least fifty years, but in the theater the sound of three really found a home. Broadway music is still full of triads even as I write this.

My "teacher" in this was Vinton Freedley of Aarons and Freedley. He made a remark about "the three-trumpet sound" in the course of a harmless chat and it suddenly dawned on me that the first-nighters were getting ahead of me.

Aarons and Freedley were already producing shows when I started working on them. A theater that appeared at the very crest of the wave of Broadway musicals and housed many lively ones is still there: the Alvin.[17] Someone recently noted that most of the playgoers that go into the Alvin have no idea

---

[16]Bennett's memory is inaccurate. He requested the three-months-only extension, which began 15 May 1929, after telling the Foundation of the financial hardship to his family "that seems at present writing inevitable if I undertake another year in Europe." (Letter to John Simon Guggenheim Foundation, 15 January 1929)

[17]The Alvin Theater has since been renamed for playwright Neil Simon.

where the name came from. Nor of course do they care—it makes a pretty good word without looking for its roots. Those of us that knew the two guys, though, get a little something out of the fact that it is the first syllables of their two first names—Alex Aarons and Vinton Freedley. Aarons and Freedley were identified with a particularly light-hearted type of musical comedy and the theater named for them must have cute ghosts floating about.

The two of them went about in just about the same type of crowd, but they were sharply different as personalities. During the years of their great vogue I saw both of them under fire a good many times. The ends of two different "run-throughs" gave a pretty complete idea of the contrast between them. I sat beside Freedley, who was suave and quite dignified at all times. This rehearsal was not a very successful one and I wondered when he would start to tear his hair and kick things around, but he did nothing of the sort. At the final curtain he said quietly, "Not quite right yet."

Aarons, at a dress rehearsal of another play, called the entire company on stage after the curtain and said, "Ladies and Gentlemen, I have just seen your dress rehearsal and I want to say that I have never before seen such a disgraceful performance in all my life. You all stink!" Whereupon he gave a vigorous nod of the head and his pince-nez landed on the floor.

I imagine a good psychiatrist would tell you at once which of the two partners the entire troupe preferred to deal with, but it surprised me. Under his rather blunt surface Alex Aarons was pretty friendly and understanding. Vinton Freedley, by all accounts, was made of steel and ice.

One of the shows that played at the Alvin was *Girl Crazy*, with Ginger Rogers, Ethel Merman, Willie Howard and William Gaxton in the cast.[18] The songs were by George and Ira Gershwin and included "I Got Rhythm," "Embraceable You," "(They're Writing Songs of Love) But Not for Me," and "Bidin' My Time." The orchestra in the pit was far from anonymous. In the first place the woodwind, brass, and drum section was an already-assembled band known as Red Nichols's orchestra, while the strings on the other side of the pit were headed by Joseph Smith, who was better known at the time than anyone else in the place. He had for years been the leader of a fine orchestra at the Hotel Plaza. The good hotels of those times often had fine orchestras.

In due course it might have been expensive to keep the *Girl Crazy* orchestra on the payroll. Our first clarinet (and saxophone) was Benny Goodman,[19] the first trumpet was Red Nichols, first trombone was Glenn

---

[18] *Girl Crazy* opened on 14 October 1930.

[19] Bennett's 1941 *Antique Suite* for clarinet and orchestra was dedicated to Goodman. It was premiered by Ralph McLane on a WOR "Russell Bennett's Notebook" broadcast shortly before the clarinetist took the first-chair position with the Philadelphia Orchestra.

Miller, drummer Gene Krupa. All of these ended up with their own internationally famous dance bands.[20]

On the first day of the company rehearsal for the show George Gershwin played his music for the assembled troupe. Alex Aarons and I were standing at the back of the empty theater as George played "I Got Rhythm" through twice. Then Earle Busby, the music director, lifted his arms and said, "Okay—everybody sing it!"

Gershwin played the good old two-bar introduction—Rum-tiddy-um-tum-tum—and the hall rang with "I Got Rhythm!" and Alex said in my ear, "Sixty liars!"

I never saw as much of Freedley as I did of Aarons, partly because Vinton didn't spend as much time with the creators and performers as Alex did. I don't even remember what we were up to once when I was leaving Freedley's office and saw a very handsome Russian girl asking for him. She was asked if she had an appointment. "No," she said, in a beautiful deep voice, "but Mister Freedley said I should look up him."

Girl Crazy was about the only Gershwin show I know of where one man was responsible for the whole job of arranging.[21] Even in this one, I had help in the form of an orchestration by the composer himself. He was developing fast at the craft and I had no need to revise or re-do anything.[22] Most of his plays through the years were orchestrated by Sears & Roebuck, which was our inelegant way of saying he passed out his numbers to four or five arrangers as they were available without type-casting in any way. Our friend William Daly and I did the scores for *Of Thee I Sing* between us [with Gershwin scoring the second-act opening himself]. Bill Daly was a fine arranger, conducted several of George's shows and was his constant advisor as he developed musically.[23]

---

[20]Bandleader-clarinetist Artie Shaw, Goodman's chief rival during the big band era, likewise "paid his dues" in New York's pit orchestras, including Gershwin's 1933 *Pardon My English.*

[21]Some historians underestimate Bennett's affinity for jazz and have given credence to speculation that Glenn Miller scored some of the "hotter" portions of *Girl Crazy.* Yet Bennett was always willing to give credit to his collaborators and would surely have acknowledged this if it were accurate.

[22]For *Girl Crazy*'s "Embraceable You," Bennett recalled that Gershwin "wanted it [the accompaniment] just as he played it—straight chords. I had [added] an undercurrent weaving in it; the song didn't need it. I don't think I ever changed anything else for George." (Bennett interview with Miles Krueger, 8 September 1978.)

[23]Gershwin's ability to orchestrate was the subject of unfounded controversy. Ferde Grofé had scored his *Rhapsody in Blue* for Paul Whiteman's orchestra in 1924, but Gershwin orchestrated all of his subsequent concert works. William Daly conducted the first reading of the *Concerto in F* and attended early rehearsals of *An American in Paris* as well, advising Gershwin on possible cuts or changes in the scoring. And he and Bennett both appeared at an early reading of Gershwin's music for *Porgy and Bess.*

George Gershwin, 28 May 1937. Photo from the Wisconsin Center for Film and Theater Research. Used by permission.

One of the last formal portraits of Gershwin—"he wasn't a one-finger thinker, he thought down through the harmony . . . and even into the harmonies of life itself." A brain tumor took his life barely six weeks later.

George used to go into the pit and conduct a performance once in a while. Conducting of any kind is a tricky assignment and in the theater so many things are involved beside just playing the music that George's producers were not very happy when it happened. Nobody could dislike him, but they hoped he would be interested in doing something else.

My guess is that George knew as well as anybody that the show wasn't going well, but he wanted to hear his music as he had conceived it, and that isn't always possible. Many of his friends referred to him laughingly as naive. Without being an old stick-in-the-mud and reminding them that they have the word in the wrong gender, let's clean this up a bit. If they meant "naive" as an antonym of "sophisticated" it won't do. He had his own special brand of sophistication, but he was so amazed at the music that came out of his piano that the little social graces seemed unimportant and even an insincerity to him. He was his own great problem and his own great fulfillment.

As for the others—what others?

He was fond of his friends, but one Monday morning after a bunch of us had spent Sunday afternoon playing baseball, George said to Harry Ruby, "Harry, you're a good ball player! You can pitch and catch and bat like a big leaguer. Trouble with me is if anything happened to my hands, I'd be sunk. With you it doesn't make any difference."

Harry laughed a little, and thought to himself that he had a few plans for his own hands also.

Some two weeks later George saw Harry again and was in a mellow mood. He was saying, "Harry, do you remember when we both played the piano at Remick's? We've always been pals, haven't we?"

Harry, with a little twinkle in his eye, said, "Yes, we have. And that's why I can't understand how you could hurt my feelings."

"I hurt your feelings!" said George. "When did I ever hurt your feelings?"

Harry said, "Do you remember a couple of weeks ago when you said if anything ever happened to your hands you'd be sunk—with me it didn't really make any difference?"

George studied a moment, smiled and said, "Well it's true!"[24]

[Bennett told author Max Wilk a bit more about Gershwin's musical studies:

> {Bill Daly} actually taught George a lot more than George could ever learn from any kind of teacher. Because George was not talented as a student. He could not study. Max Dreyfus . . . {was} very ambitious for George, as we all were. He sent George down to Artur Bodanzky, who was then conductor-in-chief for the Metropolitan Opera, so George could read scores and study classical, serious music. Bodanzky took him for six months. Then, one night, they were playing pinochle, Bodanzky and Max. "Artur," asked Dreyfus, "how's my protégé getting along?" And Artur says, "Max, you know even studying requires a certain talent."
>
> But you get plenty of examples like that. Abraham Lincoln read just the Bible and Shakespeare and became one of the wisest men in the world. As far as I know, Jesus Christ wasn't a very big student either. George just came in here with that marvelous message for us, and we're all very grateful for it.[25]]

---

[24]Bennett notes that Gershwin was in the audience for the first performance of his 1935 opera *Maria Malibran:* "What the occasion was I forget, but George was giving a party at his house that night and some of us went to it. He met me at the door with a big smile and the following note about my opera: 'Russ, you've gone far with what you had' . . . maybe Gershwin did deserve the title of most naive. There never was a trace of malice in the fellow, but 'Out of the mouth of babes and sucklings . . . '." ("From the Notes of a Music Arranger," *Theatre Arts*, November 1956, 89).

[25]Wilk, *They're Playing Our Song*, 90–91.

Chapter Six

The old job settled down into just about the same mixture of various emotions as it was before we sailed the ocean blue. While we were in Detroit with a play called *Me for You*[1] I made a rather accurate prediction. I had sent a lot of telegrams from a Western Union office in the hotel where some of us lived, so many in fact that I said to the girl at the desk, "Victoria, I've sent so many wires this week that I'll have to give you about three shares of Anaconda for a tip."

Whereupon her young assistant turned up her nose and said, "Anaconda's a copper stock. It hasn't done much lately."

I turned to the man beside me and said, "We're heading for the darndest market crash in history! She shouldn't even know Anaconda is a copper stock, but listen to her."

They didn't keep me waiting long, either.

Speaking of telegrams, a cable came about this time that read simply "So happy, Nadia." I didn't try to answer it because there was, from this angle, no way of knowing what Nadia was so happy about. I began to carry a dream around about that "honorable mention" in the big competition, but was anxious not to scare it away. Therefore I did a pretty good job of dismissing it from my mind.

There was some help in this because my big client came out of hiding all of a sudden. Jerome Kern, in spite of his opinion of sound pictures, was working on a score for Warner Brothers. He was living on a boat off the shore of Palm Beach, Florida, with his wife Eva and their daughter Betty. I joined them on the boat until my daughter Jean finished the last ten days of school, after which the Bennetts moved into Brazilian Court in West Palm Beach. The Kerns and the Bennetts sailed to Hollywood through the Panama Canal in May of 1930.

---

[1]The first version of Rodgers and Hart's 1929 *Heads Up*.

Whatever one thought of the big extension of show business called Hollywood, there were never two opinions about the real natives of Los Angeles. Our arrival at San Pedro will give a good idea of them.

When we were living in Passy our friend Quinto Maganini once introduced us to Mr. and Mrs. Harry Baxter and daughter Elise from Los Angeles. He was at the head of the Baxter-Northupp Music Company and was a flutist and devoted to woodwind music especially.[2] We all went to dinner at the Place du Tertre at the very top of Montmartre and had a most enjoyable visit.

When our boat got to the port of Los Angeles many miles from downtown and still further from the Beverly-Wilshire Hotel, a steward on the main deck handed me a written note saying, "How would you like a ride uptown? Harry Baxter."

I had written to the Baxter-Northupp Company, asking them to get hold of some music paper for me, to be called for when I got there, and here they were with a big welcome! Unfortunately we couldn't even accept their invitation because of some prior arrangement with the studio.

We felt mean, because Harry Baxter and his daughter had had to get up between four and five in the morning to meet the boat and then go back alone.

But when we had been in California a very short time we found out that such friendliness was the rule and no special deal at all. Lawyers, bankers, oilmen, real estate men—they were all alike. No matter what kind of difficult character you might get too much of in the studios (and I never had as much trouble as many report) the whole place leaves you attached to it.

I was working on a March for Two Pianos and Orchestra—a piece of considerable length that Oscar Levant and I played with the Hollywood Bowl Orchestra during the summer[3]—and of course was learning whatever I could about the film world. Many of my closest fellow-toilers of Broadway were well settled in the studios by this time. Herbert Stothart was the music man at M.G.M., Alfred Newman ditto with United Artists, Louis Silvers was music director at Warner Brothers and with him Leo Forbstein, my violin-playing leader at the five-cent movie theater in Kansas City, Kansas. At R.K.O. Studios was Victor Baravalle with Max Steiner as assistant [music] director. You might wonder who was left in New York, but the answer is plenty. At this point in this tale we needn't go into that.

Warner Brothers had moved into their big new home in Burbank, but still had their old place on Sunset Boulevard going. As I worked on Kern's

---

[2]Harry V. Baxter was an active member of the Los Angeles Flute Club as early as 1924, when he took part in a 2 March performance of Bennett's flute quartet *Rondo Capriccioso*.

[3]Levant and Bennett were soloists for the 18 July 1930 premiere; they also played the work with the New York Philharmonic at a 13 August 1931 concert in Lewisohn Stadium.

music my office was at this old place with a white picket fence around it. The Kern picture finally got the name *Men of the Sky* and the main man in the sky was my old friend Jack Whiting. The director of music was Erno Rapee of the great cinema palaces of New York.[4] I don't really know where *Men of the Sky* went because that great big collapse got around to the U.S.A. just at that time, and music went out of pictures and pictures just missed going out of our lives.[5]

After a few days at the Beverly Wilshire Hotel we settled in a little white house [number 1439] on Crescent Heights Boulevard near Sunset. One morning during our stay, my daughter Jean answered the telephone before we were really up. She called me to the phone and said, "It's Mireille." Mireille was a favorite of ours from Paris, an actress, pianist, song-composer, and a personality. I didn't think Mireille was likely to be up and calling me at seven in the morning, and I was right.

Instead, it was Irene Gallagher, Max Dreyfus's secretary in New York, and she was all excited. She said, "You got two prizes from RCA Victor!" I didn't answer right away and she said—a tone or two higher—"Five Thousand dollars each!"

In a few days the two envelopes came. They were duplicates, saying that the panel of judges had, after long deliberation, exercised their option to withhold the first prize of twenty-five thousand dollars and had awarded five scholarships of five thousand each to the composers of the five works they had chosen.

So this was what made Mlle. Boulanger "so happy." I'm sure she sent the same wire to Aaron Copland, who was her star American pupil for several years. He was among the recipients of [Boulanger's] "scholarships." The other two were Ernest Bloch (addicted to winning competitions of this sort) and Louis Gruenberg, whom I had not and have not seen since his opera *The Emperor Jones* was at the Metropolitan some years before we went to France.[6]

As for me, I had made a solemn vow, and a vow is something you don't kick around. It was a more serious vow than it may have sounded because

---

[4]Rapee (1891–1945), born and trained in Budapest, is best known as Radio City's first Music Director and the composer of two 1920s song hits, "Charmaine" and "Diane." He led the Radio City Symphony in weekly *Music Hall on the Air* network broadcasts; his programming (which occasionally featured a Bennett work) ranged from standard concert and operatic fare to Mahler's symphonies.

[5]Kern's songs were eliminated before the release of *Men of the Sky*.

[6]The other winning pieces were Copland's *Dance Symphony*, Bloch's *Helvetia*, and Gruenberg's Symphony. RCA's publicity had all but promised recordings of the winning composition(s), but only Copland's piece was so honored—and not until the 1960s. Bennett's *Abraham Lincoln* and *Sights and Sounds* were newly recorded for Naxos in 1998 [released 1999] (See Appendix D, "Selected Discography").

the whole thing was treated a little frivolously. It was, however, the most important (to me) change I could possibly make. Where was I now? Up to this moment I had never sent a note of music to the copyright office. Everything from a two-line birthday greeting to a thirty-minute symphonic work was written for fun or as part of my education. The last things I ever wrote and tried to sell were the pieces sent to *The Etude* in my teens.

So, all right now! You're a composer of music. What do you do?

Well—the first thing you do is go right ahead putting the oom-pahs under Broadway and Hollywood tunes. You do this because your family (and you) want to eat, and because by now several people are used to your oom-pahs and you are under contract to keep coming up with them.

These were sound enough thoughts. When our Muse in Montmartre—Boulanger—and I had our some serious talk on the subject she told me that of all the composers of our time who wrote what we all admire only one was able to make his way with the income that composing brought him. He was a bachelor, had written one "hit" in his early years, the *Pavane*, and made that do as his pot-boiler—Maurice Ravel. She assured me that everybody else had to edit, copy, teach, play organ or whatnot in order to keep alive and pursue his or her ideals.[7]

So much for the problem of keeping alive. But I had been told that a certain part of every day in a composer's life should be spent trying to get performances and recordings—in other words, keeping his message alive as well as his body.

I speak with no authority on this because I never tried it, in spite of the advice. Public relations, agents, propaganda—they are all a little embarrassing because you know you have no chance to be as good as they say you are.

> [Bennett never employed a press agent, and didn't exploit his friendships with conductors Reiner, Ormandy, Wallenstein, et al. He explained to author David Ewen: "I have never made an attempt to exploit my original music. . . . Were it not for the restrictions of some of the performing rights societies that I belong to, the whole world could have anything I've written in manuscript, plus my hope that the world will approach my serious efforts in the same spirit that I do."[8] Though friends encouraged him to engage in more self-promotion, he once remarked to Louis and Annette Kaufman that

---

[7]Bennett concurred: "No artist ever made a living doing his serious work. . . . Everybody has to teach, to interpret, besides creating new things" (Lucy Greenbaum, "About an Arranger," *New York Times*, 24 October 1943).

[8]David Ewen, *American Composers Today* (New York: H. W. Wilson Co., 1949), 25.

[9]Louis and Annette Kaufman interview with the editor, Los Angeles, August 1992.

"Bach was forgotten for 75 years (before his works were revived by Mendelssohn and others)—so there's no need to worry about Bennett!"[9]]

As for recordings, my impressions are rather unpopular ones. I know that fine conductors have now been raised on recorded music. They compare the tempos, the pauses, the agitations or the calming down of passages by the greatest of our generation of conductors, and that is a great privilege; but their balances are microphone balances, their hair-raising crescendi and thunderous climaxes have to be day-dreams and the magic of pianissimo may be anything from a mezzo-forte to a dead silence.

The engineers who have developed the miraculous sound of recordings are still called engineers, and rightly so. Some of them—all of the great ones—can, I do believe, hear a particle of dust as it floats by on a tiny, soft breeze. And yet one of the greatest once told me, neither in boast nor in sorrow, that the music of Vincent Youmans was about as polyphonic as he could listen to with pleasure.

We could pursue this until the embers are all ashes without proving a thing, but my heart does not leap up when I behold the word "stereo." The greatest argument for live music is not political or economic. It's just that listening to a recording is like watching baseball on television; it may all be there, but you don't know what a thrill it is if you don't hear the crack of the bat.

One of the great musical figures of our time was the conductor of the Philadelphia Orchestra, Leopold Stokowski. Hearing his performances, you could have many arguments with yourself as to just how deep he ran, but there was no argument about his magnetic power. One of his violinists once put it, "What a band-leader! The violin starts to play before the bow touches the string!"

It was good news for me that he put one of my two "winners" on a program of the Philadelphia Orchestra. Louise and I went to Philadelphia to hear him do it. With us were Robert Simon, music critic of *The New Yorker* magazine, and his brilliantly talented wife, Madeleine Marshall.

The program [24 October 1931] deserves a brief report. The first half of the concert was made up of contemporary works, ending with an Anton von Webern symphony [op. 21]. It begins with a long series of single tones coming out of various locations in the large orchestra. The audience listened in a sort of what's-going-to-happen silence for quite some time, when someone coughed and a few in the crowd tittered.

Stokowski cut the musicians off and walked quietly off the stage.

Now they really wondered what was going to happen! There we sat for what seemed like a long time until the maestro came back out, stepped up to the podium and *da capo*—started the whole symphony again. You may believe we all behaved ourselves then!

My piece, called *Abraham Lincoln—A Likeness in Symphony Form*, made up the whole second half of the performance.[10]

After the concert we went to the lovely apartment of one of Leopold Stokowski's friends, where we met for the first time. After an exchange of complimentary nothings I said, "This is a great achievement on my part. After a period of many years it's the first time I've ever been able to get into a Stokowski concert!" He laughed at this and asked me if I really wanted to get in and I certainly did. He made good, too. In a few days a note came from Carnegie Hall in New York saying that at Mr. Stokowski's request, they were holding two subscription tickets for me for the season.

At the after-the-concert party he told me that he was going to play *Abraham Lincoln* in New York in a short time and suggested I write him a letter with any suggestions I might have about the playing.

I did as he suggested. There was only one question. The performance was all I could ever desire, but the first movement, played at about one half the speed I had indicated, gave the audience a feeling of two slow movements in a row.

Back came a note: "Dear Bob—thank you for your letter, which sheds new light on the playing of your symphony. Yours sincerely, Leopold Stokowski."

So when he played it in New York he did the first movement even slower than before![11]

Maybe it's mean to tell a tale like this, but it is such a text-book example of the composer-conductor relationship! I have thumbed through some of the marked scores in Maestro Toscanini's library and have seen a few places where he "helped" a bit with the orchestration. In one I remember he had a scale in the first violins and took the seconds off what they were doing and had them join in the scale with the firsts. I suppose that if I hadn't thrown in the towel in my try for a career as a conductor I might be tempted to do similar things, but I have one question for conductors: "Do you think the composer didn't listen (inside) to it your way before he chose his way?"

---

[10]Bennett's two winners in the Victor competition, *Abraham Lincoln* and *Sights and Sounds (An Orchestral Entertainment)*, were promptly published by Harms (full scores and parts, along with the composer's piano reductions). The latter work is for an orchestra of enormous proportions, including quadruple woodwinds, four saxophones, six horns and four trumpets. Izler Solomon and the Illinois Symphony (a WPA orchestra) premiered it in Chicago in 1938; its next performance was by the Boston Symphony, in 1943.

[11]Reviewers of these concerts repeatedly mention the sameness of the first two movements of *Abraham Lincoln* due to Stokowski's too-slow tempo in the opening movement. The latter (7 November 1931) performance was by the combined orchestras of the Juilliard Graduate School and the Institute of Musical Art, dedicating the Juilliard School's new auditorium.

And one might add: "And if new inventions and new fashions have opened up new possibilities, what are you trying to prove?—that Opus 133 [Beethoven's *Grosse Fuge*] should now be played on four electronic sackbuts?

Maybe I'm touchy about Toscanini's scale because it was written by the man whose book on orchestration led me into the field in the first place: Hector Berlioz.

[The early 1930s were among Bennett's most visible years in "new music" circles. In February, 1931, his *Four Songs* (settings of Sara Teasdale's "Lyrics") were part of a League of Composers concert at New York's Art Center. The following April, the First Festival of Contemporary American Music, at Saratoga Springs' Yaddo, included his *Three Chaucer Poems* (soprano and string quartet) as well as works by Copland, Chavez, Virgil Thomson, Roger Sessions, Paul Bowles, Louis Gruenberg, Roy Harris, Marc Blitzstein, George Antheil, Nicholas Berezowsky, and Oscar Levant. It was organized by Copland with an eye to interesting critics in native works. Pianist-composer Levant wrote that "All that saved the situation as far as I was concerned was the presence of Russell Bennett, in a sense an interloper from Broadway as I was, but a musician of firm foundation and sound development, which I was not."[12]

The following year, Bennett was awarded ASCAP membership, another indication of his growing notoriety as a composer. His nomination had been submitted the previous November by Kern, and seconded by Otto Harbach.]

On Broadway near this time Oscar Hammerstein and Jerome Kern wrote a new one called *Music in the Air* .[13] It was one of Oscar's more successful plots. He told me more than once that he hated plots. Give him an outline of what happened and he was dynamite. *Music in the Air* was set somewhere in the German mountains and Walter Slezak was beautifully cast as a unsophisticated young native. With him were Natalie Hall, Katherine Carrington and Tullio Carminati. Carminati sang one of Kern's very successful songs, "The Song is You," in the show and the words by Hammerstein read like a real poem, something that simply doesn't happen.

Except that once in a great while it does:

I hear music when I look at you. A beautiful theme of ev'ry dream I ever knew.
Down deep in my heart I hear it play. I feel it start, then melt away.

---

[12]Levant, *Smattering of Ignorance* (223). Levant graciously dedicated his Sonatina for Piano—premiered at Yaddo—to Bennett.

[13]The show opened 8 November 1932.

Oscar Levant, Allen Lincoln Langley, George Gershwin, Bennett, Fritz Reiner, Deems Taylor, and William Daly at Lewisohn Stadium, 10 August 1931. Photo courtesy of Nancy Schoenberger.

Levant and Bennett were soloists with the New York Philharmonic-Symphony for Bennett's March for Two Pianos and Orchestra, which they had premiered a year earlier in Los Angeles.

I hear music when I touch your hand. A beautiful melody from some enchanted land.
Down deep in my heart. I hear it say: Is this the day?
I alone have heard this lovely strain, I alone have heard this glad refrain,
Must it be forever inside of me. Why can't I let it go? Why can't I let you know?
Why can't I let you know the song my heart would sing?
That beautiful rhapsody of love and youth and spring.
The music is sweet, the words are true. The song is you.

Precious few of the world's immortal poems have been masterpieces as songs, and not because many fine composers haven't tried. Heinrich Heine and Robert Burns, being miniaturists, can be cited as having a pretty good record, but my theory is that a great poem already has its music and needs no composer.

This does nothing to subtract from the luster of the lyric writers of the American theater. Under the strictest handicaps their verses are often little masterpieces of rhyme, rhythm, and construction—and they are so hard to write! I came to realize this all over again as I walked down the Boston Common with Richard Whiting once during the tryout of a musical he was doing with Oscar Hammerstein. Richard had written the music of many a song hit and in his kindly way he was complaining that it was hard to write with Oscar because he, Dick, was used to words that "meant something in every line."[14] It took a little thought to figure that out; the idea of Oscar not being up to something was a little unexpected.

I'm not sure I understand it, but it probably meant that every line of a pop lyric has to make its own point. "Beyond the Blue Horizon" means all it will ever mean as long as it lives. "Yes, Sir, That's My Baby" and you go and cash your ticket. "Ain't She Sweet!" That's all you need to know or ever will know. In Oscar's theater you have time to develop your story: "Fish gotta swim and birds gotta fly. I gotta love one man till I die. Can't help lovin' that man of mine."

It's hard for a dedicated snob to see the difference, or what the difference matters, but the fine points of their game made these two creative men into a misfit. It's reported here to give a glimpse of why lyric writing is such a difficult art.

One of the very successful lyric men during the "Golden Age" was the town clown, cited here before, Irving Caesar.[15] Caesar in the old days was always bubbling over, and must have spent a good deal of his life thinking up practical jokes. One of his favorite victims, if you could call them that, was Doctor Albert Sirmay,[16] Hungarian by birth and a Doctor of Philosophy at Heidelberg University. He took the title and he took life very seriously. He also took all the wags and wits ofTin Pan Alley very seriously, which was just what they wanted.

Among other things he was the original composer of the Hungarian operetta *Princess Charming*. In New York [at Chappell Music, beginning in 1927] he was our editor and arranger of nearly everybody's songs for publication and was in the middle of just about everything that happened to show music. I don't think he really resented any of the pranks and little indigna-

---

[14]Whiting's sole collaboration with Hammerstein was 1931's *Free for All*. His songwriting successes include "Japanese Sandman," "Ain't We Got Fun," "Sleepy Time Gal," and "Breezin' Along with the Breeze."

[15]Oscar Levant relates that "When Irving Caesar heard it [Bennett's *Abraham Lincoln* symphony] he commented that he'd come to the conclusion that John Wilkes Booth didn't kill Lincoln—Robert Russell Bennett did" (*Memoirs of an Amnesiac*, 81).

[16]Originally "Szirmai"; he adopted the changed spelling after emigrating to the United States.

tions they tried to heap on him, but one day he beckoned to me to come into his office and, after shutting the door behind me, he said, "Russell, in Hungary, I was a big man. People used to follow me down the street in Budapest to get my autograph. Here, they goose me!"

Once when Dr. Sirmay was in London the telephone in his room at the hotel rang and a voice with a pretty good English accent said, "Dr. Sirmay, this is the drama editor of the London *Times* speaking. We should like to have a piece by you on the present condition of the London theatre as you see it. We are prepared to pay you tuppence a word for it."

They made an appointment for the following afternoon. On the following morning the phone rang and the same voice said, "I'm terribly sorry, Dr. Sirmay, but there's been a little hitch on your article—" Dr. Sirmay rose quickly to the occasion. He said, "Oh, if tuppence is too much, I'll be glad to do it for a penny a word!"

A typical Irving Caesar masquerade.

Another with the same cast: Caesar rings Dr. Sirmay in his office on the eighth floor and in a strange, strained voice says, "Doctor, there is a man here on the third floor with a broken leg. Can you come down at once, please?"

Dr. Sirmay: "I'm sorry! I can't do anything for a broken leg."

"Why not? You're a doctor, Aren't you?"

"Yes, but not that kind of doctor."

"Well, what the hell kind of doctor are you?"

[Levant recalls an additional instance of Sirmay's serving as the butt of a prank staged by Caesar:

> This was while Sirmay was providing incidental music for *Ripples* (1930), with songs by Caesar and Levant: "An efficient woman named Murray ran {*Ripples* producer Charles Dillingham's} office. Dr. Sirmay was in mortal terror that he would have to share a room with either Caesar or me when the show opened in New Haven. Finally, he went to Miss Murray. 'With whom am I going to sleep in New Haven?' he asked timidly. Miss Murray didn't bat an eye. 'Pick any girl you want, Doctor,' she answered. Dr. Sirmay retreated in worse terror than before."[17]]

When the years had gone by Albert Sirmay, Ph.D. Heidelberg University, died. At his funeral service a truly inspired and beautiful eulogy was read with deep affection and sincerity by Irving Caesar, his long-time friend.[18]

---

[17] Levant, *Memoirs of an Amnesiac*, 82–83.

[18] Caesar outlived all the songwriters and arrangers in Bennett's 1920s–'30s "circle," passing away late in 1995 at age 101.

I carried for many years a perfectly lovely watch made for Tiffany in Switzerland, with an engraved greeting dated "June 3, 1931, from Arthur." That date was that of the opening of *The Band Wagon*, by Howard Dietz and Arthur Schwartz. Arthur, who wrote the music, was quite young and enormously talented. He is my choice for the best song demonstrator of the whole lot. He sings every word of the lyrics without hesitating over a syllable, even though he may be giving a performance of the whole show. His piano accompaniments are well arranged and always played the same way.

The show was a big hit, and stands out as one of the thoroughly professional evenings in those lean years. The cast was a joy: Fred Astaire and his sister Adele [in her final Broadway appearance], Helen Broderick, Frank Morgan, Tilly Losch—we had one of the best music directors [Al Goodman] and songs such as "Dancing in the Dark," "High and Low," and "I Love Louisa."

Howard Dietz was one of those examples of men with big jobs in business who carry around a highly charged creative potential that may or may not come out to help light up the world.[19] One of the most famous of these was Charles Ives, near the top of America's serious composers.

Another of such talents is Robert A. Simon, for years music critic of *The New Yorker* magazine, and for more years director of continuity of the Mutual Broadcasting System.

Robert A. Simon and his wife Madeleine became especially close friends of ours after a fairly novel introduction. Once day in Paris I saw a copy of *The New Yorker* magazine on somebody's table and noticed some verse in the columns of the back pages. Anything that suggests it might be poetry gets a passing glance from me, and when I looked a little more closely the words seemed familiar. Not only that, they came out of the mist as some of my own writing.

A man named Gerald Reynolds had been with us quite a bit in France, a gifted conductor who at that time was director of the Women's University Glee Club in New York. For fun (need I say?) I had done two sizable works for his group and had sent them to him.[20]

Robert Simon wrote an entertaining review of Reynolds's concert.[21] The next time we went to New York we saw more and more of the Simons. One

[19]Howard Dietz (1898–1983) had been a classmate of both Oscar Hammerstein II and Lorenz Hart at Columbia; he was for many years a publicist for MGM in addition to his work as lyricist (and sometime librettist), principally with Arthur Schwartz (1900–1984).

[20]Reynolds had previously directed the American Conservatory of Music at Fontainebleau. Bennett's two pieces for women's chorus were his *Nietschze Variations* and *Theme and Variations in the Form of a Ballade about a Lorelei*. The latter was premiered by Reynolds and his ensemble at Town Hall on 1 May 1929.

[21]Robert A. Simon, "Musical Events: About a Lorelei and Mr. Bennett—Chamber Music," *The New Yorker*, 19 May 1929, 94–96.

day Bob called me to say he had begun the libretto for "our" opera. It was about one of the great coloratura sopranos of all time. Her name was originally Maria Garcia, but as our story starts it had just become Madame Maria Malibran. The best remembered thing about her was a famous song hit that she sang and popularized around 1820: "Home Sweet Home."[22]

The play was ready in no time and the Bennetts were already looking for boats.[23] We went to Vienna, where we rented half a house from a family of bankers who previously had rented the whole place to the American Ambassador.

From our house it was a short walk to where Beethoven went for relaxation and meditation—or, if you prefer, where riots and shootings took place in the turbulent days that led to Hitler. Toward the northwest there are three "mountains" (the quotes are for all who ever saw an Ande, a Rocky, or an Alp) and they bear the names Cobenzl, Leopoldsberg, and Kahlenberg. Halfway up to the highest of these is a Heuriger where they serve May wine but just where this little drinking place is you can pause, look to the right, and understand why that would be a nice place to draw your last breath. To the left, beyond the Heuriger, is Cobenzl, with all its festive visitors circling about. Straight ahead is majestic Kahlenberg, and well around to the right Leopoldsberg rises out of the Danube mists. But turn back a little to the left and look deep down. There are the farms and arbors, and there is the "beautiful blue" river curving almost under you.

If I had published my sixth volume of poetry I might possibly have found the words to put under this picture. Probably not.

The first two acts of *Maria Malibran* got written in Vienna, in spite of an interruption of almost a week when I went to Berlin to help Fritz Kreisler do the orchestration of his music play *Sissy*. I stayed at the Eden Hotel there and went out to the Kreisler home in Grünewald, a suburb, every morning, where we worked over his manuscripts till lunch time and then talked about a little of everything all afternoon. He never practiced the violin, leaving it in its case all summer until about two weeks before his first recital in the fall.[24]

---

[22]Maria Felicita Garcia Malibran was among the first to bring Italian opera to the U.S. She married the Belgian violinist De Bériot, but died from a horse-riding accident at the age of twenty-eight. Her sister Pauline Viardot Garcia was also an acclaimed singer; their father Manuel Garcia was the original Almaviva of Rossini's *Barber of Seville*.

[23]The *New York Herald-Tribune* ("Bennett Sailing For Europe to Finish Opera," 12 May 1932) noted that the composer and his family had departed—with Simon's libretto—the previous day. The writer observes that Bennett and Simon were "interested in the idea of an American opera that would feature neither Negroes nor Indians."

[24]*Sissy* opened in Berlin 23 December 1932, shortly after a Kreisler-commissioned Bennett violin concerto had been announced ("Orchestrator on His Own," *Time*, 12 December 1932); the work was never completed. In 1941, the violinist was hit by an automobile while crossing a

The beautiful thing about spending so much time with this great musician was that it was almost impossible to think of him as a great musician. And yet you kept reminding yourself of moments of violin playing that have never been touched by any other you ever heard. And you remind yourself of his simple melodies that manage to have the very thing you spend your life missing in nearly all the simple melodies that pass in review.

But he was a simple, friendly human being who was interested in what you were thinking as well as what he was. One day we were talking about Toscanini, pretty well recognized as without an equal in our times. I said, "There is, however, one conductor that impressed me more deeply and I never seem to get over it."

Kreisler said, "I wonder who that could be. If you say one man I am going to agree with you, but only one."

I said, "I was only seventeen years old but the man has never been equaled in my thoughts. Arthur Nikisch."

He said, "You are perfectly right! I sent him the score of the Elgar concerto about a month before rehearsal with the London Symphony on the day of the concert. I came in before the second half of the rehearsal and was horrified to see him at the podium with a paper-knife cutting the pages of the score as he opened it for the first time.

"You should have heard that performance at sight. He smelt music! He simply felt and knew what was on the next page before he ever saw it."[25]

Fritz and Harriet Kreisler came to Vienna for orchestra rehearsals at the Theater an der Wien before we left for Paris and New York. We took them to dinner at our favorite restaurant, an outdoor Hungarian place in Grinzing, named Pataky. We were enjoying ourselves quietly when a man at a near table, rather noisy, flipped a spoonful of Russian salad smack in Fritz's lap. He got up and went to the man's table saying, "Do you see what you've done?" He said it twice and Harriet was terrified.

She said to us, "Oh, he's furious! There's no telling what he'll do!"

But Fritz came back and said calmly, "It's all right. He's apologized."

---

busy Manhattan intersection; Bennett responded with his orchestral *Prayer for Fritz Kreisler*, aired on WOR radio. The pair's last collaboration was Kreisler's short-lived 1944 operetta *Rhapsody*, which featured Bennett's orchestrations and "additional lyrics."

[25]Born in Hungary, Arthur Nikisch (1855–1922) worked as both permanent and guest conductor with a number of European and American orchestras, including the Boston Symphony, Budapest Opera, Berlin Philharmonic, and London Philharmonic. Slonimsky describes him as "the first of his profession that opened the era of 'the conductor as hero,' exercising a peculiar magnetism on his audiences equal to that of virtuoso artists" (*Baker's Biographical Dictionary of Music and Musicians,* 8th ed., s.v. "Nikisch, Arthur").

As we finished and I was paying the bill it started to rain a bit. At the end of the garden where the tables were there was a little resting place with a roof and my two ladies and the Kreislers went in out of the rain, which didn't amount to much. In the meantime Herr Pataky was saying he had been there eighteen years and such a thing had never happened before, apologizing for the man with the Russian salad.

I said to Pataky, "Do you know who my guests are?" thinking he might be surprised, but he said, "Oh, ja! der Herr Professor Kreisler!" I joined the rest under the little roof and in came Pataky with his autograph album. The rain ended and so did an evening we'll always think of with pleasure.

Mrs. Fritz Kreisler—Harriet—had the world believing she ruled her husband with a rod of iron. He was always gentle and gave the impression that her word was law. I've heard friends that actually felt sorry for him and wondered why he allowed her to dictate their personal lives without putting up an argument once in a while.

It happens I can reassure them on that score. He and I were sitting in the first row of the empty balcony of the theater in Vienna while the orchestra was rehearsing the new show. She and a friend were downstairs in about the sixth row of the main floor. The orchestra had just played my arrangement of the famous *Caprice Viennois*, and Fritz called down and said, "Isn't that a lovely orchestration, Harriet?"

She snapped back, "Yes, but it's too slow. It'll die like a dog at that tempo."

He started to say, "The tempo depends on the stage movement" when she went on with her loud criticism. At that point her husband answered her and at the same time answered everybody else that had any doubts about who had charge. Called down from the balcony, his words rang out like a calliope.

Poor Harriet never uttered another sound all afternoon.

On our way to New York we stayed a week or so in Paris. The stopover had no purpose except social, but we had certain roots in the place and it didn't occur to us that we could just go back to America without stopping over. Two friends that have not been much reported here were Arthur Train, son of a much-read novelist in the U.S.A.,[26] and Raoul Breton, publisher, artists' manager, and an authority on things theatrical.

Raoul published a collection of twenty pieces for piano that I wrote on the twenty precincts of Paris, and was a very unusual Frenchman. Frenchmen

---

[26] Arthur Train (Sr., 1875–1945) was the longtime Assistant District Attorney for New York County, New York. Author of some 250 short stories and novels, Train is best remembered as the creator of attorney "Mr. Ephraim Tutt," the protagonist in fifteen of his books. During his last years, Train also served as president of the National Institute of Arts and Letters.

are polite and charming—those I have known well—but almost never open an inside door to their affections.

He was with Richard Rodgers when Richard came to Paris and I met him for the first time. For quite a long time Raoul's lady-love was Damia, a celebrated comédienne with a fantastic personality. We had many visits with the two of them.

They knew all the eating places, for instance, that no foreigner could possibly know. For a quick example, we went to dinner one evening at a precious place in the Place d'Italie called "Chez Pierre l'aubergiste." During a meal that defies description the waiter asked Raoul to come to the rear and speak with the proprietor.

As we were on our way home Raoul told us what Pierre spoke to him about. He asked him not to bring in friends because they would soon have so many diners that his wife could not do all the cooking and it would never be as good again.

Arthur Train, as I recall it, was not Arthur Junior, because his middle name was not the same as that of his famous father. Arthur was a member in good standing of the "Boulangerie" but I never knew just what he did in music. I'll qualify that a little. One thing he did was sell me an armful of scores and music books that he had bought at one time or another and I hope he got half as much pleasure and benefit out of the fifty dollars as I did out of the books.

He had a dear French-speaking wife and two very young sons, a pussycat, and a doggie named Sheila. Arthur and I wrote a one-act stage work called *An Hour of Delusion* which lies snugly in the pile of things I'll never get around to looking over.[27] Since I am the only one who has heard it so far I can write my own criticism and say, with the goat in the movie studio who had eaten up a film, "I liked the book better."

The last visit we had with the Trains was on a farm in France that he had bought. It was one of those farms that are dotted all over the landscape, making no attempt to be in one piece. A patch here, another patch a kilometer down the road—at any rate the house and barn were both on the same patch of their property.

Arthur was a good nonfiction writer. I doubt that they really did any serious farming. Somehow it's hard to imagine little Nita Train as the quasi beast of burden that the neighboring farmers' wives seemed to be.

When we left France it turned out to be "The Last Time I Saw Paris" (again that [Kern-] Hammerstein song). We came back to a land in the throes of a bad depression. However predictable it was, the reality was sad every-

---

[27]Completed in 1928, Bennett's *An Hour of Delusion* remains unperformed.

where you looked. Two or three of my fellow music men (not the big money ones) were wiped out by bank failures. In Freeman, the little town of my youth, the cashier of the bank shot himself; men who were important in the evening woke up the next morning and found they were not, some of them jumping off high buildings rather than face reality.

Mr. Max Dreyfus—I'm sure he needs no further introduction—and his brother Louis had sold what I've been calling Harms to the motion picture industry before the crash came; but as soon as Max could (by terms of the sale) return to music publishing, the two brothers took over the management of Chappell and Company on both sides of the Atlantic Ocean.

I'm sure I have already betrayed the fact that again I don't really know what I am talking about, but I do know that the new name of our publisher and big client became one of the old names in music: Chappell and Company.

The "big-money" men in the world of entertainment were most of them just smart enough to get caught in the market crash. Many were in over their heads and one can only guess how many came to Max Dreyfus for salvation. He took me in his office one morning and pointed to his desk saying, "This morning I went through that desk and cleaned out everything that had to do with millions. I am no longer a millionaire."

I asked him if he meant he had sold all his holdings.

He said, "They call it selling."

"I think I know what you did with your millions," I said, "and I'm not sure any of them would have done that for you."

"That may be true," Max said, "but we don't figure that way. The only possible reason to have money is to be able to do what you want to do."

What he wanted to do was apparently to save these colorful characters from themselves even if it wiped him out. Whether his philosophy was profound or too simple, it probably worked out in his mind as a gigantic bet on his "stable" to win. For us two-dollar bettors, such thinking is out of reach.

Max and his brother Louis were equal partners in every deal but if I knew Louis Dreyfus he was not an equal partner in this one. Louis was a square shooter, but certainly was not the humanitarian—or the gambler—or the man of vision that would lay it on the line like that and risk being an absolute fool for life.

It's none of my business who or how many of our friends paid back all the money that saved their skins—each case was different, no doubt, from all the others. I did hear of one that made good in full but he was an exception, according to those who know at least a little more than I do.

Whatever they all did it's pleasant to report that Max's desk got back before very long to its concern with millions—many, many millions.

Louis Dreyfus told me his own story once. He got into the business of selling picture frames. He said he couldn't add, subtract or multiply, but when a customer came in and bought thirteen and a half feet of frame at thirty-nine cents a foot, he knew what the customer owed him. He didn't know how he knew, but he knew and he was never wrong.

When he had saved two million dollars, he put it all in U.S. Treasury Bonds yielding four percent. He told me he said, "Now that's my living. From now on I'm going to do what I want to do."

What he wanted to do was make more money. He backed his brother Max in the music publishing business and the two of them made a great combination, Max the creative pulse and Louis the keeper of the keys to the vault. Of course the line between the brains and the brawn was not that clearly drawn, but it's a good combination. Anybody who has both qualities can become a football quarterback and prevail until a two-hundred forty-five pound Thing comes through the line and sits on him.

Louis Dreyfus once told Harry Ruby and me the story of his divorce of his wife of several years in London. One day she[28] told him she wanted to quit; she didn't want to be married to him any more.

He replied, (quoting him as accurately as I can), "All right, you want to quit—what do you want?"—meaning, of course, what settlement, etc.

She was a popular leading woman and she said, "You know what I want. I want my own show in London."

At the time, he had the script on his desk of a musical that was awaiting production and she agreed not to ask for anything more than to produce it and play the lead.

So the play went into rehearsal. Shortly thereafter one of the leading theater men of London met Louis and said, "Louis I hear you are doing a show." Louis said yes, he was doing a musical. His friend said, "Well, how about letting me have a piece of it?"

Louis answered, "Sure, I'll sell you part of it. How much of it do you want?"

"I'd like to have half of it, if I may." The deal was made. The rehearsals went on.

One day the same friend came to Louis and said with an apologetic smile, that a producer friend from Paris had heard of the new play and was awfully anxious to buy part of it. To his surprise Louis said, "Okay, how much of it does he want?"

---

[28]Valli Marguerite Alice Knust, Dreyfus's first wife, known professionally as "Valli Valli." She appeared in straight plays and musical comedies, both in New York and in London, including the title role in 1919's *Miss Millions.*

"He actually wants to buy half."

And Louis sold the other half, got his divorce and the play flopped.

Harry Ruby and I agreed that even if Louis made up the whole story—and neither of us believed for a moment that he did—it was a typical Louis Dreyfus performance.

When we went with the Kern family from Palm Beach to Hollywood, California, we took railroad trains to Key West, then a boat to Havana, Cuba, and from there a large ocean liner to San Pedro, the port of Los Angeles. It was the only ocean trip I, personally, ever enjoyed. In fact we liked it so much we looked for a good excuse to do it again.

One wasn't hard to find. My mother in Kansas City had developed painful arthritis and had heard through her sister Effie of a doctor in California with a new treatment for arthritis. We left our daughter Jean with her other grandmother, Mrs. Merrill, and took my mama by train to Los Angeles. She and her sister took a small house together and we, Louise and I, took a Panama Pacific liner for New York.

What the treatment was I don't know, but the doctor made good. Mother's hands were left a little stiff, but the pain never came back as far as I ever heard.

The ocean voyage to New York was without mishap except to the ship. Going through the Panama Canal she managed to swing her "tail" around and hit the wall near one of the locks. I was standing on the deck early one morning when it seemed to me that the monstrous vessel might be swinging around a little too close to the wall while waiting for the lock to open. No real noise came to my ears, but she seemed to let out a little groan and shudder softly.

Later one of our neighbors told us that one of the lower decks took a good deal of water and they had quite a mess to clean up.

Captain Donovan—I understand he was the boss of the whole fleet of vessels—was on board, and we had one wonderful dinner with him. A prominent man of the Scripps-Howard newspaper chain had been teasing Captain Donovan about the quality of the food on board, so the Captain showed him what they could do in that line.

We had no fault to find with the daily meals, but if they had to be compared to *that* meal—!

Among the passengers was a tall, slim father with his two tall, slim daughters. The man was journalist William Field who had, among other things, founded the *New York Daily News.* He had been a tennis player but his eyes had started to fade and his retirement had amounted to settling down on a picturesque spot hear Rutland, Vermont, and publishing the *Rutland Herald.*

His wife, a daughter of the governor of Vermont when she became Mrs. Field, had died before we met him and his children. Besides Lindsay and Betsy, his two daughters, he had a son, also named William, one of whose hobbies was raising great beds of flowers.

This little cast of characters belongs with the souvenirs because the Fields and the Bennetts settled unspectacularly into one of those lasting friendships where what happens to either family has importance for both.

The Fields rented a corner of their place in Mendon, Vermont, to us and I finished writing the third act of *Maria Malibran* there. I also tried to grow a beard for almost a month, but have to count that as the greatest failure of my whole career; I gave it up after a little over three weeks.

In all honesty, I can't remember every paying them [the Fields] any rent for the nice little house, but we must have squared it with conscience in some way. The high drama of our stay there was furnished by two bears that came rather near the Fields's house on the hill and killed a cow one night. We set traps for them and caught them. One weighed a hundred and eighty pounds and the other was much bigger, at least two hundred and fifty.

They were so strong that they pulled the heavy traps loose and dragged them around. Mr. Field went up the hill behind the house one morning to look the bears over and came back before he realized that the beasts were capable of making short work of him if they wanted to go for him.

He told me the story and even laughed at how foolish he had been. The bears were shot and hauled to town for whatever one does with dead bears.

A very short time after that we visited Mr. Field in a New York hospital where they were trying to save his failing eyesight, but after another short time he went out to a spot behind his Vermont home and shot himself. Bill, his son, wrote me that his father's death was "clean and fearless, as his life had been."

Many individuals and groups of individuals believe sincerely that they understand death and even suicide, but I cast one humble vote for the theory that none of us do until we have been through it ourselves.

It's possible to make a fairly sound guess as to why William Field ended his life (fearlessly, as his son said). His sight was gone, he faced darkness and, more important, he faced giving his three children twenty years with a healthy but helpless father. A thought occurred when I first heard of his death, that the idea could have come to him from that moment he'd spent near a very unclean death—those two bears—in almost the same spot.

Something like three years had passed since my pompous pact was made with destiny. The winning of those two bits of recognition as a serious composer was supposed to usher in a mighty struggle for publications, recordings and performances, but so far not one such move had been made. It began to be apparent that none would be made.

It did no good to know that Beethoven tried to sell the same symphony to two different publishers, that Michelangelo had battles every day with churches and popes over money; that Shakespeare peddled his wares and worked purely for box-office profits. Knowing and accepting all this, an inner conviction simply will not stop shouting, "When you are allowed to take a clean score page and cover it with something you've never heard before, with whatever number of instruments you need to hear—with no orders to make a silk purse (by the definition of a completely non-musical audience) out of a sow's ear (by the definition of any first-year [college] music major)—you're having fun and you should pay them, not they, you."

Whoever "they" are.

A commissioned work may have all sorts of strings attached to it, from no suggestions at all to asking for "treatment" of this, that, or those melodies already in existence. In this case experience as an arranger of tunes has quite some importance. If the commission puts no direction or limit on the work, or if there is no commission and the composer sits down and creates his own project, he now squares off with the toughest boss he'll ever serve: musical history and the sum total of all the great works already written. Trends, style, disciplines, overtones, consonance, dissonance, percussion. Jerome Kern, who was definitely not a theorist, had a typically smart thing to say about Claude Debussy. He called Debussy the very greatest plagiarist, because he knew all music and was able to avoid it.

It doesn't pay to go too deep with Jerry Kern's music criticism but he filled the air with very apt quotes on many subjects.

Returning to our composer with no orders in his head, his first step after taking on the job is to stop by the garden where Mnemosynes's daughters[29] are and ask if there is a message for him. The answer is likely to be a tired voice saying, "No, nothing today."

But when one of the girls whispers something he must get it down quickly. She may not repeat it. The trouble now is that, even if he gets it down perfectly, it may be a long time before his world has ears to hear it or feelings to love it.

That thought must not stop him. Whether he gets money for it or pays for it he has no right to let it die unborn. That is one of his most serious responsibilities: he must save everything he has ever believed in for the generations. They will cast the final vote after the past and present have run out of ballots.

---

[29]Greek goddess Mnemosynes and Zeus parented the nine muses.

And does this also go for *The Lady with the Red Dress*?

Yes, I'm afraid it does.

One of the most quoted quotes from Oscar Levant: someone asked him if Gershwin's music would be heard a hundred years from now and he said, "It will be if Gershwin is alive." It was a frivolous answer, aimed only at teasing George about his fondness for "demonstrating." And yet that business about a hundred years from now is tantalizing. Not only what will be listened to then, but by whom.

The works of the men and women of the musical theater have shown some signs of immortality. We could be fooled by this, since radio, television and recordings—not to mention live performers—are scraping the bottom of the barrel for material twenty-four hours a day.

Immortality as we apply the word is a matter of two or three centuries in a universe billions of years old. "World-famous" may refer to a tiny part of the world, but on this accepted basis the works of these minds seem to be duly nominated.

[Bennett had earlier observed:

> Perhaps the best commentary on the term "fame" came to my notice recently. In the publishing office where I spend some time I got into the habit last winter of bringing in one of those paper horse races to which one touches a lighted cigarette and six little lines of spark crawl down the paper to a finish line, each spark representing a horse. I got everybody in the office to put up a dime and choose a horse, some fifty or sixty bets resulting. After the "running" I would take time to divide the pot among all those on the winning horse, and pay off. As I left one large room one of the secretaries who had placed a bet of ten cents on a horse, turned to the rest of the room and said, "Is that the way that poor man makes his living? I didn't have the heart to refuse him the dime."[30]]

Unfortunately I never looked to see who wrote *The Lady with the Red Dress* but the piece must be nearing its hundredth birthday. Whether it is alive is another matter, but my friend Eubie Blake is, and he is of about the same age. What has Eubie to do with it?—he still plays ragtime like nobody else, as far as I'm concerned.[31]

---

[30]Letter to Verna Arvey (Mrs. William Grant Still), 9 July 1945.

[31]Pianist-composer-songwriter Eubie Blake, much heralded during the American "ragtime revival" of the early 1970s, died in 1983, shortly after his 100th birthday. See also "Orchestrating for Broadway" (p. 283) with Bennett's recollection of an arrangement he had done for Blake's band.

A pianist who plays like nobody else brings the wandering pen back to slightly more sober questions. One of the most creative pianists in his interpretations and also a brilliant conductor of symphony [orchestras] is Jose Iturbi, whose personality simply glows.[32] He played a few of my Parisian sketches in recital in New York one evening and with them one of a collection of "fox trots" for piano.[33] The sketches were much applauded but the fox-trot was greeted with silence.

It [the "fox-trot"] was a percussive, dissonant thing of rhythms that, in the sequence of movements, leads into a direct opposite, a tender, contented little aria. One shouldn't be played without the other, perhaps, but that wouldn't be worth any space here. What I never cease to find interesting is the question of just what meaning to assign to the beating of two hands together, or to the absence of such a gesture.

Leopold Stokowski, not terribly long ago, presented a deeply serious work of Messiaen in Carnegie Hall and no sound was heard after the music faded out. A certain part of that silence was from listeners who wanted "Moonlight and Roses" and didn't get it, but I like to think that the depth of the music and its sincerity reached something in the rest of them that expressed itself in silence. I wish I were surer of it.

Robert Schumann once wrote that the only possible treatment of a work of art is silence, but he hardly meant it that way. He was actually scolding some music critic who was attempting to review a performance of Schubert's C-Major Symphony and, of course, had no idea that he was talking about a work of art, let alone one of the great works of all time.

Whatever place deep silence has at the finish of a great musical achievement (*Parsifal*, for example), audiences will have to change a great deal before they give up their claques, their palm beating and their loud bravos.

[Bennett's Concerto Grosso for Dance Band and Orchestra and *An Early American Ballade on Melodies of Stephen Foster* were created in 1932 with

---

[32]Spanish pianist and conductor Jose Iturbi (1895–1980) came to the U. S. in 1928. He led the Rochester Philharmonic for several seasons in the late 1930s, and conducted the Philadelphia Orchestra in the premiere of Bennett's *Adagio Eroico* (dedicated "To the Memory of a Soldier") in 1935. Yet it was his appearances in several of MGM's 1940s film musicals that made him a household name in the United States. Iturbi had commissioned a Bennett piano concerto in the early 1930s (the composer announced that it would be completed during his Wyoming vacation in 1935), but, as with the violin concerto for Fritz Kreisler, it was never completed. Bennett's later Piano Concerto in B Minor (1948) was played several times in Europe by Andor Foldes in the early 1950s, but Iturbi has no known connection to this work.

[33]Iturbi's Carnegie Hall program took place on 30 November 1932. The *Seven Fox Trots in Concert Form* (1928) remains unpublished.

radio airplay in mind. The Concerto Grosso, subtitled "Sketches from an American Theatre," features a typical pre-Swing-era ensemble: three saxophones doubling clarinets, two trumpets, trombone, piano, and guitar (joined often by the orchestra's first-chair bassist). Written for an NBC composition contest (it was not a winner), the work was premiered on 3 December 1932 by Howard Hanson and the Rochester Philharmonic. A month later, it was featured on three Berlin Philharmonic "All-American" programs in Berlin, Hamburg, and Leipzig, with Hanson as guest conductor. And later in 1933, Bennett was invited to lead the New York Philharmonic-Symphony in a Fourth-of-July Lewisohn Stadium performance.

The *Early American Ballade* for chamber orchestra—based on Foster's "Camptown Races" and "Ring de Banjo"—is one of several Bennett pieces that straddle the categories of "arrangement" and "composition." It was written for the Chesterfield cigarettes *Music That Satisfies* CBS program conducted by Nathaniel Shilkret. Bennett's piece (the score is lost) was premiered on the series' 15 April 1932 debut, and similar works were solicited from Percy Grainger, Ferde Grofé, Werner Janssen, John Alden Carpenter, Charles Wakefield Cadman, John Powell, David Guion, Shilkret, and Pietro Floridia (Shilkret's one-time composition teacher). The contemporary press also records Ottorino Respighi's pledge to complete a short orchestral work for the program.

Another chamber orchestra work, Bennett's well-received *Six Variations in Fox-Trot Time on a Theme by Jerome Kern*, was completed in 1933. Based on Kern's "Once in a Blue Moon" (from 1923's *Stepping Stones*), it was premiered at Town Hall on 3 December, with Bennett as *obbligato* pianist. The New Chamber Orchestra was led by Bernard Herrmann, who was later acclaimed for his dramatic underscoring for radio (including Orson Welles's "War of the Worlds" and other Mercury Theater productions at CBS) and his film scores (among them *Citizen Kane*, *The Magnificent Ambersons*, *The Day the Earth Stood Still*, and nine for Alfred Hitchcock).]

Broadway was still feeling a little dizzy from the effects of the great depression when we got back from Vienna and one of the stage pieces I remember most vividly was one I did no work on. It was not a musical and it was not a success, but it was the brilliant product of that era of uncertainty and a success. It was called *The Fabulous Invalid* and it brought the problems of the theater right out and worried about them in front of the audience.

At the end of the first act tnere was a suicide offstage and before the first act curtain we all were taken into the occult as an old doorman who had died brought William Shakespeare into the scene. They were asking him what he thought was going to happen to the fabulous invalid, the Broadway theater. He had no more idea than they did as the curtain fell.

When the second act began the house was dark and the curtain rose on the front of the theater with the word "Screen" in giant, blazing letters stretched clear across the stage. This was what was happening to some of the legitimate theaters at the time: showing movies and attracting audiences with lotto, bingo and whatnot. The play ended with a good deal about off-Broadway theater. The impression was that we might all have to go down there and start all over again.[34]

[Bennett chooses not to mention his contributions to the musical comedy *Hold Your Horses*, which debuted 25 September 1933. Russell Crouse and Corey Ford concocted a lively book based on the former's illustrated history of New York, *It Seems Like Yesterday*. Robert A. Simon wrote many of the lyrics, and Bennett was first-credited songwriter along with Owen Murphy, Lou Alter, Arthur Swanstrom, and Ben Oakland. The orchestrations, naturally, were Bennett's. The celebrity-studded opening-night audience included New York Governor Alfred E. Smith, George S. Kaufman, Condé Nast, Janet Gaynor, George Jessel, Max Gordon, Jules Glaenzer, and Walter Chrysler Jr. Featuring comedian Joe Cook, *Hold Your Horses* opened to mixed reviews but finished a respectable run of 88 performances at the Winter Garden followed by a several-week road tour. Curiously, Bennett not once remarked upon it in print.]

One musical I worked on when Broadway was a fabulous invalid was *Face the Music.*[35] The songs were by Irving Berlin, with some of his irresistible nonsense at its top. The main "ballad" was called "Soft Lights and Sweet Music." Not only was it a real money maker when no one had any money but it could be used by teachers of composition for a fine example of contemporary harmony. This by a man who almost boasted of being a musical ignoramus. Two other production numbers in the show remain with me as being right out of the times we were in: "At the Automat" and "Let's Have Another Cup of Coffee."

Two other musicals of that period, both with music by Jerome Kern, have to be worth a spot on these pages. One was a pretty flat failure. It had an original story by Oscar Hammerstein and it took us all to London for several weeks.

---

[34]Oscar Levant served as music director for the show, authored by George S. Kaufman and Moss Hart.

[35]*Face the Music* opened 17 February 1932.

Three Sisters opened at the famous Drury Lane Theatre [9 April 1934] and furnished another great example of what writing for a theater audience is like. It was a tender story about the three girls, and a report of the dress rehearsal and the opening night gives a lesson that I can't tell you how to learn.

With the house empty the end of the first act was so appealing that we were all near tears. In fact Eva (Mrs. Jerome) Kern was hardly able to speak at all. The following evening the house was packed and the end of the first act, played exactly as rehearsed, was silly and embarrassing.

The audience just sat there and wrote a new play, with the same words spoken in the same way.

One might say, "That's a British audience for you!" But Eva Kern was born and raised in Walton-on-Thames, one hundred percent British.

One also might say, "Don't write for the theater unless you are independently wealthy."

The other show with Kern music was *Roberta*, a play that is easy to remember because of two songs and two men.[36] One of the songs began as a scene with musical background and snatches of song throughout the scene.

The snatches of song were of such appeal to the audience that Otto Harbach, who wrote the libretto and the lyrics, trimmed away the scene and left a big hit-song, "Smoke Gets in Your Eyes." The other especially successful song was "Yesterdays," sung in the show by veteran actress Fay Templeton, playing the part of Mme. Roberta.

The two men that will not soon be forgotten were Bob Hope, playing the business manager of a big-time dance band in the play, and Fred MacMurray, who played the saxophone in the band.

In my own department I can report another one of those mistakes I made that never stop yapping at my heels. There was a song in *Roberta* called "I'll Be Hard to Handle." The singer was Lyda Roberti, one of the most original personalities on the stage at that time. I took a good look at her, sized up her style and missed it by nine nautical miles. I gave her an arrangement that might have been effective with a number of red-hot mamas of the day, but poor Roberti stood in the middle of the stage trying to figure out what hit her. What I had missed was the very keynote of her act.

She was a tender character trying to be tough and only succeeding in being adorable. Sweet she was, but not hot.[37]

---

[36]The show opened 18 November 1933.

[37]Roberti's trademark song was Harold Arlen's "Sweet and Hot," which she performed in his *You Said It* (1931). Theatre lyricists often tailored their songs for Roberti's distinctive Slavic accent, especially her singular pronunciation of words with an initial "h."

It took only a few minutes to take all the sassiness out of the orchestra, but a good music arranger is supposed to see those things coming.

Toward the end of the next spring—this would be in the year 1935—my family of three locked the front door and set out for a dude ranch in Wyoming, twenty-four miles from Sheridan. I took a few scores, a violin, and the libretto of a musical play by Jose Ruben.[38] He and I had become friends when he directed and played the male lead in *The Cat and the Fiddle*—music by Kern and book and lyrics by Otto Harbach some years before.[39]

Jose Ruben had great hopes for his new musical and wanted me to do the whole score from the bottom up. Whether I would have gone through with doing the tunes for a musical I don't know, but I had a few years before decided to take the composing business seriously and, in my opinion, the most serious composer in the world must have the tunes in him whether he uses them or not.

They're terribly easy to write, but the fish don't have to bite no matter how beautiful the bait, and then there is the matter of backers' auditions, playing the same tune over and over for producers, directors, collaborators and casts.

And the terrible question of the ninth (or the seventeenth) bar, where the tune has to start all over while your customers say, "Ah, there it is again! Goody! I don't have to work now until the end of the phrase." And while you say, "Oh, you again! You said that before. What else is new?"

Nothing came of the project, although the lyric writer was sure we were going to have a hit song or two.

When we got off the train at Sheridan, Wyoming, we were happy at the prospect of "roughing it." We were met by Bill Leach, the proprietor of the T.A.T. Ranch, in a ten-gallon hat and spurs. He took us around the corner to his car, a late-model Rolls Royce, and as he left us at our cottage he invited us to a polo game and a buffet dinner the next day at the Mooress's Circle M Ranch. The Circle M Ranch owned several great racehorses, but that is not exactly the kind of horses we had expected to see here. A look around at our fellow guests brought up similar thoughts. One of them was Oliver Wallop, the future Earl of Portsmouth.

Anyway, so ended our first day of roughing it.

We soon settled down to a most pleasant routine. My two girls joined the crowd of horseback riders on western saddles nearly every day. I went out

---

[38]Jose Ruben (1888–1969), born in Paris, first appeared on the New York stage in 1911. He is best known for his many roles in silent films and stage plays.

[39]*The Cat and the Fiddle* opened 15 October 1931.

once with the crowd for a hamburger roast and started to mount my horse from the left side, causing much mirth among the assembled "horsemen." Thinking it over I must have done that with all our horses in Missouri and never thought about it. The horses never complained.

Most of the day I studied scores, wrote a half dozen innocent sounding melodies for use in Jose Ruben's musical, and played a bit on the violin. Same old story on the violin—thousands of notes, but no tones.

One day we had a softball game, where two items moved in on me to stay. One was a quite stunning looking girl from St. Louis. She was there with two brothers and she was stunning because she looked powerful and was. She was playing first base, while I was at bat, and I (batting left-handed) drove a line drive at her so hard that she couldn't get her glove around it. It hit her somewhere in the middle and I was too horrified to know what to do. While I made up my mind she picked up the ball, stepped on the base and I was out.

She must have had a bullet-proof vest on. After all, those softballs are only soft by comparison.

The other item is one that makes you feel good about things. During the afternoon at the game, for who knows what reason, I left a one-hundred dollar bill in the grass by a tree behind first base. The next day I missed the money and went out to the ballgrounds to try to find out what I could about the fate of my fortune. They had mowed the grass that morning and had left a little unmowed spot around the money, which was untouched.

Toward the end of our stay on the ranch, there came a telegram asking me to come to Hollywood and arrange the music for a film called *I Dream Too Much.* The music director of the film was Max Steiner and the composer of the songs was none other than our friend Jerome Kern. Max, by this time, was as famous as any musician in Hollywood, having won the first Academy Award, or Oscar, ever given for a background score. He was a choir boy in his hometown of Vienna, as a starter, and in New York he was a musical director, a good arranger and even planned to be a musical comedy tune writer. But Hollywood got him and he got Hollywood.[40]

Among many other things on Broadway, Max was music director of *Sitting Pretty*, the Bolton, Wodehouse and Kern musical. He helped me with a few of the orchestrations on that one, and I remember him in tears once when the show was on the road during the tryout weeks. The music was not as

---

[40]The arrival of Max Steiner (1888–1971) in Hollywood coincided almost exactly with the successful synchronization of recorded sound with film in the late 1920s; his first Oscar was for 1933's *King Kong*. He was instrumental in establishing the lush, nineteenth-century orchestral style of such composers as Wagner and Richard Strauss—the latter his godfather—as the standard for Hollywood dramas and action pictures.

exciting as had been hoped and the composer was inclined to blame his music director. He sent to New York for his old conductor Victor Baravalle to come out and tell us what was wrong. Vic Baravalle was one of the very best at that job, but as a diplomat he was not talented. He was very tough on poor little Max—hence the tears on my shoulder.

After Max left my room, in came Baravalle, telling me what was wrong with Max's performance—he wasn't doing justice to the arrangements—he should accent this and accent that, etc., etc. As a matter of fact, great as he was, Vic didn't really know what he was talking about, having seen the play for the first time only a couple of hours before. What he especially didn't know was that the particular arrangements he was quoting in his criticism were ones that Max himself made while helping me through the big rush before we opened. I told him that, and he didn't stay long.

My next visitor was composer Kern. He was a tough man on these jobs, but he could be appealed to and he was smart. He realized what shape Max Steiner was in and he realized he might not have a conductor at all if too much happened to Max. Nobody else knew the show from the conductor's standpoint well enough to give a performance. Kern said to me, "You know Vic Baravalle is not a discreet and delicate personality. I'll make it up to Max somehow."

The next morning, Max showed me a check from Kern amounting to an extra week's salary, but he asked me if I didn't think it would be a good idea to send it back with a polite note of thanks. This he did and he stayed with the show as long as the show stayed with anybody, which was not very long [95 performances].

When *I Dream Too Much* came beckoning, the best way to get to Hollywood from Sheridan began with a 265-mile auto ride through the most uneventful territory in the land. Mile after mile of sand, rock, sagebrush and dead grasshoppers and jack rabbits. These creatures are completely unprepared for a great mass of metal and glass to come shooting out of the horizon at 80-odd miles an hour and their poor smashed bodies tell a somber tale.

We passed by the corner where The Virginian shot Trampas, passed through one town called Casper, and read miles of signs advertising shaving creams.

The auto ride ended in Rawlins, Wyoming, in time for Bill Leach and me to have a very welcome plate of ham and eggs before he took the same long, lonely ride back to T.A.T. Ranch, while I went down to the railroad station to get on the Los Angeles train when it came through.

The three days of my stay in California were supposed to set routines well enough for the orchestra music to be written in Wyoming. I never asked how many of my pages survived the scramble of production. It would probably have taken a couple of expert analysts to answer the question, but that is not important to this story.

The story is that as I sent the arrangements back by mail from the ranch there was an exchange of telegrams with questions and answers about each one, and the last question very amusing. Music Director [Steiner] to Arranger: "I notice you didn't write anything for the harp in the waltz. Was this intentional?"

This may or may not be funny to anyone else, but the idea of writing eighty-eight pages of full orchestra score and not noticing that one had written nothing for the harp broke me up. Especially with the question coming from a music arranger. Arranger's answer to Director: "The chromatic nature of the melody of the waltz makes it very ungrateful for the harp. However, if you have a lady harpist who needs a job by all means let us not lack in gallantry."

Knowing Max, I had hit the nail on the head. He and his beautiful harpist were married not long after and stayed so till death did them part.

I told this story to Oscar Levant once and he quoted it in his first book.[41]

During the same year, Robert Simon's and my [opera] *Maria Malibran* was given an excellent performance by the forces of the Juilliard School. The cast and the orchestra were all students there, which means that a finer presentation is not likely to be seen anywhere in the world. It would be unfair to try to list the great musical figures that have come out of that ensemble, but every so often I still hear of a new success story that began there then.[42]

The danger to a composer in a finely prepared and performed work is interesting and real. When that rare thing happens, a piece played almost entirely as he meant it to sound, it is very hard for him to conceive of it being an unsuccessful work. This can start an argument, but intelligent self-criticism can only begin with a good performance, and the pleasure of being so well understood by the players and conductors should be kept in perspective.

Bob Simon and I felt we were on the right track when the audience reaction was good, but we just wanted to sit right down and do it over. I never got very deep into his new ideas, but mine were simple.

I had tried a formula that didn't work. The period of *Maria Malibran* was around 1820, and the whole score was designed as a concert of Gavottes,

---

[41]Levant's *A Smattering of Ignorance* (1940), where he also observed (p. 102) that "Steiner never particularly liked to have [Bennett] around, as it reminded him too keenly of the days at Harms when he was the number-three orchestrator behind Bennett."

[42]Josephine Antoine, Risë Stevens, and Annamary (Annamarie) Dickey joined the Metropolitan Opera roster shortly after their April 1935 performances in *Maria Malibran*. Floyd Worthington later taught at the University of Michigan and headed voice and opera studies at Interlochen.

Bourées, Gigues, and all the other rhythms of high society, over which the play was performed with speaking voices in rhythms written out to the last syllable and only sung when the character went into song in the course of the story.

After the first act of the dress rehearsal it was obvious that the speaking voices of the singers had no chance at all unless the orchestra played so softly that not an ear in the audience would have known if they played "Dixie" or "Home on the Range."

Goodbye Gavottes, Minuets, and Allemandes!

With the singers all speaking with loud voices the evening was far from a total loss. It felt like a pretty good show, but as a work of art it was only a nice try.[43]

When, after fourteen years of speakeasies and bathtub gin, the citizens got back their beer and booze, they went out by the third post of the back fence, dug up the money they were hoarding and spent it like drunken sailors. They sang what sounded like a German drinking song slightly syncopated, called "Happy Days Are Here Again," and the resulting circulation of money put movies back in production and music back in pictures. Many of my customers, including the irrepressible Jerome Kern, moved to California.

Sigmund Romberg, whose remarks were in no way less amusing than those of the famous Samuel Goldwyn, was one of the first to go. He wrote from there to Kern in New York, "Out here you are just a clog [cog] in the wheel." Sigmund—Rommy, he was called—was Tin Pan Alley's horrible example to most of the gods of the Golden Age. He was said to have played harmonium in little gypsy bands and hotel orchestras and to have remembered all of his melodies from the folk tunes of middle Europe. Kern asked me once if one of his melodies was too much like one used by Smetana or Weinberger and I said, "Do you care?"

He answered, "Yes, because that would give Romberg the right to live."

An idea of how seriously that was meant may be had from this. When Ben Bernie opened an engagement at the Roosevelt Hotel on Hollywood

---

[43]Bennett is needlessly self-critical. Of the reviewers who commented upon the stage-to-orchestra balance, nearly all felt it had benefited from Bennett's vast musical theater experience. *Maria Malibran* was staged again in August 1935 (with many veterans of the Juilliard production) by the Chautauqua Opera Association, and in 1964 by New York City's Community Opera, Inc. Simon went on to supply libretti for Albert Stoessel (*Garrick*, 1937) and Vittorio Giannini (their one-act *Beauty and the Beast*). Bennett and Simon considered some revisions, mostly of the libretto, to *Malibran* in the early 1970s, which were apparently never undertaken.

Boulevard with his big dance band, Jerome Kern put together a fancy potpourri of appropriate tunes as a tribute to Sigmund Romberg.

We went to a rehearsal of the band on the morning of the opening and I conducted the first run-through of Kern's piece. The band played it quite nicely at sight. Up to the podium came Ben Bernie, saying, "Russell, I hereby appoint you a committee of one to conduct the performance tonight. It has retards [*ritards*] in it and I haven't made a retard since I played [Sarasate's violin piece] *Zigeunerweisen* as a kid in West Virginia and they spit tobacco juice on my fingers."

I think Kern did actually have a good deal of respect for Romberg's talent but he loved all such yarns as the one about the lady listening to Offenbach's famous *Barcarolle* and saying, "Did you write that, Mr. Romberg?" and Rommy saying, "Not yet!"

And there's the story of Rommy at an orchestra rehearsal while they were reading a can-can in one of his shows. Hans Spialek,[44] the arranger, had put a bit of the "original" can-can of the Offenbach in the orchestration. When Rommy heard it he came running to Spialek saying, "Hans! That's not my music—it's Offenbach!"

Oscar Hammerstein was standing near and said, dryly, "What's the matter with Offenbach?"

Wherever Rommy got them his tunes were plenty hard to top by any of the others.[45]

"Just One of Those Things" was just one of those things for me. If memory serves, we were in Boston with *Jubilee*—music by Cole Porter. We may have staged the number in New York before leaving, but it hadn't been arranged for the orchestra and it had to be done in one night. It didn't look so very difficult; in fact it seemed like a very pleasant assignment as I watched June Knight and Charles Walters dance and sing it. That was before I noticed a new trend in the music of Porter. This, along with "Begin the Beguine" in

---

[44]Vienna-born Hans Spialek (1894–1983) was, like Bennett, a thoroughly-schooled composer. Spialek had come to the U.S. in 1924; a few months later, after obtaining a letter of introduction from violinist Maurice Nitke, he met Bennett and was quickly offered work at Chappell. Arranging credits shared by Bennett and Spialek include Kern's *Lucky* (1927) and *Sweet Adeline* (1929) as well as *Anything Goes* (1934) and many other Porter shows of the period. Spialek did little Broadway work after the mid-1940s, yet he and Bennett were among the veterans brought in to help score 1967's *Mata Hari.* Spialek was "rediscovered" during the early-1980s revival of interest in prewar musicals; in 1983 he helped reconstruct his orchestrations for a restoration of Rodgers and Hart's 1936 *On Your Toes.*

[45]Spialek's memoirs ("A Passing Note," 166) also include this "can-can" story, which took place during out-of-town preparations for Romberg's 1931 show *East Wind.*

the same show, was one of those long, long refrains that sound so short. To make things worse I'd sprained my back playing handball and had to prop up an aching body in bed and write with a pencil. The first singing refrain took four hours to score, making it 1:00 a.m.—three more of those sixty-four-measure strains to go, and rehearsal at 1:00 p.m. the same day. It got done, and the poor men that copied the parts from the score managed to deliver it on time, but I wonder how many listeners to this lovely, sophisticated nothing could guess what a crusher it was for us who wrote it out.[46]

One morning the telephone rang and I was surprised indeed to hear Henry Hadley calling me. He was well known as a composer. The Kansas City Symphony Orchestra had played his *North-South-East-West Symphony* while I was sitting at the last desk of the second violins. He was the man considered to have broken through the barrier of prejudice against American-born conductors of symphony orchestras. His fine career included conducting the New York Philharmonic with acclaim.

He asked me to join him at a meeting of composers and conductors in his studio a few days hence. I accepted and then sat a while trying to figure out how he happened to call me. Looking back now I realize that I may not have been the least qualified musician he would call, but that little bird that sits on the other shoulder from the one with the chips reminded me that I had never conducted *Götterdämmerung* and probably never would. As Sir Winston Churchill said of the young man, "He has so much to be modest about!"

The meeting at the Hadley studio—a palatial one of two rooms two floors high—was the beginning of the National Association for American Composers and Conductors. When Henry Hadley died not a great while after this his widow never moved from their studio and she continued for years and years to be the vital center of the Association. She was quite a famous singer—Inez Barbour—when they were married but Henry Hadley was her career to the end of her own life.

We all celebrated his birthday with a big party and a birthday cake on the twentieth of every December. As in about all of the groups, leagues, guilds and the like dedicated to the Fine Arts we left all of the hard work to the women while the men got their names in the papers.

I must say that the ladies came through for us. We were able for years to give five concerts a year, plus any number of teas and studio recitals, where many composers of ambitious music were able to get good audiences and a

---

[46]Bennett's "Just One of Those Things" anecdote appears in his "From the Notes of a Music Arranger" (*Theatre Arts*, November 1956, 89). *Jubilee* opened in New York on 12 October 1935.

sympathetic atmosphere. Keeping any kind of score on how many young and little-known musicians were really helped to bigger things would be complicated, but a good many of the works and the writers who've made headlines in contemporary music can be seen on our old programs.

Sigmund Spaeth was the first president of the National Association for American Composers and Conductors and served for eleven years. Among those who followed were William Schroeder and Herman Newman. Herman Newman was for many years music director of New York's radio station WNYC where many young musicians were given a chance to be heard and every year in February ten days of American music filled the air.

The last time I saw Henry Hadley was just a few days after Victor Herbert died.[47] Victor Herbert, a heavy man, was having trouble with his heart. The story as it was told to me was that he paid a visit to his doctor, whose office was at the top of a large flight of white stone steps. The doctor had just examined him and while saying goodbye at the end of the stairs he told his patient that his condition was quite satisfactory. Herbert thanked him, shook hands and fell down the stairs. The medical examiners said he had died before he fell.

Victor Herbert was not a stranger to the bottle and neither was Henry Hadley. In fact Hadley was famous for his partiality to it.

When I told him of how Herbert had died he said, "Why, only a few days ago I met Victor coming out of the publisher's and he said, 'Henry, my boy, you and I are going to have a drink!' Of course you know me, I said, 'No, thank you very much!'"

It seemed rather a short time before Hadley himself died.

The National Association for American Composers and Conductors had a longer life than nearly all of its contemporaries, but when Inez Hadley died it was easy to predict the end of NAACC.[48] We never were able to do much for conductors, even though our name promised we should. For composers we did or didn't, according to various estimates. Some said we were going nowhere. It was reported to me that Lukas Foss, a very brilliant composer and conductor, had once voted a loud "nay!" He gave me a lovely feed-line, because I opened the next meeting of our board by announcing the title of my new song: "Lukas Don't Like Us."

47Bennett is mistaken here. Operetta composer Herbert—also a fine conductor and a virtuoso cellist—died in 1924. Hadley passed away in 1937, four years after he had helped found the NAACC. Perhaps Bennnett is thinking of Gershwin, whose death preceded Hadley's by only eight weeks.

48. Mrs. Hadley died in 1971. The NAACC—which had upwards of 1200 members at its peak—was "revived" in 1975 as the National Association of Composers, U.S.A. (NACUSA).

Chapter Seven

With all my best clients heading west we never had a chance not to "go Hollywood."[1] The first assignment was, as seems befitting and proper, *Show Boat.* It was done at Universal Pictures, with several familiar faces on the screen. There were not many scenes still to be shot when I got there. Almost all the musical numbers were sung and danced to the original scores[2] and they had our old maestro Victor Baravalle in charge of the music.[3]

Paul Robeson was Joe, singing "Ol' Man River"; Charles Winninger as Captain Andy and Helen Morgan as Julie were very close to what they were on the stage. The film was directed by James Whale, a brilliant Britisher who was clearly fascinated by Paul Robeson. Paul was indeed a striking figure, a college football star with a highly developed mind and that voice and personality.

Jimmy Whale was inclined to take strong likes, and one of them was for music marked "agitato." You should have heard him pronounce the Italian word with his English accent. It was one of our music department jokes that

---

[1]Yet Oscar Levant felt that Bennett "never particularly relished working in Hollywood, going there principally out of friendship for Kern" (*A Smattering of Ignorance*, 120–21).

[2]Later (as with Rodgers & Hammerstein's *Oklahoma!*, *The King and I*, *South Pacific* and *The Sound of Music*), more-elaborate orchestrations would routinely be created for the film versions of stage musicals, using orchestras perhaps twice the (25–33 players) size originally used in the theater pit. An exception to this rescoring practice is *The King and I*'s "March of the Siamese Children"; a larger string complement was used on the soundtrack recording, but not a note of Bennett's Broadway orchestration was changed. Though Bennett didn't work on 1958's *South Pacific* film, he was included in its main-title credits because music director Alfred Newman insisted that "any musician who had contributed germinal arrangements, orchestrations or adaptations of a composer's music be given proper screen credit" (letter, Ken Darby to the editor, 6 June 1989—Darby was vocal director for the film).

[3]This was the second film version of *Show Boat.* The first (1929) had been filmed by Universal as a silent production. Following the public success of *The Jazz Singer*, however, sound was added to the picture's second half before release. With the exception of "Ol' Man River," however, all of the songs added were newly written—and none of them by Kern.

if there was any danger of a passage of background score being cut it could be saved by calling it an agitato. In Kansas City, Kansas, we called it a "hurry."

When I last saw a running of *Show Boat* at the studio, there were two sequences in it that were headed for the cutting room floor by general agreement. And yet, after the passage of some forty years, I happened to be at a screening of the picture again and both sequences were still in!

One was a minstrel number with Irene Dunne in a burnt-cork makeup; the other a box of Aunt Jemima's Pancake Flour on Queenie-the-cook's pantry shelf.

The original Queenie being played by Aunt Jemima (Tess Gardella), the shot crept in somehow, but pancake flour (so they all agreed) hadn't been born when the show boat "Cotton Blossom" floated on the Mississippi. Technical directors are generally supposed to commit suicide when they let such things slip by.

I learned something at the first sneak preview of that picture. It was in a suburb of Los Angeles of which I had never heard and the name of which I don't remember.[4] All I ever knew about studying audience reaction was based on how attentive an audience was. In the theater or the concert hall an admiring audience is silent except for the laughs you give them or the applause they give you.

At the preview of *Show Boat* the audience sounded as if the curtain hadn't gone up yet. Talk and coughs and private laughs and moving in and out of seats. Well, there were a few spots where scattered groups laughed in the right places, and one or two fair bits of applause, but if the picture had any success at all it was not a very big one, as far as I could see. I went to the studio the next morning wondering "who would blame who" and was met by beaming faces and self-congratulations in all directions. It was a smash.

I still have trouble believing they were all at the same running I was.

By this time New York and Hollywood played the parts of the two giants of the show world, each with a somewhat exaggerated respect for the other. It was normal to go to Hollywood and pretend that New York was just a bad dream one hoped to forget. And of course to return to New York and count all your California days as camping out. We built a house in Beverly Hills and it was a nice thing to do.

We learned, I think, that New York and Hollywood are good places to work—both of them—but not ideal places to live. This is a very personal matter, and I can hear two antiphonal choirs singing "I Happen to Like New York" and "California, Here I Come." I hear them in counterpoint, since my roots are exactly between them.

---

[4]Glendale's Alexander Theatre, late April 1936.

Missing something is anyone doing creative work without the stimulus of the charged air of New York and New Yorkers to keep him bearing down—to drive him to put more of himself into it as a defense against the noises and struggles around him. Something not to be described keeps one wanting to try and wanting to excel.

Missing something equally important are those who never see the sun sinking slowly behind the Pacific Ocean, with a nearness to eternal things singing inside. If this reads like poetry it is not ambitious as such, but the need to share the feeling of that view from the Pacific Palisades is an unsatisfied need.

Fortunately nobody says that the impression has to be put on paper. Nor the snow-capped mountains of the northeast horizon, nor the friendly warmth of the real Southern Californians. These things make you feel that a contribution to beauty is expected of you.

I'm not proud of my attitude as we boarded the Twentieth Century Limited and the Chief for an indefinite stay in Hollywood. The ambition to be a film composer was roughly the same as that to be a Broadway composer—somewhere around zero, but it looked like a good place to ply my trade. Also it was a good place for the old snobbery business to have a new burst of life.

This was even more ridiculous because the look down the nose was not from Symphony Hall, but from the Folies Bergères.

From that standpoint it is true that movies were many times cheaper at the box-office than Broadway shows. Also true that the man that took your ticket at the drive-in didn't insist on your being a Phi Beta Kappa. A film director seems always to be a man who has heard a thrilling climax and tried to put it on the screen without any of the material that made it a climax. Or so it was in those days.

But here is where the unfavorable comparison with the stage goes blithely out the window. I sat near Florenz Ziegfeld as he personally directed a scene with a very fine dance team in it. At the end of their routine the boy made his exit holding his partner high over his head. Ziegfeld made them come in the same way.

Things don't add up in the musical theater; they don't have to, but the list of casualties like the carefully planned climax of the two dancers' routines is very long.

Thinking of this it's hard to see why Hollywood should have made me a present of a shiny new chip for my shoulder. All I can say is that it was not a pose, not a psychiatrist's textbook case. When I was thirteen years old, Erich Korngold was also thirteen.[5] He wrote a quite brilliant piano sonata [often

---

[5]Actually, Korngold (1897–1957) was born three years after Bennett.

programmed by Artur Schnabel] and a much admired ballet score for orchestra at that age. I made a sort of hero of him and was hungry for news of his career as we grew up.

When we were still fairly young he wrote an opera, *Die tote Stadt*, which I admired as I looked forward to great things. After a long silence, somebody in Hollywood showed me a score Korngold had written for a sequence in a movie. It was pretty, the talent was still there, and I wanted to sit down and cry. So that's what became of my hero—"Sequence 14B, 2 minutes, 13 seconds!"

There's always a good chance that musical history will say I'm one hundred percent wrong, but every time Korngold won an Oscar,[6] all I could say was "Goodbye hero!"

I never met him.

Putting the chip back in its box, where it spends most of its time, the famous merchants of entertainment in Hollywood were as easy to respect and admire as anywhere else, and the creative minds had to have something on every pitch or lose.

That doesn't mean you could always keep a straight face at some of the ideas they gave you, but they knew their market and there's no danger of anybody having too much talent for his job in pictures.

The tales and characters there were as many and varied as those around Times Square, but they were spread out and dried out in the bright sunlight and you weren't always prepared for all the reactions you got.

If you worked on music there was one fact of life you had to allow for—two facts, really: a) everybody in a studio, from the top on down, was an authority on music, and b) to a man, they believed that every musician on the lot was sent there with a mission to wreck the picture if he could. No one would ever admit this, but it would come out sooner or later.

One of the all-time great film-cutters, Billy Hamilton, was for years a top decision maker for one of the major studios. When he heard a background score the nicest compliment I ever heard him pay the music was, "I don't mind it." If he said that you were in, and you could go home and get a night's sleep.

I once told him that about himself on the scoring stage just after we had made a take with the orchestra of the Main Title of *Fifth Avenue Girl.* He turned to his companion and protested, "What did I say about the music just now?" She (Mrs. Charles Laughton)[7] said, "You said it sounded like New York."

---

[6]Korngold received Academy Awards for *Anthony Adverse* (1936) and *The Adventures of Robin Hood* (1938).

[7]Actress Elsa Lanchester.

Maybe that was nicer, but I'd still liked to have heard him say he didn't mind it.

In every production one person was always your audience, to applaud, hiss, or doze. That person was known as "He." "He won't like that," "He wants more bird noises," "He liked the other print better," etc. "He" could be a director, a producer, the head of the studio or even a cutter, as in Billy Hamilton's case, but you always knew who he was, and he was your public. As in most of show business the authors and other creators of the whole product were down near the bottom of the totem pole.

That, however, was just about as good as being second in such a special dictatorship.

Stories about these benevolent despots can be told with real feeling only by those who have had occasion to square off with one of them for a real shoot-out. This is not to imply that the shoot-out has to be unfriendly, but if you thrive on unsolvable problems, Mr. Benevolent Despot will supply them.

Earl Mounce, another great cutter (of sound rather than picture), used to tell us of his all-night cutting sessions with Howard Hughes on the sound tracks of one tenor solo, where they had many takes of the same music. He would cut from one note that pleased the boss to one or more in another performance, then back or to another "take" completely until the eventual audience hears many performances during one aria. Just how good the final soundtrack was, I never heard, but the physical effort of both the cutter and the boss must have been hard to go through.

If you press in golf, you make bogeys—in the movies in those golden days, you pressed or went back to New York.

One of the absolute monarchs that I came to know fairly well was Mark Sandrich, who once gave me an interesting weekend. I was just wrapping up a fairly heavy assignment at Paramount Pictures when Paramount's neighbor R.K.O. Studios called me and asked me to come over and talk to Mark Sandrich about the last three reels of a musical picture they were doing.

The finale of the show was a long music-filled sequence and "He" didn't like the music. It was a George Gershwin musical,[8] but I have no idea just how much Gershwin music was in it by the time Mark threw it out. It was probably one of those endless routines improvised by a choreographer and a rehearsal pianist. Or maybe several of both.

Sandrich and I sat and ran the sequence in a projection room all morning. This was on a Thursday. At noon we parted and I took the figures and

---

[8] *Shall We Dance*, released 7 May 1937.

footages up to the music building where Percival Goldenson, the head librarian, had four music copyists waiting for me. We began the new score.

Shoving each page across the table to the four copyists as soon as it was written, it took somewhere between sixty and seventy hours to get the last note down. Every eight or so hours the copyists would yawn, stretch, and go home for some sleep, while four more men would slip into their seats and keep the factory rolling.

On Sunday night on the scoring stage, Nat Shilkret's sixty-man orchestra played and recorded the new music until midnight, then got up and went home, while a new orchestra did the same thing as the copyists—slipped in and took over.

The whole film, new music and all, had to be processed and shipped out in a matter of hours and the orchestra finished some time before noon. I finished writing at 8:20 a.m.

"He" liked it.

The picture at Paramount that just preceded this affair was one that made no memorable impression on our era, but had an impressive list of ingredients.[9] The authors were two men quite familiar to you if you've come this far with me: Oscar Hammerstein and Jerome Kern. Oscar wrote the story and the lyrics.

We had a cast of players that would adorn any program, headed by Irene Dunne and Randolph Scott. One of the lesser roles was played by a very young girl who sang two songs during the course of the tale. I was given the job of teaching the songs to the young person. She was intelligent and quite musical, but I was not deeply impressed until one of the studio bosses asked me to give her all the help I could. They were going to make her a great star.

This was astonishing, but they made good. She was Dorothy Lamour, whom they later wrapped in a sarong and she delivered.

The director of our picture was Rouben Mamoulian. He was not established as the absolute dictator, the "He" of the picture. One or two other pretenders to the throne had certain credentials, but Rouben did very well indeed, considering the surroundings.

Jerome Kern fell seriously ill just as the show went into production, so all the music we needed had to come from me. This is nothing new to a music arranger, but Mamoulian was very critical of the music all through the shooting. One morning my telephone rang and someone asked me when I could get the music ready for one of the songs. The answer was "day after tomorrow."

The following day the music supervisor assigned to our production by the studio came by and told me we were asked to go to Rouben Mamoulian's

---

[9] *High, Wide and Handsome,* released 21 July 1937.

office. When we got there Rouben made a speech about all orders having to come from his office and someone had scheduled a recording for Thursday with Irene Dunne and told him about it and we weren't going to work that way and so on, and so on. This was the time to put into words just what I thought of the entire motion picture industry, but I looked at the amused expression in the eyes of the music supervisor, Sigmund Krumgold, and suddenly saw how to get along in the movies.

At the recording of the song "Can I Forget You," Rouben complained to me about the accompaniment. On the screen Irene was in a rowboat as she sang and Kern had given me a little waving figure that continued all through the refrain. With distaste in his face, Rouben asked me why that was in there. I told him what the composer had told me: it was to suggest waves gently tapping the boat. Whereupon Rouben asked a bit sarcastically, "Well! Which side of the boat are they tapping?"

Last word would have been easy, but I had known him for quite a long time so I just laughed at his joke.

Rouben Mamoulian was a fine artist and he had plenty of trouble with *High, Wide and Handsome* without any more from me.[10]

As we went through the big musical job at the end of the engagement, Rouben became my staunchest friend and supporter. Even if that had not come to pass, I should look back on the association with joy because of a party he gave for all of us who worked on the picture plus a few glamorous friends, including his father and mother. He introduced the two of them with a toast and his father got up with dignity and said, "I do not speak English very well, so I will speak to you in Russian and my son will translate what I say." He proceeded with a nice polite speech.

Rouben got up and said something like "My father says that in all his life he had never before been to such a dull party, and he says that he wouldn't mind it so much if he hadn't brought his dear wife with him to sit and suffer through the whole evening."

Of course Father sprang to his feet protesting "My son has translated very badly!" and went on to give his own speech in quite good English.

At no gathering with Irving Caesar, Harry Ruby, or any other comedian have I ever heard such a roar of laughter as went up at Rouben's "translation."

Mark Sandrich and I had another session in a projection room some time after the one reported a bit ago. We were looking at a picture starring Ginger

---

[10]Mamoulian, born in Armenia, had been brought to the U. S. by George Eastman to direct at his Rochester, N.Y., theater. His American credits include plays (many for the Theatre Guild, including the original *Porgy*), films (among them Rodgers and Hart's 1932 *Love Me Tonight*), musicals (*Oklahoma!*), and operas (*Porgy and Bess*).

Rogers, a girl I had known very well on Broadway. Her first two Broadway engagements—at least as a featured player—were *Top Speed* and *Girl Crazy*, and I'm sure she won't mind my telling you that the dancers in the chorus were not overwhelmed by her talent as a dancer. They adored her and spent quite a bit of time helping her with certain steps, but I heard more than one not predicting much success.

Show business is full of such stories, but that this lovely little comédienne with somewhat unwilling feet should become the dancing partner of one of the age's greatest is still hard to believe. Having written thousands and thousands of notes for them to dance to, both together and separately, I can assure you that this was not done with mirrors. It must have been hard work and faith.

This, however, is not a story about Ginger Rogers, star of *Fifth Avenue Girl.* That was the film Mark Sandrich and I were running because I was to do a background score for it. While we looked at the picture Mark had beside him a very vivid young person who laughed at all the funny places and was as good as a whole audience when it came to reactions and timings. After the running was over and Mark had told me all the ideas he had about the music we parted and the vivid person walked out with me and along the studio lanes, chatting away as though we were old friends.

I don't think her language was quite as rich as Frank Tinney's was in Long Branch, New Jersey, but it was full of the allusions and nuances of the farmers and laborers I was raised with in Missouri.

Then all of a sudden she said, "Well, I have to love you and leave you!," turned and made off toward the main gate. It just happened that the head man of the studio, Pandro Berman, was coming up in the other direction. I said to him, "That's quite a gal. What's her name?" He found it hard to believe I didn't know who she was but I always had trouble knowing which of those famous blondes was which unless I had known them on Broadway. I reminded him of that fact and he laughed and said, "This one is Carole Lombard."

Of course I had suspected that, just from knowing her reputation. One morning soon after that she came out to the Bel Air Country Club to play tennis with Clark Gable. I was there talking to a friend who'd been playing golf and had her two young children with her. I told her that the air might be filled with some pretty low language, but she said, "Oh, don't worry! We're quite used to things like that."

However, Carole Lombard had a way of topping every dirty expression that society had come to accept with something that had not been accepted, and after a few tennis strokes the echo rang with something that made my friend Marion Watson say, "I think I'll take my children home."

We lived in several places in Beverly Hills for quite some time before any other idea appealed to us, but eventually we bought a lot on North Arden Drive and built a house. Our architect was a friend of a couple of our oldest friends in Los Angeles, Andrew Blackmore and Madeline.

Madeline was a favorite as a student at the Merrill School and her husband, Drew Blackmore, was one of the honest-to-goodness vice presidents of the Bank of America when he retired. They were not only long friends of ours, but they had a fine tennis court as a part of the backyard.

He is a fine example of the Los Angeles businessman that has already had to take bows twice in these pages. She went on with her education, became a Phi Beta Kappa, and after their two daughters were married, became a Ph.D. and was on the faculty of the University of Southern California.

They recommended architect Sumner Spaulding, having known and liked his houses. Like all artists, he had to do something a little new to him every house he built, but we were quite happy with our new home.

The only completely unsuccessful feature was the badminton court. Because of space it had to be facing east and west and you can't do that, especially where the sun shines as it does there. We might never have tried to play badminton anyway—we belonged to the Los Angeles Tennis Club by that time and "who could ask for anything more?"

"All artists have to do something a little new to themselves," and with no particular modesty I number myself among them in this little episode, quoted by Arlene Croce in her charming book on Astaire and Rogers.[11]

When Fred and Ginger were filming *Swing Time*, the composer of the songs [Kern] called me on the telephone to say that they needed a new dance—"Go over and see Fred and find out what he wants." Composers are supposed to give their arrangers a little more than that, but they don't always do it.

After a short visit with Astaire I came up with the "Waltz in Swing Time" and Fred told me later that there were so many notes in it they had to get two pianos before they could play it. Hal Borne, who played piano for the rehearsals, added a nice treatment of one of the songs in the show, "A Fine Romance," as a sort of middle section.[12] The number was a hit with everybody until they heard my orchestration.

I had decided that the movies were ready for a new sound. They may have been but Fred and Ginger were not, at least not for the sounds I gave

---

[11] *The Fred Astaire and Ginger Rogers Book* (New York: Galahad, 1972).

[12] Arlene Croce concurs (*Astaire and Rogers*, 112) that the dance number, "The Waltz In Swing Time," contains "glancing references to [Kern's] score for the film, but it is the composition of Robert Russell Bennett."

them. I had to abandon what was new to me and let all the new come from their flying feet.

When I saw the way the picture was shot I had to be glad we did it that way.

The heads of state at R.K.O. Pictures had a great answer for a man under contract as an arranger who was not looking for screen credit as a composer. They put me on many "B" pictures—a type of movie they did with small budgets and quite a big circulation as fillers for double features or something of the kind. (Again, I don't really know what I am talking about.)[13] If I wished to enjoy seeing my name on the screen it was on these—big. I don't think I met the man that ran this department[14] but he was quoted several times as a fan of mine.

Two films for which I did quite a big job of anonymous music were officially by two of the best of all time, Alfred Newman and Franz Waxman. They were at the height of their careers and were overworked. The pictures were good ones: *The Hunchback of Notre Dame* and *Rebecca.*[15]

Sharing a score with one of these great fellows was an education, an education you can't get from any book or school. They knew all the pitfalls and all the answers of the profession. I used the word "anonymous"; perfect background scoring must be anonymous. It must sneak into the pulse of the viewer and stay out of his conscious mind. Franz Waxman ran a film with his music in it for me once. At the end of the picture he started to talk about the end of the music. It, he said, was the first example of a score that finished with two trumpets, loud, on a sustained dissonance—B and C, for instance, a half-tone apart.

I hadn't noticed it. All I noticed was that the picture ended just right. Of course, after he spoke, I could go over the last part of the music in my mind and realize what he had done, but it never had a chance of being heard while the story was coming to its end. The film was [1935's] *The Bride of Frankenstein.*

Working on the West Coast with that one-man audience (one to each picture) makes everybody more of a specialist than a trouper. All of the component parts of a production are manufactured in separate factories and you can easily see why an absolute monarchy is the best set-up to make the clear and intelligible story lines of most great films possible.

---

[13]These 1938–1939 RKO films include *Annabel Takes a Tour, Fugitives for a Night, Career, Fifth Avenue Girl* (with Ginger Rogers), *Pacific Liner* (for which "Russell Bennett" received an Academy Award nomination) and *Stanley and Livingstone.*

[14]Probably Lee Marcus, who headed RKO's "B" pictures unit in the late 1930s.

[15]Bennett also helped orchestrate Newman's music for *Gunga Din* (RKO, 1939) and *Brigham Young, Frontiersman* (Fox, 1940).

Calling on the muse, without a clear idea of just what to ask her for, leaves you with no ready answer if the high one says you missed the point. And once in a while a perfectly good "high one" misses it and we all have to man the life boats.

There was one of the R.K.O. pictures that had an especially elaborate and complicated musical episode, mostly set in a ballroom, with dances and fights and tender moments and scenes within scenes, calling for yards of music. The dancing had been shot to popular recordings of the day and new tunes had to be fitted to the movement, and all the little dramas important to the story had to look as though our music was in their ears as they fought, loved, ate, or whatever else.

On the appointed day we recorded the whole reel or so with a good big orchestra. As soon as we had a complete playing on the tape[16] I was called off the podium to go over to the producer's corner, where he cleared his throat and started in: "Now, my value to this film is to see that everything that goes into it is exactly right. Right?"

"Right."

"Well, I don't think this is right. What can you do about it?"

It takes a little time and thought to answer that question when you have devoted hours and hours to deciding what *was* right and putting it on paper note by note. For a moment you wish sincerely that you had taken the job in the lumber yard instead of practicing the piano and learning music.

But, as set forth some paragraphs ago, there is no guarantee that every department in the studio is reading the same meaning into every scene that was intended and I just accepted the idea that I was miscast. I said, after a moment of thought, "We have a preview day after tomorrow night. There's no time for a full new sequence now. Let me make a clean take of this and preview with it while we try to find out what you want."

It was agreed after some argument and, after sizing up Mr. Producer and the whole situation, I suggested calling in one of the best known "hot" arrangers to work with them—producer, director, choreographer, etc.—and give it his all.

Hollywood always insisted on typing everybody, and the word "hot"—later called "cool" and no doubt something else after that—was greeted with nods and smiles by the monarch and his coterie.

So the new version was written and recorded while I was struggling with new headaches in Studio 5, 7, 8, or 12. One day I got a call to be at the private projection room of the Top Man of the whole studio at 9:00 the next morning.

---

[16]Actually, magnetic tape recording was not used in the U.S. until after World War II; soundtrack recordings in the 1930s were typically "mastered" on lacquer discs.

Wondering what was up I went where I was told and saw all the "brass" assembled as the lights went down and a scene started to run on the screen.

It looked familiar, and should, being my old friend the ballroom sequence with the new score, and a good one, I thought. As the lights went up I was beginning to feel a little important that they should run it for my approval and I said "Great." But Mr. President said, "Now run the other one."

The other one was of course my version that had been thrown out, but the picture had been cut and re-cut until nothin' fit nothin'. Apparently that didn't bother them because someone said enthusiastically, "Oh, yes!" and somebody else said "There's no comparison!"

Now I was about to be a hero until I said, "Thank you, but there's no guarantee that the music can be cut to fit the picture as it now is."

Such chaos being nothing new to them, the Big Bosses broke up and started toward their offices, but little Mr. Producer came over and said he guessed he was wrong about it and would I please see what I could do. Of course I would see what I could do because it was my job, and in any case who could prove he was wrong? He just didn't like the music.

Some fourteen hours with a good, patient music-cutter resulted in a re-built sound track—four bars here, one chord here, a rather unconvincing modulation somewhere else—and the opus went to posterity. I never heard how the picture did, and I never saw "him" again. Maybe it wouldn't have been any better working at the lumber yard at that.

One thing we needed and didn't have at R.K.O. Pictures when I started a steady job there, was a real theater conductor, especially as long as Fred Astaire was on the lot. Playing music to keep hoofers happy is only one of the subtle talents the Broadway music directors have in their blood. Our so-often-cited Victor Baravalle had at this time had a long siege with a defective lung that kept him inactive, but I told Pan [Pandro S.] Berman that Baravalle would be a good gamble for two or three pictures coming up and Vic was engaged. It turned out to be a good move.

When he came to work he told us a priceless story about his dog, Max. Max was a big German Shepherd who lived with Vic and Alice Baravalle in Bel Air. While Vic was ill he had to spend most of his time in bed, and one of Max's duties when Alice let him out the front door in the morning was to bring in the morning paper and give it to Vic.

One morning he was out a long time and came in without the paper. So Vic, from his bed, gave Max a good scolding and told him to go right back out there and bring in that newspaper.

This time he stayed out even longer.

Finally Alice went to the window, looked out, and called, "Vic, come here! You've got to come here and look!"

Vic got out of bed, got to the window and saw Max sitting in the front yard surrounded by a dozen of the neighbors' morning papers, trying to figure out which one to take in.

One of Baravalle's first assignments was *A Damsel in Distress*, with the rather unexpected combination of Fred Astaire and Joan Fontaine featured.[17] It had songs by George Gershwin and his brother Ira.

During the filming, we did one of the numbers on location at Arturo's Ranch, a good many miles from 780 Gower Street, where the factory was. Another famous New York (and London) music director had been taken on by R.K.O., one whose career dated even further back than Vic's. He was an Englishmen named Frank Tours. That career would call for a separate book, but he went with us to Arturo's Ranch just as a kibitzer.

Vic and I were there to take notes on the routine of the song "A Foggy Day (in London Town)." On the way out to the ranch Frank Tours took me in his car and Baravalle drove alone in his. Some twenty miles out of Los Angeles Vic stopped his car at the side of the road and Frank said, with a lot of worry in his voice, "What do you suppose is wrong?" We stopped and Vic got out of his car and came back beside ours.

He looked up and said, "Frank, what do you suppose the boys at the Lambs Club [in New York] would say to having to come out forty-five miles to take down a routine?"

Then he got back in his car and went on.

Fred Astaire sang the song on an island in a little lake on Ranchero Arturo. I wasn't curious enough to find out what the location had to do with the song, but it was interesting to sit on the bank of the lake with George Stevens, the director of the picture. He talked a good deal about Joan Fontaine. He had great faith in her future, but it seemed the heads of the studio didn't agree with him.

Here was an opposite situation to the case of Dorothy Lamour, where we of the working class had so little idea of her future glamour. I certainly agreed with the director. It seemed utterly impossible to miss the beauty and distinction of the damsel in (temporary) distress.

Her career since then has certainly answered any critics that Director Stevens might have had in mind, but as for me, I had seen her once before

---

[17]Fontaine had some dance training but was ill-at-ease partnering Astaire in the film. Of *A Damsel in Distress* she wrote: "For me the title was appropriate" (*No Bed of Roses*, 1978, 101).

while they were shooting her in a scene with Mario Lanza. She wore a long blond wig and looked like Mélisande. From then on she could do no wrong.[18]

When I wrote to my librettist, Robert A. Simon, from our new home I set the street address to music. Five-Oh-Five North Arden Drive fit the first two measures of the children's march from *Carmen* perfectly. Of course he wasn't going to let me get away with that. Back came his answer with his own address, a perfect fit for the last two measures of the same strain—One-Fifty-One West Eighty-Sixth.

He wrote another stage piece for music, a story by O. Henry called "The Enchanted Kiss," and I spent quite a stretch of time setting it to music. Every time a few days or even hours were free for it, it would gain a few pages and finally it was a complete one-act opera with a big role for a strong baritone.

When it was done I did my usual great selling job on it—none. This time there was a good excuse: we did the whole piece with Lawrence Tibbett in mind as our hero, but it took me so long to finish the music that he had retired before I could show it to him.[19]

Oh, well, there's still a little room with the other things in the storage vault. Two nice commissions for symphonic works were given me in and around this time. One was from the League of Composers and the other from the Columbia Broadcasting System. For the League of Composers I did a quite ambitious scherzo for orchestra called *Hollywood.* It was full of rhythm and quite warm melody, but was scuttled by a section written personally by the chip (on my shoulder).[20] The other piece, *Eight Etudes* for Orchestra, was fairly successful and gets played once in a while. Working hard in the soft, lazy atmosphere of the southland (they sometimes call it) without New York tension to kick you out of bed was rather an experience.

[Bennett's *Eight Etudes* received its radio premiere on 17 July 1938, with Howard Barlow conducting the CBS Orchestra. It was acclaimed by both audiences and critics in Philadelphia, New York, Pittsburgh, Chicago, and Los Angeles, but has regrettably never been recorded. Bennett described the composition as serving an orchestra "in much the same way as etudes for solo instruments serve those instruments; in other words, to present an attractive exterior filled with problems in orches-

---

[18]Lanza and Fontaine starred in *Serenade* (Warner Brothers, 1956).

[19]Begun in the late 1930s, *The Enchanted Kiss* was not completed until the mid-1940s. It was premiered on a WOR broadcast on 30 December 1945, but has never been staged. Bennett is in error about Tibbett's retirement, as he sang at the Metropolitan until 1950.

[20]This "Introduction and Scherzo" promptly received its broadcast premiere (Frank Black and the NBC Symphony, 15 November 1936) as well as a 1943 Carnegie Hall performance by the National Orchestral Association, the city's best-known "training orchestra" for young professionals.

tral playing, in balance, in conducting, and (in the matter of orchestral color) for the composer himself." Each movement was provided with a dedication after its completion, the dedicatees being Walter Damrosch, Aldous Huxley, Noel Coward, pitcher Carl Hubbell, "all dictators" ("a parade of discordant and wrangling uniforms" passing by), the Grand Lama, artist Eugene Speicher, and "the ladies."]

At first glance hard work on a piece of music should be nothing unusual to an old workhorse who meets deadlines every other day, but that kind of hard work turns its back on climates and atmospheric conditions. The work that is affected is what you do far into the night and tear up the next morning.

[Late in 1937, Bennett joined forces with colleagues Johnny Green, Adolph Deutsch, Leigh Harline, Leonid Raab, Walter Scharf, and Leo Arnaud in forming the American Society of Music Arrangers; Bennett served as its first president. The ASMA ratified its constitution and bylaws in May of the following year and quickly received the endorsement of the American Federation of Musicians. The group—still active and now headquarted in Los Angeles—has done much to improve the working conditions, per-page rates, and health/pension benefits for AFM arrangers. It has been less successful in fulfilling its goal of obtaining compulsory shared copyrights between songwriters and arrangers, however; the work of AFM orchestrators, with few exceptions, remains "for-hire," one-time-payment employment.]

We settled down in our own home in Beverly Hills and became Californians except for one detail. Every evening after dinner Louise and I walked from Arden Drive along Santa Monica Boulevard to the shopping part of town to buy a paper or some necessity and walked back. As far as we could tell nobody else ever walked anywhere. That must have branded us as foreigners. The whole trip was quite a bit over a mile.

Daughter Jean finished high school at Marlboro and was much too pretty and popular for her own good. I don't honestly believe there has ever been an ugly seventeen-year-old girl, but some of them abuse the privilege. The trouble with the real beauties is their natural assumption that nothing else is expected of them. There seems no way for them to absorb that searching French proverb: the more you look at an ugly woman, the less she is ugly; the more you look at beautiful woman, the less she is beautiful.

But sayings like that are for people who think, and thinking makes wrinkles in your forehead. This may sound sarcastic, but all it is [is] the age-old amusement each generation furnishes the former one. Amusement and certain uncertainties.

Bennett playing his violin outside his Beverly Hills home, 1939. Photo courtesy of Jean Bennett.

The one-time second violinist in the Kansas City Symphony would tell his readers decades later: "The only way to have a real instinct for violin music is to get your hands on a violin. . . . Not only in your arranging, but in such conducting you need to do, is an affectionate acquaintance with the feel of a string instrument a great advantage."

The story of Whiskey and Tempo should be included here. It's not about music, nor even about the theater, movies or television. It's about love.

A friend in New York raised miniature pincers, tiny dogs that certainly do look like their big relative, the Doberman pincers, One of them was given to us; we called her Whiskey and took her to California when she was two years old. One day some friends in California gave us a black and white kitten we named Tempo. The cat and the dog hated each other and it took many anxious days before they would consent to live under the same roof. Then, as so often happens, they began to adore each other and invent games to play together. Before long, when we entertained friends, we didn't need to play bridge or have string quartets or charades. We all just sat in our chairs and watched the show the two of them put on.

One of them would hide and the other would pretend he couldn't find her (or vice-versa—Tempo was a boy cat). They had many variations on that theme. We had curtains over certain windows that reached clear to the floor and Tempo, the cat, would get behind a curtain and stick out a paw. Whiskey would dive for it but never catch it. It would disappear and come out miraculously somewhere quite a distance away. This went on as long as it got big laughs, then they would change the routine to something else—with a ball, or with a long string, or just romp as only cats and dogs can. At a given point they walked side by side out toward the kitchen.

The assembled would start to express their appreciation but I had to stop them and tell them they hadn't seen the grand finale yet. The finale was always the same. Tempo would come out alone and curl up right in the center of the room, pretending to sleep. Now came Whiskey, nonchalant, until she discovered the fluffy ball in the middle of the room. Suddenly she would stiffen, crouch, and make a great dash for Tempo, who went straight up—it looked like almost to the ceiling. Whiskey couldn't stop on the waxed floor and slid all the way to the wall.

Then they walked elegantly out, side by side again, to the kitchen. That was the grand finale.

Nobody taught them any part of this act. They wrote the whole script.

One day the little doggie turned up with one jaw badly swollen, obviously a sick pup. She was well enough to show her delight when we took her in the car, and alert enough to try to hide when the car stopped in front of the vet's. All dogs seem to love automobiles and hate dog hospitals.

That evening the doctor called to say Whiskey had died of a streptococcus infection. We were all practically in mourning. No one was prepared for such a turn of events.

Tempo the cat was nowhere to be seen.

Cats being cats, we were only mildly puzzled, but after three or four days something had to be wrong. Not with anything specifically in mind, I wandered up the broad alley behind our house and found Tempo, lying under a tree by the hedge fence.

No reason for his death could be found.

[Bennett's special fondness for cats deserves specific mention; his New York office was populated by dozens of feline figurines he'd received as gifts. A favorite was "Perky," given to him by his family in the late 1920s while working in London. The Drury Lane Theatre's rehearsal pianist, a man named Perkins ("Perky" to the chorus girls) was the animal's namesake. The cat often accompanied Bennett in his travels, receiving repairs as needed, and—when a glass eye had been lost—eventually sporting a Bennett-applied eye patch. Bennett regularly brought the

Bennett cradling cat figurine "Perky." Photo © 1940, Newsweek, Inc.

A whimsical pose with his friend and confidant, publicizing WOR radio's *Russell Bennett's Notebook.*

> statuette to the podium for recording sessions or when guest-conducting, noting that observers would "all kind of laugh and put it down as an eccentricity of some sort. Which it jolly well is!"[21] A charming photograph of Bennett and Perky accompanied a 1940 *Newsweek* article spotlighting the composer's *Notebook* radio show.]

When we were working on the music of *The Story of Vernon and Irene Castle,* Victor Baravalle said to me, "This is my—what do they call it—my swan song." He laughed, but I thought of how ill he had been and I knew he was serious. I said, "Vic, if I hadn't practically pulled you out of bed to do this work, you wouldn't be thinking those thoughts."

He was not in the habit of making pretty speeches but was obviously sincere when he assured me that he was grateful and happy. During the last

---

[21]John Ferriss, "Mr. Music and His Pal," *New York Sunday News,* 29 December 1968.

week of recordings, as he was conducting one of the biggest musical sequences I was asked to come out of the sound room to the conductor's stand, where Vic said, "Russ, you have to take over. I've got a hemorrhage."

He died three or four days later. He was a rather rough-hewn character, but he had the quality as a conductor that made your instrument begin playing before you were conscious of playing it—just as the violinist said of Stokowski.

The Story of Vernon and Irene Castle turned out to be a pretty good picture with Fred Astaire and Ginger Rogers floating through one of the prettiest true stories of the theater. We had the real Irene Castle as a consultant, with her office next to mine in the studio. They were a little ahead of me on the calendar—I saw them dance together in an Irving Berlin show, *Watch Your Step*, when it was in Kansas City.[22]

One of the other things I remember about the show is Frank Tinney doing a bit alone on the stage when the stage-hands let something drop with a big crash behind the scene. Tinney interrupted his monologue for an aside to the audience: "They're just bringing in Mrs. Castle's salary."

Two interesting trips to New York were squeezed in between jobs at R.K.O. Studios. One was by train and the other by plane. Nadia Boulanger paid a visit to New York and I went alone by train to be at a gathering of her pupils and friends. When my Union Pacific train went through Ogden, Utah, Mr. and Mrs. Samuel Dushkin and Mr. Igor Stravinsky got into my car. The Dushkins left us in Chicago and Stravinsky and I went straight to New York. I dropped him off by taxi at his hotel on Park Avenue. He was not as comfortable in English then as he became later. His French was complete.

I've been told that he only discussed his own compositions with people he liked and I must have qualified. It was a fine three days' train trip for me.[23]

Mlle. Boulanger was her same incredible self, with her excellent English and her gift for saying the right thing. I invited Boulanger and Stravinsky for a Chinese dinner the next evening, but had to back out of it. I found I was needed in Hollywood right on schedule.

---

[22] *Watch Your Step* was Berlin's first (1914) complete score for a Broadway production.

[23] Stravinsky originally asked Bennett to score his 1942 *Circus Polka* (a "ballet" for elephants) for the unique instrumentation of the Ringling Brothers–Barnum & Bailey Circus Band. Bennett, unavailable, recommended film composer David Raksin (*Laura*, *Forever Amber*), who was promptly engaged by Stravinsky. Raksin had worked alongside Bennett as a theater orchestrator in New York in the 1930s, lastly on Cole Porter's 1936 *Red, Hot and Blue*. He praised Bennett's enormous gifts and technical mastery: "Working with Russell on a project was like having a 200-watt amplifier when you only needed twenty watts!" (David Raksin interview with the editor, Los Angeles, August 1992).

Nadia Boulanger arriving in New York, 1938. From the Cleveland Public Library Photograph Collection/Corbis. Used by permission.

On this visit to America by the famed French musician, Boulanger became the first woman to conduct the Philadelphia Orchestra, and she directed the premiere of Stravinsky's "Dumbarton Oaks" Concerto in Washington, D.C. Another highlight was her appearance as organ soloist with the New York Philharmonic-Symphony.

The other trip (by plane) was on business. Monkey business, as far as Hollywood was concerned. New York was bearing down on a world's fair and one of the features of the fair was to be a fountain and fireworks display every evening at what was called the Lagoon of Nations. It would need big-sounding music and there were many ideas as to where the music was to come from.

Olin Downes, well-known music critic of the *New York Times*, was consultant for the music of the whole fair. His assistant and advisor was Gretl Urban, our friend of many years. One day Gretl phoned me and said everyone of influence seemed to have a different candidate for the music job on the fountains and Olin Downes thought that if I would sneak into New York for one day, it could be settled there and then.

I took the first flight I could get and went to dinner at the home of the Chairman of the Board of Design, Architect Stephen Frank Vorhees. He himself had to go to an architect's dinner that evening, but we shook hands and I had dinner with Mrs. Vorhees and M. Jean Labatut, who was to create the various spectacles of the fountain show. Jean Labatut, a remarkable personality from the south of France, was a Professor of Architecture at Princeton University.

As we sat down to dinner Mrs. Vorhees said, "I hope you don't mind cats. My two cats must be invited to come in. They won't do anything—just sit in that chair over there while we dine." I said, "Invite them in and see what they do."

She said, "What will they do?"

I said, "Please do let them come in. You'll see."

The door was opened and in walked Gil and Coco, two of the most gorgeous pussycats I have ever seen. They walked single-file around the table once, then one of them stopped on my left, the other stopped on my right and they met on my lap.

I got the job writing the music for the Lagoon of Nations, New York World's Fair, 1939–1940.[24]

The flight back to California was hindered by bad weather. We put down at Columbus, Ohio, instead of Louisville, Kentucky. Not more than twenty minutes out of Columbus we turned back and were taken to a hotel for the night. Even with all this delay I don't think anybody missed me in the studio.

In early Spring 1939 my family of three checked in at the Hotel La Salle on East 60th Street, New York, where I started the composing of music to be heard coming out of two enormous loud-speakers surrounded by lights, fireworks and incredible designs of water [as well as dozens of huge, gas-fired flames].

Feeding the music into the loud-speakers, about a thousand feet away, was to be a concert band of fifty musicians, conducted by Joseph Littau[25] and synchronizing with every mood and movement of the display as created by Jean Labatut. The first show was called *The Spirit of George Washington*.[26] There were four others, one every week or so, during the season.

[Two other band works, his *Fountain Lake Fanfare* (*March*) and *A TNT Cocktail*, were heard at the Fair's opening-day festivities. The magnificent World's Fair Band included eight members of the Metropolitan Opera Orchestra, four from Toscanini's NBC Symphony, three from the New York Philharmonic-Symphony and twenty-eight Sousa Band alumni. Bennett proudly described the group as "one of the best {concert bands} ever assembled"—it included Del Staigers on cornet, Simone Mantia on euphonium, and clarinetists Edmund Wall and Ross Gorman. It was Gorman who, early in his lengthy tenure with Paul Whiteman's

[24]Bennett's official position was "Consultant—Board of Design."

[25]The Fair was "held over" for 1940; the second season's band was led by cornetist Eugene LaBarre (1888–1956), an alumnus of the bands of Sousa and Pryor who was then conductor of the New York Police Band.

[26]The Fair's 30 April 1939 opening day was selected to mark the sesquicentennial of Washington's inauguration—in New York—as the nation's first president.

band, had contributed his trademark glissando to the opening of Gershwin's *Rhapsody in Blue* at its 1924 premiere.]

The best review the music got was one evening when a few of the very top directors of the fair's main features gathered for an official dinner after the fair had been open two or three weeks. We finished the dinner in time for us all to go out and stand with the crowd watching the display. Somewhere in the middle of it a young girl standing with a crowd in front of us suddenly jumped up and down and cried, "This music is marvelous!"

Back in California during that summer, my wife Louise went to a soothsayer for the fun of it, or talked to one at a party and that person said to her, "I see a great big W! Is your husband going to work for Warner Brothers?"

Alfred Wallenstein was the musical director of radio station WOR [1936–1945] and was later to be the conductor of the Los Angeles Symphony Orchestra for many years. Wallenstein, or Wally we all call him, was a close friend of Arturo Toscanini and, in my humble opinion, one of the greatest. His orchestra at WOR was certainly, man for man, as fine as any I ever heard. When Sir Thomas Beecham broadcast a concert with them once, he came to rehearsal an hour and a half late. As he started to rehearse he stopped after some twenty bars, turned to the producer and said, "Well, they make up in quality for what they lack in quantity!" He turned to the orchestra and said, "All right, gentlemen! The broadcast is at eight this evening. I'll see you then."

Alfred Wallenstein and his wife Virginia had a country place for some time near Red Bank, New Jersey. Louise and I spent a weekend there with them one summer. One of the features easiest to recall was a very large dog and his much smaller companion—Maggie his name was.

They also had a rather undistinguished cat who disappeared one day and had them somewhat worried. I volunteered toward evening to find their cat and I did. Those who know some of the fastidious habits of pussycats will appreciate the little scene I found quite a ways from the house. A neighbor farmer had just fertilized one of his fields with one of the best-known fertilizers. There was Puss, patiently pawing at the edge of the field, trying to bury it. After all, cats have a moral code about such things.

Wallenstein's career had a rather unexpected coda. Virginia was a excellent pianist and was his accompanist when he was primarily a virtuoso cellist. He was for a good many years principal cellist of the New York Philharmonic [under Toscanini]. Years after, when he had been long established as one of the most distinguished of maestri, she had a massive heart attack and died after a long struggle.

The next time I saw him I asked him what he was doing in music and he said, "Nothing. I've just been taking care of her." As far I can tell he has retired and stayed retired.[27]

None of us who know him ever realized he was that much of a one-woman man even though she looked like the heroine of a best-seller novel and had the personality to go with it.

He has made a great many very successful recordings. We were talking together once about composers and conductors and I made the somewhat pompous point that composers have a chance to live after their lives have ended; when a conductor dies, he's dead. He laughed heartily and agreed with me. But now it is no longer true. No matter what recordings do to music, conductors and performing artists have a passport to immortality.

Radio Station WOR, at Maestro Wallenstein's suggestion, offered me this beautiful orchestra, occasional soloists, and half-hour broadcasts over the Mutual Broadcasting System once a week, at which I would do the commentary and play anything I cared to write or present.

Again I thought of Alfred Newman when he heard a big, beautiful orchestra in the theater and said, "If I could have an orchestra like this, I'd work for a dollar and a half a week!" My salary at WOR was considerably more than that, but not so much as to inspire any dreams of breaking even. However, the whole thing was so much in line with my deep-down instincts about music that I never had a thought of turning the offer down.

We went back to Hollywood to sell our house and ship our worldly goods back to New York in time to try to make good with the California fortuneteller, who saw the big W.

During our last stretch as Californians there was quite a lot of work to be had and we also had to find a buyer for the house. This turned out to be relatively easy, since we weren't looking for any big profit on it. It's tempting to try to guess what we could sell it for now, these forty years later, but there is one trouble with that dream: the price we could get now is the same as we got then, but called by a different name. Some time ago now, the government of France had the courage and sense to tell the citizens to move the decimal point back where it belonged and stop pretending to be millionaires. "You think you have a one-hundred franc note there? Bring it in and get real money for it: ten francs."

---

[27]Wallenstein (1898–1983), who played "mood music" on Hollywood's silent-film sets as a teenager, also served as principal cellist with the Chicago Symphony. He led the Los Angeles Philharmonic in an April 1935 performance of Bennett's *Orchestral Fragments from the American Opera "Maria Malibran"* two months before the opera's Juilliard premiere. Wallenstein left the Los Angeles Philharmonic in 1956 and later taught conducting at Juilliard.

Bennett with Louis and Annette Kaufman, 1940s. Photo courtesy of Annette Kaufman. This picture was taken in Bennett's Park Avenue apartment. Bennett and Louis Kaufman first worked together on the 1936 Universal film of Kern and Hammerstein's *Show Boat.*

I don't look forward to anything so sensible ever happening world-wide. Nor do I suppose a good political economist would call it sensible at all, for that matter, To me it makes at least as much sense as that page in the newspaper called "Letters to the Editor" ever does.

Only a week or two before we left for the east coast we had a pleasant dinner with Louis and Annette Kaufman. For a good many years it seemed impossible to see a love scene in the movies without hearing the tender tones of Louis Kaufman's violin behind it; certainly nobody ever wanted to.[28] He, with his gifted wife Annette, has made many albums and played recitals over a good part of the globe. He has another talent that is fully as rare and com-

[28]Louis Kaufman (1905–1994) had, for several decades, a "dual" career not unlike Bennett's. Trained at New York's Institute of Musical Art with Franz Kneisel, he eventually made his home in Los Angeles. In addition to his frequent appearances internationally as recitalist and concerto soloist, he was for decades the Hollywood studios' leading concertmaster and solo violinist. He can be heard on hundreds of film soundtracks from 1934's *The Merry Widow* to 1963's *Cleopatra*, including *Gone with the Wind*, *Suspicion*, and *The Diary of Anne Frank*.

pletely beyond me to explain. He is fond of painting and painters and right before our eyes has picked out several almost unknown artists and accurately foretold their futures. I suppose the outstanding one of these is Milton Avery, whom so many of us knew without suspecting him of the quality that got him two one-man shows running concurrently at two of the very top New York galleries.[29] But this is just what happened and was just about what Louis Kaufman had predicted for many years.

Louis was almost always promoting an idea in those days, and at our dinner together he was urging me to compose something that would clothe American dance-hall material in the respectable garments of educated music.

On the way home after dinner my mind went on a search for a central idea: "jazz" was dead—believe it or not—"swing" was dying. Finally it appealed to me to make five studies for violin and piano of something not quite extinct called "jitterbugs." Approaching them as a summa cum laude graduate of Freeman, Missouri High School, I called them jitteroptera and called the five studies *Hexapoda*—a synonym of Insekta.

Our dinner was on a Friday evening. On Sunday morning I called Louis up and told him his piece was written—I just had to make a copy of the violin part and he would have it the next morning.

He surprised me by saying, "What piece?"

He and I played it at Town Hall in New York in the autumn.[30]

---

[29]Milton Avery later completed an oil portrait of Bennett.

[30]This Kaufman-Bennett premiere took place on 20 March 1940. The pair recorded the piece for Columbia Records soon after, and it was published by Chappell the following year. Kaufman also gave Bennett's *Allemande* its first performance (Town Hall, 25 March 1948, with pianist-composer Erich Itor Kahn). Bennett's Concerto for Violin in A Major (1941)—unrelated to the similarly titled but unfilled Fritz Kreisler commission nearly a decade earlier—became closely identified with Kaufman, who played it several times with orchestras in New York, Los Angeles, and London.

Chapter Eight

Less than a week before I began writing this sentence Louise and I were having lunch with some charming gentlemen who were bankers. The occasion was formal, but friendly, and our host asked me what I would consider the high spot of my long trip through the world of theater and music. The question is so often asked, but for some reason I've never polished up an answer for it. You always feel you should say something the questioner wants to hear, but after all these years of practice at it, my answer must have hit bottom, from a banker's standpoint. I picked the two years of *Russell Bennett's Notebook* and another program called *Music for an Hour*, both sustaining hours of the Mutual Network. Sustaining hours—at least in those days—were non-sponsored programs, often produced to fill up unsold air time with a gesture toward culture.

The salaries were as small as the various labor unions would countenance. This is not the stuff big bank depositors are made of. However, it definitely was a period of great personal satisfaction. The drawbacks are obvious. For one: with the green light on any style composition you choose, what do you do about the pages you have to tear up? You don't have that kind of time, with a minimum of eighteen to twenty-five minutes of music to be written, scored and copied once a week.[1]

I had imagined that young (and old) composers would line up at my door with every kind of new music looking for a performance. Three or four pieces

---

[1]The sixteen-month run of the *Notebook* program, during which he apparently did no Broadway orchestrations, was Bennett's most prolific period as a composer. More than twenty new pieces were premiered on his show, several of them appropriately patriotic—*March for America*, *March for General MacArthur*, and a narrator-with-orchestra setting of the Patrick Henry speech, *Give Me Liberty*. Bennett also aired earlier compositions, including "student" works from Kansas City, several written in Paris, and his New York World's Fair music for concert band. The Concerto for Violin in A Major—which several critics of the day proclaimed Bennett's finest composition—was premiered by *Notebook* concertmaster Joseph Coleman before it became the "exclusive" property of violinist Louis Kaufman.

were brought in, but not enough to help much.[2] Another big question mark was just how "far out" to be in the original material, even granted the time to sit and think without writing. The programs settled into a groove of browsing around among Indian tunes, Negro spirituals, almost forgotten song hits, and once a month a music-box opera. For the music-box operas we had four vocal soloists who sang the roles, and each libretto was developed from the lyrics of a folk song: "My Darling Clementine," "The Band Played On," "The Man on the Flying Trapeze," and so on and on.[3]

> ["Composer Bennett's opener last fortnight (23 March 1941) was a 'music-box opera' based upon a fine old U.S. song: "The Man on the Flying Trapeze." Throughout the opera, the ballad tune dum-diddled along, festooned with Composer Bennett's shiniest orchestral and harmonic tricks. Best original snatch was sung by a clown:
>
> Which way does a young man start when a young man's heart
> has a well-known dart stuck away down low?
> Which way does a young girl turn when her arms both yearn
> and her lips both burn with a well-known glow?
> Ah, lackaday, how do I say to you which way they go?"[4]]

The joy of the series was in the quality of the singers and the orchestra, where with the simplest gesture of the left hand one could re-balance an entire section without stopping and talking. I've told you already how I hated to practice.[5]

---

[2]Compositions by several of Bennett's commercial-music colleagues were given air time, including pieces by Hans Spialek, Dana Suesse, Nathan Van Cleave, Walter Paul, and Albert Sirmay. Bennett also programmed works by Oscar Levant, William Grant Still, Tibor Serly, and film composers Leigh Harline (best known for Disney's *Snow White* and *Pinocchio*) and Alex North (who began his film work in the 1940s doing government documentaries and rose to prominence in Hollywood in the 1950s). With few exceptions, every piece aired was written by an American. Interestingly, several native composers receiving frequent symphonic performances at the time (including Copland, Barber, Piston, Hanson, and Harris) went unperformed on the *Notebook* broadcasts.

[3]Bennett, who frequently composed light verse for holiday greetings to friends, etc., did his own libretti for the five "*Music Box Operas.*" His singers for their broadcast premieres included soprano Jean Merrill, mezzo Pauline Pierce (recipient of a Naumburg award in 1937, and a member of the *Malibran* cast at Chautauqua), tenor Robert Stuart, and basses Hugh Thompson (a Metropolitan Opera 1943–44 auditions winner) and Jack Kilty.

[4]"Russell Bennett's Notebook," *Time*, 7 April 1941, 67.

[5]Among the thirty-eight *Notebook* orchestra members was pianist Milton Kaye, who was featured on Bennett's piano-and-orchestra *Nocturne and Appassionata*—in both its broadcast premiere and a later Philadelphia Orchestra performance. Kaye went on to serve as one of Jascha Heiftez's accompanists, including several recordings and a European Theater tour performing for Allied solders during the last year of World War II.

Bennett posed with some of his music manuscripts, 1944. Photograph © Eileen Darby. Reproduced by permission.
Photographer Darby surrounded her subject with pages from his *Nocturne and Appassionata*.

No doubt it's automatic that the world takes on among its many other duties the chore of trying to side-track me as a Giant and Yale fan. When *Russell Bennett's Notebook* was on the air a few men took out their wallets and put money together to buy ball players and get the Brooklyn Dodgers out of the second division in the National League. That promoted them to the role of spoilers from the standpoint of a Giant fan and the evil genies made the most of it. My sponsors, radio station WOR and the Mutual Network, asked me to write and broadcast a piece for the Brooklyn Dodgers on one of my programs. I swallowed hard and wrote a *Symphony in D for the Dodgers.*

[Bennett provided details in his 1941 program notes:

> The Allegro con brio is in sonata form and has the subtitle "Brooklyn Wins." It means to picture the ecstatic joy of the town after the home team wins a game. The second movement is the slow movement. . . . It is called "Brooklyn Loses." Somebody has suggested that the movement be called "Brooklyn Loses—but not very often." The third movement is the Scherzo. . . . {It} pictures {then-Dodgers-president} Larry MacPhail going a-hunting for a star pitcher. . . . We hear him in Cleveland, Ohio, trying to trade for the great pitcher

> Bob Feller. He offers Prospect Park and the Brooklyn Bridge as an even trade, but the Cleveland management says "No" in the form of a big E-flat minor chord. After repeated attempts. . . he resumes the hunt in other fields. The Finale. . . like that of Beethoven's Ninth, is a choral movement. The text, again like Beethoven's Ninth Symphony, is an ode to joy. It is purely fictitious, this text, but it speaks for itself. The subtitle of this Finale is "The Giants Come to Town."]

The fourth movement of the symphony described a ninth-inning finish and I asked "Red" Barber, who broadcast the play-by-play commentary on nearly all the Dodger games, to broadcast this fictitious one with my musical accompaniment. It was all good fun except for a Giant fan. William Steinberg later played it with the New York Philharmonic at a summer concert [3 August 1941] and "Red" Barber "appeared as soloist" there, too.

I had inquiries from one or two other orchestras for it but, after allowing my friend Randolph Jones to do it once with the Jersey City Symphony, I managed to lose the score and parts and never found them. It was to me, along with Lalo's *Le Roi d'Ys* overture and Khachaturian's *Sabre Dance*, the worst music I ever heard.

There was something to learn about human beings during World War II. Radio broadcasting was coming of age and one of the favorite programs in all homes, especially of older people, was the news broadcast. The more gruesome the reports of the war and the less successful "our side" was, the more ears one saw glued to the receiving set, drinking it all in. After the war was won (they said so, anyway) the radio sets must have wondered where everybody went.

One of our favorite [WOR] commentators was Raymond Gram Swing. One fine day I was told that he, of all persons, had written a work for baritone voice and orchestra, a setting of "La Belle Dame Sans Merci" and it would be very nice if I could include it in a program of *Russell Bennett's Notebook* with his brother Dolf Swing singing the solo.

Needless to say it went right on a program and on the day it was to be broadcast I checked with the station to find out when the rehearsal was to start. The young lady said five o'clock. Ted Royal, who arranged the music for *Brigadoon* among other famous shows,[6] and I had lunch together that day

---

[6]Royal (Ted Royal Dewar) and Bennett worked together on several shows, including Porter's *Mexican Hayride* (1944) and *Around the World in 80 Days* (1946). Other musicals scored by Royal include *Guys and Dolls* (1950) and *Paint Your Wagon* (1951). Bennett was apparently not involved in orchestrating 1947's *Brigadoon*, yet was retained the following year by publisher Sam Fox (presumably with Loewe's consent) to prepare the orchestral "symphonic picture" of songs and dance music from the show.

and we talked about guess what—music. We decided after lunch was over and we were still talking about music that we should go somewhere not too public and, after some thought, went to my apartment.

The telephone was ringing as we went in and the telephone wanted to know where I was—my rehearsal at WOR was half over. "The young lady" had just received the schedules for the following week and that's what she had consulted when I asked her.

In those days you could get in a taxicab and get where you were going on the same day, so we had a run-through and went on the air on schedule. It's a good piece and Dolf Swing sang it splendidly. It was not a disaster, but certainly deserved a more relaxed performance.

World War II put an end to *Russell Bennett's Notebook*.[7] Incidentally, that was the last time I used two names instead of all three in public places. Ever since *June Twilight* (1911), anything thought up without a lead-sheet from Tin Pan Alley in front of me got the full name. It made better numerology.[8]

(Do I believe in numerology? No. Do I believe it's a hoax? An equally emphatic No. But until an official decision is handed down, it's fun.)[9]

Radio station WOR couldn't spare the air time for my show but they had a concert Sunday afternoons called *Music for an Hour* with a small choir, the same orchestra as the *Notebook*, and soloists. We rode the air waves with everything from Schumann's First Symphony to "Pistol-Packin' Mama," with a four-hour rehearsal beginning at eight in the morning. Our old friend Robert A. Simon was in charge of continuity for the network at the time and he had the job of picking out what we sang and played. For me it was a conducting job—not the one of my boyhood dreams, but with some real music in it.[10]

Every Sunday one of our features was a newly arranged medley, mostly of Broadway tunes, with all our singers involved.[11] Our music arranger was Ralph Barnhart, called Barney, and I must say he could get things on paper

---

[7]The final *Notebook* broadcast was 20 March 1942.

[8]Bennett's full name is seen on theater playbills beginning with late-1943's *Carmen Jones*. Earlier that year he was "Russell Bennett" both in *Oklahoma!*'s credits and as musical director for a short-lived network radio program starring ventriloquist Paul Winchell.

[9]In addition to numerology and the earlier-mentioned "crystal-ball" episodes, Bennett openly acknowledged his interest in such "harmless" diversions as spirit-writing and the interpretation of dreams ("Man Behind the Tune," *Newsweek*, 20 July 1953, 86).

[10]Bennett also shared conducting chores with Alfred Wallenstein, Arthur Fiedler, and others for the station's 11:30 p.m. *WOR Sinfonietta* broadcasts. Eighteenth- and nineteenth-century symphonies, overtures, and ballet scores were the mainstays of its all-classical programming.

[11]Vocal soloists on *Music for an Hour* included sopranos Annette Burford, Jean Merrill, and Mary Henderson; mezzo-soprano Margaret Harshaw; tenors Donald Dame and Earl

as fast as any of us that I ever met. Checking with him on Saturday afternoon it seemed to me that there were just not enough hours left, even without sleep, to have it ready at the unearthly hour of next morning's rehearsal. It was usually necessary to rehearse without the woodwind parts ready, but by air time, it was all there, and good!

During my particular period in and around light music there was a teacher of composition who called for arched eyebrows among the pros, but also who attracted a very large number of outstanding composers and arrangers as pupils. To mention two of these, Ted Royal, one of Broadway's very special arrangers, and George Gershwin, writer of songs and larger works. His name was Joseph Schillinger, and the number of Schillinger pupils in and around New York was impressive.[12]

He advertised his course of study with an approach that gave one pause, to say the least. It was something like this: the great masters wrote their music by instinct and didn't really know the real reason why they were great. He, Joseph Schillinger, could take anybody who wanted to compose and teach him or her how to be a Bach or a Beethoven by the time he or she finished the course. He sent me a letter when I was right in the thick of Broadway theater music and said, roughly quoted, "I realize that you are anxious to improve your work and that you are too busy to spend regular time as a pupil. I will meet you for an afternoon and will give you my course, concentrated so that you can work it out whenever you can spare the time. The price will be five hundred dollars."[13]

I didn't respond to this because I didn't know just what to say. About a year, I think, later he wrote again offering me the course free, for reasons that were not clear. I remember going to his house for tea once without talking

---

Palmer; and baritones John Barker and George Britton. Harshaw, then just beginning her career, was celebrated for her performances in a variety of Wagnerian roles—both as soprano and as a mezzo. She later established herself as one of the country's foremost teachers of singing.

[12]Schillinger (1895–1943) included Carmine Coppola, Tommy Dorsey, Vernon Duke, George Gershwin, Benny Goodman, Oscar Levant, Glenn Miller, and Ted Royal among his students. His theories are presented in a series of published texts, principally *The Schillinger System of Musical Composition* (1941). In Boston, Lawrence Berk's postwar "Schillinger House," with every course of study advertised as Schillinger-based, was the forerunner of his Berklee School of Music.

[13]Bennett's memory is admirably accurate; Schillinger also proffered his services to Bennett's arranging colleague Hans Spialek: "This special condensed course in Harmony requires only a single session of instruction of about three hours. It covers all the devices of tonal harmony. . . . The price is three hundred dollars. I can offer this course to but a few men like yourself, of independent thought and critical orientation and broad musical experience." Spialek, like Bennett, resisted Schillinger's generous offer (letter, Schillinger to Hans Spialek, November 1940, Spialek Papers, Music Division, Library of Congress).

about music particularly. By that time he was apparently no longer interested in me as a pupil, but that has nothing to do with this story.

This story is about a lawyer of considerable standing in New York, named James McInerny. Jim and I became friends when I was doing *Russell Bennett's Notebook* on the air. He got in touch with me through the big boss of WOR radio and told me that he was a pupil of Schillinger. He had graduated and also taken a post-graduate course in jazz arranging. Schillinger had told him that he was now ready to write a large work for orchestra, and Jim asked me if I would put the piece on my program and broadcast it.

My answer was yes. That was just the sort of thing my broadcasts were for, in my opinion, and I had never heard a Schillinger pupil whose orchestrations were not pretty sound. I was, however, pretty sorry for Jim and wondered just how his story could possibly turn out.

Unfortunately this happened just about the time we got into World War II, and my program was a casualty. I couldn't do anything for McInerny's new composition.

But we were all asked by a government at war to do musical things for propaganda programs and the like, and in due course James McInerny got an assignment to do the musical background for a series on radio called *The Commandos.* This was my big chance to put Joseph Schillinger's advertising to the test.

Here was his pupil, who had read the ads and bought the product, so I listened critically to the music of *The Commandos.*

It could only be described as gorgeous. It was discreet under narration or dialogue and the bridges of musical moments were of fine texture and full of power.

Schillinger stood acquitted.

[The fall of 1942 saw Bennett's return to Broadway after a two-year absence, with arrangements for Ann Ronell's *Count Me In* and Porter's *Something for the Boys.* He and office-mate Hans Spialek both provided orchestrations for CBS radio's big-budget *Great Moments in Music* program (broadcast over the Armed Forces Radio Service as *The Celanese Hour*) with singers Jan Peerce, Jean Tennyson, and Robert Weede. Spialek recalled the joys of working on such a production, along with an instance of Bennett's less-than-brilliant financial acumen:

> To be entrusted with a high-calibered commercial radio program meant then for an arranger as much, anyhow almost as much, as winning the Irish Sweepstakes. For a theatrical arranger, it meant even more: bigger and easier money, no more endless rehearsals with those inevitable, often ugly clashes of temperaments, no more chances of being told "that orchestration stinks" by some two-bit

specialty dancer whose very life ambition and pride centers in the two or three novelty steps he claims as his own; no more responsibilities to producers, composers, lyric writers, stage and dance directors, actors, singers, dancers, etc. The only person one had to please {on *Great Moments in Music*} was the conductor, not a difficult task at all because Mr. {George} Sebastian was what seventy-five percent of all musical comedy conductors were not, a profound, extremely well-educated musician, able to read an orchestra score competently.

Unable to handle in the beginning the program alone, I called on Robert Russell Bennett who had just returned from Hollywood in a somewhat less than rosy financial mood. {Completing jury duty in Manhattan} and lacking the time to do it myself, I entrusted Mr. Bennett with the financial arrangement for our services. Russell Bennett may well be the world's greatest, technically certainly {the} utmost-equipped arranger, but his talents as a businessman can best be described as pathetic. After my morning session in court, I got Russell on the phone. Learning from him the price he had agreed on, I almost fainted. Luckily, the jurors were excused for that afternoon. I contacted immediately the agency handling *Great Moments in Music*, met an hour later their representative at Toots Shor's bar and signed there an agreement for exactly three times the amount Bennett had bargained for. Finding no other piece of paper, this agreement was drawn and signed on the blank inside of an empty matchbook cover and subsequently held good for four and a half years.[14]]

One day one of my most admired conductors, Fritz Reiner, asked me to make a huge medley of music of George Gershwin's *Porgy and Bess* for him to record with the Pittsburgh Symphony Orchestra. I, by this time, had arranged so many "selections" from countless shows that the word medley was not very inspiring. As for *Porgy and Bess*, Bill Daly and I had watched it grow on Gershwin's piano and desk for some time and it was to me a little short of what I wanted a great symphony like the Pittsburgh to play. As a mature musical snob I asked myself a searching question: if it had been a medley of melodies from Puccini, Verdi, or Offenbach instead of Gershwin would I still have felt the same way about it? The answer, after honest thought, was definitely yes.

However, Fritz Reiner was not good at taking no for an answer, and about a week later Max Dreyfus called me in and asked me to do it. This put an entirely new light on the whole affair. As a music arranger with orders from the boss it was not up to me to say who should or shouldn't play it.

---

[14]Spialek, "A Passing Note," 241–42.

It was already the best orchestral music George had ever done and it was easy to see what he was getting at if the move from theater to concert music needed anything at all. Fritz had worked hard laying out the medley, which had to play exactly twenty-four minutes according to recording plans [three 78 r.p.m. discs]. He and I disagreed in two spots. Eventually I came to lean to his ideas in one place toward the end of the piece. I wanted to weave in a melody he had left out ("I Loves You, Porgy") and build up a little climax combining it with another phrase or two from the show and blossoming into the finale, "Oh Lawd, I'm on My Way." He preferred to keep it a medley and so it remains.

The other point of disagreement was a tiny cut he made, four measures, in George's original "Catfish Row" music.[15] In the middle of the tranquil opening everybody stops to listen to a single, unaccompanied line (cellos and English horn in my version) singing, "Bess, You Is My Woman Now." The calm music goes on, with the four notes of "is my woman" echoing for many bars in the middle of the harmony. This is the sort of moment that great composers leave us, but apparently great conductors don't always share our teardrops.

Sometimes a musical snob doesn't seem to have a friend in the world.

After Lorenz Hart died, Oscar Hammerstein announced to me one day that he and Dick Rodgers were signed up for a new collaboration.[16] Rodgers was a man who, in his own words, took pride in being the toughest businessman alive and at the same time writing music that made people cry. I never really saw the tough businessman side of him in our association but his reputation was such that I teased Oscar by saying "You've got yourself another Vincent Youmans there."

That was the last thing Oscar wanted me to say, because Youmans was a problem he had never solved.[17] I don't believe the firm of Rodgers and Hammerstein was full of problems between them. They were both products of a practical, commercial age and they probably agreed that temperamental clashes would be bad for business. I once saw them together with tears in their eyes, but they were tears of joy after the first performance of *South Pa-*

---

[15]The excised bars—actually, only three—appear just before rehearsal #7 (*Andantino dolente*) in Bennett's original manuscript. *Catfish Row* is also the name lyricist Ira Gershwin gave to brother George's own concert suite from his opera, all but forgotten in the 1940s and 1950s. Both Gershwin's and Bennett's creations are heard today, yet the latter's remains more frequently performed and recorded.

[16]Hart's drinking and personal problems had caused him to become an unreliable collaborator (hence Rodgers's invitation to Hammerstein) but he worked once more with Rodgers, on a revival of their 1927 *A Connecticut Yankee*. It opened 17 November 1943, six months after the debut of *Oklahoma!*; Hart passed away less than a week later.

[17]Hammerstein and Youmans worked together on *Wildflower* and *Mary Jane McKane* (both 1923) and *Rainbow* (1928).

cific. I felt like shedding a few tears myself of a different kind over the way some of it sounded and it took a little while to realize how thrilled they were.

They knew what a big fish they had on the hook.

The difference between Rodgers-and-Hart and Rodgers-and-Hammerstein songs might be material for a thesis for somebody's doctorate, but it would probably be long-winded and, like all words about music, based on impressions, instincts and reactions and entirely unprovable. The Hart songs on the surface seem gayer and younger, but the authors were indeed younger if not gayer. When you apply any deep analysis to anything so un-deep as popular songs, you're more than likely to wish you could set it to music and call it "What Was I Trying to Prove?"

The point (if we have to make one) is that the most casual listener would agree that there is quite a difference between the two collaborations. The answer would probably depend on how you ask the question.

The new partnership certainly got off to a spectacular start. Oscar took a play by Lynn Riggs about the part of the world where I was raised and with his great experience and sure instincts turned it into one of the all-time finest libretti. When those of us who were to work on the production met for a hearing of the music, it was at the home of Jules Glaenzer, theater's biggest fan of the era.[18] The audition was an unqualified success.

I did something I almost never think to do: pretended to be a music critic and congratulated Dick Rodgers on his music. He was very happy and went around telling everybody how important my opinion was to him. Of course it wasn't really even as important as that of June Jones, sitting at the end of the thirteenth row at a Wednesday matineé, but I had been impressed that the melodies were all so pure. I had only heard one note all afternoon that I was sure Irving Berlin would never have written.

En garde! Here comes a music lesson!

On page 9 above was a report of the report that Irving Berlin avoided studying music for fear it would do something to his melodies. If indeed he said that, he might not approve of one particular note in the song "Oklahoma!" where Rodgers chose the harmony before choosing the melody above it. Those of us who listen to the bottom and the middle of music as well as the top are so glad he did it that way, but he may have lost June Jones for a beat or two.[19]

When this new Rodgers-Hammerstein musical was ready for orchestration, Rodgers and I agreed on one thing at least. I told him that this might

---

[18]Glaenzer was for many years the head of Cartier. His townhouse in Manhattan's East Sixties, furnished with two Steinway grand pianos, was the site of many a lavish gathering of America's theatrical and social elite.

[19]Surely the chromatic pitch heard momentarily at "where the wind comes right behind *the* rain . . . "

very likely be the last show I would take on as music arranger. The strain of days and days with no concern for the human body was getting quite unrealistic. He understood me perfectly and said he had come to just about the same conclusion about his own work and life.

Only someone who would sit down and count the thousands—maybe millions—of little black dots on the miles of music staves we have turned out since then could possibly laugh loud enough and long enough at that interview.

This show opened with the name *Away We Go.* While they were in New Haven and Boston getting started, the Theatre Guild (I was told) offered some kind of prize for a good name for the piece. The report said that many people submitted the name "Oklahoma" but only one spelled it "Oklahoma!" with the exclamation point—and that won the contest.

Anyhow, *Oklahoma!* is its name and the real fortune would go to someone who could get a dollar for every time the exclamation point has been left out since the play started.

After *Oklahoma!* opened in New York and proved to be just what wartime New York wanted and needed, it was the fashionable thing to tell people how everybody was in despair over it in New Haven and Boston "and now look at it!"[20]

That bit of reporting is a companion piece to the one later about *My Fair Lady*, which, after one of the most exciting New York openings in theater history, was discovered by some romantic character to have been a hopeless affair on the road. If you were in the audience at those out-of-town performances and felt the electricity around you, you would find these reports a bit quaint.

[After finishing his orchestrations for *Oklahoma!* in March 1943, Bennett set to work on a new orchestral commission. The resulting symphony, *The Four Freedoms* (his fifth), proved to be one of his most-played concert works during the war years.

President Roosevelt had, during an early-1941 speech to Congress, outlined four "essential freedoms": freedom of speech and expression, freedom of religion, freedom from want, and freedom from fear. Soon after, artist Norman Rockwell (most renowned for his *Saturday Evening Post* cover illustrations) completed four paintings based on these ideals; they were exhibited nationwide by the U.S. government as part of a series of Four Freedoms War Bond Drives. The Rockwell illustrations

---

[20]Among Bennett's contributions to *Oklahoma!*'s score were the first-act ballet music, which, in the flurry of mounting the new show in New Haven, he "built up from three chords." And his "doctoring" of the title-song finale was considerable, especially his addition of the spelled-out "O-K-L-A-H-O-M-A" (Wind, "Another Opening, Another Show," 48; see also "Eight Bars and a Pencil," below).

were reprinted by the millions, quickly becoming some of the century's most widely circulated images. Bennett's symphony, commissioned by the *Post*, was completed by late summer 1943. With each movement depicting one of Roosevelt's "freedoms," it received its radio premiere by the NBC Symphony on 26 September. Frequent concert performances quickly followed, including those by the orchestras of Philadelphia, Los Angeles, and Cleveland. The work was very positively received; of all of Bennett's works, the amount of critical attention accorded *The Four Freedoms* was rivaled only by his opera *Maria Malibran*. The *Post* announced an ambitious plan to distribute copies of the published score to schools nationwide, but it was never implemented.]

The flying colors of the New York opening of *Oklahoma!* were still fluttering when Oscar Hammerstein asked me to go to lunch with him at Sardi's, where he laid out plans for the next show involving my loving touch. It turned out to be a little more loving than is sometimes the case. The composer was pretty high on the list of favorites of almost any musical snob: Georges Bizet. Oscar was converting the opera *Carmen* into a modern American version with an all-Negro cast and calling it *Carmen Jones*.

It had to be an easy job physically for me because the orchestrations were already done by a master. The new English words could have made lots of problems but, in fact, in Oscar's skillful and experienced hands, there was not much to worry about. In one place Bizet had an orchestral downbeat and began his vocal phrases on the second half of the measure. I said to Oscar when I read his new lyric, "You have your thesis on your arsis and your arsis on your thesis."

He said, "I don't know what that means but it sounds terrible!" By the time I put into words the difference between the two halves of the measure I realized that it really didn't matter enough to waste time on it. The original words were "La la la la la" anyway. It will surprise nobody to know that Oscar's English lyrics (somewhat traceable to the ancestry of Stephen Foster) were wonderfully fit and seemed happily married to Bizet's melodies. These, of course, had blood from the south in their veins to start with.

[Hammerstein had begun work on *Carmen Jones* several years earlier; his libretto was practically finished before he joined forces with Rodgers on *Oklahoma!*. In his introduction to the published *Carmen Jones* libretto (Knopf, 1945) Hammerstein argues with obvious sincerity that a wider audience for opera in the U. S. is to be gained only through English-language production. He condemns the prevailing standard set by "scholarly but untalented" translators, arguing that a good adaptation requires a librettist who is at once a skilled poet, dramatist, and showman, and that "The public has not rejected 'opera in English,' because it has never had a skillful English version of an opera submitted to it." He continues:

> I feel in my bloodstream the approach of that choleric indignation that invariably seizes me when I discuss this topic. I am beginning to sweat, and this is not a hot day. I must control myself, else I will be taking wild swipes at my list of very special hates: the dear singing teachers who instruct their pupils to broaden every "a" so that a lovely word like "romance" becomes "romonce"—no word at all; the foreign singer whose accent makes English less intelligible than his own tongue; the conductor who thinks there is more entertainment in a blast from a horn than in any English word that could possibly be sung. But. . . *Carmen Jones* is not the answer to your prayers or mine for opera in English. *Carmen Jones* is not even an opera. It is a musical play, based on an opera. *Carmen Jones*, however, does prove this much: that a surprisingly large number of the regular theatre-going public will enjoy operatic music if you let them in on the story. However unconventional may be my treatment of the original work, the score remains an operatic score, and the story, in its spirit and rendition, is an operatic story. It is a tragedy. Yet it has appealed to the same public that nightly patronizes musical comedy.]

For me it came closer to being my farmer-boy dream come true than anything so far. It was a real, honest-to-goodness, grand opera with some sublime musical moments and a producer who, to our surprise, proclaimed that in this production, the artistic thing was the commercial thing. Needless to say the idea didn't always prevail.

"Angels die broke" is a show business axiom that antedates us by quite a bit. It belongs to a time when rich men with young ideas could roll a few thousand dollar bills off their bundle and become a most welcome member of the theatrical troupe. If the show was a hit they made money—quite a lot of it—if it was not a hit, they had fun while it lasted.

In those days a hit was able to run with such a profit that it paid you back for two or three flops. Producers, even the most famous of them, were not usually rich men, although some lived like kings. When it came to financing a new show they knew the way to the rich men's doors.

This set of facts made Billy Rose a refreshing novelty when he became interested in producing *Carmen Jones.* When he said he wanted to do it we knew that he would beat no paths to rich men's doors; he didn't need to.

As noted above, he was quite up to the aims of such an experiment and in my opinion the show had an unusual amount of class. Conducting it was in line with what I most wanted to do, but I can't say I was especially good. I had all the cooperation one could expect, and of course had no pages to turn at rehearsals or performances, but the things I was not prepared for were things like groups of singers upstage whose voices I couldn't even hear and who had no experience at following a conductor no matter how far or near they were.[21] Every phase of a performance has unexpected compromises that may change from performance to performance. No doubt long experience teaches one to get used to that.

We never really fell apart but we had one moment when disaster was beckoning. This was purely my fault. We were in a preview in Philadelphia with a full house and in the second act I suddenly realized that we had cut a couple of bars out in rehearsal and I had completely forgotten to fix the orchestra parts.

I tried to make quick gestures to the men but only one clarinetist read my mind—result: Muriel Smith, our lovely Carmen,[22] with a gorgeous high A flat and one loud yelp from one clarinet. Somehow we all got back on the track and the heart-breaking finish of the opera was all in order.

After that performance Oscar Hammerstein came to me and began some kind of question about the near ship-wreck we had just had. I meant to explain about not having fixed the music, but it came over me how very little all the great specialists in the theater really know about the chemistry of the things they deal with, so I just said, "I blew it—that's all there is to it! Come down and do a performance some time and see how it goes!" It was the meanest thing I ever said to him in all our years.

In all my years in the theater I never got so overworked, or under such strain, that I would willingly change jobs with the music director of any show I knew. They are to blame for everything that doesn't come off in the musical theater. *Carmen Jones* was no worse than any other I could remember, but I had a good associate conductor in Joseph Littau (same man that conducted the band for the fountains at the New York World's Fair) and I turned over the stick to him when Billy Rose had a big idea about one of Mr. Bizet's orchestrations.[23] The experiment called for a lot of my time and was a great excuse

---

[21]*Carmen Jones* opened in New York on 2 December 1943; auditions for the "all-Negro" production had been held in several Eastern cities. Though the Negro National Opera Society had then been recently organized, black actor-singers with operatic experience reportedly proved difficult to find (Gershwin's 1935 *Porgy and Bess* had faced similar casting challenges). *Carmen Jones* was revived in New York in 1945 and again in 1959, and a film version was released in 1954 by 20th Century-Fox. It featured Dorothy Dandridge, Harry Belafonte, Pearl Bailey, and Diahann Carroll, with voice doubles employed for most of the stars.

[22]Muriel Smith alternated with Muriel Rahn; the demands of eight operatic performances weekly led to double-casting of several of *Carmen Jones*'s principal roles.

[23]His orchestra of thirty-three was larger than the Broadway standard (the Musician's Union minimum was, for many years, twenty-five or more for Manhattan's larger theaters),

for not conducting the same opera eight times a week (however great it was or however fine a performance I could achieve).

Billy's experiment was the kind of thing we worried about before we started with him, but when he asked me to make a "modern" orchestration to add excitement to the "Gypsy Song" (and dance) we had our featured drummer, Cozy Cole, doing wild and wonderful things with drums on the stage already, and I couldn't say flatly that Billy's idea was not a good one.

So I did it, and so Billy said "that's just what the doctor ordered" and the new orchestration went into the show.

As far as I knew it was never reconsidered, but here is a bit of history and a bit of audience psychology that is worth some thought: the last two times I conducted it with the original Bizet orchestration it stopped the show. They applauded and applauded, and no doubt would have liked the whole song and dance repeated. As far as I ever heard that never happened again, in spite of the new orchestration that was just what the doctor ordered.

Why do I use up so much time and space on it? Simply to offer a fragile guess about the sub-conscious of the audience—if it has one: might it be telling us that all this excitement being generated by Mr. Bizet's original sounds was an achievement, and the loud theater-sounds they were more familiar with made it less so? I don't have an answer, but I know that when you stop the show, everybody that cares at all about shows would like to know how you did it.

I first met Billy Rose in the days when he was associated with Jed Harris. Jed Harris was at the height of his popularity at that time. They were doing a revue and were playing with the idea of using the old folk-song "Frankie and Johnny" in a dramatic setting as a finale. Billy called me and we met one evening to join Jed Harris and discuss the idea.

We were to meet "the boss" at the Friars Club and on the way to keep the appointment Billy Rose was filling me in on what a partnership with Jed Harris was like. I remember particularly hearing him say, "When you work with him you sometimes feel like saying, 'Jed, I know something, too.'"

When we got to the Friars we were told Mr. Harris was waiting for us on the second floor. On the second floor we found him all alone reading a newspaper, from which he didn't look up. We sat in silence for what seemed like a long, long time. By the time he put down his paper and said, "Well, let's talk about 'Frankie and Johnny'!" I had decided that Frankie and the man that done her wrong had no place in my life. When Jed Harris asked me what I thought of it I answered, "I don't care much for it."

---

but not nearly as big as a "legitimate" opera orchestra. Critics nonetheless praised Bennett's careful adjustment of the score, a testament to his well-honed ability to make a minimum-sized ensemble sound bigger than it actually was.

This was ridiculous of me because it was fortunately not a bit important whether I liked the things I worked on or not, but Jed Harris's newspaper was apparently too much for me.

He said, "I agree with you," and who knows what undying masterpiece may have remained unborn?

I never thought to ask Billy Rose if the "Frankie and Johnny" thing was originally an idea of his.

My last association with Billy was when he opened the Billy Rose Theater with a variety show called *Seven Lively Arts.* A fairly popular story about that production is that of the two telegrams sent by Billy and the famous composer Igor Stravinsky. Stravinsky composed a ballet for Alicia Markova to dance in the show[24] and after the first preview Billy wired him, saying the ballet was a "great success" but to make it a sensation he recommended engaging Robert Russell Bennett to make a new orchestration of it. Stravinsky wired back, "Satisfied with great success."

Those who understand the story well enough laugh and think they are laughing at Billy Rose. Well, they are in a way, but only a handful of us know what went on in his mind and his sharp ears. Stravinsky was, along with several advanced composers, using a major seventh tonic and inverting it so that a trombone sang out an uninhibited B natural under the three trumpets' pure C-major triad. To Billy, and to most of his customers, this was a discord. Nothing final or satisfying about it.

When sounds like that come out of the pit in their theater they send for the arranger and he changes or redoes the arrangement. This was all Billy knew about Igor's inverted tonic major seventh and no doubt that's one of the reasons for the success he had in the theater.

About the time *Carmen Jones* settled down for its run on Broadway, things began to happen—good things and bad things. I won't try to list them with an organized mind (which I can muster when necessary), but several corners were turned into new streets, some light, some dark.

One of the bright spots for me had begun to show quite some time before when Richard Myers, a friend of ours with much talent, once accidentally let the news drop that he was a real tennis player. Around theater and publisher territory we knew him as the composer of at least one song hit called "My Darling" and I recall being at a social affair once when a most attractive lady singled me out and said, "Mr. Bennett, I'd like to ask you a question. Should I go on with Dick Myers?"

---

[24]Stravinsky's *Scènes de ballet*; the production's songs were written by Cole Porter. The show opened 7 December 1944, featuring Markova, Beatrice Lillie, Burt Lahr, and Benny Goodman's trio.

While I wrestled with some kind of answer she went on: "I'm sure he has great music in him but I'm beginning to wonder about him." Then she added, "You know, I practically put Vincent Youmans on the map."

There was, as one might imagine, a short silence before I said, "I think Dick has as much talent as anybody, He won't let you down." End of interview.

Dick Myers did fine, whether his sponsor went on with him or not, and he introduced me to an indoor tennis club that belongs in the book—almost any book. I joined the club—The Island Court Club it was called—and I must say that I played over my head for several years. I wasn't that good, but many times in doubles my partner was C. J. (Peck) Griffin, Davis Cup partner of all-time great William Johnston. Two or three times a week we had a regular foursome of William E. Hazen, retired editor of the *Wall Street Journal*, Fred W. Guild of New York Life Insurance Co., Walter Reisinger of the (Anheuser) Busch family, and me.

Even an immaculate performance of *Die Walküre* would only be slightly more exciting than some of those matches.

On the darker side of the period was a trip to Boston to open a show headed for Broadway with a young conductor named Will Irwin. Will eventually became music director at Radio City Music Hall, but this musical was his first. He had already had plenty of experience, as a pianist and assistant conductor,[25] and he prepared every detail of the music with meticulous care. Every detail but one, I should say. We all worked the usual long hours to get the scores and orchestra parts ready and on the day we transferred the whole "factory" to Boston, Will took his staff, including his music librarian, without arranging to pick up the two big stacks of music for the following morning's rehearsal. Somehow I was the last of the toilers to run for the train, with a grip and two stacks of music on my hands. That should not have been too much of a problem for an old Missouri farmer, but there was a thing called World War II going on and I stood on the back platform of the last car of the train all the way to New London before a seat was to be had.

That evening at the hotel in Boston I rang up music director Irwin and complimented him on his great attention to detail, etc., and while he was taking a smiling mental bow, I told him of one detail he had overlooked: nobody had come to pick up the music.

I thought the telephone would explode in my hand as he said, "Oh, my God! Where is it?"

---

[25]Will Irwin (b. 1907) was pianist for Gershwin's *Of Thee I Sing* and *Let 'Em Eat Cake* as well as Berlin's *As Thousands Cheer.* He also served as one of several conductors of the original production of *Oklahoma!*. Bennett is likely referring to *Men of the Sea*, which opened in New York in October 1944 after troubles with Boston's censors.

It was in my hotel room, but in a week or so I found out that the farmer-neighbor who said, "Don't try to lift that calf—you'll rupture yourself!" was telling the truth. I would have to have an operation, but in the meantime—around Christmas time of the year 1944—began a program called *Stars of the Future*, sponsored by the Ford Motor Company.

I'm afraid I'd better go back and trace my "career" in broadcasting in order to make a little sense here. Ever since *Russell Bennett's Notebook* there were occasional shows on the air that I wrote or conducted or both. The United States of America did some broadcasting for one purpose or another and people in my trade were asked to write or conduct a broadcast from time to time as part of the war effort; at one time Rudy Vallee, a home-radio-set idol, took two weeks off and they gave me a good, big orchestra and several featured artists for two luxurious one-hour broadcasts in his place. At another time we started a series with the comedy-man Ken Murray as a star, but it stayed on the air only a few weeks. I don't think I ever knew or asked why the show went off.

Friend and collaborator Robert A. Simon was music consultant to the great agency J. Walter Thompson through those years. Without ever being told I assume that my popularity there was largely due to him. Certainly no music director could possibly ask for a better spot than with *Stars of the Future*. Two regular vocal soloists from very high on the list—Jo Stafford and Lawrence Brooks—a fine chorus [of fourteen] and a fine orchestra.[26] Every week we presented a great young artist, usually making his or her first appearance on the air—and what a who's who that roll would make![27]

The temptation to sit in the old rocking chair and recall some of the personalities and some of the features of the programs is great, but the stories would be more fun to tell than to listen to. After we'd been on the air a few months I took time off to have my side sewed up (Jay Blackton, one of the

---

[26]Stafford joined the cast in April 1945 after the departure of soprano Frances Greer, who spent much of the 1940s on the Metropolitan Opera roster. Greer, while featured on *Stars of the Future*, told Bennett of her interest in a Broadway role "if the right opportunity were to appear." But he advised against such a move, with a "bitter warning" about the more unsavory, "cutthroat" aspects of commercial music and theater in New York (Frances Greer telephone interview with the editor, July 1997).

[27]*Stars of the Future* guests included singer Margaret Harshaw, violinists Ossy Renardy, Isaac Stern, and Carroll Glenn, cellist Leonard Rose, pianists Leon Fleisher and Earl Wild, duo-pianists Appleton & Field and Whittemore & Lowe, and a few well-known professionals—violinist Yehudi Menuhin, baritone Alfred Drake, and folk singer Richard Dyer-Bennett. In April 1945, the program's name was changed to *The Ford Show*; guest vocalists were all established performers with presumably broader appeal: Connee Boswell, Eileen Farrell, Jane Froman, Mary Martin, and Vaughn Monroe.

The Ford Show publicity poster, 1945, Bennett with Lawrence Brooks and Jo Stafford. From the Collections of Henry Ford Museum & Greenfield Village. Used by permission.

A poster for the Ford-sponsored network radio program.

most brilliant theater conductors,[28] took over for a month) and the program lasted exactly a year [8 December 1944 through 25 December 1945] before our sponsors joined the current rush toward comedy shows and moved to California. Mr. John Reber of J. Walter Thompson called me to express regret over the change and suggest that if I wanted to go to California it might be arranged.

My answer: "John, in my kind of show business a year's run is a hell of a run! Regrets are not in order—only thanks!"

Two men that were with me in that series—and many other engagements, it should be added—are important in the story: David Novales and Crane Calder. Crane was our chorus-master. The men that ran the show, the producers and directors from the agency, had made up their minds that the singers should all look as good as they sounded. When you think about that it's quite an order. These people are there because they have heaven-sent voices and meticulous training, to say nothing of musicianship that can't be bought at any store. In the world of personal beauty, there must be a similar set of in-

[28]Blackton, trained in Europe, conducted operetta in New York as early as 1935. Born Jacob Schwartzdorf, he Anglicized his name while conducting *Oklahoma!* in 1943—in what was perhaps a bow to World War II anti-German sentiment. His later work includes the 1969 Lincoln Center revival of that show and 1970's *Two by Two* (Rodgers, with lyrics by Martin Charnin).

gredients in each champion. What do you suppose the odds are against all those ingredients being in one person?

At rehearsal for one of the broadcasts I asked the bosses to look at the chorus and pick out the men or women who weren't pretty enough for the job. Of course they declined the invitation. Not only that, but they even got quite proud of their singers' looks.

When we were running smoothly, Crane Calder came by every week or so in his car with a friend or two and took us out to the races. One day Crane and his wife and son took Louise and me clear to Saratoga and back. Saratoga is still the most glamorous race-track I know of and we all had a marvelous time. I don't remember that any of us won or lost any money on the horses, but I remember all being awfully tired that night.

Just as Crane Calder engaged all the singers in the chorus,[29] David Novales engaged the orchestra men. How David could possibly know as much as he did about just how good the best musicians in New York were, I can't tell you, but if you didn't hear what you wanted to at the first reading there, you knew you hadn't written it.[30]

When we first met, Novales was a violin virtuoso playing recitals on the European continent. He loved tennis and we often played in Paris.

One morning on the way by taxi to a tennis court we were crossing car tracks when a train of two or three cars came down a hill at us from our left. The taxi driver got confused and stopped the cab right on the tracks. The crash sounded more deadly than it was, but the door jammed so we couldn't get out. David was eating a bun in place of breakfast. I was never calmer, but he said I turned white.

It was a matter of a few minutes to get the door open, and quite a crowd had gathered, saying, "Are you hurt? Is anybody hurt?" I couldn't resist saying, "Oh, I'm sorry, but no one is hurt."

---

[29]Calder worked occasionally as chorus master or music director on Broadway, including Albert Hague's *Plain & Fancy* (1954).

[30]*Stars of the Future* announcer Del Sharbutt once boasted on-air that "every member of the orchestra could play a solo recital tonight." The thirty-three-piece ensemble included such noted string players as first-chair violinist Jacques Gasselin (previously concertmaster at the Paris Opera and second-chair in Toscanini's NBC Symphony, later concertmaster for the Los Angeles Philharmonic) and Philip Sklar (longtime NBC Symphony principal bass). Among the wind and percussion players were Edward Powell (flute), ex-Whiteman stars Chester Hazlett (clarinet and saxophone) and Charles Margoulis (trumpet), trombonist Will Bradley (among the most fluent of big-band veterans on his instrument, and arguably Tommy Dorsey's equal in that regard), and percussionist Morris Goldenberg (who also taught at the Juilliard School and served as a WOR staff percussionist). Bennett's sole work for percussion, "Rhythm Serenade," appears in Goldenberg's *Studies in Solo Percussion* (Chappell, 1968).

However the best thing in the show was when a little train man came up from the back car and said very seriously to the taxi driver, "You shouldn't have stopped."

The program *Stars of the Future* was broadcast while World War II was using up all the automobiles, so the slogan was "There's a Ford in your Future."

One fine day I had a great idea (I thought); I wrote a song for the chorus and orchestra that went like this.

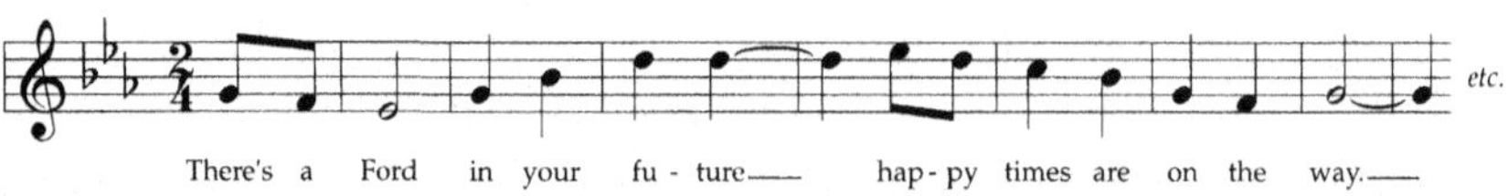

I showed it to our agency man and he smiled an indulgent smile and said, "Well, sir, you can have all the fun like that on the program that you want to, but when it comes to the commercial we have to give it to them straight from the shoulder, without trimmings."

Thirty-odd years later I was thinking about it while the merry jingles were cluttering up the air—including both good and bad for the Ford Motor Company—and I decided that Henry Ford II, whom I had met when we started our series in 1944, might well find the story as amusing as I did. I wrote him a letter and included a lead-sheet of the song in the envelope.

The manuscript of the music came back with a nice, fatherly letter from someone in the factory, saying that all their music was done by their own music department, etc., etc. I was sure that the whole thing wouldn't be funny enough to Mr. Ford to be worth my taking any more trouble with it. If I see him again I can still tell him the story.

Rodgers and Hammerstein followed *Oklahoma!* with a musical version of *Liliom*, by Ferenc Molnar. They called it *Carousel*. When it came time to arrange the music for the production I was deep in the advertising business, as per above. Richard Rodgers didn't seem inconsolable when I told him of my situation. He asked me to do some of his show that was already ready for orchestration and he would turn the big contract over to Donald Walker. No one in his right mind could shed any tears over having Don Walker's arrangements and he did one of the finest jobs that have ever been done on *Carousel*.[31]

Dick Rodgers, as just reported, didn't seem dramatically disappointed at my being unavailable for *Carousel*, but when they started plans on their next

---

[31]The show opened on 19 April 1945. Walker (1907–1989) had earlier provided orchestrations for many Porter and Rodgers and Hart shows. He later scored Berlin's *Miss Liberty* (1949) and, the following year, most of *Call Me Madam*. Among his 1960s–70s successes were *Fiddler on the Roof*, *Cabaret*, and *Shenandoah*.

collaboration (called *Allegro*) Dick called me before they had more than begun work on it themselves and asked rather plaintively if that would be enough notice for me.

When they were producing *Annie Get Your Gun* (according to someone's story) they went looking for a younger man for the music arranging job and came up with Phil Lang.

The morning after the last broadcast of the Ford program went on the air, I had a telephone call from Max Dreyfus, telling me Richard Rodgers was going to call me from New Haven and to please take care of Dick if I could. Dick called within minutes to tell me they (Rodgers and Hammerstein) had a new play just opening at the Shubert Theater in New Haven. It was all fine except the orchestrations.

I got there to see the show that evening and found one of the precious few musicals that I ever thoroughly enjoyed from top to bottom. It was produced by Dick and Oscar, but they didn't write it. The book was by Herb and Dorothy Fields and the songs were by Irving Berlin. The music was arranged by Philip Lang, and beautifully. What bothered the producers was the use of modern technique in the accompaniments under vocal solos, wherein the actual tune was left to the singer or singers and the orchestra avoided competing with the soloist on the melody. That was called "microphone technique" and was the best way to do any song for recordings of any kind.

In the theater (live sound) the music is under the singer, physically and sound-wise, and the orchestra can sing the tune along with the singer without tying him or her up in any way. That is the way those veterans of the musical theater were used to hearing their songs and it was not very difficult to get out the tools and give it to them without—I hope—unbalancing Phil's score.[32]

Annie Get Your Gun was, as far as I'm concerned, about as good as *Miss Nobody from Starland*, the first musical I ever saw. I was maybe fifteen then [the show had opened in Chicago in January 1910] and all ready to be had, but the musicals [that] passed in review through the years [were] always interesting, but seductive only in spots. Now, when the digits were reversed and I was fifty-one, I sat and enjoyed myself as though I'd paid for my ticket. I was supposed to be finding fault, and instead was rooting for Ethel Merman to get her man. Ethel Merman, a professional joy from *Girl Crazy* through show after show,

---

[32]Richard Rodgers writes that Bennett "reorchestrated the entire [*Annie Get Your Gun*] score, did his customary superlative job, and soon Irving was again calling me by my first name" (*Musical Stages*, 249). Berlin biographer Lawrence Bergreen is more directly critical of Lang's work; he tells of conductor Jay Blackton's reaction upon first examining the arrangements—"The more I looked, the worse I felt"—and summarily states that "Bennett's new orchestration rescued Berlin's score from disaster" (*As Thousands Cheer*, 456).

was exactly the type of singer that I liked the least, but here she wasn't Ethel; she was Annie Oakley and I was wishing so hard that I could help her.

In this period between (you might say) my radio and my television days, the factory was running full time in all sections—theater, broadcasting, movies, recordings. Surrounded by all those eager, creative souls, one didn't have to wait long for things to happen.

Messrs. Rodgers and Hammerstein, before they got around to *Allegro*, wrote songs for and produced a rather unusual show with my choice for the brightest of all their many stars: Helen Hayes. The show was *Happy Birthday*, written by the girl that wrote about the famous Lorelei Lee, Anita Loos. After the opening night we all sat in a big circle and Oscar Hammerstein in his quiet friendly way just tore the whole play to shreds. He took out whole characters from the story, changed the order of scenes, practically gave us all the job of writing a new show in some twenty hours. I was impressed by Anita Loos, who sat quietly taking notes on every big or little change Oscar asked for. I wondered if she didn't want to say, as Billy Rose told me he wanted to say to Jed Harris, "Oscar, I know something, too!"

But if she wanted to say it, she didn't, and one must conclude that if you have to write for the theater, seeing your brain-child kicked around that way has to be your way of life.[33]

Wondering how I would have acted in such a spot, a tiny crisis in one of the Rodgers and Hart shows came to mind. I had put a sequence of two or three striking chords at the final curtain of the first act and the authors and producers complained to Dick Rodgers that it was strange. Dick came to me about it, I showed him the chords and he played them over and over, and finally said, "There doesn't seem to be any other way to do it, does there?"

Of course there were other ways, but we both had to get the new chords out of our ears before we could change back to something our colleagues could cope with. Rodgers said something about not hurting my feelings and I'm glad I didn't say what occurred to me—that no duels will ever be fought over the last three bars of a finale act one, however I may love and admire the customers who are buying them from me. You know—the customer is always right.

This tendency to look down the nose at things that are much more important to the show than I am, brings up a short scene at Warner Brothers in California. Darryl Zanuck was talking earnestly to music director Louis Silvers about the reprise of a certain song in a current production and Jack Warner was in on the discussion. At one time Warner turned to Zanuck and said,

[33] *Happy Birthday*, with Bennett's incidental music, opened on 31 October 1946. Anita Loos (b. 1893) died on 18 August 1981—the same day as Bennett.

"You keep saying, 'Repreesal, repreesal,' all the time. The word is reprisal (rep-rye-zal)!" They argued and finally asked Lou Silvers which it was.

Silvers said, "Gentlemen, you're both wrong. The word is reprise (which he pronounced ray-preeze)."

He, also, was wrong, as is often the case.

Dumb story, but it stays with me.

A very active man, especially in motion pictures, Boris Morros,[34] produced a picture with quite an idea behind it. He took over Carnegie Hall in New York and made a picture about the place itself. I was never sure whether they were already doing a big renovating job on the hall or just accommodating their summertime client, but the old place got a good going-over.

The story of the picture was about a son of a cleaning woman of many years' service there; he was a rising young composer who finally wrote a symphonic piece that had its triumphant premiere on the Hall's hallowed stage. The music for the spot was composed by the Portnoff brothers (Wesley and Mischa) and it had a big sound when we recorded it. Conducting the big orchestra was quite a bit removed from reality. The engineers had the sections of the band spread out into groups away upstage and in the wings, walled off from one another. They all played the same music, I hope; at least what I could hear of it was what I had written, but when all the faces in the sound room were that happy over it, I wasn't sure we were all listening to the same thing.

We did get a good track, though, and we all took bows until we saw the finished picture. In the picture the young man's composition was at the end of the story as a climax—the "Fifty-Seventh Street Rhapsody," a triumph. I never heard what Wesley and Mischa thought of our baby after Beethoven, Wagner and Tchaikovsky had filled the air, but I'm afraid it had been a pretty tough assignment.[35]

When Edwin Franko Goldman arrived at his seventieth birthday it was celebrated by a concert sponsored by the League of Composers. For the concert

---

[34]Morros had conducted Bennett's orchestrations for the Kern film *High, Wide and Handsome* a decade earlier.

[35]"Russell" Bennett was credited orchestrator for 1947's *Carnegie Hall* (Federal/United Artists), the first feature film in many years to have been shot entirely in New York. Its amazing roster of featured performers included Jascha Heifetz, Gregor Piatigorsky, Artur Rubinstein, Ezio Pinza, Lily Pons, Jan Peerce, and Risë Stevens. The New York Philharmonic-Symphony, with conductors Leopold Stokowski, Fritz Reiner, Bruno Walter, Arthur Rodzinski, and Charles Previn (then Radio City Music Hall's music director) also appeared. The film's only gestures toward the popular music of the day are performances by singer Vaughn Monroe (with his orchestra) and trumpeter Harry James (featured soloist in the "Fifty Seventh Street Rhapsody" finale).

they engaged the Goldman Band of New York and asked Dr. Goldman to conduct his own band in honor of his own anniversary.[36] Louise and I went to that concert and I suddenly thought of all the beautiful sounds the American concert band could make that it hadn't yet made. That doesn't mean that the unmade sounds passed in review in my mind at all, but the sounds they made were so new to me after all my years with orchestra, dance bands and tiny "combos" that my pen was practically jumping out of my pocket begging me to give this great big instrument some more music to play.[37]

To satisfy all this urging I found time to put a good-sized piece on paper. There was really no such thing as spare time for me at that time, but somehow I got a part done here and a part done there and one day there was a piece to show Dr. Edwin Franko Goldman to see if he was interested in adding one more idiom to his great collection.

Dr. Goldman and his son Richard, also a doctor, became very warm friends indeed and gave the new piece a great send-off. It was published with the name *Suite of Old American Dances*.[38] I had a nice name for it, but you know how publishers are—they know their customers, and we authors never seem to. My name for it was *Electric Park*. Electric Park in Kansas City was a place of magic to us kids. The tricks with big electric signs, the illuminated fountains, the big band concerts, the scenic railway and the big dance hall—

---

[36]Goldman finished the 3 January 1948 program by leading the ensemble in a new march, written for the occasion and dedicated to the League. Walter Hendl, however, conducted most of the concert, which consisted of original works by Cowell, Milhaud, Schoenberg, Roussel, Auric, Honegger, Miaskovsky, Vaughan Williams, and Grainger (who took the baton for his own *The Power of Rome and the Christian Heart*). The Carnegie Hall concert was a rare indoor appearance by the Goldman unit, accustomed to playing in Central Park or in Brooklyn's Prospect Park. A reviewer approvingly noted that "Schoenberg's intricate mathematical patterns shook into place . . . as they do not in the open-air park concert." (S.S.S., "The Musical Traveler," *International Musician*, March 1948, 24.)

[37]Bennett's pieces for the 1939–1940 New York World's Fair are apparently his only previous compositions for winds, excepting some (presumably lost) works written for his father's band in Freeman.

[38]Bennett's *Suite of Old American Dances* is the most played and recorded of his pieces for band (if not of his entire output). He completed a condensed score in 1948 and, over many months, copied out individual parts without ever completing a full score. This took place while he attended to orchestrations for Porter's 1948 *Kiss Me, Kate*, Rodgers's 1949 *South Pacific*, and other shows, along with television and radio work and a few smaller compositions. Chappell's publication of his *Suite* (premiered by the Goldman Band on 17 June 1949)—and the Eastman Wind Ensemble's 1953 Mercury recording—quickly made the piece a favorite of American high school and college bands. Portions of the work's third movement are taken from an earlier orchestral *Theme and Variations* (1941) written for the *Notebook* program, and some interesting stylistic echoes are heard in his *Kiss Me, Kate* scoring, particularly the "Another Op'nin, Another Show" dance music.

Night view of Electric Park, Kansas City, c. 1908. Photo from the Kansas City Museum, Kansas City, Mo. Used by permission.

This Kansas City landmark was lit by 100,000 incandescent lights; Sousa once praised its Music Pavilion as the finest of its kind. Demolished in the late 1920s, Electric Park was memorialized in Bennett's *Suite of Old American Dances.*

all magic. In the dance hall all afternoon and evening you could hear the pieces the crowds danced to, and the five movements of my piece were samples of the dances of the day: Cake Walk, Schottische, Western One-Step, Wallflower Waltz and Rag.[39]

Way, way back on these sheets I remember writing that an old account book showed a period where I arranged music for twenty-two shows a year (complete shows, or parts of shows) for several years. Even that bit of research was reported from memory; the old account book had been thrown away more than thirty years ago. Now, however, in a drawer of this desk is the successor to that old book, and I've never seen duller reading. One would think that all these pages of song titles and names of shows strung out on list after list would yield up little dancing ghosts of tender moments in the theater, on

[39]Orchestra works are oftentimes transcribed for wind band, while the reverse is a comparative rarity. Bennett's *Suite* proved so popular that he was asked to complete an orchestral transcription in 1950; the published full score is a reproduction of his manuscript. Careful comparison of Bennett's two settings of the *Suite* provides a detailed lesson in his scoring methods for (and, one could say, his notion of the essential differences between) the two ensembles.

the screen or in the air, but about the only point of interest seems to be the gradual development of the prices we got for doing a page of score through the years.

Once during a chat with John Golden,[40] for whom a New York theater was named and who lived through nearly all of the Golden Age, he showed me a sheet of paper on which was Frank Saddler's bill for the orchestrations of an entire musical comedy John Golden produced: "Received payment with thanks, $135.00. Frank Saddler." I heard that the same material for *Camelot* in 1960 was over fifty thousand dollars.

When Kansas City was to be one hundred years old they asked me to write a piece and conduct it in a concert to celebrate the birthday. *A Kansas City Album* was the result. It was fun on one count, at least. It was fun to show my Local 34 union card and realize that I was not a guest conductor, whatever they said. It was too bad I wasn't a conductor looking for work because the review in the *Kansas City Times* would have given my press agent plenty to do with his scissors.[41]

[Bennett's orchestral compositions were performed slightly less often during the postwar years, yet there occurred a corresponding rise in his visibility within the American wind-band movement. And he became increasingly better known to the public as his name ascended to the "primary credits" on theater playbills and original-cast recordings—especially those for Rodgers and Hammerstein's *South Pacific* (1949) and *The King and I* (1951).

Late in 1951, Bennett was the subject of a portrait ("Another Opening, Another Show") in *The New Yorker* (17 November). Herbert Warren Wind's captivating essay begins with Bennett's overnight creation of the overture for Rodgers and Hammerstein's *The King and I* just before the show's New Haven opening. Bennett and his associates are liberally quoted in this, the most substantial study of its subject to appear in any periodical.]

---

[40]Producer John Golden had once been a songwriter; his most lasting contribution was the lyrics to 1916's "Poor Butterfly" (music by Raymond Hubbell). One Golden-Bennett collaboration was their *United Nations All Faith Prayer for Peace.* This choir-and-orchestra opus, performed several times in New York during the early 1950s, was published by Chappell in 1953. It has the singular distinction of published endorsements by several prominent religious leaders, including Cardinal Spellman.

[41]Though Bennett appeared fairly frequently as a guest conductor beginning in the postwar years, critics directed their attention almost exclusively toward his compositions and arrangements. The reviewer for the *Kansas City Times*, however, described Bennett on this occasion (27 February 1950) as a "tall and slender figure on the podium" who "was able to communicate to the musicians just the effects he wanted, and got them."

There are a few tiny exceptions to the general tenor of the period. One was a film about Helen Keller for which we did a score.[42] She was well toward the end of her life then. She had learned to talk without hearing a word, having been deaf and blind since she was about a year-and-a-half old. After I finished recording the background score she put out her right hand and said, "Oh, Mister Bennett, the music is beautiful!" Her companion said she really did get impressions from music and had real likes and dislikes in it.

Another one not to forget is the play that got great notices for my arrangements from almost all the reviewers. Critics very rarely take note of the orchestra, but this was the big exception. It was called *Paris '90* and had a cast of one: Cornelia Otis Skinner. She was, as usual, all the cast anyone would ever need. The orchestra was made up of ten men and the music by Kay Swift was a delight. In figuring out just what instruments we could have we began our thoughts with no brass at all, but Kay and I decided that since we had to have an overture before the curtain went up, and that since the whole audience would be talking and making noise, we'd better change one of the woodwind men for a trumpet. We did, and the trumpet played the part I gave him all through the evening.[43]

I seriously considered calling up to ask if that job in the lumber yard was still open, but the next morning I read in all the papers that the sound of the music was exactly like the sounds of old Paris and evoked just the right spirit, and so on. I'll never know where they all went in Paris to hear such god-awful sounds.

The "Golden Age" was at its most golden during these years. The account book shows several of the best remembered. Not all of them appeared before 1951, when the flirtation with TV began, but I found time to be head obstetrician at the delivery of these precious babies: *Finian's Rainbow*, *Kiss Me, Kate*, *South Pacific*, *The King and I*, *My Fair Lady*, *Flower Drum Song*, *Camelot*, *The Sound of Music*—these are the ones that had long runs.

One of the Broadway big talents was shining brightly then and I shall always regret never having put down one note for him—Frank Loesser. We only met once, that I remember, and I thoroughly enjoyed the visit. It was a dinner where people were getting awards of some kind—neither of us being

---

[42]The film was released as *Helen Keller in Her Story*, 1955; an earlier title was *The Unconquered*. The picture won an "Oscar" for Best Documentary—Feature.

[43]The show marked Swift's return to Broadway after a lengthy absence. Her best-known compositions include both the title song and "Can This Be Love" from her 1930 show *Fine and Dandy*, as well as "Can't We Be Friends," which she contributed to the 1929 revue *The Little Show*. *Paris '90*, opening on 4 March 1952, testified to Bennett's ability to make any instrumental combination "sound"—in this instance, flute, clarinet, trumpet, a septet of strings, percussion, and piano.

involved in the ceremonies. We both spoke the language, and I wondered how we had missed meeting in all those years.[44]

As for trips to Hollywood, we took one that had nothing to do with the cinema. Ralph Blaine wrote the songs for a musical called *Three Wishes for Jamie* with its opening on the west coast. Louise and I stayed at a hotel near Pershing Park where the whole pile of orchestra scores was written. The copying of the parts for the musicians took place a matter of miles away from where I worked instead of down the hall in Room 413, as it would be at an eastern tryout.

Our hotel was "near" the theater ("only" about a mile away). All communications were by auto, even to sharpen a pencil—almost. You get used to it.

When the show got to New York we rehearsed downtown on The Bowery—I suppose they were afraid we'd all miss those California distances if they didn't do it that way.

[*Three Wishes for Jamie* opened on 21 March 1952. That spring Bennett was also busy completing *Mademoiselle* (subtitled "Ballet for Band"), a new work for the Goldman Band. It was his second commission from the League of Composers (the first, for orchestra, was 1936's *Hollywood*), and was premiered by the Goldman unit, with its composer conducting, on 18 June.[45] The piece—never published or recorded—provides an interesting chronological and stylistic intermediary between the earlier *Suite of Old American Dances* and 1957's *Symphonic Songs for Band*.]

Of the three motion picture jobs of the period two were for Bobby Dolan—Robert Emmett Dolan, who was one of Broadway's best loved music directors, then went to Hollywood to write and conduct music. He became a producer, with considerable success.[46] I think he was only concerned with the music in *Lady in the Dark* (with Ginger Rogers as the "Lady" in this film version)[47] and also in *My Son John* with Helen Hayes, on which I came back and worked later.

---

[44]Loesser's biggest Broadway successes—as both composer and lyricist—were *Guys and Dolls* (1950), *The Most Happy Fella* (1956), and *How to Succeed in Business without Really Trying* (1961).

[45]In the 1950s Bennett became one of a select few "honorary members" of the Goldman Band. He appeared several times as guest conductor, usually for the premiere of a new composition or arrangement.

[46]Dolan (1908–1972) first worked on Broadway in the late 1920s as a pit musician. He also completed scores for Broadway's *Foxy* and *Texas, Li'l Darlin'* (both with Johnny Mercer's lyrics) and produced Paramount's 1954 *White Christmas*. Dolan taught at Columbia in the 1960s and authored the film-scoring text *Music in Modern Media* (G. Schirmer, 1967).

[47]*Lady in the Dark* was released by Paramount in 1944, with Dolan conducting Bennett's orchestrations. Los Angeles critic Lawrence Morton (an occasional film arranger, whose brother

Bennett with Marian Anderson, early 1960s. Photo courtesy of Jean Bennett.

It was while Bobby Dolan was working on a difficult background score for *My Son John* and I was doing my best to help him (with no conspicuous success) that I got another one of those triangular telephone calls from my New York headquarters. Max Dreyfus called to say Dick Rodgers would call me about a show for the United States Navy that was in prospect. Dick and I had a very short talk on the telephone—just long enough to change the future for both of us. He told me he had been asked to do a score for an NBC television series on World War II from the point of view of the Navy [*Victory at Sea*]. If I could do it with him he would take it on. In the years that have followed I've heard him tell people it was the best thing that ever happened

Arthur orchestrated in Hollywood for four decades) was especially complementary: "The excellence of Robert Russell Bennett's arrangements for *Lady in the Dark* could have been forecast, and of course they proved to be, as one expected, superior in skill and taste to anything that has been turned out for similar pictures" ("On The Hollywood Front," *Modern Music* 21 [1944]: 265).

Russell and Louise Bennett, 1949. Photo courtesy of Jean Bennett.
The Bennetts were attending his grandmother's 100th birthday celebration in Freeman, Mo.

to him. That would cover a bit of territory, when you think of some of the things that have happened to him, and vice versa.

There are a few notes to make before we get into the struggle with the tiny screens. There was one more session on the west coast that developed into quite a drama, but it didn't start until the Navy show was well along and I'll pay here a little more attention to chronology and get to it later.

However, there were a few persons and happenings at this point that shouldn't be left to statistics alone.

Marian Anderson [1902–1993], for instance. How can any words of mine possibly bring this beautiful person any nearer to you than even the recordings of her voice do? I arranged and conducted orchestral accompaniments on two albums of her songs. For one of those albums they printed the true story of my introduction to her voice—even that was not the live voice; it was a broadcast, wherein she sang Bach and Handel divinely. The announcer then said, "And now, Miss Anderson will sing the song we all want to hear: 'Comin' through the Rye.'"

There were very few songs I wanted to hear after Bach and Handel, and one of them was not "Comin' through the Rye"! I got up to cross the room and tune her out, but she beat me to it and sang the first phrase. By the time I got there two large tears were falling down my cheeks. Those same two snobbish tears that were reserved for the death of Mélisande or the end of King Lear!

Such is the quality of this voice and this person.

In a different way I look back with warm feelings on five albums recorded by conductor Robert Shaw with his chorus. Making the arrangements for these discs amounted to a thorough education in choral conducting. The art of balancing voices is so highly developed that the ensemble in his hands seems spontaneous and inevitable. How disciplined it has to be to achieve that perfection can only be realized by studying this master at work.[48]

One more item of the 1940s: our grandson was born. Louise and I only had one child, a daughter, and she only had one child, a son. Neither generation was the victim of driving compulsion to be a musician, as far as I know. Daughter Jean has done quite a bit of painting, far-out and pretty exciting, but grandson Kean is a member of a law firm in Philadelphia.

As I write, Kean and his wife Elizabeth have children. Being grandparents doesn't impress us much. We went to Freeman, Missouri, in 1949 to celebrate Granamy Bennett's one hundredth birthday and saw them take pictures of four generations. Granamy had a permanent wave for the occasion and was still the life of the party. When I kissed her goodbye she said, "Sonny, I'll remember this day for a long, long time."

---

[48]Two earlier Bennett–Shaw associations were *Carmen Jones* and *Seven Lively Arts*, for which Shaw was choral director.

Chapter Nine

Victory at Sea, the story of World War II from the standpoint of the Navy, had a hard time getting born. From my usual station on the good ship Hearsay I gather that the whole project was the idea of a man who became quite important to the lives of a good many of us. Henry Salomon, whom we all called Pete, was a Harvard man, a member of a club that always impressed me without my having any idea what it was: The Agawam Hunt Club. Coupled with that social and intellectual background was an inborn showmanship that belonged with Zieggy [Florenz Ziegfeld], Cecil B. [DeMille], or the inventor of the teddy bear.

"Pete" Salomon was in the Navy and (again from the crow's nest of the Hearsay) did work with historian Samuel [Eliot] Morison on the story of the conflict. The Salomon idea was to get footage from all over the world and let the viewers see and hear what the Navy did and helped to do. Reliable Sources (those snoops) say it took four years to round up a production of the series.[1] Pete wanted music, big music, all the way through the pictorial story, but at the same time a narrator had to tell the viewer what he was looking at. After a few trials they chose Leonard Graves, who was at the time understudy to Yul Brynner in *The King and I*, to do this enormous job.[2] For the music, Pete Salomon chose Richard Rodgers as the greatest American composer and went and got him.[3]

---

[1]Henry Salomon spent 1942 to 1948 collaborating with Morison on the fourteen-volume *History of United States Naval Operations in World War II.* He took his idea for a television series to NBC in the fall of 1949, but discussions became sidetracked temporarily while the network considered including the Army, Marines, et al. in the proposed series. By December 1950 the Navy had pledged its cooperation; a month later Salomon succeeded in gaining RCA president Robert Sarnoff's blessing and guarantee of funding.

[2]Actor Robert Montgomery had been Salomon's early choice (Donald Hyatt telephone interview with the editor, November 1997).

[3]Once clearance had been obtained from the American Federation of Musicians to use the NBC Symphony for the soundtrack recordings, Salomon wrote: "Mr. Chotzinoff and I

The writing of the narration was by Richard Hanser and Henry Salomon, himself. Between the two they turned out a script with enough poetry in it to set it a little apart from all the other documentaries of the period, at the same time telling a pretty intricate story against an equally intricate musical telling of the same story. *Victory at Sea* was an enormous success. It has not often been completely off the air, and from the inside I can tell you that the nature of the narration has more than carried its share of the load.

My part of the show could almost be called a dream come true. Almost.

Only "almost" because it was physically about like orchestrating a complete Broadway musical every ten days to two weeks instead of three to four weeks, as would be approximately normal—even pretending the size of a score page was nearly equal, which it wasn't. Instead of the little theater orchestras I had the full NBC Symphony and we had thirteen hours of show to get ready for twenty-six broadcasts. We just barely finished writing and recording the twenty-sixth show in time for it to go on the air.[4]

I realize that preparing and recording these big, big scores, and even broadcasting them, won't make as interesting a story for these pages as some of the less absorbing tasks in the gaily illuminated show-places of the world, but that doesn't relieve me of the need to tell why the thirteen-and-a-third-mile-long film of *Victory at Sea* represents a dream come true—almost.

In the first place no conductor alive would object to directing this great orchestra. In the second place the creating of a score for a drama that really happened and is happening again before your eyes is a new experience. None of the rules for scoring a made-up, acted-out scene are any good here. In the third and all the other places, I could say to a friend, any friend, "We are on the air at three o'clock Sunday. See it if you can."[5]

This was a new experience, indeed. If I said that about [the Youmans musical] *No, No, Nanette* I'd have to say, "How did you like it?" the next time

---

will now try to line up Richard Rodgers or someone equally competent [for the background score]" (Memorandum, Henry Salomon to Robert Sarnoff, 13 July 1951. NBC Television Papers, State Historical Society of Wisconsin, Madison). Samuel Chotzinoff was the general music director for RCA radio and television whom, in 1937, Sarnoff had sent to Italy to hire Toscanini to lead the then-proposed NBC Symphony Orchestra. Donald B. Hyatt states that Rodgers was Salomon's first choice, and that Rodgers would only accept the assignment if Bennett's assistance could be assured (Hyatt, interview).

[4]Citing the demands of his *Victory at Sea* work, Bennett declined an offer to join ASCAP's Board of Directors early in 1953.

[5]This echoes his comment upon the series' broadcast conclusion: "It is the first time I have ever urged my friends to see a work of mine." ("Man Behind the Tune," *Newsweek*, 20 July 1953, 86).

we met. With *Victory at Sea* the question of liking it had to take care of itself. It wasn't really important.

When we got down to the work of cutting the film and fitting narration and music to it Richard Rodgers had written three themes: 1) a main theme, for the opening of every episode and useful in many places where the broad waves were tossing ships about; 2) a deep and ominous passage to warn of the deadly submarines below, and a third theme that pictured the ruins of naval war washing over the dark beaches.

When he played his three themes for me I said "Bravo!" with sincerity and he was again happy to take his well-deserved bow. This time it was probably more important what I thought than in the theater because I was going right to the peoples' ears with them, unaided and unhampered by lyrics, choreography or actors.

He was surprised and delighted when I told him the three themes were all I needed from him for the first episodes. They were, in fact, plenty. We were planning to use a national tune or two of our adversaries in the earlier episodes and I did indeed have enough original material. Any one of the expert film composers will understand this perfectly, but ever since we started this super-documentary young experts have come to me with pad and pencil in hand, asking the question I spoke of some pages ago: "Where does Mr. Rodgers leave off and you begin?"

All sorts of answers occur to me and sometimes my answers are not very polite, but the fact is I don't know. You take a melody line and a mood (supplied by the picture you're scoring). A second melody line in counterpoint is called for—you take the new line and put it through the same process, always prompted by what is happening in your story. Such is the nature of serious composition and, as noted above, any expert scorer of pictures knows this. His reaction if you asked him about it might be to ask you a question: What has Bennett done to deserve to be able to call up Dick Rodgers and get a Rodgers tune brought over by a messenger when he needs it?

[Rodgers devoted only two pages of his *Musical Stages* to *Victory at Sea*, providing few details about his collaboration: "What I composed were actually musical themes. For the difficult technical task of timing, cutting, and orchestrating, I turned to my old friend Russell Bennett, who has no equal in this kind of work. He fully deserves the credit, which I give him without undue modesty, for making my music sound better than it was."[6] Rodgers had earlier shared his rationale for having others arrange his scores:

---

[6]*Musical Stages*, 279.

> The man who writes music for the theatre is directly criticized because he is incapable of doing his own orchestrations. This is true, but he is entitled to a petulant "So what?" Neither can he play the clarinet in the pit nor come out on the stage and sing one of his own songs. Since the theatre is an entirely collaborative field and orchestration is a highly specialized component, he turns naturally to an experienced specialist for assistance. While the composer is usually sufficiently intelligent to be capable of learning orchestration, it is extremely doubtful that years of study and experience would find him as satisfactory in scoring his own show as Robert Russell Bennett, who has devoted his life to the business and brings to it a rare and high talent.[7]]

This brings me back to the "almost" that qualified *Victory at Sea* when considered as a dream come true. No film score that I know of has ever brought out a master work for orchestra and very possibly none ever will. I'm ashamed to confess I never have studied Prokofiev's *Lieutenant Kije* music—it, along with a few excerpts from rather experimental scores, may be an exception for the sake of argument, but the very nature of background scoring makes the odds against it prohibitive.

Two or three times that bit about calling up and having a tune sent over really happened. The most famous tune in the whole score ["Beneath the Southern Cross"] was the answer to such a phone call. It was later borrowed for use in *Me and Juliet*, a Rodgers & Hammerstein musical. It became "No Other Love." I saw an episode in our picture coming up that could use a warm, southern melody and phoned Dick about it. He didn't get around to writing it for a week or so. I had already scored the first two of the three reels of the picture when he called to say he was sending me a very nice tango.

It would be inconceivable that Rodgers could do a score for any show without a song hit, and this turned out to be our song hit (song without words in this case). When it arrived at the office I called [in] Pete Salomon, Don Hyatt, his assistant director, and Dick Hanser, writer of the narration. I spread Rodgers's manuscript out on the piano and then couldn't read it. After trying to puzzle it out I gave up and took a taxi to the theater where Rodgers was. On the way over I looked at the paper again and it dawned on me that he had put the whole left-hand part of the piece in the treble clef by mistake. It should have been obvious after all my years with songwriters, but, since I was on my way I went on over and got him to play it for me.

---

[7]"Music for the American Theatre," *Music Publishers Journal*, September-October 1943, 13.

Victory at Sea; Bennett with Richard Rodgers and Henry Salomon, 1952. From the Cleveland Public Library Photograph Collection. Used by permission.

Henry Salomon is flanked by *Victory at Sea*'s musical partnership, Rodgers and Bennett, who had first worked together a quarter-century earlier.

After I finally played it for our group Pete Salomon said, "It's a hit!"

He should have been a music publisher, because he was right.

Since two reels of the picture were already scored without this music in it I made up for lost time by filling the air with it in the third reel. Our film editors were inclined to fidget about this but it wasn't too bad a fit and was worth a lot to the whole series. After the episode was on the air we got letters about this music. I don't know just how many letters, because nobody ever seems to count them and give an honest report on how many there are.

If I got any letters the film editors may have been right to fidget—you'll recall my firm conviction that background scores are not for conscious hearing—but there's a difference here. The scene on the screen is real, not trying to make a point in a plot. Whether good or bad scoring it brings up the point again of how powerful a string of musical notes can be in human ears.

Looking back on the actual work of putting all the music for the big orchestra on paper I wonder why my right arm didn't fall off. Twenty-six half-hours of picture didn't mean thirteen hours of music because some three or four minutes of each separate show had short conversations among important men of the Navy or other appropriate material with no call for music, but it couldn't have been less than eleven hours of playing by any estimate.[8]

I never tried to count all the bars or the pages of score involved, but I never called in any help. The job of copying and binding the orchestra parts was under the direction of George Zevitas, another Harvard man, as it happened. From time to time none of us in the music department got much sleep, the least going to Zevitas, who nearly always turned up at the recording session in the morning still proofreading and binding the parts.[9]

The orchestra was not only good but tough. Only a few times they showed signs of strain. When we recorded the music for the attack on Pearl Harbor I apologized for the number of notes they had to play, and Mischa Mischakoff, the concert-master, said, "We had the old man this morning, and nothing will bother us after that."

But when we ended the first reading of the first-reel music the violinists were waving their arms to see if they were still there. I said, "You want to go back to Toscanini now, don't you?" And they all said "Yes!"[10]

At the mixing sessions, where we put together narration, music and sound effects (which Pete Salomon detested and held to a minimum) we had some long sessions, even though we had less disagreement than is normal in motion pictures. We had less disagreement, I suppose, because there was no "he," no absolute monarch, in the offing to make our product fit any preconceived standards or policies. The buck for every department stopped right in that room.

Our "monarch," Salomon, was inclined to mix the music too loud for J. Q. Public to hear the narration. He was likely to say, "But the music tells the

---

[8]Rodgers's contribution totaled twelve themes—about thirty minutes of music. Their working titles, during the series' production, were "The Song of the Sea," "The Submarine Menace," "From Naples to Rome," "Landing on D-Day," "Fiddle and Geetar," "Defeat and Discouragement," "Hawaiian Mood," "On Board a Carrier," "Mustering of Forces," "The Victory," "Guadalcanal March," and "Beneath the Southern Cross" (the tango which later appeared in 1953's *Me and Juliet* as "No Other Love"). A good deal of the underscoring is wholly Bennett's, based not at all on any of the Rodgers themes.

[9]Zevitas states that proofreading before a recording session "was usually an all-night undertaking." According to Zevitas, the production of each of the twenty-six *Victory at Sea* episodes usually allowed about ten days between Bennett's receipt of a completed script and shot-list (with timings) and the six-hour recording session with the NBC Symphony. Zevitas's team of copyists included Bennett's colleague Hans Spialek (George Zevitas telephone interview with the editor, July 1993).

[10]Throughout the many months of recording sessions, the NBC Symphony's musicians remained devoted to their leader and were well aware of how much of the score was entirely of Bennett's devising. Donald Hyatt reports that the musicians honored Bennett with a standing ovation at the end of the first day's recording session, held in Rockefeller Center's Center Theater (Hyatt, interview).

story better than the narration!" Since he wrote the narration (with Hanser) himself one would be tempted to listen to him, but we had to remind him that his viewers didn't speak the language of music quite as well as he seemed to.

Once in a while we did get letters complaining that they couldn't hear the words for the music, but the complaint was not a new one. The movie studios had many a theory about it through the years and one experiment was a favorite with the music departments: they tried running scenes entirely without music and found that the complainers still couldn't understand the words.

When, after some hesitation, RCA Records issued discs and tapes of the music alone that also proved to be a big success.[11] It gave me two nice feelings: one was because it was a conducting job. No need to stress the fact that, in spite of the reams of composition of many qualities and purposes, conducting a great orchestra is still top for me. The other nice feeling is because "the man in the street" has finally changed his greeting when we are introduced. For oh-so-many years, when he heard my name, he, being on the ball, would say as we shook hands, "Oh, yes, I know your *Symphonic Picture of Porgy and Bess.*" Now he says, "Oh yes! *Victory at Sea*!"

When I meet the admissions jury up there, I shall probably not submit either of these as a big contribution here below, but I am thankful for the change!

Even with all these side excursions came a fairly constant stream of orchestra and band arrangements, mostly of "selections" from current shows.[12] Medleys, as I believe I said before, are not a delight to the soul of the classic-minded. For the uncritical a good potpourri of pop tunes is satisfying enough. It might be likened to a meal of nothing but candy. A real gourmet chooses dishes with considerably more thought. Because of the plethora of ditties written during the Golden Age I should not be surprised to hear that no one else in history has ever written more of those things than I have, but I don't remember being filled with admiration and affection for one since *The For-*

---

[11]Part of the Musician's Union (AFM) agreement with NBC was that excerpts from the soundtracks themselves could not be issued commercially—they would have to be re-recorded at prevailing AFM wage scales. Bennett first recorded his quickly assembled nine-part concert suite in July 1953. Later that year, he led some eighteen hours of recording sessions for *Victory at Sea*'s theatrical release. Newer technologies have been embraced in turn: stereophonic versions of the suites (with Bennett again conducting) in 1958 and 1959, and remastering for compact disc in the 1980s. The music, with credits for Rodgers ("original musical score") and Bennett ("arranged and conducted by") unchanged, has thus remained continuously "in print" for four decades.

[12]Bennett completed many "symphonic pictures" while under contract to Chappell. Those from *Oklahoma!*, *South Pacific*, *The King and I*, *My Fair Lady*, and *The Sound of Music*, especially, continue to be widely performed by student, community, and professional orchestras across the U.S. (see Appendix B). Students of Bennett's scoring technique have long been disappointed because—with few exceptions—no full scores of these Broadway medleys are available.

tune Teller by Victor Herbert, so I can only guess who did this one. (It could be looked up but that is not the way these pages are being written.)[13]

Two arranging jobs that were good for a little fun came from Arthur Fiedler and his great Boston Pops Orchestra. It seems that Johann Strauss, the famous waltz man, had once written a *Jubilee Waltz* to celebrate a jubilee in Boston,[14] but the Boston orchestra could find only an arrangement for piano solo—no orchestra score or parts. Mr. Fiedler asked me to make the needed orchestration. This was too good a chance to miss. I wrote a letter in my German, regretting the loss of the score and saying I would write it over for him. I signed the letter "Johann."

Not only that, but a couple of years later the same orchestra did a waltz by Jacques Offenbach, called *Les Belles Américaines*, calling for a similar bit of correspondence in French in the same vein. I never heard whether the arrangements turned out well or not, but nothing Arthur Fiedler did ever turned out badly, played by that orchestra.

He and I were born the same year but I beat him here by just over six months. Something amusing happened to us just a few months before he died. I got a letter from the manager of the Boston Symphony Orchestra saying that he was delighted to hear that I was writing a composition for the orchestra to celebrate an important anniversary of Arthur Fiedler and the Boston Pops, and would I please let them know when the score and parts would be ready for rehearsal. It was the first I had heard of it.

I tried to telephone the manager in Boston and was told he was on the phone with an important call and would ring me back as soon as he was free. But he didn't, and a day or so later the librarian of the orchestra sent me a note asking me to have the material in his hands by a certain date. In the meantime I had written them asking who was crazy. I told them I was tied up and could not have done the piece in any case, much as I should like to have helped my "twin brother" celebrate his anniversary.

Finally a letter came explaining the mix-up. The story was that Fiedler had called an old number of mine that was seven years out of date. The number had been reassigned and when Arthur called he said, "This is Arthur Fiedler." The man at the other end of the line thought some friend was clowning, so he played his part well and accepted the commission and promised to write the piece.

---

[13]Probably the published arrangement by Otto Langey (1851–1922), recorded by Eugene Ormandy and the Philadelphia Pops Orchestra in the early 1950s (Columbia AAL29).

[14]The International Peace Jubilee of 1872 followed the Franco-Prussian war. Strauss came to the U.S. and wrote many pieces for the Jubilee as well as for America's 1876 centennial observance.

Poor Arthur thought it was all set. The letter also reported that a man in Boston took on the job and turned out the needed music in time for the celebration.

The whole episode took me back to another bit of drama with a cast of four: Mr. and Mrs. Arthur Fiedler, the telephone and I. When television was just beginning to cope with the problem of the round surface of the globe the Gillette Razor Company put on a big Christmas show with live broadcasts from New York, Boston and Los Angeles all on the same show. The Boston part of it was the Boston Pops, for which I made some nice, loud arrangements. When I asked at the agency about where to deliver the music when it was copied the answer was: take it to them and somebody would be going to Boston and would take the music with him. About two-thirty the afternoon before the morning of the rehearsal I called. There was nobody going to Boston and nobody knew anything about the music.

I bundled it up and hurried over to Grand Central Station, catching a train to Boston. I got off at Back Bay Station and called my worried wife to tell her the story. Then I sat down to figure out how to find out a few things, the main one being where, when—and who gets the material. I looked in the telephone book for Arthur Fiedler. His number was not listed but away back somewhere in my mind a number came up. I have no idea at what point in our lives the unlisted number was given to me, but how beautiful the voice of Mrs. Fiedler sounded when she answered the telephone!

This last escapade does not seem like yesterday. It was, to be statistical for a moment, December twenty-third, nineteen hundred and fifty-three.

These "escapades" seem to be reasonably named so, as they chatter at me from the past. The word—I never looked it up as a lexicographer would—seems related to an escape, and the escape may very likely be from the business of grinding out a respectable living. Some very highly endowed economics professor would have at least one grateful reader if he would make a dispassionate study of the financial story of every great artist he could think of, so that coming generations might really know how each great soul kept its body alive.

Nadia Boulanger's general observation on the subject needs, in my mind, a completely practical analysis of every individual case in order to clear away the cobwebs of ignorance and speculation. Mlle. Boulanger's big favorite, Igor Stravinsky, is reported to have left a million dollars when he died. If this is at all accurate it tempts me to write him off as a durable musical force, especially as you compare him with Bartok, who was near starvation in his last years.

Had nothing to do with it? Maybe the professor's book will help us to know where to place out bets.

Next escapade: a trip to Enid, Oklahoma, to be a judge at the Tri-State Band Festival, where ninety bands from first grade kiddies to high school seniors were in competition. It was the first real chance I'd had to hear what the youngsters do with band music in this country and it was a bit hard to believe. All ninety of them marched in a parade past the reviewing stand, the youngest of them just playing their tune in unison, with the drums for accompaniment, and all of them well rehearsed and disciplined.

When you are a judge in such a contest you find yourself judging teachers and band-leaders as much or more than the players. The winner of the main prize at the judging was from Stillwater, Oklahoma, and the playing of the *Die Fledermaus* overture was just about flawless. It came down to some of the really fine points, and that's where the teachers come in. Somebody has to show the kids what to do.

The first oboe player of the winning band played his solo in the overture with all the style of the best of them, and he looked like a tough little boy with big ears who might have milked the cows before he got on the bus to come to Enid. I happened to be conducting the Toronto Symphony Orchestra in a concert only a short time after that [2 February 1956], and had the same *Fledermaus* overture on the program. When we came to the oboe solo there was nothing to criticize in the performance, but I must say the little farmer boy from Oklahoma had more style and more beauty than the pro.

> [Enid's Tri-State Festival, begun in 1939, typically includes bands from ten or more states and has long promoted itself as "the world's largest." It retains its popularity decades later, and the closing of longtime sponsor Phillips University in the 1990s appears not to threaten its continuation. A few days after his May 1954 visit, Bennett disclosed his awareness that America's growing school band movement was proving harmful to school and professional orchestras. He remarked to a hometown reporter that "{the strings} are the foundation of an orchestra. . . . At {Enid's} tri-state band festival last week there were ninety bands with 8,490 children enrolled, a tremendous display. But the music directors said they couldn't put together enough string players any more to make a good showing. The band instruments are easier to learn than the strings, which are the most difficult."[15]]

With *Victory at Sea* started on its long career our same group started making one hour-long broadcast after the other on every subject the inspired

---

[15] *Kansas City Times*, 18 May 1954.

brain of Henry (Pete) Salomon felt like pursuing.[16] The first one—"Three–Two–One–Zero"—was on some of the up-to-date sources of energy and power. I wrote five or six themes for this one, but had to leave the scoring and general music direction to Morris Mamorsky while I defected to the west again and took up the battle of *Oklahoma!* in an ambitious production housed by MGM Studios. This was a pioneer in Todd-AO sound and wide-screen picture. A lot of the film was shot on location in southern Arizona. It seems they couldn't find an Oklahoma farm that was not surrounded by oil wells, and oil wells didn't exist as they look now when the State of Oklahoma began its existence.

The production was directed by one of the best, Fred Zinneman, who had just added to his fame with a big hit called *High Noon.* Our producer was none other than Arthur Hornblow, Jr.. He it was who produced *High, Wide and Handsome* eighteen years earlier. At that time, Arthur Hornblow used to speak to the director, Rouben Mamoulian, in French when I was in the room with them. It was not obviously an attempt to keep secrets from me, but it was hard not to feel that his conversation was not for my ears. I told Rouben at the time not to remind Arthur that I was especially happy when I could parade my Parisian accent before people.

Now, with Fred Zinneman and Arthur in the room with me, the temptation was too great to resist. I put Fred up to it, and we went in German a couple of times, just for Arthur's benefit. It really wasn't as much fun as I thought it would be. We rather enjoyed German though—even without our friend in the room. German is a harder language to keep fluent in than it seems like it ought to be, and his German was beautiful to listen to.

Oklahoma! was a long and rather difficult task. As we worked on it, it seemed impossible for it not to be a hit. But somebody or some combination of somebodies did the impossible. I may have overestimated it as a work of art but approached the whole story very thoughtfully. Since we had such fine songs and musical moments in the play I tried to keep the music behind the whole production very free of speaking unless it was spoken to, letting the songs and dances have fresh ears to listen to them. That didn't mean silence, but it meant avoiding "orchestrator's music," music that would compete in any way with the melodies to come. It didn't work. Too many ears were there that had seen too many movies, maybe.

And of course they may have been right. As I tried compromises and some arguments I realized there was no hope for the tender little idea. Fred Hynes, who was the overall director of the Todd-AO sound and equipment, was often

---

[16]The NBC *Project 20* series of films for television eventually totaled more than thirty. All feature scores composed or arranged by Bennett, who also conducted the soundtrack recording sessions.

at the studio restaurant at tea time and we discussed and reported our defeats and disillusionments. Each had an almost daily report of the disappointments.

We came to a delay in the production and Louise and I went to New York, where I now had a contract with NBC. It is put this way because, at the luncheon in the Rainbow Room where I first met Henry Salomon we had a very few words about my salary for *Victory at Sea.* None of us having any idea of what the whole project would be worth to civilization I named a figure that would just about make ends meet.

Did I want a contract? No, just a letter would take care of it. He would see that I got the letter right away.

We started the recordings and my stipend was ready every payday. One day "Pete" said to me, "I was worrying about something last night. Did you ever get that letter?"

"No, but I've been paid every week!"

"But how embarrassing! I'll see that you get the letter right away."

For some reason I never did. You'd think some matter-of-fact person in the business office of the National Broadcasting Company would wonder after a year and more what this fellow Bennett was getting that money for, but the money came up and no questions were asked. Ah well-a-day!

But now there was an agreement on paper and the group that was to be called *Project 20*[17] was already at work. Not because they were far enough along for me to roll up my sleeves, but because the condition of *Oklahoma!* at MGM was a problem that needed solving. I called Dick Rodgers to recommend my not going back on salary there and letting them clean up the final details with one of their highly qualified music men.

Rodgers seemed surprisingly indifferent about the whole affair, and I surmised that they had already considered the same idea in Hollywood. They engaged my long-time friend and co-worker Adolph Deutsch [and orchestrator Alexander Courage]—a winner by this time of two or three Academy Awards for his scoring—and it would be hard to make a better choice.

They finally had a sneak preview of the film on Long Island near New York City and a few of us got over to see it. As I sat through the running I thought of Director Fred Zinneman's good-bye to me on the last evening we were together at the studio, trying to put something together that would get us past the front office. It hadn't occurred to me that he had any such problem, but as we shook hands I said "Also gute Nacht, Herr Kunstler!" (I always called him Mr. Artist.)

---

[17] NBC's press releases regularly explained that the title "derives from the 20th Century and our aim to dramatize its major themes with a blending of film, music, and spoken narrative." Bennett usually spelled out the word twenty.

He replied, "Mit der Kunst hat es nichts zu tun!" ("It has nothing to do with art.")

I have neither the equipment nor the desire to write a review of what we saw at the preview. Mentally, beyond wondering why a group of wise, experienced showmen would choose a darling little show of vignettes of little people to show off the world's biggest screen, I didn't even allow myself the luxury of an opinion.

I still kept it out of my mind until one morning a long and beautifully worded telegram came from Arthur Hornblow congratulating me on a nomination for the Academy Award for the background score of *Oklahoma!* We went to the big evening, and sure enough, two features of the film got Oscars: one was for the score, with statuettes for Jay Blackton, who conducted the music, Adolph Deutsch, and me. The other was for Fred Hynes with his Todd-AO sound. My tea-time companion![18]

I happened to see Rodgers and Hammerstein standing together at a theater the next day and they looked up and said "Congratulations" without much of an exclamation point. I said "Oh boy! was that ever a bad show!" and Rodgers said, "There's too much talent." It may have been said many times by many people, but to me it is a brilliant comment on those Oscar, Emmy, Tony,[19] Grammy evenings.

[Bennett fails to mention his spirited *Symphonic Songs for Band*, commissioned by the Kappa Kappa Psi fraternity and Tau Beta Sigma sorority. It was premiered on 24 August 1957 at the Salt Lake City Tabernacle by the National Intercollegiate Band. The 125 student musicians, from 52 colleges and universities, were led by Lt. Col. William F. Santelmann, retired conductor of the Marine Band. *Symphonic Songs* was promptly published by Chappell and—like his *Suite of Old American Dances*—was championed by Frederick Fennell and his Eastman Wind Ensemble. Mercury Records' Fennell/EWE recordings (beginning in 1953) proved to be influential in establishing the American concert band's "standard repertory" and ensuring the widespread popularity of the *Suite* and *Symphonic Songs*.[20]]

---

[18]Fred Hynes's Oscar (as head of the Todd-AO sound unit) for *Oklahoma!* was followed by similar honors for his work on *South Pacific*, *The Sound of Music*, and *West Side Story*. The Academy of Motion Picture Arts and Sciences also singled out Hynes for two special awards in the 1980s.

[19]The Antoinette Perry "Tony" awards did not specifically honor theater orchestrations until the 1990s, but Bennett was presented with one of the organization's "Special Awards" in 1957.

[20]The editor's orchestral transcription of the *Symphonic Songs* was premiered by the Wisconsin Chamber Orchestra in 1995.

Robert Austin Boudreau had come into this narrative by this time. Robert Austin Boudreau, with a rich background of music, especially band music, had founded the American Wind Symphony, with a luxurious instrumentation of woodwind and brass [and percussion] and no strings.[21] It had a big barge for a concert stage. His season tour began [in Pittsburgh] at the point where the Allegheny, the Monongahela, and the Ohio Rivers all joined together. The barge sailed down the Ohio to the Mississippi and down the Mississippi to its mouth, giving nightly concerts to large crowds in amphitheaters carved out in the river banks. The programs were uncompromising, giving those who gathered on the river music they had mostly not heard before. All of the crowds were big and some of them were enormous.

Sitting among them and feeling their reaction to, for instance, a contemporary work of a Japanese composer who had no concern for consonance and dissonance as we label them was indeed an experience.

They branched out and traveled up the Mississippi to Minnesota, on the Great Lakes, up the Thames in England, and elsewhere. The only comparison of audiences I ever heard was from a member of the orchestra. What he said, not too admiringly, was that all the New York audiences wanted to hear was marches.

I don't think I ever heard where Robert Boudreau heard of me, but he asked me to write a work for his second season.[22] The orchestra was made up of carefully selected young musicians from all over the country and even from abroad, and nothing was too difficult for them. The Bennetts became quasi-members of the "family." I wrote a number of pieces for them, including a whole program to conduct on my birthday one year.[23]

One of the features of that concert was an *Ohio River Suite*, describing the three rivers that meet in Pittsburgh. We were taken through a steel mill

---

[21]The American Wind Symphony was renamed "American Waterways Wind Orchestra" in the 1980s. Its instrumentation differs from the typical American concert band by incorporating a multiplicity of "auxiliary" woodwinds (piccolos, alto flutes, English horns, contrabassoons, etc.) while eliminating saxophones and euphoniums. The latter two instruments—generally agreed to be the easiest to play of the standard woodwinds and brasses—are longtime mainstays of the band, but remain rarely used by orchestral composers.

[22]Bennett's first piece for the American Wind Symphony was the Concerto Grosso for Woodwind Quintet and Wind Orchestra; premiered 6 July 1958, it remains the best-known and most-played of his AWS works. Juilliard graduate Boudreau tells of meeting Bennett while playing trumpet in the Goldman Band in the late 1940s and notes that Bennett also assisted him in obtaining free-lance engagements in New York (Robert Austin Boudreau telephone interview with the editor, March 1990).

[23]This "birthday" concert was 15 June 1961; the program included Bennett's *Overture to Ty, Tris, and Willie* (Pittsburgh baseball greats Cobb, Speaker, and Stargell, respectively) and his *Three Humoresques* (one each for the ensemble's woodwinds, brasses, and percussion/harps).

for "inspiration." As is often the case we went for the inspiration after I had written the piece (in Bermuda) and was already rehearsing it.

We enjoyed visiting Pittsburgh for two reasons. The second one was really the first, calendar-wise. Some time before all this the Pittsburgh Symphony played my *Eight Etudes*, and almost a month before the concert a letter came to me on the stationery of the Pittsburgh Pirates (National League baseball team). It said (roughly remembered) "Dear Mr. Bennett, It may surprise you to know that, beside being the owner of the Pittsburgh Pirates, I am also program annotator for the Pittsburgh Symphony Orchestra. We are presenting your *Eight Etudes* under the direction of Fritz Reiner and I would appreciate anything you would like to tell me about the piece—" and so on, signed "William Benswanger."

I wrote back, "Dear Bill, you don't have to introduce yourself. I met you at Harry Ruby's house in Beverly Hills with Pie Traynor, Harry Danni, Bill Rigrey and others a couple of years ago," and went on with notes on the music.

Harry Ruby, who is no stranger to these pages, was also no stranger to big league ball players. He used to walk into the club house at almost any ball park and somebody would say, "Get your glove, Harry!" I don't know what they thought of him as a ball player but he had them all in stitches most of the time.

The American Wind Symphony, and Bill and Eleanor Benswanger (her father was the original owner of the Pirates as we know them) made Pittsburgh, Pa. a nice place to stop off on any pretext.

And there were pretexts. On the one-hundred-fiftieth anniversary of the city we did *A Commemoration Symphony* built of the tunes of Pittsburgher Stephen Collins Foster. William Steinberg, the Pittsburgh Symphony and the Mendelssohn Choir did a fine performance.

> [Bennett approached the 1959 work as a would-be "period piece"—as if Foster, unable to construct a piece of symphonic proportions from his beautiful melodies, had engaged him to complete the task. In the program notes for the first performance, Bennett confessed an initial suspicion that Foster's songs (twelve are used in the work's four movements) wouldn't be "substantial enough" for symphonic treatment. He never did consider himself the work's composer, thus his "specially arranged and orchestrated by" program credit.]

At another time Steinberg recorded a disk with [my] special arrangements of *My Fair Lady* and *The Sound of Music* for symphony orchestra.[24] This was

---

[24]The works were recorded in April 1968. The elaborate, extended medley from *My Fair Lady* was commissioned by the Pittsburgh Symphony as a parallel to the Gershwin-Bennett

recorded there and that called for another visit. William Benswanger's favorite music was very like mine. The scores on his piano were usually the ones I studied and still don't really know well enough if fate ever calls my bluff!

The second documentary of our *Project 20* series [for NBC television] was a study of communism as it was developing in Russia. We still had our team together and we gave it our all. You don't hear thunderous applause or see long lines at the box office to tell you how you're doin' with this medium but the smile of success was on everybody's face.

The title Pete Salomon chose for this one [broadcast 27 December 1955] was "Nightmare in Red." His titles were always pretty apt. Each of the *Victory at Sea* episodes had had a strikingly thoughtful title. I wrote a march for this latest one and since it was to be published I asked Pete to give me a name for "a piece about dictators and totalitarians in general." He suggested "The March of Might."

The first public performance of it was at a [summer 1956] concert of the Goldman Band in New York. Trust the dear old morning newspaper to set an example for accuracy. In announcing the concert they listed the new march as "The March of Night" from "Nightmare in Bed"!

We came next to a study of the years of the great depression of all-too-recent-memory. Pete called it "The Jazz Age" and engaged the great Fred Allen to do the narration for the [6 December 1956] broadcast. He was never anything but lovable and for me a real nostalgic joy. Comedy changes a bit every twenty-four hours of our lives, and what makes people laugh today can easily fall flat tomorrow. Personalities do not change, nor are they ever quite replaced.

"The Jazz Age" was certainly not a comedy—after all this—it was much more like a tragedy. It dealt mostly with that stock market and country-wide crash. Pete Salomon was quite inclined to the left and you could almost hear him smack his lips over the plight of Wall Street. With this mixture of bad news and worse on the screen the personality of Fred Allen seemed to be just the right thing to keep at least a few of us listening to the story.

Salomon, in this film and one or two others, picked out a lot of his favorite pop tunes for the background score. He went by titles, and you can guess what a bit of music-arranging was needed to make the music fit the scenes. The extreme of this came in a study of World War One, where, in a long scene about the mud and the bugs and the rats of the trenches, he chose "The Roses of Picardy"!

Symphonic Picture of "Porgy and Bess" that Reiner and the orchestra had commissioned a quarter-century earlier. It and Bennett's *The Sound of Music* arrangement are more elaborate and symphonic in conception than the "print" medleys he had completed for Chappell.

[Composer-arranger Eddy Lawrence Manson, one-time president of the American Society of Music Arrangers, noted:

> I watched Russell conduct an intricate {*Project 20*} film score once. He had a top-notch orchestra of the best men in N.Y. at the time. Instead of dividing his score, as we all do, into short two or three minute cues, he conducted an ENTIRE REEL {*sic*} at a time, which attested to his immaculate musicianship, sense of timing, and faultless orchestration. A reel, by the way, runs approximately eight to ten minutes and in those days—the fifties—if a mistake was made, the entire reel had to be re-wound at sound speed, and done over again, which of course could take an enormous amount of expensive time over the course of a recording session. So you can see the chance he took. . . . Professionally, the man had no peer. He was fast, accurate, terribly creative, and had no patience with inferior or sloppy musicianship.[25]]

What with these elaborate documentaries coming out of our *Project 20* factory about as frequently as these hard-working creative minds could conceive and produce them, and the Broadway scene bringing in some of the prime productions of the Golden Age in high gear, and Chappell and Company, my publishers, needing a number of ambitious selections from the Broadway shows, and an active schedule of doubles and singles sessions at the West Side Tennis Club, there was not much chance of sitting around and getting bored during the years that followed *Victory at Sea.*

Just in case it might get monotonous, Destiny amused herself by bringing me another weekly show (live) for TV in which I think the sponsors actually wanted to set all records for variety and outlay. It was the sort of show wherein, if I needed a nice tenor soloist for a short passage in an arrangement and asked the bosses for him they would say, "Let's see: whom shall we get—Caruso?—no, he's dead" and they would proceed down the list of the greatest until they got me a tenor!

Well, we went on the air for two broadcasts in which we had Leontyne Price and William Warfield sing "Bess, You Is My Woman Now" and paraded that quality of performance before one's eyes and ears all the way.[26]

There was no conceivable way to fit such a series into my life and it's hard to see why I allowed it to go so far as these two broadcasts—like [*Oklahoma!*'s] Ado Annie, I guess I couldn't say no, but a disastrous conflict was down the street waiting for me.

---

[25]Eddy Lawrence Manson letter to the editor, 19 February 1989.

[26]The show was the *Scott Music Hall*; Bennett was host, conductor, and arranger for its 3 and 17 June 1953 broadcasts.

Bennett at the podium during the recording session. Photo courtesy of Donald B. Hyatt.

Note "Perky" on the conductor's stand.

Bennett conducting one of the *Project 20* soundtracks for NBC at Manhattan's Center Theatre, early 1960s. Photo courtesy of Donald B. Hyatt.

These recording sessions with the NBC recording orchestra never failed to thrill Bennett, who had gone to Europe decades earlier with a conducting career as perhaps his foremost ambition.

Good old NBC took me off the hook, although their action had nothing to do with me. They simply didn't want a musical show of any kind in the spot and the new extravaganza had no home.

From me a big sigh of relief. Even with nothing else on his mind a show of that kind is a full-time worry for a music director. It was an interesting experience to see a head-line personality no matter which way one looked, but I'd been in a similar spot before and knew some of the drawbacks.

Back at the beginning of the roaring forties, when ASCAP was in a dispute with the major networks, Oscar Hammerstein designed and produced an elaborate revue to be broadcast by independent stations as propaganda for the ASCAP side. As music director of that I enjoyed meeting all the great stars who joined us and did some of their famous turns, but before very long fun wasn't fun any more. You seemed to spend the most of your time with your heart in your mouth.[27]

In this new revue that died abornin' [*Scott Music Hall*], Patricia Morison had the stage to herself for a lovely performance of a song that was not from *Kiss Me, Kate*, even though she was Kate in that Shakespeare-Spewack-Cole Porter gem.[28] I single her out here because I overheard her say something backstage at *Kiss Me, Kate* that is among my keepsakes. She was sitting not far from the two comedians, Harry Clark and Jack Diamond, while they were having a lively discussion of psychoanalysis as they waited for whatever it was. Their conversation was getting more and more "basic."

She began to demur a bit at the level of the humor. Finally she protested, "Boys! This is getting a little rough for me."

Harry turned to her and said, "What's the matter—haven't you ever been psychoanalyzed?"

Pat: "No, I never have."

Harry: "Then how do you know whether you're a boy or a girl?"

Pat: "I had pink booties."

Harry: "Well . . . that stops me!"

---

[27]The first of the projected thirteen weekly *ASCAP on Parade* radio programs aired on 25 January 1941. The Society's strike having begun with the new year, this was the only commercial broadcast on which songs by ASCAP members were aired. Bennett's own *Notebook* program was permitted to return to the airwaves late in March—well before the official end of the strike—because the Bennett compositions performed on his show were not considered "commercial."

[28]Decades later, Morison would flatteringly recall Bennett's work on the show: "When we were rehearsing *Kate*, we rehearsed with piano, of course. . . . It was disjointed, and we didn't think we had a hit. . . . It wasn't until we heard Robert Russell Bennett's orchestrations that all of a sudden we got really excited" (Patricia Morison interview with Miles Krueger, Los Angeles, 24 May 1990, in liner notes for EMI CD D230278, 1990).

I finally ran into a serious jam even without the one that almost was: *My Fair Lady* on Broadway and "The Twisted Cross" on TV.[29] "The Twisted Cross" was a fine study of World War Two and the end of Hitler. Either of these without the other was a full-time headache. I had no right to consider their relative importance. Looking back without deep thought it would be easy to say that the Broadway musical became a classic, etc., but suppose we answer the question, "How long would the musical have to play in theaters to reach the audience that 'The Twisted Cross' did, without being repeated?" And how many members of each family might look and listen—could and should look and listen?

These two questions refer only to the number of persons we are to reach and says nothing about the message we have for them.

The size of the audience may or may not be interesting but adds up to another way of saying I had no right to choose between the two jobs. I had to do them both with as near one hundred percent of what I had to offer as I could.

For "The Twisted Cross" I did what practically every Hollywood composer does: composed and fit the entire score to the picture and then turned it over to "my orchestrator" (who happened to be a fine musician named Robert Noeltner[30]). Bob did the full orchestra score and I don't see how it could have been better done. For *My Fair Lady* our old friend Phil Lang took on several numbers by the time we opened in New York.[31]

One morning some extra-sensory something called to me and said, "Hey! Philip J. Lang has done quite a bit of this and he would probably like you to give him credit on the program."[32] If anybody thinks it normal for me to stop and think of program credits in a jam like this I haven't given a very accurate idea of my thinking habits up to here. But the idea struck me very clearly, wherever it came from. And, wherever it came from I'm so glad it did. The nature of Broadway being what it is, I heard that the milkman in the Long

---

[29]NBC's "The Twisted Cross" aired 14 March 1956; *My Fair Lady* opened in New York the following day.

[30]Noeltner prepared the published piano-vocal scores for a number of Broadway shows beginning in the 1960s; this had earlier been Albert Sirmay's specialty at Chappell.

[31]Philip J. Lang's work in the 1940s and 50s included arrangements for Alfred Wallenstein, Arthur Fiedler, and Morton Gould, as well as the Victor Borge and *Your Show of Shows* television programs. Among Lang's Broadway credits are orchestrations for *High Button Shoes* (1947), *Take Me Along* (1959), *Carnival* (1961), *Hello, Dolly!* (1964) and *Mame* (1966). He also scored some of the 1969 film version of *Dolly* and the soundtracks for *The Night They Raided Minsky's* (1968) and *The Molly Maguires* (1970). Most of his original works and arrangements for concert band were published by Mills Music, as was his valuable 1950 text *Scoring for the Band.*

[32]On Broadway, it was long common to credit only the "lead" or principal orchestrator.

Island town [Freeport] where Phil Lang lived said to Mrs. Lang one morning, "Is it true that your husband arranged the music for *My Fair Lady*?" Mrs. Lang said, "Yes" and Phil was a famous man.

> [Students of theater orchestration, aware that the majority of musicals are collaboratively scored, listen intently to original-cast recordings, keen to notice stylistic differences that might hint at which orchestrator had scored a given song. Lang takes credit for *My Fair Lady*'s "With a Little Bit of Luck," "The Ascot Gavotte," "On the Street Where You Live," "The Embassy Waltz," "Get Me to the Church on Time," and "Without You," the remainder (including the Overture) being Bennett's contributions.]

The television hour ["The Twisted Cross"] had a different aftermath. We went on the air and off with the great tragedy. There was nothing to applaud and any criticism had to be an expert, technical one. It simply left its viewers with the feeling that was well expressed by General Dwight Eisenhower when he returned from his assignment in Europe: "It must never happen again."

The only criticism of the hour as a show that I saw was in *Variety*, the theatrical weekly newspaper. The reviewer (I forget which one) said my music was an "inferior score." Pete Salomon, who was particularly pleased with the music, told me he was going to call up the editor and ask him not to have the same writer review any show of ours again.

After we talked for a few minutes about it Pete promised me he would not do anything of the kind. Critics can only express an opinion, and history has never shown me a criticism that could change the career of a musical composition. It is very hard to believe that any symphony orchestra conductor, in his seat of authority, would allow any critic alive to influence his opinion of works he might put on his program. Nor any other person, for that matter. An example comes to mind: I once went to Arthur Judson with a timid suggestion (timid as was befitting, with my complete lack of background as a conductor) that I be given a chance to be a guest conductor in my home town, Kansas City, when they announced publicly that they were going to engage some guest conductors. Arthur Judson was a name to frighten naughty little musicians with in those days.[33]

He was very gracious, and almost patted me on the head as he told me that I was a great composer, and the New York Philharmonic must play a

[33]Judson (1881–1975) managed the Philadelphia Orchestra (1915–1936) and, later, the New York Philharmonic (1922–1956). In the 1930s he formed what later became Columbia Artists Management, Inc. (CAMI), the agency that effectively dominated the booking of artist performers and conductors in the U.S. for many years.

work of mine. He would speak to Stokowski about it.[34] I had visions of Stokie throwing him out the front door, but he did worse: he agreed to play a piece of mine. I sent him my [1946] *Overture to an Imaginary Drama*, which I had conducted twice as a guest conductor with pretty good success. Two conductor friends of mine had done it and also reported a good reception.[35]

I went to the [26 November 1949] concert of the Philharmonic. The maestro made sure that Arthur Judson would never interfere with his programming again. Members of the orchestra apologized to me for the performance.

Among other stage shows I should stop to note was one called *Bells Are Ringing*. It had one of the stars to remember as a leading lady, Judy Holliday, but I pause to single out the play because of the composer of the songs. He was Jule Styne, and his story in my life has been almost like Frank Loesser's, for whom I never did a page of orchestration. For Jule Styne I only did one show in which I had to take full blame for all the music arranging. This was it. Jule had one of the biggest talents and also knew a lot about planning, casting and producing. Nearly all the tune and lyric writers think they are capable of producing and directing but it isn't usually evident to us whose work is so dependent on operating and timing and spacing.

Jule Styne is another who seldom wrote a show that didn't have a song hit in it. *Bells Are Ringing* had two songs that one hears frequently, "The Party's Over" and "Just in Time." I'm not sure that by his standards either of these would be called a hit, but they both refuse to disappear.

Rodgers and Hammerstein took a slightly unusual turn and did a musical for television in the spring of 1957. They made it out of *Cinderella* and Julie Andrews played *the* part. We worked very hard indeed on it, it cost a lot of money and every department was manned by experts. We did a complete show, tore it down and did another, repeated the same effort twice and finally went on the air. It sounds like the birth of a masterpiece, but I'm afraid I used the right word for it when I called it an effort.

Project 20—over the NBC network—was in good health these days, putting a new documentary on the air at fairly regular intervals, but one night our boss, Henry Salomon Jr. died. Possibly we should have been prepared in some way for this, because I remember Louise and I paid him a visit at a hospital some time before. Nobody spelled out his ailment and he seemed lively and full of

---

[34]The N. Y. Philharmonic had, however, already performed the *Symphony in D for the Dodgers* (1941) and *Eight Etudes* (1942). Stokowski, too, had judged the earlier *Musical America* and Victor Records composition contests and led the Philadelphia Orchestra in Bennett's *Abraham Lincoln* symphony.

[35]Howard Mitchell (twice with the National Symphony) and Fritz Mahler (Toronto Philharmonic).

ideas for the future. He was only in his forties. His assistant, Donald B. Hyatt, was a brilliant and alert member of our production team and he slipped into the driver's seat without slowing down. Pete Salomon might have had many criticisms of the details of the shows that followed, but I think he would have been delighted with the way his great off-spring never missed a beat.

One of the documentaries that came soon after Pete died was "Meet Mr. Lincoln" [11 February 1959], a pretty elaborate example of the technique Don Hyatt developed of using "stills" and moving around them.[36] A still (if there is anyone who doesn't recognize the term) is merely a photograph that doesn't move. Some of the very primitive ones of Lincoln's time are simply wonderful considering how young and how complicated photography was. They ran a preview at a formal gathering in Washington the evening before we went on the air. The then-president Dwight Eisenhower, Vice President Richard Nixon,[37] members of the Cabinet, the Supreme Court, and "everybody who's anybody" were there.

The following morning we took an eight o'clock train for New York, got as far as Baltimore and learned that the seven o'clock train had been scattered all over the track when the electric engine jumped the track and rammed its nose into the ground.

The rest of my troupe decided to go to the airport and get on the first plane they could, but I bought two paperback whodunits and went back into our car. In about twenty minutes the train moved out toward New York. There was one track undamaged, over which our train crawled, and when I looked at the wreck, with cars making a series of big W's across the rails, I discovered we were at an exact spot that I had noticed and even inquired about for several years. It was a clearing in a wooded sector, amounted to an enormous green lawn, with what looked like a very modern factory at the far edge of it. Surely a good solid man of business would not only have inquired about it, he would have found out about it, but the whole scene had more music in it if it remained a mystery, if that's any excuse.

---

[36]Donald Hyatt's "stills-in-motion" technique has since become ubiquitous in the production of television and film documentaries.

[37]Nixon described the *Victory at Sea* music as "one of my favorites" in his *Memoirs* (Grosset & Dunlap, 1978). At home, the evening after his 1968 election, he "put it [the LP] on and turned the volume up high. My thoughts meshed with the music. The battle had been long and arduous. We had suffered reverses and won victories. The struggle had been hard fought. But now we had won the final victory. The music captured the moment for me better than anything I could say or think or write" (335). Nixon later thanked Bennett (letter, 23 June 1971) for his gift of some specially-packaged *Victory at Sea* LPs.

There is absolutely no reason known to me why the seven o'clock train chose this exact hundred yards to crash in.

It was reported that there were no serious injuries, and I beat my crowd to New York.

My three careers [broadcasting, theater, and composing], none of them spectacular, were nonetheless active and clearly defined. *Project 20* was on the air periodically with a pretty thorough study of a variety of subjects: historical, political, religious, artistic and so on. Besides well over twenty under the label of *Project 20* we went up several side streets and back alleys to visit trends and events as they would come up. As an example, Ragtime, when the younger ears started to rediscover it. For an hour's visit with ragtime our narrator was Hoagy Carmichael, famous as the composer of one of America's top pop classics, "Star Dust." Hoagy had one difficulty: he couldn't keep from saying "jazz" when he came to the word "ragtime" in his script. Since our main point was to show the difference between those two and we were putting the show on long stretches of tape, each time he made the mistake we had to throw the tape away and make a new one. This was not only expensive in time and tape but everyone who played or sang on that particular section had to come up with a new performance in his or her best vein. I felt sorry for dear old Eubie Blake, nearly ninety years old,[38] who had to play a ragtime solo in top form three or four times in a row. To get keyed up and play over and over like that kills you a little each time.

Among our broadcasts was "The Coming of Christ" [21 December 1960], quite faithfully pictured with the paintings of the masters, narration of great beauty written by Richard Hanser and read by Alexander Scourby. Scourby's voice and deep sincerity are something not to miss. Later, in the same way, we did "He Is Risen" [15 April 1962], the second half of Jesus's story, and some time after that "The Law and the Prophets" [23 April 1967], a study of the Old Testament.

The National Academy of Television Arts and Sciences gave me their little statuette, called an Emmy, for the music of "He Is Risen."[39] I took Emmy

---

[38]Composer-pianist Blake (1883–1983) was actually only 77 years old at the time. "Those Ragtime Years" aired on 22 November 1960, including such songs as "Under the Bamboo Tree" and "Bill Bailey." It anticipated by a decade America's "ragtime revival" of the 1970s, when Blake's audiences could marvel at the spirited television and concert performances the pianist gave as he approached his 100th birthday.

[39]Syndicated television columnist Jack Gould asserted that Bennett's Emmy was "much the most deserved" of the entertainment awards. . . . "That he received the night's most sustained ovation in New York was fitting" (*New York Times*, 2 June 1963).

home and was afraid she would lord it over Oscar; at the time Emmys seemed more important than Oscars, but it was a happy marriage.

The thing I remember best about the music is behind the scene of the Crucifixion. At the recording my orchestra played it tenderly and sincerely. Soft, sustained strings seemed to fill the sky, harp notes came out of the hills and trees of the horizon, and low horns chanted a Gregorian melody. The picture and the music faded out together and left a silence in the whole studio. At this point a second violin man turned to the first horn player nearby and said, "You played that like a Christian!"

There were so many of those shows with memories, and some of the memories are sad ones. One of our especially thoughtful studies was of the cowboy country that really existed as compared with the whoopin' and a-hollerin' that anybody seemed to be able to write and everybody seemed to buy.

We called it "The Real West" [29 March 1961] and our narrator was somebody that knew what he was narrating about: Gary Cooper. No wide-eyed schoolgirl fan ever overestimated the genuine character of that real man.

The sad part of the memory is that while he was recording his narration he could only work two hours and go back to bed for four before he came back to work another two hours. He finished the job but lasted only a matter of days after that.[40]

Another sad memory was "The End of the Trail" [16 March 1967] but the sadness was only that shared by the viewers when we went on the air. It told the story of what the white men did to the American natives as they pushed west on the continent and it brought on some sober thoughts. For music I remembered Indian melodies from the collection my old teacher Sir Carl Busch had in Kansas City. With five flutes in four different sizes it sounded pretty to us, but I wonder if any of it sounded so to any Indians.[41]

The only other of our broadcasts that goes on the memories list will be "Down to the Sea In Ships" [11 December 1968]. It had a lot to tell us about our struggles, triumphs, and defeats on the mighty ocean and my department had a lot of excitement with sea chanteys and wild winds and Franz Schubert's

---

[40]Producer Don Hyatt, Bennett, and the *Project 20* team later eulogized the star in their "The Tall American—Gary Cooper" (26 March 1963).

[41]Even after the late-1950s demise of the NBC Symphony, the network continued to provide New York's best musicians for Bennett's recording sessions. *Project 20*'s "The Story of Will Rogers" (which aired 28 March 1961) was typical; his superb clarinet-saxophone section included Leonard Portnoy, Theodore Gompers, Walt Levinsky, Al Gallodoro (ex-Whiteman and NBC Symphony), Paul Ricci, Harold Feldman, Joe Allard (longtime member of the Juilliard faculty), and ace big-band veterans Al Klink and Hymie Shertzer.

beautiful song, "Am Meer (On The Sea)." A good deal of the music is played at band concerts wherever there are bands.[42]

Our *Project 20* met with a sudden end. We were doing a series of ten broadcasts to go on the air as the U.S.A. celebrated its two-hundredth birthday. Three of the ten episodes were written and recorded, the star of the show being Chet Huntley. I doubt that there has ever been a more clear-thinking, articulate and convincing personality on the air. Recordings of his narration were a joy. He read from Richard Hanser's script as though he were saying his own words right from the heart.

But after we had put the third episode together—ready for the air—I wrote a note and sent it to his Montana address. A nice reply, thanking me for telling him how pleased we were with it, came back to me in a few days. The date of the postmark was the date of his death from lung cancer.

For one reason or another *Project 20* went with him. The titles chosen for the first three [bicentennial] episodes were "The Fabulous Country," "Strange and Terrible Times," and "Faith of Our Fathers." Our whole group scattered without undue stir. We all had work of some kind waiting for us, no tears were shed that I know of, yet all of us look back with affection on the team we were playing for.[43]

Some of the most highly toasted [Broadway] shows still came along, and one or two that were not successful have entertaining histories. Another one of the Rodgers and Hammerstein shows (inclined to be overlooked for some reason) is *Flower Drum Song.* It was quite an appealing play, with one or two unforgettable members of the cast. The two authors had reached a plateau that all enormously successful show people seem to reach, where the smarties and the critics take the good for granted and fill the lake with crocodile tears if the hero has to blow his nose. After this play had run exactly one year with very few unsold seats I happened to pick up a New York paper with an article that began, "After the dismal failure of *Flower Drum Song* . . . "—that's all I read.[44]

---

[42]Warner Brothers published a concert suite from *Down to the Sea in Ships*, transcribed by its composer from the orchestral original. It was premiered by the Goldman Band on a July 1969 concert celebrating Bennett's 75th birthday.

[43]Donald Hyatt's *Project 20* scripts—as well as nearly all of Bennett's holograph scores for those productions—are housed at the State Historical Society of Wisconsin (Madison, Wisc.).

[44]The first of *Flower Drum Song*'s 600 performances was on 1 December 1958. Many musical theater professionals doubted Bennett's ability to do full justice to the jazz-flavored numbers of the era's musicals (see Glenn Miller's supposed contributions to *Girl Crazy* [p. 115]). Bruce Pomahac, of the Rodgers and Hammerstein organization, reports that *Flower Drum Song*'s "Grant Avenue"—first scored by Bennett—was reworked by at least two other orchestrators, Joe Glover and Luther Henderson (Bruce Pomahac interview with the editor, New York, November 1996).

A dismal failure—I mean a real one—was called *Juno.* It was a musical setting of *Juno and the Paycock* of Sean O'Casey. The man who wrote the songs—words and music—was a real musician, Marc Blitzstein.[45] His music as a serious composer is of great distinction and I felt him to be headed for real importance. On Broadway he had already had some success, being the author and composer of *The Cradle Will Rock*, for example. We opened *Juno* in Washington and worked hard on it. Bobby Dolan was our musical director and did his usual meticulous job, and when we got to the New York opening [9 March 1959] it felt to me like a better than average show. Shirley Booth gave an impressive performance as Juno. At the premiere there were more than the usual bravos and salvos of applause, it seemed to me, but the next morning the reviews were murderous and the show died at birth. Marc Blitzstein called me on the telephone to tell me they were closing the thing, and he thanked me with great sincerity for my help—which was a very rare experience for me, but Marc was a rare musician.

He went somewhere in the Caribbean and was murdered in some kind of assault, the details of which I never learned.[46] All of this happened in a very short space of time.

---

[45]Decades earlier, the two had attended the first Yaddo Festival. Blitzstein's musical criticism appeared regularly in the journal *Modern Music*; among his assignments was a December 1930 Women's University Glee Club program, for which he praised Bennett's *Three Chaucer Poems* and a Virgil Thomson work as "the best things" on the program ("New York Chronicle of New Music," *Modern Music* 8 [1931]: 40).

[46]January, 1964, in Martinique; it has been suggested that his killing grew out of a political argument.

Chapter Ten

In September of 1959 Richard Rodgers told me of his new show, *The Sound of Music*, and also told me that he liked the men that usually helped me—he liked them socially—but he wanted to get every bit requiring music ready in time for me to write every one without any assistance at all. Anywhere along the line this would have been a rare accomplishment and the calendar insisted that I was sixty-five years old. It is a very well accepted theory that the older one gets the less sleep one needs, but I've never been able to prove it. Maybe that conversation that Dick and I had on the subject many years before[1] was still funny to me. Anyhow I laughed the sandman off and scored *The Sound of Music* from cover to cover.

Dick and Oscar only did the music part of this one. The principal writer of the play was a great favorite of mine, a man of rare stature in the theater, Howard Lindsay. If I have used one of my snobbish assessments of the men of the theater as big talents in not-as-big people, that never could apply to Howard. He gave out a real ray of personal dimension.[2]

The play has another distinction in my story (if it ever wants it). During the tryout weeks it is the only show at which I ever got the habit of sitting out front even when there was nothing I needed to see or hear in the orchestration. If that doesn't seem remarkable to anyone it is because he hasn't been with me through nearly three hundred shows the way I have.

[Letter, Bennett (Hotel Touraine, Boston) to Louis and Annette Kaufman (Los Angeles), 26 October 1959: "I'm here with the Mary Martin show, which is a honey—at least they got me to go back to see nearly all the performances since it opened. That's very much more than

---

[1]In the early 1940s, when the pair agreed that *Oklahoma!* might be their last theatrical venture.

[2]Russel Crouse, who wrote *The Sound of Music* with Lindsay, had earlier co-authored the book for Bennett's 1933 musical comedy *Hold Your Horses*.

I ever did for *South Pacific*, *Oklahoma!*, *My Fair Lady*, or any of the others. . . . I'm dying to get back to my present effort, which is a concerto for violin, piano and orchestra.[3] It's tough to get back from Richard's one, five and four oompahs to a concerto. What makes it harder is that his music is exceptionally appealing in this show. . . ."]

One of the heroes of the play had to be the casting director who found the Trapp family children, perfect "stair-steps" as they stood in line. In the movie they made of the show the first thing that lets you down is the heights of the young ones.

That whole picture recalled my original ideas about the moving-picture industry when I first went west. It is said to be the biggest box-office success in movie history, so it must have been a divine imp from up there that told me my shoulder would be needing its chip in Hollywood.

How the picture people knew enough to take out the most wonderfully dramatic moment in the stage play and replace it with a gag about a naughty nun tampering with an automobile part is well over my head. But Louise and I were once driving from our motel to a rehearsal in Emporia, Kansas,[4] and passed a drive-in movie on which big letters said "*The Sound of Music*—Second Year."

How do these people know these things?[5]

I'm grateful to Alan Jay Lerner for having written about *Camelot* in his book *On the Street Where You Live.* When I went out to Manhasset, Long Island, where Lerner and Fritz Loewe showed me the show, it was a great show. I looked for a spot that would have the same theatrical punch as these two men had achieved with "The Rain in Spain" in *My Fair Lady.* Not quite as obvious as that, but very moving was Sir Lancelot bringing his jousting adversary to life by prayer, after having felled him. It was a moment to be powerful for grown-ups, but should have been magic for everybody.

The whole piece was magic, as I heard it with those two fellows at the piano in Manhasset, Long Island. I had another conflict of schedules coming up, and after going to Toronto for the openings I had to wish the obstet-

---

[3]Benno and Sylvia Rabinov premiered the Concerto for Violin, Piano, and Orchestra with the Portland (Oregon) Symphony Orchestra on 18 March 1963.

[4]Bennett was the guest conductor at a 10 May 1966 band concert at Kansas State Teachers College (now Emporia State University).

[5]*The Sound of Music* was revived in New York early in 1998, with Bennett's original orchestrations adapted by Bruce Coughlin. Several columnists reminded their readers that there were crucial differences between the stage and film versions, with the "Nazi menace" more overt in the former.

rical job on my friend Phil Lang. He ended up doing more pages of orchestration on the show than I did. I suppose there is some underlying reason why my second conflict had to come with the same two writers as before (with *My Fair Lady*) being affected.

In Toronto I saw the over-long opening performance. It still didn't tie *Show Boat* in length, but it was close. The low orchestra pit in the newly-built theater was of great concern to them all because it was swallowing up the sound. It didn't bother me quite as much, probably because two-thirds of all I ever wrote for the theater was swallowed up. I had to admit, however, that it all sounded pretty unimpressive.

From Alan's account I was able to piece together some of the reports that came in from the tryout. The only musical casualty that was damaging to my good impression of the show—my original good impression—was a song called "Guenevere." Never in any staging that I saw was the slightest evidence of a feeling for what the number meant to me on first hearing.

It may be that an audience of tin ears and seismographic souls simply can't stay with a refrain that starts in C and ends in B major, but the charm and verve of that song is apparently a secret well kept from too many of our contemporaries. If I sound unbearably conceited I'll try to get in touch with Hector Berlioz and Richard Wagner and ask them what to do with that kind of conceit.

Looking over that old account book I see a good lot of work listed for the stage version of *Cinderella.* It must have been too recently done for me to remember it very clearly. This is seriously said, and quite in line with many experiences with human memory. The dates on the new version show it to be four years later than the television show, but the various songs, dances and musical moments still refer to the original titles and routine numbers as in the TV broadcast.[6]

It would be quite appropriate to report on how this version compared in success with the one four years before. Appropriate but impossible, after a moment's thought. I'm sure I've said enough about the difference between the stage and television as to success and failure, in any case.

Not counting two elaborate revivals of two great favorites there were four or five more productions that tried to get started, all of them highly promising but unsuccessful. *The Girl Who Came to Supper* was produced by the man

[6]Rodgers and Hammerstein's made-for-television *Cinderella* (starring Julie Andrews) aired 31 March 1957; CBS reported that the evening's audience exceeded 107 million. The stage version followed, as did 1965's television remake (with a new script by Joseph Schrank). Yet another incarnation—with an ethnically diverse cast and new mix of Rodgers songs (several of them from his theater scores)—aired in November 1997.

who did *My Fair Lady*—Herman Levin. It opened in Boston like a hit. One of the greatest figures of the modern theater wrote the whole thing and the newspaper reviews took it very seriously after the premiere. Noel Coward was such a remarkable talent that you found yourself looking at him and trying to see where he kept all his many selves. He not only created things, he could interpret and perform them with utter brilliance. He could be old or young, a woman or a man, a child, a youth, a servant or a master. With all this as much music and poetry in him as any of the great songwriters start with.

Florence Henderson and José Ferrer played the two main characters. Things began to happen during the tryout, similar things to those of *Camelot.* The director [Joe Layton] had an accident and was lost to them, the theaters on the tour and in New York were ideal for a *Ziegfeld Follies* but not for a charming play with music. It didn't run long and some awfully nice theater died with it.[7]

Very high on my list of favorite libretti would be *On a Clear Day You Can See Forever* by Alan Jay Lerner, who seemed to haunt my history during the last years of my show arranging. The appeal of this libretto was in its maturity—for want of a better word. All of our forages into the world of Dr. J. B. Rhine[8] may lead to some universe quite different from the one we see from here now, but the scared shudders of a vast number of people (and the reassuring research of their newspapers, who find that Morris Bernstein's Bridey Murphy[9] is a cousin of Glinda, the Good Witch of the South) are best understood as immaturity.

On a Clear Day had a fine cast when we opened [October 1965] in Boston. The music[10] was pretty and the whole show had but one fundamental weakness: I doubt that the twentieth century will last long enough to fill theaters with audiences of comfortable people following excursions into the time past, future, and complicated present. Precognition, post-cognition, ESP, PPS—these are for grown-ups.

---

[7]The first of the show's 112 performances took place on 8 December 1963, only a few weeks after President Kennedy's assassination. *The Noel Coward Diaries* (Boston: Little, Brown and Co., 1982) include the playwright's detailed account of the creation and demise of *The Girl Who Came to Supper.*

[8]Joseph Banks Rhine (1895–1980) was, with his wife Louisa, a leading investigator of extrasensory perception (he coined the term in the 1930s) at Duke University. A prolific author of books and essays on the subject, Rhine founded the *Journal of Parapsychology* in 1937.

[9]Morey Bernstein's novel *The Search for Bridey Murphy* was a surprise bestseller that was brought to the screen by Paramount in 1956. The title character, aided by hypnosis, goes back in time to a previous life as a nineteenth-century Irish lass.

[10]By Burton Lane, whose 1947 *Finian's Rainbow* had also been orchestrated by Bennett.

The two big revivals of old favorites were of *Annie Get Your Gun* and *Show Boat.* They were played at Lincoln Center in New York, they cost a lot of money and tried very hard. The orchestras of the two productions were much larger than the original ones and called for a lot of writing in my department, but we didn't make history with the sounds we made.[11] I thought as I listened to them that my life-long feeling of clipped wings with small orchestras trying to sound big may have been artistic naiveté on my part. A luxurious group of fiddles with the tiny phrases of Irving Berlin and Jerome Kern to play may have something for the intellect—which theater audiences ain't got—but nothing for the deeper instincts, which they certainly do have.

And now for the last of my work on Broadway. One producer, David Merrick, who was setting records for hit shows, was another man I had completely missed until he did one about the famous spy (or was she?) Mata Hari. The show was named for the girl. When he bombed, Mr. Merrick bombed. Not entirely due to the quality of the piece, it was a disaster. My friend hearsay told me that we were not by any means ready to open on the date announced, but we were in Washington, and a Very Important Person had invited an international crowd of equally important persons (almost) to the opening. We had to open [18 November 1967] whether we could or not.

There were only two big laughs in the show. One when a man jumped off a boat that was split in two and landed on the bare stage and the other when poor Mata Hari died tied to the stake and had to hang there with no curtain coming down until she couldn't stand it any more and straightened up to look around and see what happened.[12]

It's impossible to turn away from Broadway without a final thought or two about a few immortal hitch-hikers we picked up along the way.

---

[11]The shows opened on 30 May and 19 July 1966 respectively. Bennett's cover-to-cover rescoring of *Annie Get Your Gun* included several changes in instrumentation, most noticeably in the woodwinds. Saxophones were eliminated, with doubling limited to traditional "legitimate" practice: flute/piccolo, oboe/English horn, clarinet/bass clarinet, etc. The newer script and orchestrations constitute the currently licensed version, the original materials having been withdrawn. The *Show Boat* orchestrations (which had been once reworked for its 1946 revival) were likewise totally redone for the expanded orchestra. Yet another Music Theatre of Lincoln Center revival was *Oklahoma!* (June 1969); Bennett's enlargement of his 1943 orchestrations included an added bassoon, third trumpet, and second trombone.

[12]*Mata Hari* never opened in New York. A year later, retitled *Ballad for a Firing Squad,* it was produced off-Broadway by Edward Thomas at the Theater de Lys, lasting only seven performances. Bennett made minor scoring contributions to two later shows—*The Grass Harp* (2 November 1971) and *Rodgers and Hart* (13 May 1975).

Chapter Eleven

IRVING BERLIN

I started talking about Irving Berlin in Paragraph One, refer to him as just about songwriter number one, at least in our era, and look back on many a page written for him, but the fact is we never spent a great deal of time together. In the first place he was his own publisher,[1] and when he needed me he had to come to my publisher and ask for me. That must have been a little distasteful to him, although no evidence of that was ever visible. We never visited with the Berlins like we did with the Kerns, the Hammersteins and the Harry Rubys, for instance, but if any youngster is ambitious as a songwriter a long look at Irving Berlin should be a required study.

Many who are fond of songs are slightly upset to hear me class him with or above the most famous composers for the theater. Those who listen to a lot of the music in the air begin to get choosy and feel they have outgrown the primitive idiom. They should hear, as I have, the reaction of two of the composers they probably admire most to those completely down-to-earth songs—Jerome Kern and Cole Porter. Both of them always surprised me with their sincere admiration for songs that had no touch of their sophistication in them. No one can tell us what to love, but Johannes Brahms is reported to have put it subtly, writing on his program after hearing a Strauss waltz, "Unfortunately not by Johannes Brahms."

What can a young songwriter learn from Irving Berlin? "Practically nothing" is too easy an answer. Those of us who stayed in to practice and write exercises while the shouts of ball players leaked through the window don't like that kind of answer, even though we know that the man and his music just happened, and happened before he played or sang his first note.

---

[1]Early in his career, Berlin (unlike most of the major songwriters of his day) formed his own publishing firm, renowned (or, to some, "notorious") for its tight control of the licensing of his songs and shows.

Irving Berlin, 1938. From the Cleveland Public Library Photograph Collection. Used by permission.

"Irving . . . never broke down in his refusal to know the treble clef when he saw it, and he went from rags to riches."

His harmonies are not venturesome but they are sound and hard to improve on. He hears them without being able to find them on the keyboard once in a while. I have already described his delight when we could find the chord for him. Maybe our young songwriter can learn one thing from that. Such as, for instance, "the harmony comes from the same place as the melody—hear it before you fish for it on the keyboard!" And then again maybe he already senses that or he wouldn't want to write songs in the first place.

Irving's personal modesty is sometimes called exaggerated, but humility is not too rare among big, big talents. Anyway he's always been that way so it's a little bit late to worry about how sincerely humble he was when he was waiting on tables.

What Mrs. Irving Berlin told me about Irving's mother, whom she greatly admired, is proof of a good heritage, but indicates no source of poetry or music.[2]

And that story we are told about his making up songs as a waiter in a restaurant without being conscious of the music that went with the words. I

---

[2]This reference is obscure, as Bennett never explains it.

believe the story but what can my young songwriter learn from it—wait on tables and sing?

One odd characteristic nearly all of us have noticed in the past is that Irving Berlin never seemed to laugh when we told him a joke, no matter how funny it was. Neither did he look as though he were not listening. A good guess is that he was working. He could have been weighing the joke and filing it for possible use in a future song.

If this has anything to do with it we may see something to learn there. A funny idea for a song has a high price on the market.

I've seen the opening of a second act in one of Berlin's musicals where a line of some sixteen pretty chorus girls sang without props or gestures and got screams of laughter at the end of every line of lyric. These girls were not comedians nor could they sing especially well, but the fun was in the words and music. Who knows how many of these great gags come from jokes that Irving didn't laugh at?

As to the way he worked, his usual approach whenever I have worked with him was simple. First came the idea—what the song was about. Then came the title and the melody of the title, often but not always at the beginning of the refrain, like "Say It with Music," "What'll I Do?," or "God Bless America." When the title was not at the top it usually came at the end of the first phrase, like "Alexander's Ragtime Band," "Always," and "I've Got My Love to Keep Me Warm."

After the title (words and music) came the music of the whole refrain, which he improvised on the black keys (mostly) of the piano. Finally he set words to the whole strain as now composed. To those who would like to pin the operation down more closely than this I would say "don't waste too much time on it." It may easily be that the first words and music of "Alexander's Ragtime Band" were "Come on and hear, Come on and hear," for instance. I doubt if he could be sure himself just what he did in many cases. He improvises words and music like Gershwin and many others improvised the tune alone.

Nearly all American popular songs have been written music-first, more or less as Irving did it, but the latter part of Oscar Hammerstein's life he was able to do his entire lyric with no music composed. This is the classical approach—poems set to music—but not many songwriters have Dick Rodgers's gift for finding a popular tune to fit words already written. With Irving Berlin he had his choice and it's nobody's business which came first.

I believe I have come to the end of what I know of the gentleman now, except to say that his was the first name I ever noticed on a popular song. The song was called "That Mesmerizing Mendelssohn Tune."

VINCENT YOUMANS

Vincent Youmans was a champion whistler through his teeth. I don't suppose he won any cups at it but he deserved something. When you think how many beautiful tunes have come into the world through Vincent Youmans's teeth you feel your musical education enriched. The whole idea appeals to me somewhat because it was partly for me that he did it. Whistling the tune left the fingers of his right hand free to fish for harmonies and added notes to use in the orchestration. No one would call his harmonic idiom experimental but it was personal, and he was very particular about what went on under the melody.

As I think of it I'm not sure he wrote out much of the music his right hand played under the whistled melody when he made the copy he furnished us, but you can be assured that we arrangers pounced on it when it was good. In other words he proceeded very much like Irving Berlin: 1) Title, 2) Music, 3) Words (in this case by somebody else).

Who thought up the title "Tea for Two" is in doubt in my mind. Vince told me about the song one day in such a way that I certainly understood him to be the author of the whole phrase "Tea for two and two for tea, me for you and you for me," and yet it is such a typical Irving Caesar couplet that I'll never be sure. Irving did the lyrics for the show *No, No, Nanette* where the song first appeared. In the same show was another song, "I Want to Be Happy," with a certain past.

Much earlier [1923] Arthur Hammerstein had produced a show with music by Youmans and Herb Stothart, called *Mary Jane McKane.* Youmans had written a song called "Come On and Pet Me" for the show, lyrics by Oscar Hammerstein and Otto Harbach. One day during rehearsal Vince Youmans said to me, "I'm going to save 'Come On and Pet Me.'" Of course what he meant was that the bosses had cut the number out. Youmans hated so much to be told what was in and what was out that he later became a producer and lost a great part of the money his tunes had brought in.

It turned out that he used exactly the right expression this time. He saved the melody of "Come On and Pet Me," Irving Caesar wrote a new lyric for it, and under the name of "I Want to Be Happy" it made big money.

This dread of having material cut out of the show seemed always to be a part of writers' worries, but it was never one of my problems. Many times certain orchestrations that were especially liked had to be lost in the final version of the play and somebody would break the news gently to me. I always had an inelegant answer to their kind words: "I never mind what's cut out of my arrangements; what I mind is what's left in and stinks."

The only way Vincent could be sure his tunes wouldn't be cut out by somebody else was to be the absolute boss of the whole works. Being a producer-manager, however, is a job for a very special talent, and most creative artists don't have it, as I noted when talking about Jule Styne.

Somehow it doesn't seem to fit the character of Vincent Youmans. This is again something I don't know and have only heard, but *Hit the Deck*, one of Vinnie's productions, was a great hit, playing its first year to absolute capacity crowds and losing eight hundred dollars a week. Whatever the truth is the story is one of the easy ones to believe.

He was, by all accounts, hard to work with. His contemporaries seemed to agree that his father's hat factory was having trouble to make a hat big enough for Vinnie. In personal contact he never seemed swell-headed, considering how explosive his success was at his age. Something awful happens to very young people who see a lot of money coming in, but (to balance that a little) tune-writers are fundamentally a bit awed by their music arrangers.

Knowing what was being said about him I tried once to take him apart and went into a pocket-sized sermon on the subject of self-esteem. The stars being so vast and wonderful, the arts being so big and man being so small—and so on. He was able to assure me that his thoughts were very similar and he couldn't conceive of being conceited over a few pieces of music.

I realized as he spoke that none of us were going to influence him much with our philosophies. His complexes were complex indeed but he was going where he was going and none of us were going to stop him.

Very early in his career he gave me an amusing bit of autobiography. It seems he had something in common with George Frederick Handel: his parents were determined not to let music interfere with his taking over the family business. They made men's hats and the firm had a big name in the hat business.

However Vincent had no dreams but music—popular music. Almost behind the backs of Father and Mother Youmans the son began to make big waves in Broadway music. This went on for a certain length of time while Vincent collected checks. The attitude of the parents didn't change but one day he went home (in Larchmont) a little early and saw his father in the living room reading *Variety*, the show business bible. Music had won the day!

The hat business eventually went down and out, but people still sing "Tea for Two," "Great Day," "Hallelujah!" and so many others.

Youmans had a sharp and sensitive ear for music. A fellow music arranger of mine did a good deal of work on Vince's theater music, and he told me something quite impressive about that sharp and sensitive ear. Hans Spialek, my fellow arranger, European born, was fond of opera and knew plenty about it. He said he once took Vince Youmans to a matinee performance of *Tristan*

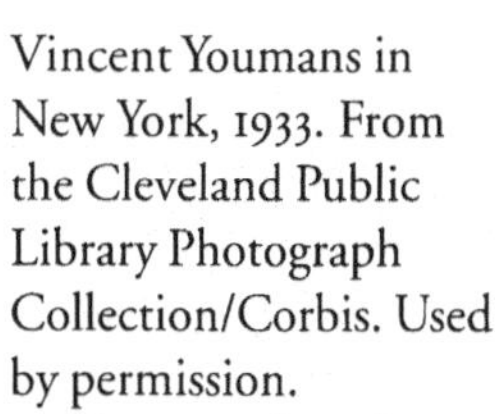

Vincent Youmans in New York, 1933. From the Cleveland Public Library Photograph Collection/Corbis. Used by permission.

Youmans "may have been the most talented of all our tune writers."

and Isolde, which Youmans had never seen. After the opera they were at the piano in the course of doing a little work and Vince played just about all the themes of the third act of *Tristan* by ear before they settled down to the business at hand.

Of course I don't know just how much he did of it but if it impressed Spialek (a brilliant, conservatory-trained composer and conductor) that much it had to be pretty remarkable as a stunt.[3] The Youmans ear impressed me in another way. He seemed to hear the individual sections of an orchestra no matter how many were playing at the same time. I would see him chuckle over something I had given the woodwind to play while the whole orchestra

---

[3]Spialek recalled the incident, characterizing the songwriter as an "exquisite natural pianist [who] had an uncanny musical memory." Yet Youmans "never had heard a Wagnerian opera before and considered Wagner as so many, so erroneously still do—just a big noise-maker. . . . After the [*Tristan*] performance he took me to his office, where he proceeded directly to the piano, giving me a résumé of the opera's themes and an almost complete rendition of the famous Love Death. True, he played most everything in different keys but otherwise astonishingly correct" (Hans Spialek, "A Passing Note" [unpublished memoirs], 150).

was sounding off. I knew the parts were there because I wrote them, but he seemed to hear and enjoy them even though strings, brass and drums were doing other things.[4]

Youmans's music usually went fairly successfully into the orchestra. There seemed at one time to be an idea among the professionals that he was hard on voices. Singers, being interested in survival, need places to breathe in, and some melodists have a sure instinct for meeting that problem as they conceive a song. I must say I never heard a singer complain about Youmans on that score but the criticism got around somehow.

As for the orchestra, no one could possibly forget how the orchestra sounded in Steve Jones's arrangement of "The Bambalina" in *Wildflower.* Unforgettable for me was the verse of another song in an early show of Youmans (they always had verses and choruses in show songs in those days). Perhaps nobody in the audience ever took the trouble to listen to it, but at the rehearsal with orchestra a lot of oohs and ahs were generated by a certain combination of low woodwinds and I never forgot it because they wouldn't let me. For some time I kept getting requests to put that same "haunting" sound into other songs and other shows. It couldn't be done by me or by anybody else. The sound of music begins with the music itself—I almost said begins and ends. A pretty girl has a pretty dress and she is devastating. Another pretty girl has the same dress made for her and should have saved her money.[5]

Precious few women ever make that mistake. I have said and believe I am the world's worst music teacher, but if a young arranger of music can truly learn that lesson in dressmaking he doesn't really need to know much more.

Vince and I drifted apart rather early in his career. I drifted to Hollywood and he drifted (if that's the word) into producing shows. He also came to Hollywood, I believe, but composers of songs never seem to have the same active part in the production there that they have in the New York theaters. What happened in the last years of his too-short life is only hearsay from where I sit, and not much of that. It's nice to carry around the memory I have of him whistling his satisfying melodies through his teeth, sitting at the piano at Jules Glaenzer's big parties, enchanting the revelers with his modest presentation after Gershwin had torn the piano to bits with his improvisations

---

[4]Violinist-conductor David Sackson (concertmaster in the pit for a number of Bennett-arranged musicals) notes that, "having conducted *Carousel* and other shows, I learned one of RRB's very well-guarded secrets in his [theater] orchestrations, and a musical hallmark known to very few: namely, he always 'buried' a Tchaikovsky bit [quotation] where only the cognoscenti would find it!" (David Sackson letter to the editor, 24 August 1989).

[5]A recurring simile in Bennett's writing; see his "A Pretty Girl is Like a Melody" below.

and Bert Kalmar and Harry Ruby have had us rolling on the floor with their comedy.

He and his melodies will always be young to us who knew him then.

COLE PORTER

When one adds up the hundreds of hours I've spent with Cole Porter's music it's hard to realize how little I knew him. We had not one quarrel that I remember; I was in his house in the rue Monsieur in Paris as we prepared a show for London,[6] spent time with him in one of his two large suites at the Waldorf in New York and was with him at countless rehearsals of the many shows he did, but when he died I still had to confess that I didn't know him very well.

Part of this is because he called on one or two or three other men to work with him at the piano to prepare his voice-and-piano copies as the songs first went on paper. He was left-handed and wrote with his left elbow above the top of the page and the hand above the staff instead of below it or ahead of the writing the way we right-handers do. The bulk of the writing was done by the arranger-editor from Cole's dictation. His not writing out every detail of the harmony himself surprised me because he was a pupil of Gédalge in Paris, studying harmony with about the most famous contrapuntist in Europe at the time.[7] Porter, like Kern, liked to play the music on the piano and let an arranger put it in shape to face the world. Unlike Kern he didn't come to one of us who were to do the orchestrations.

His fine musical education, the fact that we both enjoyed France and the French language, and the fact that we both had a stake in the success and quality of his music, should have brought us together socially, but we lived on different planets. No antipathy, but also no common ground.

Cole Porter was of a level of society where all problems, however deep, could be solved by engaging somebody to solve them. When somebody attacks us we wonder where to put his head after we knock it off. If somebody attacked Cole Porter in the same way he called his lawyer. One of his music directors got angry at him one time and was heard to say what he would like to do to him. It was said under the man's breath but in no time at all Cole turned up with a bodyguard. The music director and the bodyguard got to be friends and went out for drinks together during the next two weeks.

Cole at an orchestra reading of a new show would sit in the back of the empty theater with his principal music editor, Dr. Albert Sirmay, and every

---

[6]Almost certainly 1929's *Wake Up and Dream.*

[7]André Gédalge (1856–1926) also included Ravel, Milhaud, Honegger, and Florent Schmitt among his pupils.

time he wanted to make a little change Dr. Sirmay—large, rotund, and a Doctor of Philosophy at Heidelberg—would have to come running down the aisle to tell the conductor to tell the oboe player to accent the F sharp a little more. That went on all day.[8]

It doesn't seem too odd when you think how little taste Cole had for running down the aisle, even before he became so lame. But he might have gathered up his courage and sat in the second row where he could make his suggestions simply and more effectively.

Something tells me that poor Cole was a little afraid the oboe player might say that in his opinion the F sharp was not much of a note to begin with. I say this not with derision but in sympathy, because I've been a little afraid of that oboe player myself on occasion.

Judged from a purely artistic standpoint Cole Porter had points of superiority over nearly all the other musicians of the theater. His cafe-society poetry and his moments of ten-cent-store ragtime will never dim the brilliance of some of his truly divine inventions: the first measures of the refrain of "Night and Day," the design of "I Get a Kick Out of You" with his original accompaniment (which all the dance bands and their arrangers I ever heard missed completely), the long lines of "Begin the Beguine," the texture of "Were Thine That Special Face" . . . something for the boys to shoot at during another long Golden Age when it comes.

Since Cole Porter, like Irving Berlin, wrote whole songs instead of just piano pieces or just poetry—collaborating only with himself—I owe it to you to tell you how he put the words and music together, as I did briefly with Berlin, but it's a debt I can't pay, I'm sorry to say. Analyzing his songs, as I had to do with every song that was ready for orchestration, I would guess that they were worked out phrase by phrase, word by word and bar by bar—that both words and music went together more like mosaics than in the case of most songsmiths. This is only a guess based on the subtlest bits of evidence.

There could be someone who knows more but he worked out his forms and structures in the strictest privacy, and by the time he got to his aides who were to put the first simple copy on paper he himself may have forgotten just how the song was built. The fact that he worked out his songs behind closed doors suggests to me that maybe none of us who worked with him knew him very well.

---

[8]Hans Spialek similarly observed that "Porter conveyed once to me through Harms, Inc.'s errand boy deluxe, Dr. Sirmay, his displeasure about my being too familiar with some of the principals in a show" ("A Passing Note," 172).

Cole Porter, 1938. From the Cleveland Public Library Photograph Collection/ Corbis. Used by permission.

Porter once observed, "Most arrangers are so anxious to display their creative talent that they swamp the composer's melody. Russell has a tremendous amount of originality, but he uses it to give the song a texture and shading the composer has in mind. He has superb taste."

Before leaving this complex and incredible man I'll say goodbye to him by telling of another piece of gaucherie to add to my substantial collection. I joined Cole at a [Spring 1936] meeting of studio heads who were planning a large film [MGM's *Born to Dance*] with Porter songs. He played and sang a brand new song just added to the score of the picture. For a reason I have now forgotten he was playing it now for me. At the end of it, while everybody applauded, I said "You've changed it a bit." This calmed them all down somewhat and after we broke up Cole told me why. He had brought the song in as having been written the night before and was taking bows as a great hero to turn out such a song in twenty-four hours. All this was before I got there.

It was a song he had had for several months. He'd made some changes to avoid trouble with film censors, but I'm not at all sure he did even that in twenty-four hours.[9]

I must say he was nice about it. Instead of saying "Why Grandma! What a big mouth you have!" he just chuckled as he told me what I had done.

[9]The revision took place on 13 April, according to Porter's diary. The song had first been written for 1934's *Anything Goes*.

I claim that it would have been very hard for anybody to keep silent about the change that opened up my big mouth. The song was "You'd Be So Easy to Love" and he had taken out one of the cutest little couplets he or anybody else ever wrote. The refrain started, "You'd be so easy to love, So easy to idolize, all others above" and here is the couplet: "So sweet to waken with! So nice to sit down to eggs and bacon with!" If it is accurate to say that Cole Porter and his music arrangers hail from two different planets, then what of Cole Porter and his enchanted public? Two different solar systems, maybe.

The term "Café Society" grew up as sort of twin with Cole Porter, and songs like "Anything Goes," "Miss Otis Regrets," "Begin the Beguine," "You're the Top," and "I Get a Kick Out of You" add up to his public image. They must have been in there somewhere but you'd have to peel away a lot of layers to find them. He was ambitious and not instinctively generous, as (for example) Kern and Gershwin were. He set out to prove that his music and poetry could put him in as high brackets financially as any of his social companions from the world of big business.

He proved it conclusively but died tragically. My friend Dr. Albert Sirmay worked very closely with Cole and saw him every day in the course of editing his music. Sirmay came to me one morning practically in tears of envy as he described a trip around the world Cole was about to take. He knew exactly at what hour he would look at the Taj Mahal, exactly what day he would ride an elephant, etc., etc. I didn't share his envy, exactly. I said, "Albert, if I had a program like that the only possible entertainment would be to find the elephant with a sore foot, so that I would have to change something."

Cole's trip was to end on January 1 in California, when his movie contract [for *Rosalie*, 1937] was to start. I should not have worded my pronouncement exactly as I did, superstition being what it is. Cole's first disappointment came when they postponed his movie job until June 1. Then he went riding and his horse threw him and started a long series of operations to save two broken legs. Every time I asked Sirmay how many operations there had been the number was greater. I lost count after thirty-two or three.

And with it all these joyous bursts of words and music—shows like *Kiss Me, Kate*, *Panama Hattie*, and *Silk Stockings*. The rehearsals for one play were in a hall one flight higher than the elevators went. Cole had a big strong "gentleman's gentleman" who picked him up and carried him up the stairs, where every day he taught the company his gay songs.

Then he lost the battle. After a good many years one leg could no longer be saved. Nothing seemed to console him. He lay there and wanted to die, and did.

Others have lost similar and bitter battles. Others, many others, have had to sing "Laugh, Clown!" while their hearts were being torn to bits, but Cole Porter, because the world he tried to create was light, gay and make-believe, gets my vote as one of the bitterest tragedies.

RICHARD RODGERS

There could be a point made of the similarity between the long, losing fight of Cole Porter to save his legs and Richard Rodgers's great battle against cancer. When we were in rehearsal with Rodgers and Hammerstein's *Pipe Dream*, their [1955] musical-play version of John Steinbeck's "Sweet Thursday," Dick Rodgers had to leave us for between two and three weeks while surgeons took out a cancerous jaw-bone and replaced it with a certain part of the chest. It was one of those miracles of surgery that you hear and read about, but when I told my tennis partner J. Gordon Cole that they had cured Rodgers of cancer he was shaking his head.

Gordon Cole was one of the finest eye surgeons and was therefore an authority on just that type of emergency. He was shaking his head because, in his experience, it had been impossible to get at the master malignancy by removing the affected area in nearly all cases.

But Dick refused to surrender for almost twenty-five years, and, like Cole Porter, turned out some of his most successful songs during that time.

As to our personal relationship, I have already said that his own appraisal of himself as a man who was ruthless, hard-boiled, inflexible (I don't recall just what his adjectives were) in business and then sat down to write music that made people cry never seemed to apply in any of our collaborations. Others have been wounded in battle and reported it to me but if I'm on the casualty list I'm not sharp enough to know it. As for tears, one note, sung twice in *Aida* at the end of the opera, is guaranteed to choke me up, as is the most of Act Five of *Pelléas.* And that devil Puccini has a thing called *Suor Angelica* that never lets up on me. These spots are picked because they have words with their music, for the sake of comparison. The truth is, music that needs words usually doesn't need me and doesn't send for me. Of course there are big exceptions to that rule.

I said of Cole Porter that I never knew him very well and perhaps none of us did. As for truly knowing Dick Rodgers, I once spoke with his and Oscar Hammerstein's secretary, Lillian Leff, who was with them for many years. She had been with him or near him in every kind of crisis, but she simply didn't know him. She said, "I've seen him cry, I've seen him happy, worried, angry, thrilled, even. But never once did I know what was going on inside. With

Richard Rodgers and Oscar Hammerstein II, 1957. From the Cleveland Public Library Photograph Collection. Used by permission.

Rodgers and Hammerstein are on the set of their 1957 television production *Cinderella*. Bennett was perhaps the most consistent member of the Rodgers and Hammerstein production team.

the other man I always felt I could help him think, if he needed me, but not with Rodgers."

I hope the quote is fairly accurate. It was not said during a serious consultation, but it supported my conviction that Richard Rodgers took great satisfaction in hiding all the warmth and tenderness he ever had in order to come out with it in song and surprise us all. By his own estimate that was he.

Rodgers and Kern were opposites when it came to spoiling us who worked on their music. Kern was almost impossible to buy an ice cream soda for. Oscar Hammerstein used to say, "Jerry comes from a long line of check payers." He never said anything of the kind about his other great collaborator, Dick Rodgers.

When *Oklahoma!* had just opened in New York, Oscar invited me to lunch at Sardi's for the purpose of discussing our upcoming work on *Carmen Jones*, and when Dick was with him I suddenly had an idea Dick might burst out with something like "Russ, this is a good chance to buy you a drink!" because he had been so happy with the work I did for him on *Oklahoma!*. Some day I may know why such a thought entered my head. What happened was: the three of us had about finished the main course of the lunch and he turned to Oscar and said, "Oscar, will you find out what I owe for lunch? I don't feel very well and I think I'll go home."

Oscar said, "I'm buying your lunch today," and Dick said, "Oh, are you buying the lunch? Thanks, very much!" and away he went. Thinking back, I remembered then that he and I had gone one day to Boston to join one of his shows. On the train we went into the dining car and I asked him to have lunch with me. He accepted with alacrity that surprised an old orchestrator of Jerome Kern's music! Not that he owed me a lunch, or anything else, for that matter.

We who toil through the night on their tunes certainly don't expect any such generosity from the composers as was shown by Jerome Kern, but he spoiled us all.

There's no question in my mind but that that was just another of those features of Richard's self-proclaimed toughness that may not have been his real down-deep character as much as the tender little tunes were.

And if it came to a hand-to-hand, face-to-face, duel to see who could out-tough the other my money would certainly go on Jerome D. Kern.

JEROME KERN

Jerome David Kern was an apostle of the unexpected. Any time he could cause a gasp of surprise his life was a success. One afternoon at a tea in London I was talking with Oscar Hammerstein, who was torn between amusement and exasperation.

He had just had to interrupt Jerry Kern at tea with two or three charming people to ask him to make a business decision. Someone had just offered some considerable sum of money for something to the two of them. I'm sorry I wasn't concerned enough to remember now just what it was they wanted to buy, but according to Oscar it was found money for Kern and Hammerstein.

He said he knew it was not a good idea to bring it up in front of the charming people but the offer couldn't wait and only needed a nod of Kern's head to consummate the deal. In this case the unthinkable was predictable. Kern said, "Tell them to go hell!"

"Found money!" Oscar was mourning through his amusement. "Found money!"

Kern came clear across the dining room of an ocean liner to where my wife, daughter and I were sitting one evening, cocked his head on one side in a characteristic pose and said, "You can all say what you like, Brahms is just a lot of academic futzing around with material that Lew Alter could write!"

And he looked me right in the eye.[10]

---

[10]The Cleveland Orchestra brought Kern's new *Show Boat* "Scenario for Orchestra" to Carnegie Hall on 19 November 1941, at which time the composer similarly informed the press

In my pathological musical snobbishness the distance from Johannes Brahms to Lew Alter was not significantly greater than the distance from Johannes Brahms to Jerome Kern, and I said something I regret saying: "Well, Jerry, congratulations—you don't have to listen to Brahms unless you want to."

He turned without a word and went back to his table. Of course my narrow-mindedness was well known to him, and for all I know my answer was just what he expected and maybe even wanted, but I'm not proud of it.[11]

Working on Kern's music was a joy, compared with working on the usual successful theater music. He was rather better schooled than the majority and was very sensitive to harmony and orchestral color. In a medium where too much originality condemns a writer to posthumous success his melodies were never likely to be completely obvious. There was a touch of aristocracy in his self-assurance, a feeling of proceeding with dignity no matter how trivial or nonsensical the message was. When you do my work, where twenty seconds of music can take an hour or two (or more) to put on paper, you say, "Thank God for the Jerome Kerns!"—if indeed there can ever be more than one.

He created the music, as far as I ever knew, before any words were written. He must have set tunes to some of the titles, but if at any time he set a poem it was when my back was turned. As noted before, he liked to improvise everything at the piano and then write it down, or have one of us write it for him. He was very conscious of the basses and harmonies under his tunes and by the time he was satisfied with them they were very hard to improve.

He was actually the composer of a great deal of the background music behind scenes, and some of the counter-melodies (where two tunes are going on at the same time) were completely his invention. We arrangers get credit for them in the trade, but we didn't always write them.

One case where I did do a countermelody had an amusing story. It was a simple strain, light-hearted and sort of Tyrolean, and the melody that went with it was more sustained and romantic. As soon as I turned the piano copy over to him he had Oscar Hammerstein write words for both tunes. They

---

that "The object of many of the older symphonies was to say as little as possible in the most grandiloquent, ponderous and intellectual forms. What I tried to do was to say as much as I could as briefly as I could" (quoted in Bordman, *Jerome Kern: His Life and Music*, 388).

[11]Witholding Kern's name, Bennett recalled the incident in another essay, and concluded: "His opinion, based on his own special gift for the top line of music, had only this much importance: his ears were exactly as simple as the ears of the great multitude for whom he wrote, and his inability to recognize the profound inspiration of Bach's counterpoint was merely an honest betrayal of how little the average ear takes in of polyphony" ("A Master Arranger Speaks," 20).

Jerome Kern, 1935. From the Cleveland Public Library Photograph Collection/Corbis. Used by permission.

Kern, "the life of every party," was being interviewed by radio station XERC while on a Spring 1935 visit to Tijuana's Agua Caliente race track: "If there ever was anybody that was not anybody else, it was Jerome Kern."

were both sung in a scene at the end of Act I in *Very Warm for May* [1939]. Then they were both sung at the same time and the effect was nice.

The amusing thing is that both of us tried honestly to remember a few years later which tune was his and which was the one I wrote to go with it, but we had to give up. We couldn't remember.

My introduction to Jerome Kern's music was before I ever came to New York. A musical called *Nobody Home*, with Charlotte Greenwood and Lawrence Grossmith in it, came to Kansas City. The whole thing was adorable to my young thinking and the music of Kern had a special spot in my life from then on. A couple of years later when I gathered up my worldly goods—one hundred forty dollars—and went to New York I looked in the papers (I forget whether they were one or two cents a copy then) to see if any shows by Jerome Kern were playing. There were two and I scraped up the money for balcony seats to both of them. The charm of Kern had not worn off.

His music was an acknowledged model for the type of show music most in favor and the entertainment world was very conscious of the royal triumvirate: Bolton, Wodehouse and Kern. The names stood for pure nonsense, really, but it was nonsense you wanted to throw your arms around and hug. All three of them devoted their lives to making life a little less serious.

This is not a good time to stomp in with my muddy feet but I can't resist thinking again what a nice turn of fate it was for me to be a fourth at what we called bridge during the long tryout of *Sitting Pretty.* Their careers at that point had only just begun, as a matter of fact, however fine their success was as a team.

With all the delicate magic of his melodies in those days, and with all his unexpected pranks and boyish humor, Kern was not an easy man to deal with. As was the case with Richard Rodgers, I never had a flare-up with him but I saw the smoke of battle on many occasions. He brooked no nonsense, to put it the way he sometimes did, and only a fantastic sense of humor saved him from being a little tyrant.

This was of course when he was at work in the theater and dealing with producers, directors, agents and the like. Socially it was a different story. During the time I spent with him on boat off the coast of Palm Beach, Florida [in 1930], I got a good chance to see that side of him.

And there was plenty to see—the life of every party, getting up games, playing his many song hits on the piano, getting laughs and squeals of surprise in every direction. In those days of quizzes and trick questions he was always amazingly well informed and articulate. As far as I could tell he was never at a loss socially whatever the question. He spoke the language.

I suppose a composite of all those talents went into every tune he ever wrote, if you want to go that deep. Somehow he and his music belonged together but I'm glad I don't have to prove it or explain it.

Just before the Kerns moved to California and built their house in Beverly Hills he sat at the piano and improvised tune after tune while I wrote out the melody of each one and labeled it simply by a number. From California he would call me and tell me to make a piano and voice arrangement of the tunes he needed, identifying them by number. I didn't count how many of them I sent but there were quite a lot. When they did a screen version of *Roberta* we began to hear in New York of the new number they had put in the show, and what a hit it was becoming. Finally I heard someone sing it on the radio and I let out a small yell. It was No. 12! Its new name was "Lovely to Look at."

Even more of a surprise was a little line at the end of our list that didn't even have a number, I believe. It was, as Jerry Kern said, just a little phrase for something like a Tiller Girls dance routine. This is all it amounted to.

It didn't look much like what it became: "The Way You Look Tonight" [from *Swing Time*, 1936].

Every Broadway musical or Hollywood movie we ever worked on together would yield some kind of out-of-the-ordinary story, amusing in varying degrees to varying listeners, but there has to be an end somewhere, and the end of Jerry Kern was about as unpredictable as anything he ever did.

Doctors said he died twice. He had a severe stroke just as *High, Wide and Handsome* went into production at Paramount [in 1937] and a miracle of modern medicine brought him back after his heart had stopped beating. Brought him back to compose some of his loveliest songs, such as "Dearly Beloved," "Long Ago and Far Away," and "All the Things You Are."

He took great pleasure in having done these (on borrowed time, he said) and when you think how long the journey back from the shadow was, how he slapped his thighs to be sure there was feeling in them, hardly daring to believe he was still there, you think how good it is that he could bring back the songs with him.

Then one day while he was visiting New York he dropped in the street and they had a terrible time finding out who he was.[12]

At a comparatively simple ceremony Oscar Hammerstein delivered the appropriate words. Oscar's poetic and beautiful words at a service in Los Angeles for George Gershwin when George was being buried in New York will never be forgotten, but his words of farewell to Jerome Kern had a much more intimate tone. One felt he was deeply involved, and when he started by saying there should be no tears shed for Jerry, who always stood for smiles rather than tears, I wondered just how deep our feelings for this wonderful little show-off were. Oscar himself got almost to the end of his eulogy and choked up, having to apologize for breaking his promise about the tears.

As I walked away from the gathering with my wife I thought deeply and honestly that this famous and fabulous person had, in spite of the many

---

[12]Following his collapse, Kern was taken to Welfare Island's City Hospital. He was identified by means of his ASCAP membership card and eventually transferred to a Manhattan facility, where he died a few days later (11 November 1945).

problems we had solved together, never knocked at the door of my inner feelings, however attractive and entertaining he was to me. I would therefore not pretend to mourn his loss—just close the book with respect, put it on the shelf and take down the next book. And as I was thinking these thoughts I suddenly realized that tears were in my eyes and I couldn't talk.[13]

[13]Bennett memorialized Kern the following year in his *A Symphonic Story of Jerome Kern*. The lavish orchestral medley includes ten of the songwriter's creations, arranged chronologically, beginning with "Babes in the Wood" (*Very Good Eddie*, 1915) and concluding with "All the Things You Are" (*Very Warm for May*, 1939).

Chapter Twelve

My introduction to "The Bohemians" (the name has the quotes when properly spelled) was sometime in the late 1930s, when my much admired friend Eugene Heffley took me to a meeting as a guest. I was enormously impressed with the group of famous men I met there. The main entertainment of the evening was by a man I had never heard of named Charles Stafford—I may not even have his name exactly right, but I'll never forget him. He played and sang a cantata (so he called it) with a lyric that he recited for us before taking off with a G. F. Handel-style vamp on the piano.

The lyric was, "When Tyrus Cobb steps up to the plate then I rejoice. But the crafty Miller Huggins slyly beats out a bunt."

One wondered what he could do with those words but one soon found out. Nothing could be more devastating than his legitimate-sounding presentation of utter nonsense. When I met him at the end of the evening he told me his job was so deadly serious that he did this for his own relaxation. I gather that he was an organist and choir director. He was the first thing I thought of when Dolf Swing offered to propose me for membership [in 1947].

I was a member for only one meeting when president Hughes[1] called me and asked me to be a member of the Board of Directors—and that didn't last long either. After only a few months he called again and asked me to be a vice-president. That lasted longer. The Musicians Foundation, the great charity of "The Bohemians," gives out thousands of dollars every year to musicians that have fallen on evil days. Cases of which I have had personal knowledge have been rescued from disaster and humiliation and tided over, or in some cases have been able to die with their minds at peace.

As a social club we meet every month except in the summer and at every meeting the finest groups and soloists join us and play or sing for us. I said to

[1]American pianist and teacher Edwin Hughes (1884–1965), a student of Rafael Joseffy and Theodore Leschetizky, is best known for his work as editor of piano music for G. Schirmer in the 1920s.

pianist Vladimir Horowitz once that I had the impression that the performing artists were always at their very best on these occasions. He agreed with obvious sincerity, saying something about an audience that knows exactly what you are doing helping you do it.

For me, sitting with great human beings like Georges Enesco, Paolo Gallico, Alec Templeton, Ruggiero Ricci and the like (except that there isn't really any like) makes me glad I took music lessons. One evening Enesco and I were sitting together listening to a nice performance of a Beethoven sonata for violin and piano, and after it was over I wrote out two measures of it on a sheet of paper to ask him a question about it. He answered the question and noted that what I wrote was not in one tiny detail the way Mr. Beethoven wrote it. I hadn't thought of it since my mother and I played the sonata and it may be that I never had really noticed just what the piano did under my violin at the spot. The point is that with all the thousands of such passages he knew, he knew them in such detail that my little inaccuracy bothered him.

That same Georges Enesco, composer of brilliant works for orchestra and famous for writing, playing and conducting, gave me an evening once that I wish I could share with more people. Benno and Sylvia Rabinof[2] asked us to join them at Enesco's apartment in New York and we got there some time later than they did. This was planned because Benno was to go over the six sonatas of Bach for violin alone under Enesco's coaching—or whatever you would call it.

The Bach sonatas are just about as wonderful as they are difficult technically. Not many violinists get very far with them, I've been told. When we got to the Enescos' apartment-studio we were met by Mrs. Enesco, whose charm was evidence of her genuine royal breeding.

Benno Rabinof was truly a virtuoso and he was playing the sonatas with the music on the stand in front of him while Master Enesco sat just behind the music stand, looking at no music and playing it all in unison with Benno. As he played he spoke continuously about the phrases and the style of playing, etc., and they never stopped until the last note was over.

We all settled down for a visit, but before I could talk about my pitiful attempts to play the Bach sonatas the door-bell rang and a French violinist at the door reminded Mr. Enesco of his offer to play the Fauré violin-and-piano sonata with him. Enesco said, "Come in" and they played Gabriel Fauré's sonata. The master kept up his running comment (from the piano) just as he had with Rabinof in the Bach.

Again we went about the business of visiting and nibbling cookies until we began to feel it was going-home time. But Madame Enesco urged us to

[2]The couple to whom Bennett dedicated his *A Song Sonata* for violin and piano (1947).

stay twenty minutes more because it was Good Friday, and every year her husband played the "Good Friday" music from *Parsifal* just for her.

Which he proceeded to do, playing the voice parts on the piano along with the orchestra parts and ending with a sublime pianissimo that faded into silence. After a long silence I said, "Merci" and my voice sounded a little profane to me. However, he said quite simply, "Il n'y a pas de quoi" and we came back to earth.

As we said good night I asked him how one man could hold so much music. He said, "You have your baseball and tennis. I have only music." I'm sure he knew that that didn't answer my question at all.

It may be a little top-heavy to single out one great artist from among the "who's who" members of "The Bohemians" beside whom one sits at meetings, but it's not an unusual approach in this narrative. When our admired and beloved Edwin Hughes died I had to try to take his place. One of the worst things I ever did as president was to go completely tongue-tied when, at the first annual dinner over which I presided, I wanted so much to say something graceful about Edwin. The words were in my heart but so many things happened one on top of the other that I failed my friend.

You don't get a second chance on such occasions. There was one time and place to do it and I blew it.

The president of "The Bohemians" has certain duties and responsibilities, but the hard workers are the secretary and the treasurer. The secretary while I served as president was a powerful man, Clyde Burrows, who in his youth pitched major league baseball for a while. He was succeeded by another powerful man, Brent Williams, for whom Clyde Burrows had great affection and admiration. And so say we all. The secretary is also secretary and treasurer of the Musicians Foundation, and must sleep less than a music arranger with his personal attention to the delicate work with the needy.

After I'd been president for quite a number of years I got so I wanted very much to straggle in as a member with no duties except to enjoy the music. This pleasure, as noted above, had been mine for exactly one meeting. And it was a pleasure, but when one of the board members retired and they asked me to come back it seemed good to get back to the inside works where I recognized the scenery.

"The Bohemians," NAACC, the Los Angeles Tennis Club and the West Side Tennis Club of Forest Hills, Long Island—even an inveterate "joiner" could hardly name four nicer clubs to belong to.

[Bennett was awarded the honorary Doctor of Humane Letters in June, 1965 by Franklin & Marshall College in Lancaster, Pennsylvania. Fellow members of his honorary "class" that day were Agnes DeMille, artist Andrew

Wyeth, and theater director Tyrone Guthrie.] The doctorate at Franklin and Marshall was particularly welcome because there was a very nice man that never seemed to miss a public function of NAACC and always called me "Dr. Bennett." Franklin and Marshall finally made an honest man of him.

In 1966 I had another visit with the young band players of the U.S.A. in a very different setting. The Soap Box Derby in Akron, Ohio, was one of the sights everybody ought to see. Every year boys made their own cars out of boxes and on the big day, in many sections of the world, races would be run to pick the entrants in one big race. That one big race in Akron was an affair no one would ever forget.

There were about ninety finalists on the day we joined the program. My job was to conduct a march I'd written for them [*Soap Box Derby March*], and also *The Star Spangled Banner*—with a band of seven hundred! On this occasion I had another one of those criticisms that a performer loves to remember. Just after I cut off the last chord of the National Anthem the master of ceremonies sent his voice booming out of the loudspeakers with "wasn't that thrilling!"

Conducting a band of seven hundred schoolboys and girls has to have its mechanical problems, but he was right; it was thrilling—for me!

One more experience with the young musicians, but this time not so young, quite. A performance of one of the rather few compositions that I am glad to think back on. It was written purely for myself, with no commission, sponsor or performance in mind, and was not done to prove or disprove anything. Fritz Reiner had asked me some time before to do a piece for him, but there was no chance for me to accept the invitation at that time. He put my *Eight Etudes* for Orchestra on his program then [13–14 November 1958, in Chicago], but when I had the new work almost done[3] it seemed like something nice to do to dedicate it to Fritz and offer it to him.

Sometimes the dedicatee at the top of page one of a work is far and away the best part of it, and I was sincerely humble about offering this to my friend. He seemed truly pleased about it. I may have said this back there somewhere, but I'll say it again: Dr. Fritz Reiner was one of the rarest of conductors when it comes to reading a page of music and playing exactly what the composer heard as he wrote it.

We went to Chicago to hear the Chicago Symphony play the first two performances. The audience cheered the playing, the men of the orchestra

---

[3]Bennett noted that the Symphony had been "sketched between jobs . . . and was orchestrated in May [1962] during a three-week visit in Rome" (Chicago Symphony Orchestra program notes, 11–12 April 1963).

were most pleased with it, and Dr. Reiner said, "I think it is a successful work." And the four critics of the big newspapers gave it the most contemptuous reviews I ever read. Claudia Cassidy, famous for damning criticisms, was by far the least vicious.

Indiana State University at Terre Haute, Indiana had an ambitious music department and a better than average symphony orchestra when we paid them a visit in 1966. They tackled the "Fritz Reiner" symphony [Bennett's seventh] under my direction in a program of considerable variety. Only a few spots were too much for them and working with these sincere and courageous youngsters was my idea of what serious music is for in many ways. I wish I could put on these pages the religious level of companionship such an unselfish and intimate effort brings.

It rises above mere entertainment, and the fine response of the audience makes one flatter oneself that more than the ear has been touched.

A lovely memory indeed.

One last bit about Fritz Reiner and the symphony: the Steinways (piano company) gave a big party in Steinway Hall for Van Cliburn, celebrating his great success as a pianist. We went to the party. I had never met Van Cliburn but was hoping for a chance to introduce myself and add my congratulations. He was, however, completely surrounded by adoring fans. Louise and I went into the next big room, where we met our longtime friend Theodore Fitch, pianist, composer, and musicologist. When I spoke of my disappointment at not meeting the guest of honor he said, "Just a minute" and disappeared. In a matter of two minutes he came back bringing Van Cliburn with him. Before I could find appropriate words he said, "Oh, Mr. Bennett, I have a sort of message for you. From Doctor Reiner. I had a visit with him only a short time before he died, and he showed me your symphony and told me what a fine work it is!"

Such a surprise brings out all the "ham" in one. I've never developed a decent response to such a kindly speech. I knew that Fritz Reiner would never have said anything like that to anybody's face, although he was obviously pleased with the success of the Symphony at his concerts.

That seems to take care of the escapade business, but one or two episodes involving some interesting people ought to be reported from my point of vantage, episodes that are not likely to be reported anywhere else.

The United States Navy shot a most interesting movie on the history of that branch of the service. Bruce Catton, eminent historian, walked through the whole story with easy grace and he certainly knew what he was talking about.

The music score was played by the U.S. Navy Band in Washington, D.C. and conducted by their leader, Commander Ned Muffley. This was a rather unusual experience for me in that almost no original motion picture music in my "catalog" was conducted by somebody else. It worked out quite well, but the main story is something else.

It took us nine hours to record the score for the picture, three three-hour sessions. Commander Muffley, in the times between sessions, changed into his running pants and ran six miles—both intermissions.

Certainly I don't need to punctuate this with any exclamation points. This was the last picture score I've done (as I write) and who was it that said there's nothing new under the sun?

The picture is called *Born of the Sea.* It was done for the Navy and I don't really know from here whether it will be seen by the general public or not. Maybe they'll change their slogan from "Join the Navy and see the world" to "Join the Navy and see *Born of the Sea.*"

It's impossible to put together a lot of memories like these without, as Cornelia Otis Skinner used to say, "dropping names with a dull, sickening thud." Some of mine make a tinkle and a few shake windows. I'll drop one of the heavy ones with a rather appealing little nothing about a very great musician, Sergei Rachmaninov.

(Without speaking a sentence of the language, I once learned five hundred Russian words in their native spelling but I never can be sure how they convert them into our script. Most of the time I'm not sure how to write them in either script.)

Our first meeting was at a time when Mr. Fritz Kreisler and I were working something out together, and we happened by chance to meet in a studio which, if my memory serves me, was one of Mr. Rachmaninov's workshops. I was at that time working on the arrangements for *Of Thee I Sing* with music by George Gershwin [opening 26 December 1931]. I had to excuse myself rather early during the afternoon because I had to begin work on the overture for the play. Mr. Rachmaninov asked me when I had to finish it, and I told him that the orchestra was rehearsing it the following afternoon at 4 p.m. He looked at me very gravely and said, "That is too little time" and he was perfectly right, but he understood already that that was show business in the U.S.A.[4]

I can't leave him without reporting the time when he was my pupil for a day. He had written his three *Symphonic Dances* and wanted to hear the sound of a saxophone solo on the second subject of the first movement. His manager, Charles Foley, was a friend of Max Dreyfus and also of mine, and I'm

[4]This paragraph is taken from Bennett's 29 October 1949 letter to Rachmaninov's biographer Serge Bertensson. Its description of the pair's "first meeting" contradicts Bennett's assertion in chapter five that they'd met in Paris in the late 1920s.

sure it was he who suggested Rachmaninov ask me to help him choose and write for the instrument. Saxophones come in many sizes and have several different sounds, all of them on the plebeian side.

I happened to have a booklet that gave the fingerings, more or less the same on all sizes, and this I left with him after we went over his melody and picked out the E-flat alto sax as having the right "personality."

After the discussion of the mechanics and the transposition necessary, he gave me a real treat. Without my asking him he sat at the piano and played the whole composition from his original sketch. It was unforgettable in many ways, but the feature was hearing this greatest of pianists play, pound, sing and stomp, just like any of us trying to make the piano sound like a symphony orchestra.

A few days later Louise and I were asked to have lunch at the Rachmaninovs' summer home on Long Island. We went out on the train with Charles Foley and Sergei Rachmaninov drove his own car to the station to meet us. We all got in the car, he drove a short distance to a stopping place, turned around to me and said, "I start on A sharp?"

I said, "Right!" He said, "Right!" and drove on to the house, where we all had a lovely luncheon.[5]

At the beginning of the autumn of 1972 we took it into our heads to move to a place where Louise could do the retiring, at least from the monotony of housekeeping. Practically all our life together she had kept books on our income, output, taxes, charities and such and from that she didn't retire. We moved to a hotel we had always liked [the Warwick] and the moving was an education. Selling all the furniture at auction was made practically painless by a good firm and, not knowing much of anything about the process, I could only stand first on one foot and then on the other and wait to see the box-score. One thing was good for a small chuckle: a big drawing board on which I did nearly all the manuscripts was bought the week we returned from our honeymoon for thirteen dollars and some cents. It sold for eighty dollars.

Much less pleasant is the story of our books and scores. Going to a hotel meant having no room for a "library." A man who I had always admired a great deal was Ben Grauer, radio and television announcer, newscaster, member of the Légion d'Honneur of France, a man of grace and substance. We had become more and more friends as the years went by. He was a collector

---

[5]One additional Rachmaninov-Bennett "collaboration" is the former's Piano Concerto No. 4, Op. 40 (1926, revised 1941). Rachmaninov's two-piano reduction was left unfinished at his death in 1943; his widow then asked Bennett to complete the transcription, which was published three years later by Charles Foley.

of fine books and came by our apartment to see what we had one day. He saw the hodge-podge of volumes that had collected in the course of everyday living, and saw a number of things he thought might have some value. He asked a dealer friend to come in and look over the lot. The gentleman came over in immaculate dress and turned up his nose.

A second-hand dealer recommended by my fellow music arranger Hans Spialek had come in [previously] and relieved me of all my scores and music books for as little as he could offer without laughing.

The apartment manager of our building was of a branch of the human race of whom it had been said that if you have him for a friend you don't need an enemy. He was very friendly. He said his brother was with a college on Long Island and would be glad to accept our books for the college if I would just leave them there.

We left them, and I hope they got to the college.

I have met some of the faculty and I'm afraid to ask them especially after what happened when we left. Our lease was up on a Saturday. On Saturday when we left we took trip after trip by taxi with a seemingly endless lot of boxes and packages, but still had to leave three boxes in the middle of the bare living-room floor. We came back to pick them up Sunday morning at about nine. Nobody knew anything about them, including our helpful "friend." One box contained about one dozen new shirts, a second one was filled with liqueurs and kindred spirits while the third had a beautifully bound original manuscript of the opera *Maria Malibran* with its vocal scores and two or three other pieces I had wanted to save.[6]

At some time or another we got into a habit of fleeing the unpredictable New York winters and spending a few weeks in the southwest desert, first in Palm Springs, California and then in Scottsdale, Arizona. Not only are these spots great to breathe in but they are great to work in. Some years before we began our visits I was surprised to learn how many famous English authors, poets and the like had become attached to the region.

In Palm Springs I wrote no music, but did some thinking about an American opera that seemed to me to need writing. The reasons for writing it, in a hand-to-hand battle with the reasons why it has not been done by someone already, might be a dull spectacle here, but it took a little honest pondering and ended with writing a first draft of the libretto. Name of opera: *Crystal.* Aim of opera: to make prior acquaintance with the entire story unnecessary. Chance of success with the typical grand opera audience—well—?

---

[6]The orchestral holograph of *Maria Malibran* has never resurfaced. A copy of the piano-vocal score, however, is housed in the Archives at the Juilliard School.

Richard Wagner had more or less the same purpose, but he was fundamentally a poet whose poetry was not easy for all hearers. The result was that most ears depended on the powerful music for the story. Claude Debussy put his delicious music to poetry that calls for thought. Thought has never been plentiful in the theater. Most of the great and famous operas could almost exchange stories without losing their audiences. Almost.

The major part of *Crystal*, both words and music, was written in Arizona. It is guaranteed to make potential backers blanch with horror, with its elaborate scenery, large chorus and large orchestra, but it is on paper. Mainly it is a statement of my idea of the form a new American opera could take.[7]

[Bennett's long-awaited arranging text, *Instrumentally Speaking*, was published by Belwin Mills in 1975. It begins with a concise (yet personal) examination of each instrument's range and capabilities, and then takes the reader through the scoring of a hypothetical new Broadway musical. Bennett describes the challenges and potential pitfalls confronting the theater orchestrator, while giving a candid and engrossing first-hand account of his working methods. The text concludes with brief chapters on "legitimate" arranging for concert band and orchestra, where he transcribes Beethoven's "Hammerklavier" sonata for the two mediums.

Several reviewers expressed their disappointment, having expected a revelation of Bennett's supposed "secret formulas." One of the clear messages of his book, however, is precisely what he had insisted in his earlier essays: that formulas are no substitute for creativity, and that careful study of the canon of orchestral masterworks—plus first-hand arranging experience—provide the best possible training for an aspiring orchestrator. It was more than modesty that had once compelled him to write: "I am sometimes asked to give lessons in arranging. The answer is simple: 'What I actually *know* about it, I can tell in about twenty minutes—not even enough for a half-hour lesson. As to the other elements that go into a beautiful arrangement, your guess has every chance to be as good as mine.'"[8]]

Two works to celebrate the two hundredth birthday of the U.S.A. were largely put on paper in Scottsdale. One [*Zimmer's American Greeting*] was for Robert Boudreau's American Wind Symphony and was a music setting and background for a big poem written by Paul Zimmer for the anniversary. The author read his poem at the inaugural concert of the ensemble that year, 1976.

---

[7]Bennett's opera *Crystal* remains unperformed. Piano-vocal scores are in the New York Public Library and Library of Congress collections.

[8]From his "All I Know about Arranging Music," below.

The other work was called *The Fun and Faith of William Billings, American* and was commissioned by the National Symphony Orchestra of Washington. Antal Dorati conducted the first performance with the chorus of the University of Maryland and the orchestra at the Inaugural Concert of the season of concerts celebrating the Bicentennial. Dorati had asked me to use some of the songs of Billings, who was our first great songwriter. He died in 1800 and of course lived through the American Revolution and the first two decades of the young republic. William Billings was branded an ignoramus by his educated contemporaries. He did indeed do some rather primitive things, but he wrote out all his songs in four-part vocal arrangements and wrote the alto line in the alto clef. I'd love to call a meeting of the composers of our Golden Age and invite them to do one of their big song hits that way and call the choir in for rehearsal.

Billings's counterpoint was often a bit rough-shod, but he aimed at making each part a kind of song-hit in itself and that's a large order for anybody. In my piece I laid it on the line, so to speak, for him by presenting three of the four parts, each with its own new orchestral accompaniment, and used the fourth line as a sort of obbligato to the third. This was done with the song "When Jesus Wept" and the effect was truly moving when done thus separately and finally all together.

The man's faith was absolute. Those who have chosen their gods and are even anxious to fight to defend their choice don't like the idea, but there's a lot of evidence to support the idea that faith in itself has the power to move the mountains. It's possible to believe that the great source of this universe is so powerful that all prayers get to him as the ultimate god, through whatsoever being is named in our prayers. I like to think of that God, with His million right answers to the million problems we give Him, as the being to whom all our gods must report.

On that basis we can work and live with people of all faiths, and segregation is not merely wrong, it is an impossibility. The faith of William Billings warms one's heart, however we choose to compare his faith with our own.

Which bit of philosophizing brings my report to two of the last three major efforts. The success of Robert Shaw's (and my) recordings of *The Many Moods of Christmas* for chorus and orchestra led a very talented and imaginative music director of the First Presbyterian Church of Orlando, Florida, whose name is Jack Wilson, to call me and ask me to do about twenty more Christmas carols. The result was four so-called *Carol Cantatas*, which he did with his fine choir and the Florida Symphony Orchestra at his church on two Christmas Eves. Not satisfied with that we brought into the world *The Easter*

Story, presented on two consecutive Sundays [in April 1978] and made up of Easter songs into a substantial part of the Easter service.

The four *Carol Cantatas* were first sung and played to celebrate the one hundredth anniversary of the church, a fact that reminded me that I, who never joined a church, just about began my whole musical career as a leader and first violinist in the Presbyterian Church of Freeman, Missouri, at the age of eleven. Somehow it seemed to me to fit.

Now, the latest of my published pieces for band and last I'll quote—I promise. It is called *Autobiography* and was another piece built under the Arizona sun. Some friends got the idea that I might have seen something they missed (probably not in Arizona) and seemed anxious to have my doings put on paper. The band piece was my attempt to fill the order. Here is the form of it, with the titles, dates, and commercial-sounding jingles:

I. Cherry Street (1894)
Born on a hill by a railroad track—
our house was a mansion—or was it a shack?
II. South Omaha (1899)
The mind said più vivo! The feet said retard!
Talking was easy but walking was hard,
Limping around in a lumber yard.
III. Corn, Cows and Music (1900)
Haying the horses and slopping the pigs
And playing sonatas and rags and jigs.
IV. Missouri to New York (1916)
To Broadway! What was I waiting for?
My country came up with the answer: War!
V. The Merrill Miracle (1919)
Our destinies danced to far different themes
But counterpoint showed us the way to our dreams
The ghost of old Johann Sebastian beams.
VI. A Parisian in Paris (1926)
Sometimes our French was a little bit broken
But English, chez nous, she was not often spoken.
VII. —What Was The Question? (1933)
Man's ages are seven, but I must admit
That I tried them all on and none of them fit.
So, Mr. Shakespeare, this is it.
[copyright G. Schirmer, Inc. 1978]

Editor's Epilogue

Epilogue

Bennett remained active putting pen to paper in his final years; his associates seem certain that "there's nothing he'd rather have done." Among the last of his more that 175 original works were an *Arabesque* commissioned by the American Brass Quintet (1978) and the last of his eleven pieces for the American Wind Symphony—*Christmas Overture* (1980) and *Fanfare* (1981).

In 1979 he was awarded a citation by the American Society of Music Arrangers, which he had helped found more than forty years earlier. It was the last of a lifetime of honors that included:

Academy of Motion Picture Arts and Sciences (Oscar), 1955 (for *Oklahoma!*)
Christopher Award (television), 1960
National Academy of Television Arts and Sciences (Emmy), 1962
Doctor of Humane Letters, Franklin and Marshall College, 1965
George Frederick Handel Medallion, City of New York, 1967
Henry Hadley Medal, National Association for American Composers and Conductors, 1969
Phi Mu Alpha Sinfonia Fraternity, Citation, 1972
Kappa Kappa Psi, Citation, 1975
Honorary Life Member, Alumni Association, University of Missouri-Kansas City, 1977
Scroll, City of Los Angeles, 1979

He had also been nominated for a Pulitzer in the 1960s (among his supporters was Avery Fisher), but the honor proved to be one prize that eluded him.

Though Bennett hadn't contributed to a new musical since 1975's *Rodgers and Hart*, he lived to see splashy New York revivals of several of the "Golden Age" productions he had been associated with. Among these were *My Fair Lady* (1976), *The King and I* (1977, with Yul Brynner in the role he had originated in 1951), *Oklahoma!* (1979, in a spirited production that ran for nine months), and *Camelot* (1980, with Richard Burton returning). The Bennett arrangements, so well known via their best-selling original-cast LPs, survived more-or-less intact. And these and several other Bennett-orchestrated shows would remain among the musicals most often staged by amateur and stock companies.

Another emergent trend was the revival of Broadway's prewar shows. It had long been held that original libretti would prove dated and slow, and the orchestrations thin and unsatisfying—hence the extensive reworking of *Good News* (DeSylva, Brown, and Henderson, 1927/1974), *No, No, Nanette* (Youmans, 1925/1971), and *Very Good Eddie* (Kern, 1915/1975) for their latter-day Broadway productions.

Yet many musical theater devotees were determined to authentically resurrect—if only for a concert performance and perhaps a commercial recording—some of the most-celebrated "Golden Age" shows. Bennett visited the Rodgers and Hammerstein 52nd Street warehouse with Miles Krueger[1] in 1978 to retrieve the orchestra parts for the 1927 and 1946 productions of *Show Boat*, which eventually led to a recording of a completely restored version in 1988, with Bennett's 1927 arrangements used whenever possible. And Hans Spialek, shortly before his death, refashioned his 1936 orchestrations for Rodgers and Hart's *On Your Toes* (1936); the revival was produced on Broadway in 1983 and documented on long-playing disc.

The movement blossomed, with Lenore (Mrs. Ira) Gershwin sponsoring new recordings of the complete scores of George Gershwin's *Lady Be Good*, *Oh, Kay!*, *Strike Up the Band*, *Girl Crazy*, *Of Three I Sing*, *Let 'Em Eat Cake*, and *Pardon My English*. All extant 1920s–30s orchestrations (many by Bennett) were used; lost materials were refashioned as authentically as possible by a new generation of orchestrators, principally Russell Warner, William David Brohn, and Larry Wilcox. Conductors John Mauceri, John McGlinn, Eric Stern, Michael Tilson Thomas, and Rob Fisher led these and other recordings, which would eventually include such vintage scores as Porter's *Anything Goes* and *Kiss Me, Kate*, Berlin's *Annie Get Your Gun* (in its original, 1946, guise) and *Louisiana Purchase*, and Kern's *Sitting Pretty* and *Very Warm for May*.

Just as a digital-recording boom had been fueled by consumer acceptance of compact disc technology, the dramatic growth in videocassette recorder sales prompted the marketing of thousands of Hollywood films. The landmark RKO musicals that featured Bennett's orchestrations were widely available for purchase or rental, no longer limited to screenings at big-city revival

---

[1]Author of *Show Boat: The Story of a Classic American Musical* (Oxford, 1977) and director of the Institute of the American Musical (Los Angeles).

houses or on late-night television. *Victory at Sea*, too, was likewise more widely seen than it had been in years.

Although Bennett perpetually questioned the ultimate worth of the theater music he arranged for most of his adult life, he too could be seduced by its charms. Orchestrator William David Brohn recently recalled a special moment:

> The setting was the New York State Theater at Lincoln Center, the house lights out and the stage lighting a romantic midnight blue with the follow spot picking the leading couple for *Show Boat* in their final dress rehearsal. My job as assistant conductor was to check the sonic balance (unamplified, of course—this was 1966) by wandering about the mostly empty house where the first audience was due that night. "You are love, here in my arms, where you belong . . . " sang the Magnolia to her Ravenal. Suddenly my progress down the left aisle was interrupted by the presence of a long limb that I hadn't spied in the dark, extending as it did from the aisle seat. "Oh, excuse me, Mr. Bennett," I exclaimed *sotto voce* to the orchestrator of that sublime duet swelling forth from the stage and pit. And as I crouched down just in front of him I gazed at that patrician-looking face to see that tears were trickling down, and he was tenderly holding his wife's hand. I fancifully imagined that perhaps they had done the same thing those many years before at the Ziegfeld Theater as his orchestrations soared with the voices in that first performance of *Show Boat*. He must have noticed the embarrassment, coupled with admiration, that I felt, for he responded to this unwitting intrusion into a private emotional moment: "Oh, hello there, Bill. Isn't this just one of the most beautiful songs that Jerry ever wrote? I still feel this way about it. . . ." The great heart that informed his enormous talent was manifest at that moment as now.[2]

Bennett passed away on 18 August 1981—the same day that a revival of *My Fair Lady* opened in New York, with Rex Harrison recreating his 1956 role. Russell Bennett claimed to have no concerns about posterity and his particular place in it; yet his compositions and arrangements endure, permitting new generations to get to know him through his witty, elegant, and charming contributions to the American music of his century.

---

[2]William D. Brohn letter to the editor, November 1997. Brohn, a Bennett protégé, is especially renowned for his sensitive revisions of orchestrations for several 1990s revivals of "Golden Age" Broadway shows, including *Carousel* and *Show Boat*. In 1998 he received a "Tony" award for his *Ragtime* orchestrations.

Eight Selected Essays by Robert Russell Bennett

Orchestrating for Broadway[1]

I make orchestrations for musical comedies, operettas, radio shows, etc. In Tin-Pan Alley, where tunes are born so fast that their progenitors would be next to helpless without the aid of my particular type of musical obstetrics. It is my job to nurse to a life of from a day or so to about six months each ditty, jingle or roundelay that my many talented patients are able to bring to a fairly healthy embryonic state.

Orchestrators just happen. All the education in the world will not develop the peculiar gift required unless it is already there, and if it is there education alone is still inadequate to bring the gift up to specialist requirements. There must also be experience of such a wide range that its gaining must in many details be accidental. Less successful men are usually so because of a shortage of such accidental experience. More successful ones always bear out the same theory.

When I was nine my father gave me a trumpet and after a little preliminary sparring I set about playing a piece with my sister (at the piano). The piece was called "The Naughty Pixie Mocking His Mother," the upper part of which I had already copied out for the violin. To my dismay the first note didn't fit and suddenly the meaning of "Trumpet in B flat" dawned on me, whereupon we got a fresh start and gave a successful rendition of the piece, to the great astonishment and delight of our doting father. At the age of eleven I was given the job of conducting our family orchestra while doing things to the first violin part, my father much preferring to play the trumpet, which he did most capably. At sixteen I had had my hands on a large majority of known instruments and soon began making a living playing the piano, my then current studies in harmony and counterpoint being the excuse and reason

---

[1]*Modern Music* 9, no. 4 (May–June 1932): 148–52. Reprinted by permission of The Estate of Robert Russell Bennett.

for rearranging every piano part handed me, a practice not uncommon to professional pianists, alas, but of great benefit to me at the time.

Coming to New York a few years later, a period of copying the parts from musical comedy scores gave me the first urge to do the scoring, followed by a much greater urge when I learned how much orchestrators were paid per page for the work. Eventually the chance came to make what is known as print arrangements, arrangements of music for dancing playable by any likely combination of instruments at any reasonable tempo. I made several hundred of these and finally graduated, meaning in this case: I was promoted to the "shows."

Taking anything from a whistled melody to a piano sketch from its author to the lighted orchestra pit of a theatrical production demands, as indicated above, a great many things beside theoretical training but if I were asked what the great asset one can have in this work is, I should have to answer, "counterpoint." Here is where the admonition of the teacher to his pupil to avoid forced voice-leading comes into its own. The audience, sitting there watching dimpled knees and listening to tiny voices singing out familiar intervals in praise of familiar emotions, has no idea what counterpoint is; but let it be stiff, forced or badly distributed and the knees seem less dimpled, the tiny voices grow tinier and the general atmosphere becomes charged with an unmistakable So What? What the public doesn't know, which is plenty, it very nearly always feels, and that applies to the good things as well as the bad.

Let me say that at no time in all the ten years I have been at this work have I felt that one note of the miles of exercises I did as a student was wasted on it. Rather am I tempted to get out the old worn-out book and start all over again, cleaning up, purifying the counters, making them—in the language of those who pay to listen to them—prettier.

Now besides this most important point come many others, such as the fact that the whole style of tune-writing and orchestrating changes from season to season, almost from week to week. The change is gradual, but after a few months in Europe, on repeated occasions I have found it necessary to stop, look and do a lot of listening before daring to start afresh at the old work-bench. I have even, as Tin-Pan Alley calls it, "flopped" on one or two plays, meaning that I had quite some rewriting to do before the result was fit for the sophisticated first-nighters.

Another hazard of the métier is the art of scoring for an orchestra to accompany voiceless voices. The operatic type of voice is far too hard-boiled to hold the sympathy of an American music comedy audience; they want youth, simplicity and tenderness rather than brilliance or "style." This is all to the good except for the poor orchestras, who are obliged to learn a pianissimo on their instruments that has no precedent anywhere else. It is the orchestrator's place to know exactly which of these and what combinations of these instruments are at the moment within the exalted circle of the elect, i.e., capable of "playing under" the voice of the particular actor or actress who is to present the song or musical scene in question. This is perhaps the most difficult mechanical problem in the business, and one of the constant worries of the musical director, who is in the last analysis responsible both to the singer for colorful support without overpowering, and to the composer and the orchestrator for such individuality as they have invested in the number on paper.

In the case of dancing on the stage a new set of problems arises. Solo dancers and teams are the *bête noire* of the arranger. They seldom know what they want to dance to and, if they do, have no terms to communicate their wants to a musician. In nearly every case in a large production they are called on to dance to a new melody, which is a part of the composer's "score." Imagine the joy of the orchestrator when he is asked to set the old orchestration to the new tune without even a deaf-and-dumb language indication from the dancer as to what features of the arrangement of the old number were valuable.

Chorus dancing is staged by a director, who has names for all of the thousand and one tricky rhythms, steps and formations he uses. Everything he creates should be echoed in the perfect orchestration, so, rather than spend months at a dancing school, this humble orchestrator takes down a sketch of every step, hop, twist, entrance, exit, stop, break, back-bend, split, nip-up or what-have-you—measure by measure. Then after going home and spending the night wrestling with his figures and translating them into exciting concord he often gets a phone call saying the "boss" didn't like the routine, so the director has to restage the number. All things considered, we are a peaceful, law-abiding lot, we arrangers.

I have already mentioned conductors and musicians of theatre orchestras. There are fewer really fine conductors than there are great symphony conductors; in fact the fingers of one hand are more than sufficient to count them in New York from whence practically all shows spring. When an inefficient musical director is on the job nothing can sound good; the finest bands, the greatest productions, the most charming music, the most brilliant arrangements all go down the sink when the man in the middle hasn't "got rhythm." This, like all others in the theatre, is a highly specialized art, and is not for any but born troupers, as the expression goes. More than once have I done two shows simultaneously and seen one draw unending favorable notice on its orchestration while the other limped along and remained unsung as far as I was concerned. This solely according to who conducted, and it is usually very hard to put your finger on the exact thing that distinguishes the one from the other, though you recognize the difference almost before either lifts his baton.

The difference in style of playing by musicians is one of the greatest reasons why the orchestral colors keep progressing (in one direction or another). This is particularly true of brass players and the wise orchestrator keeps his acquaintance with many a trumpeter and trombonist. Ever so often some one invents a new mute, or a new way of attacking a tone or a completely new timbre by a new position of the lips. There are many names for what brass players do, such as "rip," "flair" ["flare"], "hot break," "sixteen measure ride-out," etc., etc., most of which material is to be found in good music; but the names and the particular manner of playing are unique to Broadway. The brasses are almost as constantly in use as in the military bands, but are much of the time kept softly underneath the strings and woodwinds so that the fullness of the ensemble is not lost in the quieter moments.

Woodwind sections nowadays often consist of three men, playing piccolo, flute, oboe, English horn, clarinet, bass clarinet, alto, tenor and baritone saxophone, naturally not all at the same time. It is simply fantastic what feats of versatility these men perform, and in orchestrating an important show it is necessary to know exactly who is to be there and what instruments he plays.

String players are the least changeable in tone color but it is sometimes a bit of a shock to hear a violinist who plays five or six concerti and reads the most involved passages with ease get "hot" and start "goin' to town"—which means outdoing the wow-wow trumpets in the matter of off-beat improvisation.

Many interesting memories have already piled up during the period I have spent at the "racket." I shall never forget, for instance, one of the leading producers, on hearing a dance I had written in several shifting keys (using the device a little ahead of its subsequent vogue), saying he thought the orchestration was too "fuguey"!

Also a letter from Herbert Stothart, conductor and part composer of *Rose Marie*, asking me to come to Atlantic City to help him with some new material, as he thought the show was going to turn out all right. While I was in Paris the French version of the play gave its thirteen-hundredth performance and I had to admit he was right; the show turned out "all right."

The most striking memory I keep of *Show Boat* is having to finish the work in a very short space of time, spending nine days on an average of sixty-two pages of full orchestral score per day. In the course of this play, which covers a period of fifty years, I tried the experiment of treating the banjo in each number exactly as it would have been played at the time the number was supposed to have taken place, saving the modern fox-trot rhythm until the last five minutes of the performance. Picture my thoughts when I attended a rehearsal in Paris and the conductor told me, not without some pride, that he had given the banjo a "blues" part and had added a hot trumpet and jazz drummer to Julie's song in the first act (1880!).

Many such reminiscences could be recounted but I must leave myself room to tell you of the only genuine thrill the job has ever given me. It came when I was asked to make a real low-down overture for the eleven-piece jazz band of Eubie Blake, whose blackness is only exceeded by that of his band. Then I knew once and for all I belonged to Tin-Pan Alley.

Orchestration of Theatre and Dance Music[1]

More progress is seen in the orchestral treatment of light music than in any other feature of this type of entertainment, not excluding the melodic and harmonic substance of the pieces themselves. Music designed for immediate popular appeal must, of course, work in the direction of the obvious, therefore it can add not more than one experimental feature to what is already well planted in the public ear, and composers do best when they can avoid even that *one* and still be fresh and appealing.

Instrumentation is not so limited; in fact great inventiveness is often shown. Its more imaginative flights are protected from popular failure by the success of the tune and the almost barbaric simplicity of the underlying rhythm, and the arranger finds himself free to borrow at will from all the striking orchestral effects of the masters with no necessity for the hearer to "analyze and understand" him. With the development of recorded music and broadcasting, orchestration assumes greater and greater importance. Robbed of one of its primary ingredients, namely the personal magnetism of the performers, music must look to so-called orchestral color for a great portion of its individuality, if any is to be achieved. This point is hardly controversial, but if anyone questions it let him make a list of the human imperfections of playing freely pardoned and often enjoyed in the concert-hall, yet simply unpleasant when recorded or transmitted by mechanical instruments.

---

[1]This essay appears in the *Music Lovers' Encyclopedia*, compiled by Rupert Hughes, rev. and ed. by Deems Taylor and Russell Kerr (New York: Doubleday, © 1955), as well as previous editions. Used by permission of Doubleday, a division of Bantam Doubleday Dell Publishing Group, Inc. It would seem to date from the late 1930s. In all editions, one British spelling—"colour"—is, for an unknown reason, used, though no prior appearance of the essay in a British publication is known. The editor has adopted the American form.

In other words, the spread of radio and phonograph over the world has tended largely to reduce ensemble playing to a chemical mixture whose component parts must be as pure as possible. (For the purposes of this article, the term *music* will refer to what is known as "popular," "light," "commercial," etc., and is not to be confused with the great art of music for musicians and cultured listeners, who might pardonably wonder why we spend time on the details of the scherzo—so to speak—without taking up the profounder movements of life's symphony.)

The vast majority of this music is first introduced in the form of songs. Every arrangement for orchestra of these songs falls into one or another formula, depending on the nature of performance intended. This formula changes and develops in each branch as new combinations are successfully tried, but there is never any very revolutionary novelty introduced with success—as a deep study of every new development will reveal. The introduction of greater or smaller combinations, the addition of unusual instruments, the sudden discovery of new playing tricks of instruments and groups of instruments already in use, and the use of the voice or voices with the orchestra to present the words of the song; all these "innovations" are made to cling desperately to the original tune or the semi-barbaric rhythms already mentioned, or both, and the result will not go down as revolutionary.

THEATRE ORCHESTRAS

With no attempt to go deeply into its history one can say that theater music has always been composed of songs, dances, and incidental music. For many, many years the formula for the orchestral score of a "number" for the theater was something as follows:

In general, a transcription for orchestra of the piano copy as printed and sold. More specifically, an introduction, vamp, verse, and chorus. The chorus was marked to repeat, with certain instruments playing the second time only, and certain others playing an octave higher on the repeat. This repeat version served either for an accompaniment to the ensemble on the stage, singing *fortissimo*, or for dancing, either by the chorus or by the "principals" (actors or actresses who went into their dance after singing the song through).

This loud refrain, or chorus—both of which terms are avoided as confusing in the music of Jerome Kern, where the word "burthen" supplants them—merits a little deeper study, as it has long remained the basis of all arrangements for the purposes enumerated above. Examining briefly the instruments and their treatment, we find something like this:

Flute or Flutes: portions of the melody and little variations at frequent intervals, all placed an octave higher than the soprano voice would be on the melody.

Oboe: the melody, in the register of the soprano voice, with certain allowances for breathing.

Clarinets (2): the second and third voices of the flute part.

Bassoon: a mixture and 'cello and bass parts, with sometimes both bass notes and afterbeats.

Horns (2): mostly afterbeats with an occasional sustained note or a doubling of the counter-melody of the 'cello for a few measures.

Trumpets (2): the melody and an accompanying line in thirds, sixths, or other pleasant-sounding harmony notes for the second trumpet. These parts were marked "second time only."

Trombone, bass notes, occasionally the melody and occasionally the counter-melody of the 'cello, also marked "second time only."

Drums: "oom-pahs" in the loud version—that is—bass drum and attached cymbal on the bass beats and snare-drum on the afterbeats. Sometimes the strain was written out, with bells (glockenspiel) playing the first time through, principally on the melody, and drums for the repeat.

First Violin or Violins: the melody, marked "8va 2nd time."

Second Violin: afterbeats, arranged so as to form a full chord with the viola, for the most part by means of double stops, the lower note of which was usually lower than the higher note of the:

Viola, which served as a "big second fiddle" and completed the harmony of the afterbeats.

'Cello: a counter-melody, or low harmony note under the melody of the first violin. This counter was preferably on the A string and was sustained in character especially if the tune of the composition was not.

Bass: the bass notes, *arco* or *pizzicato.*

It is to be borne in mind that this whole strain served, played softly and as marked, for a vocal accompaniment to solo voices on the stage the first time through. All instruments marked "2nd time only" joined in during the "1st Ending" (or "First Time Bars," as they call it in England) and proceed with the repeat version, *ff* as just described. This briefly detailed résumé is given, not to indicate that it was the first orchestral makeup of a popular refrain, nor that it continued in vogue for a longer period than some other way has or will in the future, but chiefly because it assumes importance as the starting point for all that has followed.

It is well to avoid individual names in a study of this kind, but two names, one well known and the other quite obscure, are indispensable. These names are Victor Herbert and Frank Saddler. The former influenced theater orchestration tremendously by enriching the pattern described above in several details; the latter by the introduction of combinations of colors and flights of imagination that lead to practically all the subsequent styles employed by the countless band arrangers of our era. Victor Herbert was a great musician in every sense of the word—his knowledge of the classics was such that he conducted symphony orchestras for many seasons without reference to scores during rehearsal or concert, and his feeling for the structure of a sound orchestration was infallible. His only concern in the arrangement of his operettas was the simplest, most effective method of presenting his charming melodies, and his technical contributions to our formula were the result of no search for unusual sounds, but merely of his desire to make his music sound as beautiful as possible. Frank Saddler, however, was not at home with the broader beauties of a Victor Herbert style of arrangement. He was a champion of small orchestras, filling up his refrain with the charming tricks of muted brass, unexpected bass progressions, *pizzicato* effects, duets for two violins against the melody in the lower instruments and many other devices. The main addition of Victor Herbert was the dividing of the violins into three or more expressive parts, the high vibrant 'cello just beneath the melody, and the dramatic, full-sounding brass choir at the climaxes. He detested the usual variations of the flutes and clarinets and kept them low, simple and sonorous.

Frank Saddler wrote no operettas of his own. He was an *orchestrator*, versatile and inventive, with a fine ear for every novel effect of the great writers of symphonic music and a genius for adapting their tricks to the current musical-comedy tunes. His arrangements fairly sparkled and a melody of no distinction whatsoever became alluring in his interpretation. No subsequent arranging has done more for the tunes themselves than Saddler's although much has been added to his technique. It is not too much to say that he established once and for all the position of the orchestrator as a personality quite apart from the composer of the songs. He is responsible for the fact that even composers who can make creditable arrangements for the orchestra decline to do so in view of the great advantage of their melodies of having new and equally inspired brains create the orchestrations.

Continuing a bit on the technical side, one feature that both of these men struggled for was not fully realized until after their death. Both had visions of emancipating the second violins and violas so that they might play *cantabile*—with the first violins and 'celli—instead of incessant short afterbeats. Saddler eliminated second violins or rather included them with the firsts, and left the rhythm to two or more divided violas. (See the opening bars of Mozart's G Minor Symphony [No. 40] for a perfect example of this distribution.) Herbert at times left the rhythm to the harp, often used in metropolitan theaters, whilst his second fiddles soared away with the firsts. After both of these gifted men had passed away a new style of guitar playing came into being and, with a piano or two and a very much refined and softened pulse of drums, solved the oom-pah problem completely and left all other instruments free to indulge in counterpoint or their particular rendition of the melody. Not all music will admit of such an accompaniment but the majority will and the seconds and violas have gone free!

Theatre orchestration was undoubtedly the main source of ideas for dance orchestras, at first in its effect on the printed arrangements from which all dance bands played and, later, as the bands elaborated on these printed arrangements, in its more imaginative combinations. However, the use of saxophones, which dates back much farther than one might think, added great possibilities to the dance combinations, and eventually the saxes, plus the rhythm combination of the piano (or pianos) and guitar, invaded the theater and colored its music. Saxophones are of great value because they are easy to play and can almost be "sung" on without great concern over technical difficulties such as beset flutes, oboes, bassoons, and even clarinets. This does not mean that anyone with a good ear can play them, but a good clarinetist, for example, feels he is on a vacation when playing alto or tenor saxophone.

Naturally their development has taken a turn not purely technical. They have grown in warmth of tone and lip and tongue effects, and they are the last answer (up to this writing) to an arranger's prayer when he deals with small bands. They can play loud enough not to be drowned out by trumpets and trombones, and in the softer bits, their peculiar timbre seems to combine low strings, horn, bassoon, and human voice tone, so that (always remembering the simple chord structure of the type of music we are concerned with) the sensitive ear of the sincere musician must acknowledge the live, vibrant pulse they add to an orchestra with inadequate strings, horns and low winds.

This becomes even more important where rhythm is the prime factor, since it is almost axiomatic that the smaller the group the better and cleaner the rhythm.

In the theater as one sits in the back rows of a crowded house with a "legitimate" (i.e., saxless) orchestra, the impression is that there are two moods in the orchestration—with brass, and without brass. With saxophones added one is distinctly conscious of three colors: one with predominating brass, and one with wood-wind and saxes. This leaves the "without brass" mood still to be used for the tenderer, more delicate moments and we have actually gained one whole color. This is of course speaking very broadly of the effect when seeing the show for the first time, and wasting no time listening consciously to the orchestra.

It would be silly to say that theater music cannot do without saxophones. Many productions are so conceived that the tone would be entirely out of place—vulgar and blasphemous. Their great value to the majority of shows is nevertheless incontestable.

This is not meant to be a lesson in theater arrangements for orchestrators, yet a few of the problems of this most limited of all orchestration jobs will be interesting to all music-lovers.

In the first place the general rule to observe is that we are not arranging for the concert stage but for the orchestra pit, and the broad brush of the opera composer is more our pattern than the more precious pastels of symphonists. Not at any time during the performance are we given the undivided attention of the audience. Even overtures, entr'actes and outmarches are accompaniments to a babble of the audience's own conversation and movement, and the orchestra must either be so garish as to stop momentarily the flow of talk or resign itself to the enhancing of a general mood of enjoyment while being practically ignored. The latter is by far the safer plan.

In accompanying singers of the musical-comedy stage, a great problem was presented when the popular fancy turned away from big voice to little, thin ones of personal appeal but no vocal power. This necessitated for years the presence of the melody strongly played in the orchestra, since the singer would leave some doubt as to just what the melody was if left to his or her own devices in the matter. Not until the use of microphones, which transform a "croon" into a full vocal tone, was it thought possible to make the orchestration into a pure accompaniment. Somehow a wave of such orchestration followed the radio and motion-picture boom. High sustained violins (divided), piano, guitars, and *pizzicato* bass for rhythm, low sustained wood-wind (maybe sax, *pianissimo*) or a harmless counter-melody in low unison clarinets, with trumpets and trombones chirping out the moment the voice pauses for breath—that became the accepted architecture of song orchestration when voices were "miked."

It is also used where no loud-speaker system is present. The reason is vague but somehow the hammering of the public ear by "miked" music has caused voices to grow fuller and more penetrating when left unaided.

When the full chorus comes on and the dance begins the orchestra comes nearer to being the feature than at any other time in the show. As suggested above, before the use of saxophones the full brass was indispensable throughout the whole dance except on rare occasions when a delicate four-measure phrase came as a surprise (and "got by" the producer of the show). After the development of the sax it was possible to carry a few measures on the winds for variety, giving the brass a short rest for higher and louder doings later.

If we take up the cinema as part of theater orchestration we are concerned not so much with music as with sound. In recording, a solo muted violin can be made to drown out a full orchestra playing *fff* by means of a small dial.[2] This may bring up many different possibilities in the facile mind, but the final condition is something like this: The limit of effect is merely the limit of the orchestrator's imagination. There is practically nothing ineffective, there are no boundaries of safe combination of instruments, there is no art in doubling or reinforcing different sections of the orchestra. All this is theoretically true because of the curious feature known as sound-mixing. However, a sound, well-balanced orchestration renders the task of recording, both by the conductor of the orchestra and by the sound-mixer, very much easier.[3] Although it harnesses the mind of the orchestrator very much as the original art of theater orchestration has, it makes possible a much simpler system of microphones, and brings a consequent saving in terms of the great deal of time and money for the studios. At least one of the film industry's best musical directors prefers to play the music all into one "mike" and of course the orchestration must in this case be practically as well made as for the concert platform. The orchestras used are in most cases larger than for the theaters and an experienced arranger knows that the larger the band the easier his task. As one fine orchestrator, Stephen O. Jones, once said when told of a great orchestration someone had made for a fifty-piece band, "Who *can't* make a good one for that sized bunch?"

DANCE ORCHESTRAS

Years ago when trumpets were more than hazardous in their upper tones, a colored band had a star player who, after many attempts at a high C

[2]He made the point more vividly in 1975's *Instrumentally Speaking* (12–13): "Recorded music . . . removes all dynamic distinction between a muted viola and the Battle of the Marne. . . ."

[3]Oscar Levant, writing at about the same time, echoed: "Much of the fine work these men [Hollywood's orchestrators] do is conditioned by the characteristics of sound-track recording. I don't know whether their work would come off nearly so well without a microphone. (This does not apply at all to Bennett, who is much more flexible.)" (*A Smattering of Ignorance*, 121).

sounding B flat, finally resigned himself to missing it and substituting the major second lower which comes out with the same fingering and less effort for the lips (for the studious reader, he sounded the seventh tone of the harmonic series—rather false in intonation—instead of the eighth, for which he was striving). Who shall say that this resultant seventh was not the sire of the W. C. Handy–George Gershwin–Darius Milhaud line of "blues" chords that found such a vogue?

Likewise in the heart of Kansas there was (also years ago) a small orchestra with no 'cello player. One harness maker had an E flat alto saxophone and one day he discovered that he could read the 'cello part. Looking at a 'cello part one sees at once that all he had to do was use a little imagination in the key signature and read it in the G (treble) clef, and the missing 'cello was missed no more. Who will take the trouble to go farther in a search for the birth of the sax choir in our dance bands? The treatment of this choir by the best dance-arrangers lends credence to the theory at least. This of course ceases to apply when the saxes are doubling other instruments, a practice that has grown universal since they were introduced.

The art of doubling, an art so advanced that many an arrangement for the modern dance orchestra has the names of persons in place of the names of instruments in the wood-wind section, has carried the matter of coloring to an almost fantastic point. Instead of the accustomed "1st Clarinet in B flat" we see on the score "Elmer," followed by the first measure of his part over which appears "Flute in G"[4] or "Oboe" or "B flat tenor" or whatever other instrument Elmer owns and the orchestrator needs. A woodwind section of six players will give you at various intervals all the tone combinations of a full symphony orchestra's wood-wind, plus beautifully-played saxophones, plus a light-hearted and enthusiastic quality to whatever phrase is played, making up for the lack of virtuosity with spirit and a feeling for ensemble not always obtainable in the larger orchestras.

Dance orchestration has long since taken its place as the most imaginative and productive of all arranging. Bands that remain together for long periods develop what is known by the over-worked name of "style" to a degree not possible in any other group. Very much as the old glee clubs and minstrels used to do, the modern dance band discovers its most striking effects in rehearsal and playing. Usually the arranger is one of the band himself and he is thus "in" at the inception of any new twist the players discover. To

[4]The alto flute was, at the time, all but unknown in theatre orchestras and dance bands. Bennett's occasional use of the instrument in his late-30s film scoring, a time of rapid improvement in the quality of soundtrack recording and reproduction, had much to do with its subsequent vogue on Hollywood's sound stages.

make the point clearer, a trombonist may arrive at a rehearsal and, in warming his instrument up, play some phrase with a certain personal amplification—some slur with lips instead of the slide, a "rip" which is a series of grace notes up to a high tone, made possible by the harmonic series, playable with no change of slide or valve position, or a hundred other little variations on the usual. Another player hears it or he calls the other's attention to it, they gather in one or two more players and a new find in orchestration is realized. If the effect is sufficiently appealing it sweeps the land; if not it is tried and soon discarded.

A glossary of terms such as "rip," "flare," "lick," "break," "release," "redow," etc., provocative as they are, would be of little value because they are outmoded so quickly that a student who took the trouble to learn them would risk that most damning of all stigmas—"corny" (originally "corn-fed," the jazz player's translation of the French "rococo").

Each of these terms and a great many others may be safely assumed to have grown up in the course of rehearsal and playing by individual instrumentalists, as already described. Not all of the names were originated with the players who discovered the tricks, in fact the majority of the names spring from the picturesque vernacular of the Negro bands. These Negro bands, incidentally, are in a class by themselves as to rhythm, a fact probably due to a simpler set of vibrations in the bodies themselves, but that would be for a student of something besides music to say. In many ways they are pioneers in dance music and a number of them can boast of splendid musicians as their arrangers. They have influenced enormously all popular music, which is not surprising if we consider that the American contribution to popular music is the direct offspring of the "Coon Song." Were it not for the Viennese and English ingredients in our finest operettas we could merely say, "The Negroes continue to set the pace in light music."

The "Coon Song" got a new name in Ragtime. Ragtime was later christened Jazz. Jazz became trite as a name before the music did, so its name was again changed to Swing Music. Swing Music became rococo—corny if you like—as a title, but hearts still beat oom-pah, oom-pah, and so do dancing feet; and all nature, bisected, according to Emerson, by an inevitable dualism, continues under different names to go oom-pah, oom-pah, oom-pah, oom-pah.

Backstage with the Orchestrator[1]: A Conference with Russell Bennett

One of the hardest things a musician has to overcome is the aura that attaches to being known as a good orchestrator. For some inexplicable reason, the public critical mind seems unwilling to grant the craft serious connection with music. Just about the time that I began to get a good grip on musical comedy orchestration, the public discovered the term, "orchestration." After that, the term was used in season and out. Serious musical reviews have been known to comment on a piece in terms of its "poor music" but "good orchestration." Now, in all my experience, I have never found a poor piece of music that lent itself to good orchestration! Orchestration, actually, is the rounding out and filling out of the melodic line by means of instrumentation, harmonic color (and all that goes with it) and rhythmic emphases. If the original melody is poor, none of these added embellishments can give it new life or luster. The music itself always comes first and must always be judged first. And, in order to work with music, the orchestrator must first of all be a musician.

SPECIAL REQUIREMENTS

Like any other specialized branch of the larger field of music, orchestration requires both special gifts and special studies. One does not "learn" orchestration, any more than one "learns" a gift for tune creation, or for violin playing. The gift must first be there, inborn, After that, one develops it. Harmony, counterpoint, composition, and instrumentation are vitally necessary studies to bring about the development, but such studies alone do not and never can produce a first-class orchestrator. The attainment of that happy state depends upon a gift for orchestral color and for harmonic variations. It

---

[1]From *Etude Music Magazine*, April 1943.

also depends upon long and often arduous experience. . . . [Bennett tells the "Naughty Pixie" story of his first childhood "arrangement."]

What are the requirements of a good orchestrator? Generally, that deep in his heart, he set himself a goal higher than mere orchestrating! All of our best orchestrators are—or have been, or hope to be and could be—composers. Thus, they need to draw on a gift for melody, for inspired harmonization, for musical balance, exactly as a composer does. These gifts must be developed by a thorough study of harmony and counterpoint, and of several instruments as well. The piano is valuable for its harmonic possibilities; orchestral instruments are valuable for their practice in color and in blending. Added to this, the young orchestrator needs the gift and the ability to make arrangements. Most of all, perhaps, he needs the ability to hear instrumental coloring clearly; he should have, for example, a keen reaction to the color of the oboe as opposed to that of the English horn—the difference between three flutes and three violins. He hears these differences, catalogs them in his mind, and draws on them in his future work.

The best preliminary experience he can get is to play with a small group—preferably a dance band, where the instruments are of all colors with the exception of violoncellos, harps, and horns—learning the feeling of these instruments, as well as the sensation of making his own combine with the others, for color and balance. One of our finest orchestrators was Victor Herbert, who played, not with bands, but as violoncellist in orchestral groups, including the Metropolitan Opera orchestra; early in his life he got the feeling of group balance and color. Later, the young orchestrator needs the experience of working at his craft under the conditions imposed by the work itself—conditions for which it is not exactly easy to prepare academically. Let me outline for you the process of orchestrating a light tune (great music does not require the services of an orchestrator, as a rule—the composer attends to his own orchestrations).

First, an author writes a play for music and gets a composer and a lyric writer to do the songs. These two read the play and work out a number of song *titles*, based on episodes in the story. Usually, a good suitable title is all an experienced composer needs to get to work. Often, a song writer can make an acceptable piano sketch, but in most cases he beats out, whistles, or sings a chorus (maybe a verse, too) and makes certain the lyricist's on hand to witness the process of creation and acquaint himself with the tune. Next, the lyric writer sets words (lyrics) to the newborn melody—and a song is ready. Now the various creative spirits in the process go to the producer, read him the play, and beat out, whistle, or sing him the songs. Not a line is properly written down as yet—neither has the orchestrator made his appearance, although this is to be his life-story, professionally speaking. The producer hears all and agrees to produce the show, whereupon all activity is interrupted for exclamations of joy!

Next, all hands go to the music publisher, who agrees to bring out the music in view of the promised production. He listens to the tunes and sends for his arranger to take down the lead sheet (the first pencil written version of the melodies alone). The arranger takes down the tunes, from the composer's dictation, and sketches in the harmonies. Next he makes several copies of a piano arrangement. Then the show goes into production. (Patience, the orchestrator will soon arrive.)

Production begins with the dance director, who assembles the singing and dancing chorus, teaches them the songs, the words, and the rhythmic accents. When the songs are thus learned, the dance director lines the chorus up and outlines the dance routines. In about two weeks, the dance numbers are ready to give a good idea of the completed product. Then it is that the orchestrator is called in.

He is given the piano copies of the music, watches the dance routines, and begins his work of constructing a singing routine and a dancing routine, all based on the original melodies. He must fill in the harmonies, set the instrumentation, and, often enough, invent new tunes for moments that the original tunes do not cover, interpolate countermelodies of his own and, generally transform the simple melody that the composer beat out, whistled, or sang, into the finished, polished version that the audience hears on opening night and thereafter. It is a colossal job, inasmuch as he has something less than three weeks in which to turn out the six hundred to a thousand pages of manuscript that clothe the average musical show.

Exactly how does the orchestrator go to work? There is no set, single way. Each man proceeds according to his own aptitudes. When I orchestrate for a musical show, I hear at once, in my mind's ear, the harmonies and instrumental combinations I am to make. As I watch the dance routines, and consult the piano copy of the tunes, I hear in my mind exactly the instrumental combinations I am to make. When I go home to work, I need only set down what is in my mind. I always work this way—and never in my experience have two melodies called for exactly the same harmonic or instrumental combinations—nor could they, since each melody carries its own requirements with it. The orchestrator must discover, from nowhere but his own ear and his own good taste, based on experience, just what these exactly suitable combinations are to be.

That, then, is the process of craftsmanship to which the young orchestrator may look forward. How is he to get into it? If he plays in a band, he will undoubtedly be burning to try his hand at arrangements for his own group to play. He grows from that point on. If he makes enough good arrangements in home territory, his work will be spotted. If it is spotted and played often enough, he may have an opportunity to do some arranging for a "big name" band. After that, he is on his own, making the best effects he can, according to the gifts and the craftsmanship over which he can dispose. Successful arrangements attract the attention of music publishers; and, up to now, the music publishers have the most say about who shall be called in to orchestrate which shows.

Orchestrators are often asked why they exist at all—are not the composers capable of turning out their own scores complete? That is a difficult question—also a diplomatic one!—to tackle. Practice rather than theory must supply the answer. There's no use talking of what "ought to be" or what Beethoven and Brahms did. The fact is that many of our popular composers are quite unable to complete a score. They are endowed with their inborn gift for melody, and simply turn out tunes. Some of then know academic composition; some do not. There have been cases where a popular composer was not even certain of his own harmonies. The orchestrator suggests one harmonization, and the composer says, "No, that' s not it." After another few suggestions, he exclaims, "Yes, you've got it now—that's what I mean!"

A good orchestrator can make a very fine living at his craft. But my most earnest counsel is that he regard it as a craft—something to be done as a potboiler while he prepares himself for the higher demands of independent creative artistry. If ever he lets go the hope of writing his own music and gives himself up to orchestrating completely, the chances are that he will never do anything else. If he feels that, potentially at least, he has his own work before him and never means to let it go, the chances are that, even along with his orchestrating, he may be able to round out his stature as a creative artist. If a man is capable of making himself a really fine orchestrator at all, he has the musical feeling and the imagination that would carry him further. And he should never quite let that go. Actually, it is difficult to draw the one line that completely separates good music from trash. Only time draws that line. In the mind of the people, however, there is a very definite pathway from the cheap to the good. In my broadcasts, my viewpoint is that all music is fun, but the greater it is, the more exciting it becomes. This standard of taste can be worked up in any musical medium. The orchestrator can do his share by clinging to his best ideals. After all, both Brahms and Wagner began as orchestrators!

A Pretty Girl Is Like a Melody[1]

Sometimes a song writer utters a lasting truth and even sells it over the counter to a buying public which is usually known as "John Q." The last thing John Q. really wants to spend his money for is a lasting truth, but Irving Berlin outsmarted him in this and other instances. "A Pretty Girl Is Like a Melody," sang Irving in G-flat major and John Q. Public bought a million copies.

I am taking Irving Berlin's song title as a sort of text just as the preacher used to take his text in the little church which I attended as a boy in Freeman, Missouri. The following are the informal thoughts of an arranger of music, who makes possible the tune-writer's entrée into John Q's front yard.

First, let's consider the tune itself. It starts out by being a "pretty girl." One of the world's most difficult questions to answer is, "What is a pretty girl?" Your best friend says, "Gosh, I met a pretty girl last night! Is she a *dish!,*" or words to that effect. You say, "Well, trot her out and let me have a look at her." And he does. Do *you* think she's pretty? The chances are that you don't. Certainly not so pretty as he thinks she is. Oh, yes, she's attractive in a way, but that silly hat! And those too vivid nails! And so on.

Now just see how right the philosopher Irving Berlin was. What is the difference between your friend's girl friend and a new melody? There is none. What to him is a gorgeous tune is to you merely pleasant, or even worse, in many cases. Quite a bit depends on how it is dressed up, orchestrally or vocally. And that is where music arrangers, the Mainbochers and Adrians of music, step in.[2]

---

[1]*Music Publishers Journal,* September–October 1944. Reprinted by permission of The Estate of Robert Russell Bennett.

[2]Mainbocher (Main Rousseau Bocher, 1890–1976) was born in Chicago and acquired a fine background in design, theatre, and music. His Broadway costume designs include those for *One Touch of Venus* (1943), *Call Me Madam* (1950), *Wonderful Town* (1953), and *The Sound of Music* (1959). In the 1940s he also designed uniforms for the Girl Scouts, Red Cross, and the

A melody is like a pretty girl—neither of them is pretty enough to go around unclad. Even those ladies who would deny this should concede at least a few flowers in their hair. And that goes equally for the melodies. Some of them are lovely but they'd better get some "clothes" on before they venture forth.

The fact is that in both cases a lot of very beautiful clothes have been designed to emphasize every good feature of a lot of very dull-looking damsels. The result often justifies the effort, and in music many large, impressive pieces have started as a few bars of nothing much. But, by and large, we musical dressmakers handle a pretty nice class of customers.

"BECOMING" ARRANGEMENTS

The perfect arrangement is the one that manages to be most "becoming" to the melody at all points. Some melodies defy a sensitive treatment in the orchestration. They sound good sung and they go well on the piano, but they drive us to the verge of mayhem as we sit up all night trying to spread them out over a small, or large, band of musicians. That's our problem. We never escape it entirely because there never is a perfect melody. Doubtless if human expression attained perfection a craft such as music arranging would be unnecessary and almost sacrilege.

My idea of the most *effective* (ruling out the word "perfect") arrangement of a piece of music is identical with my idea of the most effective dress, make-up, coiffure, and jewelry of an attractive woman. I don't know one thing about designing a dress for a woman, but I share the average man's appreciation of the finished product. I expect the listeners in a theater or on the radio to know just about the same regarding the "dresses" we put on the tunes and I expect them to like or be bored with them in more or less the same ratio.

When we are given a pretty tune we can't make it any prettier than it is but we can put on it clothes which will call for that "second look." We can give the average man the maximum of pleasure with our scheme of colors, texture, line, etc.,—all of which are musical terms as well as sartorial.

We can also overdress a tune outrageously, and sometimes we have to. The struggle for novelty and uniqueness among bands has a deplorable effect on the poor little melodies. If you ever sit through a evening a few tables away from one of our popular bands, try to name a few of the tunes that they

---

women's branches of the U.S. Navy (the "Waves") and Marines. Gilbert Adrian (1903–1959) designed for Broadway as early as 1921 (Berlin's *Music Box Revue*) but is most renowned for his work in Hollywood, especially at MGM, where many a production was graced with "Gowns by Adrian." Among the stars he outfitted were Greta Garbo, Katharine Hepburn, Joan Crawford, and (future wife) Janet Gaynor.

play, especially when they are broadcasting. If you can name three out of five your ears are keener than mine. I can name only about half the tunes that I hear even though I know all the titles, so elaborately and ambitiously are they orchestrated. It's an arranger's field day, but I imagine that they sometimes wish that they didn't even have to start with a tune. That would leave them freer in their wild flights of imagination.

Most of my own "dressmaking" has been done in theaters and motion-picture studios where the tunes are getting their very first hearing. Here it is important that we dress our "babies" simply and in such a way as to bring out their naked charms, if any. It's no good starting the tunes out covered with a thousand and one adornments unless we know that they won't be listened to in any other form. This would be a great responsibility to take, especially as no one in the theater ever *knows* anything. This is not a "crack"; it is a statement of fact that any great showman will corroborate. Public reaction is harder to handicap than horse racing!

So far as I am concerned, any melody is good as soon as the people have bought enough copies to pay for the printing—and I'm not a publisher. I am, by virtue of my job, sensitive to every nuance of every tune I ever hear, but each in its entirety leaves me cold until John Q. begins to send in his money.

I don't supposed that couturiers have any different experience to report. They must be sensitive to every feature of a woman's appearance—they must be affected by every curve and color—but they are probably all very happy to go home and pet the cat at five or six in the afternoon.

PLEASANT EXPERIENCE

One of our finest arrangers, who works in Hollywood, said to me: "I like to work in pictures because I am never bothered with 'composers.'" I know what he meant, although my own experience with the melodists has been practically one hundred per cent pleasant. There is a strange "meanie-genie" perched on the shoulder of some tune composers, and it keeps whispering into their ears such remarks as "Now be nice to that orchestrator, he can make or break you." or "Leave that big dramatic sequence to him. You've given him the tunes. Let him develop them. That's his job." Or, indeed, "Give the arrangers and copyists all the rehearsal time they need. We certainly can't open the show until they get the music on paper."

Then comes the opening of the show, the worry, and the final triumph with critics and public in New York. Don't look now, but there's that "meanie-genie" again, whispering into the composer's ear, "Listen, don't let them tell you that that orchestrator made your music wonderful! After all, you did practically all his work for him. Where would he be without your melodies?" And so on far into the night.

Mother brings a beautiful baby into the world, nourishes it, brings it up into a radiant, enchanting young girl. But she suffers because she never learned to design her daughter's clothes.

Eight Bars and a Pencil[1]

It might be interesting to collar a member of a theatre audience some time to get him to tell you just how he imagines a particular tune was prepared for his entertainment. If he has a clear idea of the long, and usually painful, hours of struggle with the details of composing, lyricizing, staging, arranging, copying, and rehearsing involved, the number probably didn't entertain him much.

It's a never-ending amusement to me to watch the reaction of a theatre full of people to a gay and frothy little song. After the composer has pounded it out for the lyricist, and the lyricist has jumped for joy and said "colossal," after the two of them have presented it to the producer, and he has called it "the greatest thing ever heard," after the arranger of the chorus parts is told he has done something "absolutely sensational with the number," after the orchestration has been rehearsed and the whole thing branded by all as the dawn of a new theatre, comes Mister Ultimate Consumer.

He starts a half-pleased smile, loses it, starts to pat his foot and gets out of rhythm and finally decides that the tall showgirls' knees would be just as cute as the dancers' if you could see them. Thus the number is a success.

SLEEP COMES SECOND

The first thing you study, to become a famous music arranger, is to do without sleep. Whenever you hear a flute play a pretty "noodle" in an orchestra you can put down a bet the man who wrote it should already have been in bed two hours before he did it. So long and tedious is the work of preparing a full orchestral score that it just never gets done in time for normal bedtime. The last play I orchestrated opened on Christmas night.[2] On

---

[1] *New York Times*, 8 June 1947. Copyright © 1947 by the New York Times Co. Reprinted by permission.

[2] 1946's *In Gay New Orleans* debuted in Boston, but never reached New York.

Dec. 24 I got up, after three and a half hours of sleep, at 6 in the morning and went back to bed at 2 the morning of the twenty-sixth. I was writing, writing, writing—feeding score to the poor, tired copyists.

The question all of my uninitiated friends ask is, "Why not start sooner and have more time?" The answer is the key to the main value of theatre orchestrations. Rehearsals for a musical usually last about four and a half weeks. The first week or ten days is lost time because the directors and cast are not at all set with their business. An effective orchestration must be sensitive to every move on the stage, every trick of the singer and even the timbre of the singer's voice. Until these "colors" and movements are established the arranger can do more harm than good by guessing at what the scene will feel like.

I say this is the main value of orchestration, though I know that the listener is not conscious of what is going on. He must, however, feel better about the whole thing if it fits—and if it all fits, the arranger hasn't been sleeping eight hours a day.

MEALS DON'T MATTER

The second lesson for the famous-to-be arranger is: Learn to do without regular food. When two or three copyists, who have even more notes to get on paper than you (because of certain duplications), are waiting for you to finish a strain, you'll do well to finish it and grab a sandwich when you can. The main consideration is the finishing of a section of the arrangement in the same mood and general color as you began it.

Yes, you can do without sleep if you are a "trouper," and you can do without regular meals, even good air, but what you can not do without is a tune.

The genus Song Writer, variously considered as everything from a significant force to the lowest form of animal life, is the begin-all and end-all of light music. To a serious student of music, his tune may be obvious, unoriginal and banal, but it has something—a very big something. It is that something that makes Wagner more exciting than Mendelssohn, who was a vastly superior musician. No orchestral treatment can do much more for it if it doesn't have that certain thing.

In these days when the music arranger is being "discovered" on the fronts of theatres, on the first page of the program and in the newspapers, there is a great tendency for producers and writers to expect the orchestrator to do miracles and make an uninspired melody sound inspired. They ought to know better.

Some of the best song writers can't write or read a note of music, and almost all of them read badly. That doesn't keep them from having not only a definite style of their own as to melody, but also a most solid instinct for the right harmony to go with their melodies. They are usually easy to work with because their musical thoughts are simple and friendly and require no revolutionary invention as to counterpoint and instrumentation.

In fact, my trade secret is to approach all such music with the least possible embellishment. Let the phrases of the melody and the sense of the words bring their own orchestral color; then do the same thing with the dance routines as worked out by an untiring dance director and an equally untiring rehearsal pianist, and you have a sound job. This will work except when the tunes are not good tunes, and the poor desperate souls look up to you with big eyes and say they know you will make it all sound wonderful.

For a fairly typical history of a number from composition through arrangement, take the case of a song that begins to qualify as an American classic—"Oklahoma!" Richard Rodgers and Oscar Hammerstein 2d worked out the words and music together, part of it words first and part the other way 'round. Rodgers played the melody for Margot Hopkins, rehearsal pianist, who learned it by ear. He then made a pencil copy of his own piano arrangement, which was copied and blue-printed for all departments of the show. Rodgers, Jay Blackton (musical director), and Margot Hopkins all played it for and taught it to the singers who were to sing it. Agnes deMille, with her own rehearsal pianist, Buddy Lewis,[3] worked out the routine (repeats, special rhythms, etc.) and staged pantomime and dances.

LISTEN INWARDLY

I, as arranger, heard the singers sing it to piano accompaniment, helped decide what keys were best for their voices, and then went to another hall where Agnes had her dancers do part of the number for me. I took notes of every movement and listened in my own mind to the complete orchestrated number. I went home and wrote what I had listened to (inwardly) on a score, which was copied into separate parts for the various members of the orchestra.

We opened. The number was entertaining, but seemed too elaborate for the late spot in the show that it occupied. After a few performances we tried having the whole company come downstage and sing it—all on the melody. This had a good feel to it, so Rodgers and Hammerstein had a new idea—a big choral arrangement.

---

[3]Morgan "Buddy" Lewis also wrote songs for producer Nancy Hamilton's series of revues, *One for the Money* (1939), *Two for the Show* (1940), and *Three to Make Ready* (1946). His most enduring creation is *Two for the Show*'s "How High the Moon," which quickly became the virtual "anthem" of bebop jazz.

I wrote out a new vocal score, in harmony, with additions of new vocal vamps and a special ending spelling out the word Oklahoma and took it to the theatre, where I played it through for the whole company, and Jay Blackton taught each one his or her individual part. I had to go back and make a new [orchestral] score to fit this version, have it copied and get it ready for a special rehearsal with company and orchestra. The number went into the show as it is now heard, we all had a big six hours of sleep, and went on to another number.

All I Know about Arranging Music[1]: A Few Notes Not Meant for the Laymen

I. MUSIC IN GENERAL AND STRINGS IN PARTICULAR

My first brush with the job of arranging music for two or more human beings to play came when I was nine years old. My sister, age seven, was practicing a piece in canon form called "The Naughty Pixie Mocking His Mother." I hit on the idea that it would be fun to get my violin and play the Pixie's part while my sister played the other on the piano. It went very well and we both got the giggles over the result. As I could never let well enough alone, I then got into a little difficulty by trying to do the same thing with my new cornet, but after playing two bars in F major I had to play the rest of it in G to make it sound right.

Mother assured me that there was nothing wrong with the cornet; cornets were just made that way. If you played in C they sounded in B flat. All I could say was "Oh."

I am glad to be able to talk about orchestration and orchestras to professionals. It would shock you to know how few otherwise intelligent men and women in the great big world know what the word "orchestration" means. The poor dears, especially the young poor dears, have in but a few years added the word to their vocabulary, and, oh boy! Even to some of the best-known producers and directors of pictures and plays a piece played at M.M. quarter note = 80 is a different orchestration at M.M. = 96.

Knowledge is Not Enough

I am sometimes asked to give lessons in arranging. The answer is simple: "What I actually know about it, I can tell in about twenty minutes,

[1]*International Musician*, February, March, and April 1949. Reprinted with permission of *International Musician, the Official Journal of the American Federation of Musicians*. The subheadings, though almost certainly not Bennett's, have been retained from the original printing.

not even enough for a half-hour lesson. As to the other elements that go into a beautiful arrangement, your guess has every chance to be as good as mine."

So here, in three chapters, is all I know; beginning with what I know about strings:

To write beautifully for strings is a simple task. That is, of course, if you are an arranger. All you have to do is to have played violin, viola, cello and bass since you were a child. (What! No viola da gamba?)

Read Scores—and Listen!

[If there's] Any chance you spent your youth in pool rooms, milking cows, or going to college [then] the thing to playing stringed instruments is to muse over scores, especially the chamber music of the masters, and then to listen—not to phonographs and radios, but to live players.

What the four fingers of the left hand can do on a stringed instrument is either a life study or a simple matter, depending on what you want to get out of life. A violinist friend of mine recommended Dounis's violin exercises[2] to me one time. I bought a copy and started to practice, with the effect on my left hand that following Saturday I muffed a throw from the outfield and let two runs score. To play Dounis's exercises well you ought to have two violins. There isn't room on one for all he makes you do.

But on the subject of what to write for the violin, rather than how to play it, experience shows that the number of tone colors and technical tricks you can get out of fiddlers is relatively small. Strings give beauty and personality—even emotion—but not very much "Wow! What was that?" The string section remains the staff of life for an orchestrator, no matter what garish ear-tickling turns up in the passing parade of tone color, but, like bread, it keeps you reaching for the butter and jam.

Nix on Octaves

A personal note on violins, and indeed all strings: If ever, years after my death, any man discovers a passage written by me in octaves where the fingering is 1–4, 1–4, 1–4, etc., that man is hereby requested to dig me up and kick me. This means that with the first finger on the A string and the little finger on the E the player starts sliding around from octave to octave, as in Wilhelmj's[3] arrangement of Schubert's "Ave Maria." Violinists, who have spent

---

[2]Greek-American violinist Demetrius Constantine Dounis (1886–1954) completed several technical treatises, including *The Absolute Independence of the Fingers* and *Advanced Studies for the Development of the Independence of the Fingers in Violin Playing on a Scientific Basis.*

[3]August Wilhelmj, a protégé of Ferdinand David, also transcribed an air from Bach's *Orchestral Suite* in D Major which has become universally known as the *Air on the G String.*

your lives getting these passages in tune, why are you kidding yourselves? Some time in the dark past a violinist heard a pianist play octaves and decided, by golly, he could do it too! So now violin students sit and hear virtuosi do it and all gasp with admiration, while the sounds are simply unbearable to the sensitive ear. The first finger on the lower string has an entirely different vibrato and a different "timbre" from the fourth finger on the higher string, and the only time it is any good is when it is a little out of tune, to depict savagery or bitter complaint.

Cellists and bassists can do the same damage by bringing the thumb into play, but their literature is much more innocent in this respect. As for violists, what literature there is for the "big second fiddle" is also comparatively free from octaves.

It's Not in the Books

Many treatises exist on the subject of instrumentation. Many of them are sound and sober, and can be a great help to inexperienced arrangers. The large chapters devoted to strings are useful, but there is no way to cover string writing and string playing in a book. The problems are too simple, fundamentally, being problems of "How does it sound?" or "What does it make you think of?"—and you can't write books for the human soul. It can't read. Take for instance the sound of cellos at the top voice of a four-part, or any-part, harmony: What is your impression, with the crying tones leading the quietly sedate harmony-notes of low violins and violas? What is *my* impression? Is it the same as yours or even similar? How will you describe your impression in print?

And again the problems are too extensive, if one is to take up the actual art of playing the instruments. Read your scores, study them, listen outwardly to good players, and, more important, listen inwardly to yourself. Then you'll be a good arranger, and can look for work.

Doubling Strings and Woodwinds

Almost without exception, in the case of small orchestras especially, the strings get the greatest admiration when they are doubled in unison by the "color sections" of the orchestra. Never have so many compliments been flung at the arrangers of theatre music on their writing for strings as when they were also writing for oboes, flutes, horns, etc., to play the same music at the same time. Ironic, isn't it? But it's all a part of the subtler workings of the human ear, I suppose. And it's all a part of the baffling insensitivity of the usual listener, who, if you call his attention to the fact that the woodwind is also playing the same thing, will nearly always say, "Yes, I hear that, but I just *love* strings."

Strings are like show business, and orthodox religions; they keep going out of fashion and then coming back stronger than ever every few years. How low they can sink in popular favor is indicated by the true story many of you have heard of a friend of mine [perhaps Robert A. Simon?] who was looking over some bands for a proposed radio show. One very fine band had about six saxophones, six or seven brass, two pianos, two drummers, etc., etc., and one violin. When he saw the violinist sawing away in the midst of this carnival of riotous sound he asked a little sarcastically, "What is the violin for?" The leader of the group answered, most seriously, "That's in case of a waltz."

II. WOODWINDS

As I sit down to carry this learned treatise into the woodwind family I have before me a fine interview with William Kincaid in the February [1949] *International Musician* by Miss Hope Stoddard. Any reader who doesn't know a lot about who William Kincaid is will kindly put this down at once: Get out the February number and read Miss Stoddard's article.

THE KINCAID MOTIF

Then, as an extra dessert, here is something a little private about this wonderful flutist. A very select handful of his friends make it a point when in Philadelphia to go to a hotel just a few yards from the apartment building where he lives. As soon as the bell-boy shows them into their rooms he usually opens a window. Just hotel routine, but at this point the new guest goes over to the window and, drawing a deep breath, whistles as loudly as possible,[4] and waits. In a minute or two there floats over the breeze the same phrase in the most beautiful flute tones that man has yet achieved, and that is a date for a drink and a lot of laughs.[5]

This has been going on for many years, and as an arranger for Broadway shows I am always glad to open the tryout in Philadelphia, just for those three bars. (The third one isn't shown above).

---

[4]An excerpt—rhythmically simplified by Bennett—from Rimsky-Korsakov's opera *Le Coq d'or* ("The Golden Cockerel").

[5]Bennett met Kincaid shortly after arriving in New York in 1916. The flutist was one of George Barrère's students at the Institute of Musical Art who joined their teacher in premier-

Everything But Wood

Woodwinds are so called because there used to be some wood in them somewhere. Now we have silver woodwinds, brass woodwinds, gold and even platinum woodwinds.[6] We also have plastic woodwinds that you can bounce on the floor, but it isn't recommended; it might make marks on the floor.

Let me begin this lesson on woodwinds by saying that I know nothing about them, but literally! My father was always about to buy me a flute and a piccolo when I was playing in his band in Missouri, but somehow I always ended up with brass or drums outdoors, and strings or piano in the front parlor. Speaking of writing for strings, last month I said you could do it by listening to others play if you can't play yourself. I know that, because you can hardly imagine how bad I can make a clarinet sound, or how mixed up I can get with fingerings. And incidentally, there is a big plot on among beginners' books to keep the fingerings a secret. They usually give you a chart and then offer a substantial prize for anyone who can make it out. So far as I know no one ever won the prize.

In spite of this, one of the few pupils I ever had was on the saxophone. I gave him one lesson, and his name was Sergei Rachmaninov. Yes, *the* Sergei Rachmaninov! He was writing his "Symphonic Dances" and he wanted to write a saxophone solo in the second part of the first movement. He picked me out as the man to show him how to write for the instrument, and I played a mean trick on him. I gave him a fingering chart. But I don't think he ever looked at it. The solo sounded too good.

Woodwind Doubling

If one wanted to pick out the most remarkable development in orchestra music within the past twenty-five years it would be hard to eliminate woodwind playing, woodwind construction, and, above all, woodwind doubling. When you think what this doubling has done for us in the way of color combinations in small bands it gives you something to ponder on. But it has done more. Only the very great artists on flutes, oboes, clarinets and bassoons are able to sing on their instruments (or, to be more pointed, talk on them), but saxophonists for some reason are a race of Bing Crosbys when it comes to wooing the ear with cantabile playing. This seems to go with the job, somehow, and when they begin serious study on their doubles they carry over a

---

ing Bennett's flute quartet, *Rondo Capriccioso.* Kincaid was for many years principal flute for the Philadelphia Orchestra. With his first-chair colleagues, he gave Bennett's woodwind quintet *Toy Symphony* its first performance in 1931.

[6]Edgard Varèse's *Density 21.5* (the title referring to the specific gravity of platinum) was written for Barrère, whose instrument was one of the first crafted of the precious metal.

quality of expression that would have sent Mozart, or even Wagner, into a heaven of ecstasy. In other words, an ordinary sax player is easier to listen to than an ordinary legitimate wind man, unless you and I have very different ears.

Will you pardon me just one moment while I speak to a group of young orchestrators about the ranges of instruments? Thank you. (Young ladies and gentlemen, when you study the ranges of the woodwind choir, please hold the book so that your right thumb covers the three or four highest notes of each scale. Don't move your thumb, and don't peek. And don't tell me Richard Strauss used those notes, or that your brother-in-law can go even higher. These notes are loud, unpleasant, very hard on reeds and lips, and will do you no good. Rather use your pretty little heads to see how exciting you can be with some of the lower tones. They will reward you handsomely.)

I once heard one of our big league music arrangers arguing with a reed section during a rehearsal, and what I overheard him say was, "Albert, you ought to know by now how I treat the clarinet!" I wonder what he meant.

How you "treat" an orchestral instrument depends on many elements. The first thing is the tune. Every new tune presents new problems and new possibilities, and no one ever gets anywhere by trying to apply Orchestration A to Tune B. They may have raved about Orchestration A for Tune A, but the sooner you forget that the better for your success with Tune B.

Each Arranging Problem Is Unique

Then there is the matter of what the playing is to be for—vocal, dance, microphone, silent audience or noisy audience (as in theatre overtures), and many others.

Then again the key of the piece adds its own colors and its own handicaps to your arrangement. And many other little headaches here and there pop up to change your approach to each instrument. Sometimes the instrument won't stand for it. Through no fault of yours or of the music, something has happened to make the whole thing awkward and ineffective for the very instruments that should play it. Such occasions are far from rare, and that is where a lot of the orchestrator's sleep is lost.

And sleep is what the orchestrator loses. In the busy season when I see a man giving up with a big yawn on the street I'm tempted to go up to him and say, "Which show are you arranging?" The question would stand a good chance of getting a serious answer.

Beware That Solo Effect

In general the woodwind choir is a gathering of individuals. They are best understood if we think of each as a soloist who will be good enough to join the big group when he is not busy playing solos. In combining the various members of the section you find them liking or disliking one another just like a lot of backyard neighbors. If they all play at once the oboes seem to take charge, just as the trumpets do in a full band or orchestra. This is strange, because they are not the loudest by any means. They simply reach for you. Putting them on middle harmony notes is inviting trouble.

The work-horse is the clarinet. When you carry a set of parts to a rehearsal you wish you had left out the clarinets, because their part weighs so much. The flute and the bassoon are in love with each other. That's one of the scandals of the trade—why should this great oaf with double reeds forsake his kinswoman, the oboe, and whisper sweet nothings to a very responsive young lady with no reeds at all? But there it is; they're just that way, and personally, I'm glad, no matter how the clarinets may chuckle and smack their single reeds.

Saxophone Rivals the Brass

It's always hard for me to consider saxophones as woodwinds. In the first place, sax players, as mentioned above, double on everything from the sackbut to the Burmese harp and bi-va, and in the second place they are so powerful that they can square off with the brass and come out none the worse for it. When they are good they are very good—and you know the rest.

Even the best have a vibrato like the roller-coaster at Luna Park, and when they get into a symphony orchestra the "long-haired" conductors are inclined to have dizzy spells. Nevertheless, the saxes have put many an arranger's child through college during the last forty years. Nothing takes their place in a small band when you want a real middle for your chords.

I'm sorry I don't really know the woodwind section better from the players' standpoint, but I'm doing something about it. I bought one of Eddie Powell's[7] Chromettes, and next time I go to Philadelphia I'm going to surprise Billy Kincaid by going to the open window and playing:

[7]The reference remains obscure. Bennett's "Eddie Powell" is either a) the New York symphonic and free-lance flutist, earlier a member of Bennett's superb *Stars of the Future* radio orchestra; or 2) the Hollywood orchestrator who had, as a fellow Harms/Chappell arranger, worked alongside Bennett on several early-30s musicals.

Note: I have been often been asked to recommend a text-book on instrumentation. For an excellent guide to the various instruments, without examples from any scores, I like *The Orchestrator's Handbook* by Maurice Gardner very much. For popular music, especially dance, Glenn Miller's book [*Glenn Miller's Method for Orchestral Arranging*, 1943] is the work of a real professional. As a general authority on the larger phases of the art of orchestration, I believe Cecil Forsythe [*Orchestration*] has never been surpassed, but, as you may guess from these articles, I think you can learn more from the scores of Wagner or Debussy. Or Beethoven or Prokofiev.

III. NOTES ON BRASS AND PERCUSSION

My career as a percussion player has been confined to one afternoon when I played bass drum for a Labor Day parade in the rain. The strap over my shoulder kept coming loose, and the two snare drummers were trying to be helpful. They were playing afterbeats with one hand and with the other helping me locate the big drum in time for the down beats. About the middle of the trio we looked up and saw the rest of the band a block ahead turning a corner.

These notes on music arranging have often said, directly or indirectly, that the best way to make good arrangements is best found through experience. The experience above is among the most valuable of my career. What did I learn? I learned that the one most important instrument in the whole band or orchestra is the bass drum. There may be instruments that can be learned and played well without much natural gift for music in the performer, but such an instrument is not the bass drum.

Percussion Men Set the Rhythms

The great percussion players are always real musicians. Most of them play the piano or other instruments, and all of them have that fantastic set of vibration frequencies (I'm sure you know what I mean even if science has a better name for it) that enables them to feel every rhythm and counter-rhythm down to the tiniest impulse. The drums keep music going forward. They yield their powerful influence over the entire sound even when they are silent and waiting to roll a backward rhythm into line. They are the "contact men" with the public ear, and they can make or break an orchestration.

Fusion Creates New Choirs

In dividing an orchestra into three large sections as I am discussing it, I am really not being fair to such readers as might take the serious notes seriously. Firstly there is a new alignment in dance bands—brass, sax, and rhythm; secondly, I leave out of account a most important group, the military or concert band; and, thirdly, the finest arrangements always mix the tone colors up until no one stays identified with his own section for long at a time. Examples are found in every properly written orchestra piece, but for now look at the "Prelude" to *Parsifal* by one of the two great Wagners—Richard. (The other is Hans of the Pittsburgh Pirates.) When the trumpet soars out in unison with the violins on the main motif you realize that the trumpet is no longer brass and the violins are no longer strings, but a new instrument is singing to you. This destroys the idea of "sections" completely, and you have as many choirs as our inventive inner ears have been able to create up to this point.

The Brasses Are Versatile

The beauty of brasses is their great range of dynamic power. Nothing in band or orchestra can play any softer than trumpets and trombones, and certainly nothing can be any louder. The brass choir can be majestic, cruel, religious, mocking, sentimental, mysterious, triumphant—almost anything. Nothing can make for more tender beauty that a sweet trombone tone with strings and clarinets around it, nor can any sound be tougher and rougher than this same trombone when occasion demands. The long line of mutes that can be strung out in front of a brass player is a subject for some study, and multiplies the colors of the section many times. Many of them belong only to dance music. In the theatres we use mostly straight mutes or cups, but every so often a number calls for Harmon, plunger, "stuffy," or indeed one or two that I can't even name. One color that was always ear-catching to me is the color of derby hats over the bells of trumpets and trombones. This is particularly exciting when the playing is loud without being too much of a climax. Don't try to get the effect unless you are prepared to buy the hats; for some reason the boys never have them, and unless they *all* do the effect is no good.[8]

Hazards of the Horn

The aristocrats of the brasses are the horns, not because they are never identified with small bands, but because their depth and their power let you know at once they are not kidding. They are treacherous fellows if their players happen to have a dry lip or any other discomfort in playing them. They

---

[8]A quarter-century later, in *Instrumentally Speaking*, Bennett again observed (43) that brass players "are not fond of carrying these as standard equipment," noting that "music directors and arrangers have been known to bring them and present them to the brass sections at the first rehearsal."

crack, snort, spit like a cat, or otherwise befoul the air waves at the slightest provocation. Likewise they, almost above any other member of the orchestra, have it in them to bring the listener to bring to his knees before his God, so noble and inspiring is their sound. I'm sure that Gabriel's trumpet is really a French horn.

We profane them often by using them on after-beats, but even then they bring a touch of distinction with them. In bands, the euphonium (B-flat baritone) has almost as much nobility as the horn. It is a thing of beauty in the hands of a real artist, not as versatile as the horn, but also not as temperamental. It (taking the place in bands that the cellos take in orchestras) is one of the reasons why I have a fondness for bands. I played one for an entire division to pass in review one afternoon. The other euphonium player had fallen ill on the march, and as we stood in front of the general's stand I had to play one march eighteen times through without taking the mouthpiece away from my lips. After about the third repeat I got used to it, but it was quite a chore. I still like the euphonium.

I also like the tubas, but there is very little I can say about them that you don't know. Maybe you didn't know that the double C tuba, the one used in most orchestras, is the only brass instrument that actually is fingered in the key it sounds.[9] In spite of how they may read, trombones are all in B-flat (or D for the bottom of the bass trombone), horns are in E-flat and F, trumpets in B-flat and A. (There is a C trumpet used on the European continent, but I wouldn't give it house room.[10]) Properly written, a band tuba part should be written in octaves, so that the E-flat tuba reads the lower note, the actual sound, and plays it in treble clef with three less flats; the BB-flat reads the upper octave like a string bass, sounding an octave lower, while the CC reads the lower part as he does in orchestra music.[11]

But even John Philip Sousa, the greatest band writer, often ignored this rule. Tuba players therefore mostly pick their own register and the writer is not always sure just which octave he will hear.

---

[9]I.e., an instrument whose "open" harmonic series has C as its fundamental.

[10]As this article was being written, the Boston Symphony's Roger Voisin and Marcel Lafosse were pioneering the C trumpet's use in U.S. orchestras. The B-flat instrument remains ubiquitous in American concert bands, pit orchestras, and jazz ensembles.

[11]Use of the E-flat tuba has declined in the U.S., and present practice is to write only the sounds desired. The tuba parts ("Basses") for some of Bennett's earlier band works—*Suite of Old American Dances*, particularly—must be scrutinized for octaves where the upper note is clearly intended not to be played, especially when it would interfere with the tenor-register harmonies. Orchestral tuba writing, by contrast, has never had such "which octave?" ambiguities.

DRUMMERS ROLL THEIR OWN

Going back to percussion, I should never tell a pupil what to write for drums because in popular music they never play what you write anyway. In symphonic writing you can have any effect you want, and there are always men to get it for you. In popular music the art of drumming has undergone years of development, and no charts have been designed that even resemble what a good hot man will do. Look over a printed arrangement of Jack Mason for a good simple way to guide the drummer to his fantastic doings.

MASTER CHART FOR SONORITY

As a conclusion to these informal observations I would like to describe a *forte* chord in the full orchestra. The chart also applies to whole passages as well as one chord. If you listen to one big down beat for full symphony orchestra wherein all players are playing "out full" without advice from the conductor's left hand, these are the sounds that strike your ear, in the order of their effect on you:

1. Cymbals (piatti)
2. Tympani and bass drum
3. Snare Drum
4. Horns (with bells up)
5. Trumpets
6. Bells and xylophone
7. Trombones
8. Piccolo (not the low octave)
9. Tuba
10. Horns (normal)
11. Saxophones
12. Harp and piano
13. Violins
14. Oboes
15. Clarinets
16. Flutes
17. Basses
18. Cellos
19. Bassoons
20. Violas

This order can be upset by many devices: putting certain instruments high, and others low; bringing the whole chord to a *mezzo-forte*; making strings *pizzicato*; muting brass, etc., etc. However, the study of any combination within this ensemble will reveal all I can tell a pupil about orchestration. The rest is up to him and the source of his inspiration.

On Writing Harp Music[1]

Probably the majority of those who pause to read these lines will be well-schooled harpists who can call my shots before I make them. They will be inclined to say, "Who doesn't know that already?" However, they may agree with me that there are a good many writers of music who either do not know or do not care what the boundaries of good expression on the harp are, and who might possibly be exposed with benefit to some of the problems touched on here.

Every arranger of orchestra music probably has a certain section of the orchestra whose technics and effects he has had to take from a treatise on the art of orchestration, or from driving his instrumentalist friends crazy with childish questions on the play and sound of many, many passages. It is hardly possible for an arranger to play enough different instruments to have the "feel" of all of them. Even if, as has happened, his childhood was spent in a music store and at band rehearsals where he developed into a sort of utility man who could fill in on almost any missing instrument, he still misses that final attachment to each one that can only come with years of study and experience.

An instrument as complicated and difficult as the harp takes such long application and deep affection that it is to be wondered whether a poor fellow could have time even to become an arranger at all, were he a true authority on the harp. What I know and, more important, what I feel about this fantastic instrument was nurtured mostly by the second method quoted above, namely by boring my harp-playing friends with questions and requests for lessons for which I never paid. I never cease to marvel at the things fine harpists can do on the harp, although it is my privilege to have as friends a real Who's Who of the great instrument.[2]

---

[1]*Harp News* 1, no. 10 (Fall 1954). Reprinted by permission of the American Harp Society.

[2]Including Carlos Salzedo, Laura Newell, and Assunta Dell'Aquila. Newell, the longtime NBC Symphony harpist, also played in the *Russell Bennett's Notebook* radio orchestra, where she and Milton Katims premiered his Concerto for Viola, Harp, and Orchestra. She also shared

The first point in the job of writing is the usual one of love. How much do you love the harp? Does it "send" you by the very nature of its tone? Or is the middle of the harp exciting and the upper tones unpleasant to you? Do the deep bass notes hold you up and carry you, or do you feel like you might fall through them into darkness? Personally I feel only happiness through all of its register, and even lean on it for dynamic support in some of the most unexpected places. If you love it, it will respond to you according to the respect you have for it. If you love it it will be impossible for you to prostitute it with dominant seventh and tonic sixth "oceans" every time the orchestra comes to a pause. Glissandi are effective if no one dreamed that they were coming, but when the average listener can spot them on the way, they amount to plain vulgarity, and that is not the way to treat a dear friend. Unhappily, this rule is much abused by many who should be ashamed of themselves thereby.[3] The moguls of popular music have come to miss the voluptuous sound when they do not hear it, but that fact cannot change the rule.

As to the technique of harp-writing (and here is where the harpists may make a cut in their reading), the main point, with some footnotes, is that all chords, arpeggi, and scales are based on a hand of four fingers and not five. The first footnote, and it should be read and memorized by all writers, is that the two hands are exactly the same as to the balance of a chord. That is to say, the thumb is the top of the chord in the right hand as well as the left, and not the opposite as it is on the piano. So, when a *bisbigliando* is played the chord is traded from hand to hand with the very same fingers all the way down. When a melody is played at the tops of the chords in the right hand the strongest fingers are assigned to the tune. What a lot of piano-playing song writers would give if that could also be so on the piano.

The second footnote is that an arpeggio on a triad may be played three by three, with the hands trading the same chord, or it may be traded four by four if that lands one on a better finger at the end. Good harpists do not seem to care much which hand finishes the arpeggio at the top, although neatness seems to call for the right when possible. The speed with which they can play arpeggi and many ostinato figures never loses its fascination for me.

Another point to keep in mind is that once the C-flat pedal is down it changes every C on the harp to C natural. An obvious point? Try a modern flight of chromatic imagination on an organ-point and see how the chords begin to thin out just when the dramatic calls for them to be rich. It does not

---

the first performance of his *Sonatine pour Sopran et Harpe* at Town Hall in 1947 with Australian singer Jean Love.

[3]Bennett's orchestrations for both Hollywood and Broadway—as well as his concert works—are distinguished by his sparing use of harp glissandi.

have to be so, but in certain keys it is. This thought also gets a footnote that a tone cannot be held beyond a change of its pedal. A pretty trick is to strike a low octave and then move it around chromatically with the pedal—a pretty trick, but one that makes me feel a little apologetic to my friends, like those big glissandi.

More points could come showering us from all sides as we warm up to the subject, but I can already see some of my audience beginning to leave, so only one more mechanical point will be mentioned. It has to do with harmonics. The sound of harmonics is quite striking, and there seems to be small difference in quality between the two hands, even though they are very differently played. Theoretically the effect should be good up to the top of the register but actually it loses out somewhere toward the top of the middle. No tone can be set as a limit upward since harps and harpists vary a little, but see your local harpist for a general idea.

Now for some of the joys of harp writing in chamber music and orchestra. In waltzes and oom-pah music the entire rhythm of the after-beats can be left to the harp no matter how rich the sound of the rest of the ensemble may be. It is equally fine doubling the after-beats of horns or strings if you like that better as sonority. It is majestic as a punctuation of octaves or chords in the brass, especially *mezzo-forte*. It puts lovely vitality in wood and divisi string passages when allowed to wander around through the harmonies with a little movement. Astonishingly it adds a lot of lift to a marching strain, especially in six-eight time, when you send it through the upper harmony with short four and five-note arpeggi. Nothing is more gripping than a few discreet tones *sulla tuvola* during a low string tremolo *sul ponticello* or muted. And of course, our old ghost friend, the *bisbigliando*, or murmur, has many charming uses.[4]

Most modern composers show a lot of respect for the harp, and it is not rare at all to see intelligent pedal graphs throughout their scores. Their fondness for the instrument is probably no greater than that of the two Richards, but their love is certainly much more disciplined and understanding. On second thought Wagner and Strauss did not confine their technical impossibilities[5] to the harp. They—and who is big enough to chide them for immodesty—merely assumed that instrument makers and instrumentalists would simply have to get together and make their dreams come true.

---

[4]All of these devices can be seen (and heard) in his scoring for *Victory at Sea*, completed shortly before this article was written.

[5]Their most common error being the writing of a five-finger chord or arpeggio for one hand, forgetting that harpists don't use their "little" finger.

Fools Give You Reasons[1]

That endearing character, Oscar Hammerstein, wrote in a very popular song, "Fools give you reasons, wise men never try." The random thoughts that follow here may probably strike the reader as a study in name-dropping. Cornelia Otis Skinner (to drop the first one) referred the other day to "the dull, sickening thud of a dropped name." It can't be helped, and all apologies to her, in advance.

Pembroke Davenport, who conducted the original production of a new, affectionately remembered theatre success called *Kiss Me, Kate*, was once sitting beside me at the run-through of another good show called *Bells Are Ringing*. As they came to a particularly pretty melodic phrase on the stage he whispered in my ear, "There's no substitute for talent." This is one of those little remarks that stay big in one's thoughts and I might have trouble forgetting it even if I wanted to.

I sat with two great men one afternoon, talking (and listening) about music. Fritz Kreisler was his usual radiant self and spent a lot of time at the piano, which he played brilliantly. Well toward the end of the visit Sergei Rachmaninov was making a point that took him to the piano. Speaking and walking slowly he sat down and started to play the scherzo from Beethoven's Fifth Symphony. As the fifth finger of his right hand struck the four Gs of the horn melody something came out of that small piano that had not been heard before. One note filled the whole room and, seemingly, the whole universe.

When Rachmaninov came into this world he brought that sound with him, and of course Kreisler would have done the same thing to us with a violin in his hand. Forgetting that here were two musician-composers who may well have achieved immortality as creators, the mere sound of one tone on their

---

[1]*Music Journal* 25, no. 5 (May 1967). Reprinted by permission of The Estate of Robert Russell Bennett.

instruments is enough to prove their claim. Education can tell us how to get the greatest good from what we bring to the scene, but Sergei Rachmaninov's G came from no music school.

You wake up in the morning and say to the looking glass, "Do I have Talent?" or you say, "Do I have Personality?" The voice of Truth, if Truth cares to reveal itself, probably says, "Poor baby! You'll never know for sure about either. You can look at all the evidence and try to guess its meaning, but you'll have to take your talent on faith and work your head off to give it every possible chance."

Farther than that, a great number of your contemporaries are as much in the dark about your talents as you are. Some of the best reading I can think of is to be found at the beginning of the (King James) Bible. After a formal and dutiful note to His majesty the translators wrote an introduction "to the reader." It is recommended reading, perhaps not all of it, but at least the first page or two. They begin with a beautifully worded essay on criticism, some time before the famous one of Alexander Pope. It tries to show you what you are up against if you bring anything new into the world. "Zeal," they say, "to promote the common good, whether it be by devising anything ourselves, or revising that which hath been labored by others, deserveth certainly much respect and esteem, but yet findeth but cold entertainment in the world. It is welcomed with suspicion instead of love, and with emulation instead of thanks; and if there be any hole left for cavil to enter, (and cavil, if it does not find a hole, will make one) it is sure to be misconstrued, and in danger to be condemned." And this in the year 1611!

I pursue these thoughts as I wonder at the mystery of one of the world's most elusive talents, the talent for melody—one-fingered, small-range, popular melody. I pursue the subject, speaking as a musician to musicians, because it seems to indicate that a lot of the frantic search for new sounds among our serious composers, the big hunt for a new musical language, has a sobering example in what communication the tune writers can achieve without one new word in their vocabulary. In the course of a music arranger's day he is given over and over again phrases to set that seem so obvious and over-worked that he can't imagine writing them and calling them "my music," but he is often deceived. What is it in a millionaire composer's tune that makes it step out and corner the market? Certainly thousands of others try most eagerly to compete with him but he makes it and the others don't. Why? It isn't hard to write, sometimes even being improvised on a piano in exactly the time it takes to play it. Even a lead-sheet (melody and maybe chord symbols) only requires ten to twenty minutes to write. "Fools give you reasons, wise men never try."

Now for another highly droppable name: Sigmund Spaeth and I were mostly on two different sides of the fence in this. On my side, a few lively tears had been shed over the fact that such gifts as those of Kern, Gershwin, Youmans and the others should be confined to words-and-music messages to tired businessmen, café society expense-account visitors and such. Great composers have always found things to save out of the gist of pop music, and perhaps none of it is in vain: gypsy ragtime, country fiddlin', blues, rock 'n' roll, the more the merrier. Chopin, Grieg, Bartok, and, yea verily, Bach, Mozart and Beethoven, found sublime utterance in profanity used at just the right time. But does a talent like Cole Porter's have to settle for that as a fulfillment of its destiny?

Sigmund Spaeth, on the other hand, gave each of these men the full title of Genius, and was content with each as a branch of the art. This was especially interesting because his beautiful wife once told me that when she first met Sigmund he scolded her for loving Tchaikovsky and Puccini, as they were not quite worthy to sit in the high places. You gather as you read that Sigmund and I eventually came much closer in point of view, and that the adjustment was mostly mine.

Wherever the real values lie in this, it all comes back to what can't be taught or imitated: Talent, that miserable word that accounts for tears, laughter, and monuments. [Bennett tells the story of Kern's creation of "Why Do I Love You?" for *Show Boat*, with Hammerstein sending his comic "cupid rules the day. . ." lyric to Kern, followed by the "real" words; see Chapter Five.] I think it must have been a good song. I couldn't tell at the time.

Afterword
A Tribute by Robert Shaw

Among those who know him and have worked with him in the theatre, recordings, motion pictures, or radio and television, it is not easy to be "objective" about Robert Russell Bennett—and there are decades of reasons for a just accounting to this remarkable musician.

The trouble comes from the fact that "Robert Russell" is so exceptional a human being—wears so comfortably those attributes of kindness, honesty, humor, and wisdom in a time when these are suspect as a press agent's "image"—that it takes an inverted sort of hindsight to see that perhaps once a generation nice guys finish first.

Someone else will have to document Bennett's "commercial credits." That would take columns. But let me list here three things which from a musician's point of view are his in unique degree and combination.

First—his unrivaled knowledge of the orchestra. Because of his vast experience and know-how, everything sounds: it balances, it blends, or it isolates; it does what it's supposed to do; it needs no doctoring. And because of his great imagination—everything sounds *fresh*: (Want to recall a New York organ-grinder? "Russell Bennett" can do it with a few solo winds playing a precise prescription of right and wrong notes.)

Second—his gift for the development of subsidiary and—until he touches them—hidden musical elements: the just-right accompaniment figure, the second chorus with an accumulative device that makes the song and the show a "hit," overtures or "symphonic syntheses" out of a fistful of disparate tunes, hours upon hours upon hours of distinguished motion picture scoring from a moment or two of "original" themes.

Third, and rarest of all—his great good taste: he matches manner to the material, style to content. Like charity, his music "vaunteth not itself, is not puffed up." Patriotism is not allowed to become pompous. Musical comedy is not confused or compounded with Schubert or Mozart, nor operetta with Verdi. No great classical composer has been plagiarized, caricatured, or demeaned by Bennett's expertise, though few speak the language so well. Music for fun is to be taken seriously and precisely as music for fun.

Of course, it is exactly because he knows the vast classical symphonic, operatic, and chamber music literatures so intimately and so lovingly that this taste and invention remain unique in their entertainment roles.

And it is just as certainly because of his kindness, honesty, humor, and wisdom that our hearts are warmed to see Robert Russell Bennett without peer in his field.[1]

[The esteemed career of conductor Robert Shaw (1916–1999) spanned six decades of leadership in his field. Shaw founded the Collegiate Chorale in 1941, directed choral departments at Juilliard and Tanglewood, and for many years led the internationally recognized Robert Shaw Chorale. His directorship of the San Diego Symphony preceded a position as asssociate conductor of the Cleveland Orchestra under George Szell. Shaw became the Atlanta Symphony's Music Director in 1967, which organization he served, later as Music Director Emeritus, until his passing on 25 January 1999.]

[1]This tribute, slightly revised by Robert Shaw for inclusion in this volume, is taken from the program for the Army Band concert, 10 November 1981, "A Salute to America's Veterans" (an all-Robert Russell Bennett concert), at the D.A.R. Constitution Hall. First half: Col. Eugene W. Allen conducting the Army Band; second half: The United States Army Band and Chorus (with soloists) performing Bennett's arrangements of music by Rodgers and Kern.

Appendix A: Selected Compositions

Works within each genre are listed chronologically. A complete list, along with details of publication, instrumentation, duration, etc., may be found in the editor's *Robert Russell Bennett: A Bio-Bibliography*.

Orchestra

Symphony [#1] (1926)
Charleston Rhapsody (1926)
Endimion (1927)
Paysage ("Landscape") (1928)
Sights and Sounds (1929)
Abraham Lincoln: A Likeness in Symphony Form (1929)
March for Two Pianos and Orchestra (1930)
Adagio Eroico (c. 1932)
Concerto Grosso for Dance Band and Orchestra (1932)
An Early American Ballade on Melodies of Stephen Foster (1932)
Six Variations in Fox-Trot Time on a Theme by Jerome Kern (1933)
Orchestral Fragments from "Maria Malibran" (1934)
Hollywood (1936)
Eight Etudes for Symphony Orchestra (1938)
Antique Suite for Clarinet and Orchestra (1941)
Classic Serenade for Strings (1941)
Concerto for Violin in A Major ("In the popular style") (1941)
Symphony in D for the Dodgers [#3] (1941)
Concerto for Viola, Harp, and Orchestra (1940 or 1941; revised as Concerto for Harp, Cello, and Orchestra, 1959 or 1960)
March for America (1942)
"The Four Freedoms": A Symphony after Four Paintings by Norman Rockwell (1943)

Symphony [#6] (1946)
A Dry Weather Legend (flute and orchestra, 1946)
Overture to an Imaginary Drama (1946)
Piano Concerto in B minor (1947)
Concert Variations on a Crooner's Theme (violin and orchestra, 1949)
Kansas City Album (1950)
Overture to the Mississippi (1950)
Suite of Old American Dances (originally for band, 1950)
A Commemoration Symphony (with chorus, 1959)
Concerto for Violin, Piano and Orchestra (1959)
Symphony [#7] (1962)
Concerto for Harmonica and Orchestra (1971 or 1972)
The Fun and Faith of William Billings, American (with chorus, 1975)

Concert Band or Wind Orchestra

Tone Poems for Band (1939)
Fountain Lake Fanfare (March) (1939)
A TNT Cocktail (1939)
Suite of Old American Dances (1949)
Mademoiselle (1952)
Rose Variations (trumpet and band, 1955)
Symphonic Songs for Band (1957)
Concerto Grosso for Woodwind Quintet and Wind Orchestra (1958)
Ohio River Suite (1959)
Overture to Ty, Tris, and Willie (1960)
West Virginia Epic (1960)
Track Meet (1960 or 1961)
Kentucky (c. 1961)
Three Humoresques (1961)
Down to the Sea in Ships (1968)
Twain and the River (1968)
Jazz? (1969)
Four Preludes for Band (1974)
Zimmer's American Greeting (1974)
Autobiography for Band (1977)
Christmas Overture (1980)
Fanfare (1981)

Stage Works

An Hour of Delusion (one-act opera, 1928)
Hold Your Horses (musical comedy, 1933)

Maria Malibran (opera, 1934)
The Enchanted Kiss (opera, 1944 or 1945)
Crystal (opera, 1972)

Incidental Music

Macbeth (1921)
Hamlet (1922)
Romeo and Juliet (1922)
The Firebrand (1924)
Happy Birthday (1946)

Chamber Music

Sonata (violin and piano, 1927)
Toy Symphony (wind quintet, 1928)
Dance (flute and piano, 1928)
Nocturne (flute and piano, 1928)
Water Music (string quartet, 1937)
Dance Scherzo (wind quintet, 1937)
Hexapoda (violin and piano, 1940)
Clarinet Quartet (1941)
Suite (violin and piano, 1945)
A Song Sonata (violin and piano, 1947)
Five Improvisations on Exotic Scales (flute, cello, and piano, 1947)
Sonatine pour Sopran et Harpe (1947)
Allemande (violin and piano, 1948)
Six Souvenirs (2 flutes and piano, 1948)
Five Tune Cartoons (violin and piano, 1949)
Trio (flute, cello, and piano, 1950 or 1951)
A Flute at Dusk (solo flute, 1952)
Four Dances for Piano Trio (1953 or 1954)
String Quartet (1956)
Four Nocturnes (accordion, 1959)
Trio for Harp, Cello, and Flute (c. 1960)
Quintette (string quartet and accordion, 1962)
Rhythm Serenade (solo percussion, 1968)
Suite for Flute and B-flat Clarinet (1973)
Arabesque (2 trumpets, horn, trombone, and bass trombone, 1978)

Keyboard Works

Seven Fox-Trots in Concert Form (piano, 1928)
Sonata in G for Organ (1929)
Second Sonatina (piano, 1944)

Tema Sporca con Variazoni (2 pianos, 1946)
Sonata ("Ragtime") (piano, c. 1970)

Vocal Works

Three Chaucer Poems (woman's voice or voices with piano or string quartet, 1926)
Four Songs (Teasdale) (voice and piano, 1928)
Aux Quatre Coins (four voices, SSAA, 1929)
Nietzsche Variations (women's chorus and piano, 1929)
Theme and Variations in the Form of a Ballade about a Lorelei (women's chorus, soloists, and piano, 1929)
Sonatine pour Sopran et Harpe (1947)
United Nations All Faith Prayer for Peace (SATB chorus, solo voice, and piano or orchestra, 1950)
Carol Cantatas I–II–III–IV (SATB chorus, solo voice, and piano or orchestra, 1977)
The Easter Story (SATB chorus and piano or orchestra, 1978)

Appendix B: Selected Concert Arrangements

It might be supposed that these medleys, scored without the limitations imposed by a minimum pit orchestra, would represent to their arranger a luxurious kind of freedom. In reality these assignments involved trading off an important set of Broadway certainties (a specific, if modest, complement—including woodwind doublers—staffed by New York's highest-caliber instrumentalists) for some crucial "unknowns": the often incomplete or imbalanced instrumentation of amateur and semi-professional groups, and the varying technical abilities of their members.[1]

Some of the Broadway medleys were specifically conceived for a symphonic, fully professional instrumentation (especially the 1968 *Sound of Music* and *My Fair Lady* for William Steinberg); for others, segments of the original production's overture, entr'acte, or exit music are used with only slight changes in instrumentation.

One "secret" of Bennett's success with his "selections" and "symphonic pictures" was an ability to forecast the vagaries of performance to which his arrangements would be subjected. As he advised prospective commercial orchestrators:

> Hovering around your career as an arranger for big [concert] bands and orchestra, particularly when you are writing for publication, is the fact that they will not always be big. When you go to a ball game or the horse races and hear a band of twenty playing a piece you have written for bands of up to a hundred, you are entitled to a little self-satisfaction if nothing essential is entirely missing. This is not an ultimate goal for you as a dedicated mu-

---

[1]This is paralleled in the dichotomy of Bennett's works for wind and percussion—the concert band pieces (most of them published by Chappell) for America's high-school and college groups vs. the American Wind Symphony scores (written for a "known," unique ensemble of first-rate players).

> sician, as you will agree, and yet careful attention to the details of who plays what will bring you many tiny rewards of this kind. The music they would play at a ball game is not very profound, but the sound structure of your arrangement is put to a pretty good test.[2]

Yet Bennett's show "selections" seem, to the listener, so effortless and inevitable that one is unaware of their arranger's constraints. Jonathan Tunick, a veteran of theater and film work who is best known for his many collaborations with Stephen Sondheim, wrote:

> In selecting overtures and entr'actes for concert performance—one should seek out not only the best-loved music, but also the most distinguished orchestrators—Robert Russell Bennett, Don Walker, Hershy Kay, Robert Hinzler [Ginzler], Sid Ramin, and Ralph Burns are just a few. I am especially partial to the arrangements of Robert Russell Bennett, the late dean of Broadway orchestrators, who arranged some of the best-known works of Kern, Gershwin, Porter, Rodgers, and Berlin. He adapted their music magnificently for orchestra, employing delightfully clever and original transitional material and developmental devices.
>
> Bennett eschewed the futile attempt to make the symphony orchestra "swing" by having a sit-down drummer try to "drive" it the way he would a jazz band. The "time" or rhythmic continuo played in a dance or show band by the rhythm section of piano, guitar, drums and pizzicato bass (only one, please) must, in the symphony orchestra, be scored for sections of the orchestra itself—the horns, violins, violas and harp must be used to "comp" the orchestra. Because he was aware of this, Bennett's arrangements "swing" more than those written by bona fide jazz arrangers who write for the symphony orchestra as though it were merely an enormous studio band. His symphonic arrangements of *Porgy and Bess, Show Boat*, and other musicals prove him to be the all-time master of this form.[3]

Nearly all of the orchestrations listed below were completed under contract to Chappell; most of the unpublished ones are on deposit at the Library of Congress. Though some are presently out of print, Bennett's show medleys sold very well and are held in the performing libraries of many secondary school, college/university, and professional ensembles. Many of the orchestra scores are also available from Luck's Music Library and similar rental firms. The Rodgers & Hammerstein Concert Library contains more than 200 of

---

[2]*Instrumentally Speaking*, 137.

[3]Jonathan Tunick, "Broadway in the Concert Hall: By Special Arrangement Only," *Symphony* (Feb.–Mar. 1987): 6.

Bennett's musical theater arrangements for orchestra, including some Porter, Kern, and Berlin in addition to the Rodgers & Hart-or-Hammerstein items. Most of these rental materials are accompaniments for vocal soloists or chorus—individual songs as well as several "concert package" medleys. The Rodgers & Hammerstein Concert Library also has many of the "symphonic pictures" and original Broadway overtures as well as some *Victory at Sea* music.[4]

ORCHESTRA

A Symphonic Picture of "Porgy and Bess" (1943)
Oklahoma! ("Selections," c. 1944)
Around the World in 80 Days (Three songs from the Porter show, 1946)
Show Boat ("Symphonic Selections," 1946)
A Symphonic Story of Jerome Kern ("Ten Highlights of Jerome Kern Melodies Down the Years from 1915 to 1940," 1946)
Gershwin in Hollywood (c. 1946)
Carousel ("Symphonic Picture," 1947)
Allegro ("Selections," 1947)
Finian's Rainbow ("Symphonic Picture" 1947)
Brigadoon ("Symphonic Picture," 1948)
Irving Berlin's "White Christmas" (1948)
Lady in the Dark ("A Symphonic Nocturne," 1949)
Kiss Me, Kate ("Selections," 1949)
South Pacific ("Symphonic Scenario," 1949)
Symphonic Memories of "Roberta" (1949)
The King and I ("Symphonic Picture," 1951)
My Fair Lady ("Selections," 1957)
Gigi ("Selections," 1958)
Flower Drum Song ("Selections," 1958)
The Sound of Music ("Symphonic Picture," 1960)
Camelot ("Concert Medley," 1961)
On a Clear Day You Can See Forever (1965)
Funny Girl ("Selections," c. 1968)
Symphonic Picture of "The Sound of Music" (1968)
Symphonic Picture of "My Fair Lady" (1968)

CONCERT BAND

Porgy and Bess ("Selections," 1942)
Cole Porter Songs ("Selections," 1946)
Irving Berlin's "White Christmas" (1948)

---

[4]Rodgers & Hammerstein Concert Library, 328 W. 28th Street, New York, N.Y. 10019; their catalog may be perused online at <www.rnh.com>.

Carousel Waltzes (c. 1949)
The King and I ("Selections," 1951)
Me and Juliet ("Selections," 1953)
Victory at Sea ("Symphonic Scenario," 1953)
Silk Stockings ("Selections," 1955)
My Fair Lady ("Selections," c. 1957)
Gigi ("Selections," 1958)
The Sound of Music ("Selections," c. 1960)
H.M.S. Pinafore (Arthur Sullivan) ("Selections," 1961)
Do I Hear a Waltz? (c. 1965)
Funny Girl ("Selections,"1968)
Gershwin: A Medley (SATB chorus and band, 1972)
Picasso Suite (Michel Legrand) (1973)
Cole Porter: A Medley for Concert Band (1973)
Noel Coward: A Medley for Concert Band (1974)

Appendix C: Selected Stage and Film Credits

Bennett did some or all of the orchestrations for each of the following productions, listed chronologically by composer. Additional details, including names of the collaborating orchestrators on each production, may be found in the editor's *Robert Russell Bennett: A Bio-Bibliography.*

Harold Arlen
Bloomer Girl (1944).

Irving Berlin
Face the Music (1932), *Louisiana Purchase* (1940), *Annie Get Your Gun* (1946, and 1966 revival).

Vernon Duke
Walk a Little Faster (1932), *Ziegfeld Follies of 1936, The Show is On* (1936, music by Duke, et al.), *Jackpot* (1944).[1]

George Gershwin
George White's Scandals (1924 and 1925 editions), *Lady, Be Good!* (1924), *Tell Me More* (1925), *Song of the Flame* (1925, music by Gershwin and

---

[1]When asked "What was your toughest orchestral assignment?," Bennett replied, "I could name a few composers who were awfully hard to arrange beautifully for. Vernon Duke—whom I loved—his music was always hard to put on paper. He was a modern composer . . . who I thought had a fine talent and a great future. . . . Whenever I had to orchestrate his music for popular consumption, what it really needed was four trumpets and plenty of strings; you were always having to interlace different [timbres], which you do in musical shows all the time. You never had a chance to sit down and say 'one lovely chord of four flutes would be just ideal'—you don't *have* four flutes. So you have two flutes and two clarinets; that's not a very good substitute, but it's the best you can do. . . . Duke, I found, was more of a problem like that than any other thing I ever did, [putting] more things into chords than you can possibly get out of a theater orchestra." (Bennett interview with George J. Guilbaut for WGBH radio, Boston, 1 October 1977.)

H. Stothart), *Funny Face* (1927), *Girl Crazy* (1930), *Of Thee I Sing* (1931), *Pardon My English* (1933). Films: *A Damsel in Distress* (1937), *Shall We Dance* (1937).

Jerome Kern
Hitchy-Koo of 1920, *Daffy Dill* (1922), *Sitting Pretty* (1924), *Dear Sir* (1924), *Sunny* (1925), *The City Chap* (1925), *Criss Cross* (1926), *Lucky* (1927), *Show Boat* (1927, also 1946 and 1966 revivals), *Blue Eyes* (London, 1928), *Sweet Adeline* (1929), *The Cat and the Fiddle* (1931), *Music in the Air* (1932, and 1951 revival), *Roberta* (1933), *Three Sisters* (London, 1934), *Gentleman Unafraid* (St. Louis, 1938), *Very Warm for May* (1939), *Sally* (1948 revival of the 1920 musical). Films: *Men of the Sky* (1931), *I Dream Too Much* (1935), *Show Boat* (1936), *Swing Time* (1936), *High, Wide and Handsome* (1937).

Burton Lane
Finian's Rainbow (1947), *On a Clear Day You Can See Forever* (1965).

Fritz Loewe
My Fair Lady (1956), *Camelot* (1960).

Cole Porter
Fifty Million Frenchmen (1929), *Gay Divorce* (1932), *Anything Goes* (1934), *Jubilee* (1935), *Red, Hot and Blue!* (1936), *Dubarry Was a Lady* (1939), *Panama Hattie* (1940), *Something for the Boys* (1943), *Mexican Hayride* (1944), *Seven Lively Arts* (1944, music by Porter, Stravinsky, et al.), *Around the World in Eighty Days* (1946), *Kiss Me, Kate* (1948), *Out of This World* (1950), *Alladin* (1958 television production).

Richard Rodgers
One Dam Thing After Another (London, 1927), *A Connecticut Yankee* (1927), *She's My Baby* (1928), *Heads Up* (1929), *Ever Green* (London, 1930), *America's Sweetheart* (1931), *Jumbo* (1935), *Oklahoma!* (1943), *Allegro* (1947), *South Pacific* (1949), *The King and I* (1951), *Pipe Dream* (1955), *Cinderella* (1957 television production and its stage adaptation), *Flower Drum Song* (1958), *The Sound of Music* (1959), *Androcles and the Lion* (1967 television production). Films: *Victory at Sea* (1954), *Oklahoma!* (1955).

Arthur Schwartz
The Band Wagon (1931), *Flying Colors* (1932), *Revenge with Music* (1934), *At Home Abroad* (1935), *Inside U.S.A.* (1948), *A Tree Grows in Brooklyn* (1951), *By the Beautiful Sea* (1954), *Jennie* (1963).

Kurt Weill
Film: *Lady in the Dark* (1944).[2]

Vincent Youmans
Wildflower (1923, music by Youmans and H. Stothart), *Mary Jane McKane* (1923, Youmans/Stothart), *Lollipop* (1925), *No, No, Nanette* (1925).

---

[2]Following the composer's death, Bennett was asked to orchestrate selections from the never-finished Weill–Maxwell Anderson musical *Huckleberry Finn*. The resulting *Five Songs from "Huckleberry Finn"* were first performed in New York in 1952.

Appendix D: Selected Discography

Except as noted, all pre-1980 items are 33 rpm LPs; those post-1980 are compact discs (new releases or reissues). Not included below are original-cast recordings of Bennett-orchestrated musicals; these are catalogued in several exhaustive reference works, including Jack Raymond's *Show Music on Record from the 1890s to the 1980s* (New York: Ungar, 1982). Archival recordings of Bennett's work are listed in the editor's *Robert Russell Bennett: A Bio-Bibliography*.

Concert Works

Abraham Lincoln: A Likeness in Symphony Form
Moscow Symphony Orchestra, William Stromberg cond., Naxos 8.559004 (1999)

A Commemoration Symphony: Stephen Collins Foster
Pittsburgh Symphony Orchestra, Mendelssohn Choir of Pittsburgh, William Steinberg cond., Everest LPBR 6063, SDBR 3063 (1960); Everest EVC 9027 (1996)

Concerto for Violin in A Major
Louis Kaufman, violin, London Symphony Orchestra, Bernard Herrmann cond. (rec. 1956), Citadel CT-6005 (1976); Musical Heritage Society MHS 3974 (1978); Bay Cities 1008 (1989)

Concerto Grosso for Woodwind Quintet and Wind Orchestra
American Wind Symphony, Robert Austin Boudreau cond., AWS-109 (c. 1985)

The Fun and Faith of William Billings, American
National Symphony Orchestra, U. of Maryland Chorus, Antal Dorati cond., London OS 26442 (1976)

Hexapoda (violin and piano)

Louis Kaufman and Bennett, Columbia 70727D (12" 78 rpm, 1941); Orion OC800 (cassette, c. 1980); Bay Cities BCD 1019 (1990)
Jascha Heifetz and Milton Kaye, Decca DA-23659 (78 rpm, 1945); MCA MCAD 42212 (1988)
Louis and Annette Kaufman, Citadel CT 6005 (1976), Musical Heritage Society MHS 3974 (1978)

Rondo Capriccioso (flute quartet)

Members of the New York Flute Club, Musical Heritage Society MHS 3578 (1977)

Rose Variations (trumpet and piano)

David Hickman and Pauline Soderholm, Crystal S-363 (1978); Crystal CD-668 (c. 1990)

Sonata in G (organ)

David Britton, Delos DE 3111 (1991)

Second Sonatina (piano)

Milton Kaye Golden Crest CRDG 4195 (1975)

Sights and Sounds

Moscow Symphony Orchestra, William Stromberg cond., Naxos 8.559004 (1999)

A Song Sonata (violin and piano)

Jascha Heifetz and Brooks Smith, RCA LM-2382 (1960) [mvts. 2–3–4 only]
Louis Kaufman and Theodore Saidenberg, Concert Hall CHS-1062 (1951)
Louis and Annette Kaufman, Citadel CT 6004 (1976); Musical Heritage Society MHS 3974 (1978); Cambria 1078 (1996)
Roy Malan and Robin Sutherland, Orion ORS 82439 (1982)

Suite for Flute and B-flat Clarinet

Glennda Dove, flute, Paul Drusler or Larry Combs, clarinet, Mark MES-57590 (1980s)

Suite of Old American Dances

Eastman Wind Ensemble, Frederick Fennell cond., Mercury LPs 40006 (1953), MG50079 (1957), SRI 75086 (1977)
Cincinnati College–Conservatory of Music Wind Symphony, Eugene Corporon cond., Klavier KCD 11060 (1994)

Symphonic Songs for Band

Eastman Wind Ensemble, Frederick Fennell cond., Mercury MG 50220, SR90220 (1960); Mercury 432 009-2 (1990)

Northwestern U. Wind Ensemble, John Paynter, cond., New World NW211 (1977), NW80211-2 (1990s)

Tokyo Kosei Wind Orchestra, Frederick Fennell cond., Kosei KOCD 3562 (1988)

A Symphonic Story of Jerome Kern

Pittsburgh Symphony, William Steinberg cond., Everest LPBR 6063, SDBR 3063 (1960); Everest EVC 9027 (1996)

Victory at Sea music (selections and concert medleys)

NBC Symphony Orchestra, Bennett cond., RCA Red Seal 6660-2-RC (1987; reissue of late-1950s LPs)

Cincinnati Pops Orchestra, Eric Kunzel cond., Telarc 80175 (1990s)

ORIGINAL WORKS AND ARRANGEMENTS FOR LONG-PLAYING RECORDS

An Adventure in High Fidelity

RCA Symphony Orchestra, Bennett cond., RCA LM 1802 (1954)

RCA commissioned Bennett to compose this "demonstration disc" of fanciful music for large studio orchestra. Among its nine selections are "The Circular Serenade of the Diamond Stylus" and "Waltz of the Vinylite Biscuits."

"America The Beautiful"

Robert Shaw Chorale, RCA Victor Symphony Orchestra, RCA LSC-2662 (1964)

Armed Forces Suite (1960)

RCA Symphony Orchestra, Symphony Band, and "Combo," Bennett cond., RCA LM 2445, LSC 2445, 1960

"Christmas Carols"

Marian Anderson, contralto; Franz Rupp, piano, chorus and orchestra, Bennett cond., RCA LM-2613 (1962)

The Many Moods of Christmas

Robert Shaw Chorale, RCA Victor Symphony Orchestra, RCA LM-2684 (1963)

Atlanta Symphony Orchestra and Chorus, Robert Shaw cond., Telarc 80087 (1983)

"The Robert Shaw Chorale and Orchestra on Broadway," RCA LM/LSC-2799 (1965)

"Songs at Eventide"

Marian Anderson, contralto; Franz Rupp, harpsichord, chamber ensemble, Bennett cond., RCA LM/LSC2769 (1964)

"Songs of Faith and Inspiration"

Robert Shaw Chorale, RCA Victor Symphony Orchestra, arr. Bennett, RCA LSC 2760 (1964)

"Yours Is My Heart Alone—Operetta Favorites"

Robert Shaw Chorale, RCA Victor Symphony Orchestra, RCA VCM/VCS-7023 (1963)

Broadway "Symphonic Picture" Medleys

"Gershwin in Hollywood"

Hollywood Bowl Orchestra, Gregory Hines and Patti Austin, vocals, John Mauceri cond., Philips 434274-2 (1990s)

The only commercial recording of the title-track Gershwin medley; also contains instrumental and vocal music—in their original orchestrations—from Gershwin's 1930s film musicals.

"Gershwin Overtures"

New Princess Theater Orchestra, McGlinn, cond., EMI D 170391 (1987)

Music from Gershwin's *Girl Crazy*, *Of Thee I Sing*, *Tip-Toes*, *Primrose*, and *Oh, Kay!*—along with the film *A Damsel in Distress*—most of it orchestrated by Bennett.

A Symphonic Picture of "Porgy and Bess"

Pittsburgh Symphony Orchestra, Fritz Reiner cond., Columbia MM-572 (original 78 rpm release, 1940s)

The work has received dozens of commercial recordings. Bennett's own late-1950s reading, with the RCA Symphony Orchestra, has been reissued on RCA 09026-68334-2 [CD].

"Jerome Kern Treasury"

London Sinfonietta and Chorus, McGlinn cond., Angel 7-54883-2 (1993)

Eighteen of Kern's show and film songs, spanning the years 1912–1940. Nearly all of the orchestrations are the "originals" by Bennett or Frank Saddler. Soloists include Thomas Hampson and Rebecca Luker.

"Lerner & Loewe Songbook for Orchestra"

Cincinnati Pops, Kunzel cond., Telarc 80375 (1994)

Includes Bennett's medleys of music from *Brigadoon*, *My Fair Lady*, *Gigi* (the 1958 film, reworked for Broadway in 1973), and *Camelot*.

My Fair Lady (concert band medley; Loewe)
Ohlone College Wind Orchestra, Philip Zahorsky cond., Ohlone CDOC-5015-2 (1994)

"Rodgers & Hammerstein: Opening Night"
Hollywood Bowl Orchestra, Mauceri cond., Philips 434-932-2 (1992)
Overtures from all of the Rogers & Hammerstein original productions, their 1945 film *State Fair*, and the 1965 remake of television's 1957 *Cinderella*. Bennett's work is heard on seven of the eleven tracks.

"Rodgers & Hammerstein Songbook for Orchestra"
Cincinnati Pops, Kunzel cond., Telarc 80278 (1992)
Includes Bennett's "symphonic picture" medleys from *Oklahoma!*, *South Pacific*, *The King and I*, *Flower Drum Song*, and *The Sound of Music*, along with his scoring of Rodgers's *Cinderella Waltz*.

MUSICAL THEATER "RESTORATIONS"

Anything Goes (Porter)
London Sinfonietta, Ambrosian Chorus, McGlinn cond., EMI 7 49848 2 (1989)
Original orchestrations by Bennett and Hans Spialek, with missing items rescored by Russell Warner.

Girl Crazy (Gershwin)
Elektra Nonesuch 79250-2 (CD, 1990)
Conducted by John Mauceri, this is one of the "Roxbury Recordings" restorations funded by Ira Gershwin's widow, Lenore. All of the surviving Bennett-orchestrated material is heard, along with some songs sympathetically scored by Larry Moore and Russell Warner.

Kiss Me, Kate (Porter)
London Sinfonietta, Ambrosian Chorus, McGlinn cond., EMI D 230278 (2 CDs, 1990)
Though the original cast recording (1949) has been reissued on compact disc, this is a complete recording of the score, including dance music and some songs dropped from the production early in its run.

Lady, Be Good! (Gershwin)
Elektra Nonesuch 79308-2 (1992)
Conducted by Eric Stern. The few original orchestrations (by Bennett, Daly, Charles Grant, Stephen O. Jones, Paul Lannin, and Max Steiner) that survive are included; the rest have been faithfully recreated by Larry Wilcox and Russell Warner.

Louisiana Purchase (Berlin)

Rob Fisher, cond., DRG 94766 (1996)

This is a studio recording of the "Carnegie Hall–Weill Recital Hall" concert presentation of the full score, its first hearing since the original 1940 production. The 1940 orchestrations (Bennett's, with a few by Nathan Lang Van Cleave) belie the notion that Bennett was too stiff or conservative an arranger to turn out propulsive, swinging charts like these.

Of Thee I Sing and *Let 'Em Eat Cake* (Gershwin)

CBS M2K 42522 (2 CDs, 1987)

Orchestra of St. Luke's, New York Choral Artists, conducted by Michael Tilson Thomas, featuring singers Maureen McGovern, Larry Kert, and Jack Gilford.

Of Thee I Sing uses the original Bennett/Daly/Gershwin orchestrations. Russell Warner reconstructed the lost arrangements from *Let 'Em Eat Cake.*

Pardon My English (Gershwin)

Elektra Nonesuch 79338-2 (1994)

Another "Roxbury Records" restoration, conducted by Eric Stern. The original orchestrations by Bennett, William Daly, and Adolph Deutsch are heard, with some recent scoring for the project by Russell Warner.

Show Boat (Kern)

London Sinfonietta, Ambrosian Chorus, McGlinn cond., EMI/Angel CDS 7–49108–2 (1988).

An exhaustive restoration of the 1927 version of the show, nearly all of it using Bennett's original orchestrations.

Bibliography

Anderson, George. "Robert Russell Bennett: Music Man." Pittsburgh *Post-Gazette*, 27 May 1974.

Behrman, S.N. "Profiles: Accoucheur." *The New Yorker*, 6 February 1932, 20–24.

Bennett, Robert Russell. "All I Know about Arranging Music." *International Musician*, February 1949, 9, 33.

———. "Another Chapter on Arranging Music." *International Musician*, March 1949, 16, 33.

———. "Another Chapter on Arranging Music." *International Musician*, April 1949, 49.

———. "Backstage with the Orchestrator." *Etude* 61, no. 4 (April 1943), 233, 273, 288.

———. "Eight Bars and a Pencil." *New York Times*, 8 June 1947.

———. "Fools Give You Reasons." *Music Journal* 25, no. 5 (May 1967), 44, 88.

———. "From the Notes of a Music Arranger." *Theater Arts*, November 1956, 88–89.

———. *Instrumentally Speaking*. Melville, N.Y.: Belwin Mills, Inc., 1975.

———. "A Master Arranger Speaks." *The Musical Digest*, October–November 1948, 5, 20.

———. "On Writing Harp Music." *Harp News* 1, no. 10 (Fall 1954), 2–3.

———. "Orchestrating for Broadway." *Modern Music* 9, no. 4 (May–June 1932), 148–152.

———. "Orchestration of Theatre and Dance Music." In *Music Lovers' Encyclopedia*, compiled by Rupert Hughes, rev. and ed. by Deems Taylor and Russell Kerr. Garden City, N. Y.: Garden City Books, 1950.

———. "A Pretty Girl is Like a Melody." *Music Publishers Journal* 2, no. 5 (September–October 1944), 15, 30–31.

Bergreen, Lawrence. *As Thousands Cheer*. New York: Viking, 1990.

Blitzstein, Mark. "New York Chronicle of New Music," *Modern Music* 8 (1931), 39–42.

Bordman, Gerald. *Jerome Kern: His Life and Music.* New York: Oxford University Press, 1980.

"The Boys That Make the Noise." *Time*, 5 July 1943, 65.

Chapman, John. "Mainly about Manhattan." *New York Daily News*, 17 May 1937.

Collinson, Francis M. *Orchestration for the Theatre.* London: John Lane, The Bodley Head, 1941.

Donald B. Hyatt Papers. State Historical Society of Wisconsin, Madison.

Ewen, David. *American Composers Today.* New York: H.W. Wilson Co., 1949.

Ferencz, George J. *Robert Russell Bennett: A Bio-Bibliography.* Westport, Conn.: Greenwood Press, 1990.

Ferriss, John. "Mr. Music and His Pal," *New York Sunday News*, 29 December 1968.

Gelatt, Roland. "Music Makers: Bruckner and a Loewe-Bennett Fair Lady from Pittsburgh." *High Fidelity*, July 1968, 20, 22.

Greenbaum, Lucy. "About an Arranger." *New York Times*, 24 October 1943.

Hawkins, Roy Benton. "The Life and Work of Robert Russell Bennett." Ph.D. diss., Texas Tech University, 1989.

Krueger, Miles. *Show Boat: The Story of a Classic American Musical.* New York: Oxford University Press, 1977.

Levant, Oscar. *Memoirs of an Amnesiac.* New York: G.P. Putnam's Sons, 1965.

———. *A Smattering of Ignorance.* Garden City, N.Y.: Garden City Publishing Co., Inc. 1940.

Lowe, Donald Robert. "Sir Carl Busch: His Life and Work as a Teacher, Conductor and Composer." D.M.A. diss., University of Missouri–Kansas City, 1972.

"Man behind the Tune." *Newsweek*, 20 July 1953, 86.

McCarty, Clifford. *Film Composers in America: A Checklist of Their Work.* Glendale, Cal.: Valentine, 1953. Reprint, New York: Da Capo, 1972.

Mordden, Ethan. *Rodgers & Hammerstein.* New York: Harry N. Abrams, Inc., 1992.

Morley, Sheridan, with Graham Payn. *The Noel Coward Diaries.* New York: Little, Brown and Co., 1982.

Morton, Lawrence. "On the Hollywood Front." *Modern Music* 21 (1944), 264–266.

NBC Television Papers. State Historical Society of Wisconsin, Madison.

Nixon, Richard M. *RN: The Memoirs of Richard Nixon.* New York: Grosset & Dunlap, 1978.

Rodgers, Richard. *Musical Stages: An Autobiography.* New York: Random House, 1975.

Sheehan, Vincent. *Oscar Hammerstein I: The Life and Exploits of an Impresario.* New York: Simon and Schuster, 1956.

Simon, Robert A. "Musical Events: About a Lorelei and Mr. Bennett—Chamber Music," *The New Yorker*, 19 May 1929, 94–96.

Spialek, Hans. "A Passing Note." Unpublished memoirs, c. 1956. Alice Gruber, Andover, N.J.

S.S.S. "The Musical Traveler." *International Musician*, March 1948, 24.

Tunick, Jonathan. "Broadway in the Concert Hall: By Special Arrangement Only." *Symphony*, February–March 1987, 6.

Waters, Edward N. *Victor Herbert: A Life in Music*. New York: Macmillan, 1955.

Wilk, Max. *OK! The Story of "Oklahoma!"* New York: Grove Press, 1993.

———. *They're Playing Our Song*. New York: Atheneum, 1973.

Wind, Herbert Warren. "Profiles: Another Opening, Another Show." *The New Yorker*, 17 November 1951, 46–71.

Index

The remarkable career of composer-orchestrator Robert Russell Bennett (1894–1981) encompassed a wide variety of both "legitimate" and popular music-making on Broadway, in Hollywood, and for television. Bennett is principally responsible for what is known worldwide as the "Broadway sound" and for greatly elevating the status of the theater orchestrator. He worked alongside Jerome Kern, Cole Porter, George Gershwin, Irving Berlin, Richard Rodgers, and Frederick Loewe on much of the Broadway canon. Among the more than 300 musicals on which he worked between 1920 and 1975 are *Oklahoma!*, *My Fair Lady*, *Show Boat*, *South Pacific*, and *The Sound of Music*. He also arranged and orchestrated all the music in the memorable 26-part NBC television series *Victory at Sea*.

"The Broadway Sound" is the first publication of Bennett's autobiography, which was written in the late 1970s. It also includes eight of his most important essays on the art of orchestration.

George J. Ferencz is Professor of Music at the University of Wisconsin–Whitewater. He is the author of *Robert Russell Bennett: A Bio-Bibliography* (Westport, Conn.: Greenwood Press, 1990).

Praise for *"The Broadway Sound"*

"*'The Broadway Sound'* is utterly fascinating. It solidifies my admiration for the orchestrations he did with all the great theater composers. Robert Russell Bennett *was* the dean of Broadway orchestrators, and these memoirs provide an amazing glimpse into an era that no one knew at the time would be considered golden."

—Theodore S. Chapin,
President and Executive Director,
The Rodgers and Hammerstein Organization

"There has probably never been a better personal history of Broadway and Hollywood's Golden Age than *'The Broadway Sound'*. Every page dazzles the reader with some new insight or little-known story of the American musical stage. How lucky we are to have this treasure published for the first time! It is of extraordinary importance."

—John Mauceri,
Music Director of Broadway shows
and the Hollywood Bowl Orchestra

"When I was growing up, I wondered who this Bennett was who devised the fascinating orchestral sounds on the original-cast albums I was buying, like *Oklahoma!* and *Kiss Me, Kate*. Bennett's autobiography proves to be charmingly personal in tone and richly informative in its narrative."

—Jon Alan Conrad (University of Delaware),
musicologist specializing in the Broadway orchestra and its history

Lightning Source UK Ltd.
Milton Keynes UK
UKOW05f1051121216
289776UK00002B/557/P

9 781580 460828